SEXUAL RESTRAINT AND AESTHETIC EXPERIENCE IN VICTORIAN LITERARY DECADENCE

Can sexual restraint be good for you? Many Victorians thought so. This book explores the surprisingly positive construction of sexual restraint in an unlikely place: late nineteenth-century Decadence. Reading Decadent texts alongside Victorian writing about sexual health, including medical literature, adverts, advice books, and periodical articles, identifies an intellectual Paterian tradition of sensuous continence, in which 'healthy' pleasure is distinguished from its 'harmful' counterpart. Recent work on Decadent sexuality concentrates on transgression and subversion, with restraint interpreted ahistorically as evidence of repression/sublimation or queer coding. Here Sarah Green examines the work of Walter Pater, Lionel Johnson, Vernon Lee, and George Moore to outline a co-extensive alternative approach to sexuality where restraint figured as a productive part of the 'aesthetic life', or a practical ethics shaped by aesthetic principles. Attending to this tradition reveals neglected connections within and beyond Decadence, bringing fresh perspective to its reception in the late nineteenth and twentieth centuries.

SARAH GREEN is a researcher with interests in the intersections between nineteenth-century literature and sexuality. She has worked as a postdoctoral researcher on the University of Oxford ERC-funded project 'Diseases of Modern Life: Nineteenth Century Perspectives' (PI Sally Shuttleworth).

SEXUAL RESTRAINT AND AESTHETIC EXPERIENCE IN VICTORIAN LITERARY DECADENCE

SARAH GREEN

University of Oxford

CAMBRIDGE
UNIVERSITY PRESS

Shaftesbury Road, Cambridge CB2 8EA, United Kingdom

One Liberty Plaza, 20th Floor, New York, NY 10006, USA

477 Williamstown Road, Port Melbourne, VIC 3207, Australia

314–321, 3rd Floor, Plot 3, Splendor Forum, Jasola District Centre, New Delhi – 110025, India

103 Penang Road, #05–06/07, Visioncrest Commercial, Singapore 238467

Cambridge University Press is part of Cambridge University Press & Assessment, a department of the University of Cambridge.

We share the University's mission to contribute to society through the pursuit of education, learning and research at the highest international levels of excellence.

www.cambridge.org
Information on this title: www.cambridge.org/9781108831512

DOI: 10.1017/9781108917490

First published 2023

A catalogue record for this publication is available from the British Library.

Library of Congress Cataloging-in-Publication Data
NAMES: Green, Sarah, 1989– author.
TITLE: Sexual restraint and aesthetic experience in Victorian literary decadence / Sarah Green, University of Oxford.
DESCRIPTION: Cambridge, United Kingdom : New York, NY : Cambridge University Press, 2023. | Series: Cambridge studies in nineteenth-century literature and culture | Includes bibliographical references and index.
IDENTIFIERS: LCCN 2022038890 | ISBN 9781108831512 (hardback) | ISBN 9781108917490 (ebook)
SUBJECTS: LCSH: English literature – 19th century – History and criticism. | Sexual abstinence in literature. | Sexual ethics in literature. | Sex customs in literature. | Decadence (Literary movement) – Great Britain. | LCGFT: Literary criticism.
CLASSIFICATION: LCC PR468.S486 G74 2023 | DDC 820.9/3538–dc23/eng/20221004
LC record available at https://lccn.loc.gov/2022038890

ISBN 978-1-108-83151-2 Hardback

Contents

Acknowledgements

The research for this book was funded by the European Research Council as part of the Oxford University project 'Diseases of Modern Life: Nineteenth Century Perspectives' (PI Sally Shuttleworth), as well as by an Arts and Humanities Research Council doctoral award, and supplementary grants from Merton College, Oxford. I would like to thank these bodies for their crucial support. Very little, however, would have been done without the sustained guidance of Sally Shuttleworth, Stefano Evangelista, and Sophie Ratcliffe, as well as those who read and commented upon sections in progress – Matthew Bradley, Sos Eltis, Helen Small, Michèle Mendelssohn, Robert Douglas-Fairhurst, Ruth Derham, and of course all the anonymous but no less helpful readers along the way. Moreover, both the book and I would have been poorer without the friendship, conversation, and interdisciplinary expertise of all members of the 'Diseases' project, especially Sally Frampton, Jean-Michel Johnston, Emilie Taylor-Pirie, and Hosanna Krienke.

My sincere thanks go to those who assisted me in archive enquiries: the staff of Loras College Library, Dubuque, Iowa, especially Joyce Meldrem and Heidi Pettitt; Fran Baker of John Rylands Library, Manchester; Kate Jarman of St Bartholomew's Hospital Archives; Suzanne Foster of Winchester College Archives; Professor Julian Patrick of the University of Toronto; and all those who so kindly responded to my requests for information about Adrian Earle. I would further like to express my gratitude to Andrew Auge, Erin VanLaningham, and Kevin Koch, for their much-appreciated hospitality during my week at Loras College, and to Martin Dyar for so serendipitously facilitating that connection; as well as to the attendees of the International George Moore Conference 2015, especially Elizabeth Grubgeld and Mary Pierse, for their comments on a paper that would become Chapter 5 and their subsequent encouragement. A version of Chapter 5 was published as 'Impotence and the Male Artist: The Case of George Moore' in the *Journal of Victorian Culture*, 24:2 (April 2019),

179–192; I thank the editors for permission to repurpose some of this material here.

Finally, I want to thank Bethany Thomas and the staff at Cambridge University Press who bore with me so patiently when long COVID temporarily derailed this project; Rebecca Shuttleworth and Ushashi Dasgupta for getting me through that delay; Alex Wong for all his patience, help, and love; and my family, for everything.

Introduction

Walter Pater, in his 1889 essay 'Hippolytus Veiled: A Study from Euripides', elaborates upon a familiar scene from the Greek myth of Hippolytus and Phaedra. The lustful Phaedra lures the chaste youth Hippolytus into her private chamber and attempts to seduce him. 'A peculiar glow', Pater writes, 'such as he had never before seen, like heady lamplight, or sunshine to some sleeper in a delirious dream, hung upon the bold, naked, shameful imageries'. Hippolytus is, in accordance with tradition, disgusted rather than seduced by Phaedra's voluptuousness. And yet Pater does not describe him here or elsewhere as sexually anxious or 'repressed' as we might expect of a Decadent retelling, but rather as cheerfully and healthfully celibate. Throughout the essay we are told of Hippolytus' 'invincible happiness', and that 'healthily white and red, he had a marvellous discretion about him'. His sexual abstention provides a felicity that suffuses his entire being, and we see him 'singing always audaciously [...] so visibly happy, occupied, popular'.[1] Why does Pater go to such lengths to represent Hippolytus' continence as positive, social, and productive?

In this as in other translations and retellings, Hippolytus' chastity is readily readable as a cypher or coding for something else. Does his horrified reaction to his stepmother's advances signify a wider, misogynistic disgust for female sexuality? Is it a version of what Eve Kosofsky Sedgwick calls 'sexual anaesthesia' caused by 'male homosexual panic', either on the part of Hippolytus himself or his author?[2] Or does his disinclination simply indicate a secret liking for something that Phaedra cannot provide? Yopie Prins has argued that when late nineteenth-century aesthetes write about Hippolytus, it is often as a gender-crossing figure whose opting out of heterosexual love allows him to inhabit 'the space of homoerotic aestheticism'.[3] As a beautiful, athletic Hellenic youth who recoiled from female sexual advances, Hippolytus speaks easily to a discourse of pederastic 'Greek love' that was familiar to many Victorian readers regardless of their own sexual affiliations.⁴ Prins argues, for instance, that it was in this guise that Hippolytus featured in the writing of John Addington Symonds and A. Mary F. Robinson, whose friendship can be imagined as a 'period of "queer" tutelage' that resulted in Robinson dedicating her translation of Euripides' *Hippolytus* to Symonds.⁵

Like that of Symonds and Robinson, Pater's admiration for the beauty of male youth, both Ancient Greek and modern, is widely understood as an expression of homosexual desire. But while any of the above interpretations may well be relevant to 'Hippolytus Veiled', none account fully for Pater's unusual retelling (notably a 'study', not a straight translation, from Euripides). In particular, they do not account for his unusual representation of Phaedra and her fate. Lene Østermark-Johansen has observed that Pater departs from tradition to focus on the figure of Hippolytus at the expense of his stepmother: 'Phaedra's status as undisputed tragic heroine is significantly downplayed: there is no suicide, and her lust, jealousy, and deceit are quickly passed over'.⁶ But while it is true that these traditional elements of the story are neglected, Pater introduces something new in their place. His Phaedra is driven mad not so much by lust, as by her frustrated attempts to interpret her stepson's restraint.

Pater's Phaedra is at first attracted precisely by Hippolytus' resistance – 'Ah! it was that very reluctance that chiefly stirred her'. But she becomes increasingly frustrated as it emerges that she lacks available categories through which to make sense of him. She tries first to account for his lack of interest through a narrative of arrested development: 'Is he indeed but a child still', she wonders, 'to be a child always?' Then, as if this explanation were immediately unsatisfactory, she asks whether he might be a 'wily priest'. To a nineteenth-century reader this phrase may have suggested an anachronistic anti-Catholicism, as it imitates the rhetoric of manipulative hypocrisy commonly used to denigrate Catholic priestly celibacy.⁷ Traditionally Phaedra is driven mad by her passion, whether this passion is portrayed as inherent or Goddess-imposed. But in Pater's retelling of the myth it is not her frustrated desire, but rather her inability to comprehend a lack of sexual appetite, that causes Phaedra's insanity – described as a physical as well as a moral collapse. Her failed attempts at understanding, at categorization, drive Phaedra into a 'bodily sickness at last, [...] her thoughts running madly on what she fancies his secret business'. She tells her husband 'a false story of violence to her bed', and this story too can be read as a further attempt at understanding, in which continence is interpreted as a suppressed sexuality that gathers violence in the suppression and must inevitably erupt in time.⁸

Late nineteenth-century British culture often had difficulty conceptualizing genuine restraint of the sexual instinct in anything other than negative terms: as evidence of perversity or pathological lack; as disease, immaturity, or inhumanity. Pater's retelling of the Hippolytus myth engages with that difficulty; but the weight of his critique also relies upon the plausibility to his readers of a viable alternative. Pater suggests that sexual restraint might form a significant part of a healthy life – that it can enhance the individual's experience of the world, as well as their relationship with the society of which they are inevitably a part. And with his account of Phaedra's failed attempts to reinscribe this restraint as something closer to her own experience, he warns against a too ready interpretation of unfamiliar sexual behaviours according to familiar terms.

This book makes two main arguments. More generally, its purpose is to suggest that the idea of a productive sexual continence, like that of Pater's Hippolytus, pervaded Victorian culture, as a recognizable part of the complex, messy, often contradictory web of discourse that constituted late nineteenth-century sexuality. This ideal of continence had both normative and non-normative potential, allowing it to be woven into many different ideological positions at all points on the political spectrum, and was deeply rooted in nineteenth-century models of bodily function. Attending to the prevalence of this concept enriches our understanding of the sexual history, and in the process, other histories, of that culture, by suggesting new connections, affiliations, and canons.

Secondly, the book argues that this manner of imagining sexual restraint had a far greater influence on late nineteenth-century British literary Decadence than has previously been recognized. This influence produced a relatively coherent intellectual and affective tradition that existed alongside, interacted with, and occasionally supplemented the now more familiar queer discourses unquestionably utilized by the same writers, often in the same texts. Whether or not it was actually practiced (about which this book makes no claims), an ideal of continence often formed part of the late nineteenth-century aesthete's impulse to conceptualize an aesthetic mode of life. Sexual restraint held a wide range of positive and often surprising associations in the late nineteenth century, giving it a flexibility that earned it a remarkably persistent place in many a writer's intellectual artillery. For the aesthetically inclined, continence was frequently imagined as a viable response to elements in their culture that could be felt to make an aesthetic life (whatever that meant to the writer in question) difficult: ugliness, unhealthiness, selfishness, sensuality (not the same as sensuousness, a distinction that this book frequently has cause to dwell on).

Late nineteenth-century aesthetes approached such difficulties in different ways – by claiming that ugliness was itself beautiful, for instance, or that one could simply ignore such things through aesthetic retreat. Positive sexual continence offered a solution that was potentially more socially engaged and embedded than other more commonly explored modes of Decadent thought, via lines of association perhaps more readily comprehensible to a nineteenth- than a twenty-first-century reader. The networks of discourses surrounding continence that made this flexibility and sociability possible are explored in Chapter 1.

Although my subject is a specific sexual discourse, then, this has also come to be a book about the intersection of many ideas important to late Victorian intellectual culture. The authors explored here – Lionel Johnson, Vernon Lee, and George Moore – all associate their idealizations of sexual continence with Walter Pater. In part, then, this is a book about an alternative Paterianism to that generally explored by Decadent Studies. Recent readings of Pater and Paterianism mostly emphasize the undoubted presence of queer sexuality in that work. This emphasis, combined with Pater's relative reticence or coyness in such matters, has led to the habitual reading of sexuality into its very absence: a method of reading in which, as Heather Love puts it, Pater's '"circumspection and displacement" […] are not seen as impediments to thinking about sexuality in Pater's work – rather, they *are* that sexuality'.[9] Such readings have revealed the crucial importance of sexual discourse to British Aesthetic and Decadent writing. I build upon this heritage by exploring a further possibility that is neither impediment nor sexualization, but instead reads Pater's representations of sexual restraint as typical productions of his culture's sexual discourse, in which he theorizes an embodied sensuousness that is aware of sexual/sensual potential, and yet relies upon physical continence for its most effective elaborations. And although I outline points at which Pater allows readers to eroticize this continence if they wish, especially where aesthetic experience focuses on the sensuous beauty of male bodies, the recognition that such eroticization is rarely essential to his thinking is crucial to a fuller understanding of his late nineteenth-century reception.

I do not, however, want to suggest that the sexual continence described in the work of Lee, Johnson, and Moore is only a Paterian inheritance. This book is also about the distinction that many aesthetes attempted to draw – at least sometimes – between sensuous experience and sensuality; about the efforts that so many writers made to reconcile the competing claims of the individual and society, the desire for self-cultivation and the sense of social responsibility; about their tendency to think of all wellbeing, individual and social, in terms of 'health'; about their frequent elaboration of the idea of 'love' not as a possessive desire for another person, but as what Benjamin Morgan has called a set of 'transformative affective relationships to a world of things', an ideal, disinterested attitude towards people and objects alike;[10] and, perhaps more than anything, about the constant connections that they made between ethics and everything else, treating all ideas, at least in theory, as part of the process of living rather than as abstract concepts.

This expansion and intermingling of categories is a testament to the Victorian habit of thinking about the body and the mind, and indeed society and even the spiritual world, as a holistic system that worked to one rough set of principles, whatever those principles happened to be. As Bruce Haley has it:

> Victorian intellectuals insisted on the reality of a spiritual life higher than that of the body, but in one way or another they all thought physiologically: they adopted the well-knit body as their model for the well-formed mind, and the mind-body harmony as their model for spiritual health, the harmony of the self with external principles of growth and order.[11]

The late Victorian Decadent writers explored here are no different in this sense from the majority of Victorian intellectuals. But the ideological nexus that their thinking created around sexual continence, in which this bodily state could have physical, intellectual, creative, social, and spiritual implications, has not previously been described.

In writing about this discourse, I prefer the very Victorian term 'sexual continence', along with the occasional 'sexual restraint', to 'virginity', 'celibacy', 'chastity', or even for the most part 'abstinence'. This is because the former terms are able to refer to both temporary and permanent states (real or imagined) of restraint from *all* sexual activity – whether the activity abstained from is auto- or alloerotic, homo- or heterosexual, physiological or psychological – without undue burden of moralistic or religious connotation.[12] 'Continence', furthermore, was by far the term of choice in non-religious late nineteenth-century writing about sexual health, whether medical or otherwise. Unlike the alternatives, it suits the period's conception of the sexual body as part of a regulatory system in which sex involved the loss of something, whether that something was a physical substance or some more abstract quality such as energy or spiritual vitality, whereas restraint involved the conservation, redistribution, and even cultivation of that quality or substance.[13]

It is likely that today's readers, in attempting to conceive of a productive sexual continence, will be put in mind of Freud's theory of sublimation, in which sexual energy is imagined to be redirected towards non-sexual ends.[14] 'Observation of men's daily lives', writes Freud, 'shows us that most people succeed in directing very considerable portions of their sexual instinctual forces to their professional activity'. Artists, in Freud's thinking, were particularly good at this act of conversion: 'artistic talent and capacity are intimately connected with sublimation'.[15] And towards the end of his career Freud posited this mechanism as one of the driving forces behind civilization itself, as a means of processing and making use of potentially anti-social instincts.[16]

Freudian sublimation is, however, only the most famous product of a web of discourses concerning the control of sexual desires that can be found in many cultures throughout time and space. For Freud, it is crucial that this converted energy (a thermodynamic metaphor that was important to many writers before him) is *originally* sexual, and to a certain extent remains so despite producing non-sexual behaviour. 'What an artist creates', he claims, 'provides at the same time an outlet for his sexual desire'.[17] The result for Freud is therefore to a certain extent unstable, always liable to lapse again into the sexual, and inevitably leaving readable traces of the sexual origins of which the creator may or may not be conscious. There is a world of difference between this and the Victorian model of energy that was converted for various uses but had few properties in its own right; in which art was not an outlet for an already sexual energy, but rather called on the same reserves of basic energy that sex called upon. And although this book's first chapter will explore the discursive slipperiness that existed in relation to continence in the late nineteenth century, in which the same terms could describe a genuinely non-sexual or an intensely autoerotic state, yet the potential for non-erotic sexual restraint is emphasized as the least recognizable, and therefore most likely to be overlooked, discourse. In practice writers often exploited the ambiguity created by such slipperiness, especially those such as Pater who explored socially proscribed sexual objects.

Freud did not leave a full account of sublimation; but the very haziness of its conception is perhaps responsible for its twentieth- and twenty-first-century popular success as an explanation for any seemingly positive – that is, not openly destructive or unstable – state of sexual continence. When critics of nineteenth-century Decadent literature address references to sexual continence in those texts, they are usually read as a pseudo-Freudian sublimation (whether or not the term itself is used) that takes advantage of the potential that Freud always left for sublimated energy to either return to sexuality, and therefore create an intense, always-deferred sexuality expressed in activities other than genital acts – what Kate Hext (with regard to Pater) has called 'the frisson of unrequited desire'[18] – or to at least be readable as the product of unsatisfied sexual desire. Ellis Hanson, for example, writes of 'the tendency of the decadents to displace sexuality onto textuality', creating a situation 'in which sexuality was more likely to find articulation in the stylistic excesses of gothic and baroque art than in any genital transgression', because 'the ecstasies of art and religion [...] are a spiritualization and an intensification of desire'.[19] And Jeff Nunokawa, in his reading of Wilde's work as developing a management of sexual desire that would 'remove the element of compulsion from the chemistry of the erotic', finds that 'managing passions is merely a matter of giving them form or expression'.[20] Nunokawa represents Wilde as setting out to control desire, but actually finding desire in a different form. Such an approach harmonizes well with Wilde's treatments of sexuality, but less well with those of the writers examined here.

Reading representations of continence as the product of an ahistorical psychological mechanism may shed light on the potential motivations behind some of these representations. Occasionally, however, it obscures historical understandings of what it meant to avoid sex, and in the process obscures also those networks of meaning that grew up around such understandings. The discourse described in this book differs from pseudo-Freudian sublimation primarily in the confidence with which it presented genuine non-sexuality as a perfectly possible state (however difficult of achievement and however temporarily achieved) even if eroticized forms of continence are also acknowledged, as well as in its imagining of such continence as productive rather than unstable, whether of health, (non-sexual) pleasure, energy, or social potential. Pater, for instance, emphasizes the general social success that Hippolytus' continence inspires: people 'instinctively admired his wonderful placidity, and would fain have shared its secret, as it were the carelessness of some fair flower upon his face'. There is even a suggestion that his very lack of sexual activity creates a mysterious connection between him, the natural world, and the rest of mankind, as we are told that 'his continual singing' was 'like the earth itself made audible in all its humanities'.[21] Continence gives to every aspect of Hippolytus' experience what Pater calls in another context (describing Giordano Bruno's reading of Plato) 'borrowed fire and wings'.[22] And though Hippolytus does reach his usual violent ending in this retelling, in which he is dragged to death by his chariot horses, Pater allows this violence to be interpreted as the result of a failure of others to understand, rather than inherent unworthiness or repressive outbreak.

* * *

Decadent literature has for the past thirty years or so been primarily approached as expressive of a queer sensual radicalism, as what Dennis Denisoff describes as an essentially 'anti-conformist' movement, its writers 'flaunting their dissident passions before the British public'.[23] For Richard Dellamora, for instance, 'decadence is always radical in its opposition to the organization of modern urban, industrial, and commercial society', and this radicalism is expressed largely in what he calls 'sexual dissidence'.[24] As Stefano Evangelista writes, 'Today the aesthetes are retrospectively seen as having made a shaping contribution to the formation of a twentieth-century "gay" identity, and their received critical reputation has subsequently shifted from that of art historians and moralists to sexual radicals'.[25]

As a supplement to this reading of the aesthete as queer sexual radical, the remainder of this introduction briefly indicates an alternative and co-existent Decadent means of representing sexuality that the book describes in more detail, in which sexual continence was used to address and counteract accusations of excessive individualism and sensuality that were levelled at Aestheticism and Decadence throughout the period. It then claims that this continent Decadence makes sense as part of a common Victorian mode of imagining the sexuality of the post-Romantic artist, which itself draws on a wider discourse of productive sexual continence that is outlined more fully in Chapter 1. This less explicitly radical continent Decadence and an overtly sexually radical Decadence were by no means mutually exclusive, however; indeed many writers shuttled between these postures, as will be seen in the case of Moore and Pater.

Nineteenth-century Aesthetic – and to a certain extent, Decadent – writers commonly concerned themselves with ethical as well as artistic questions; as Sara Lyons puts it, 'aestheticism had ambitions to be not simply a philosophy of beauty but a philosophy of happiness', and this was true whether its proponents wrote criticism, poetry, fiction, or in some cases letters, though the solutions they presented to these questions varied.[26] This ethical concern was partly with what Foucault calls 'arts of existence' or 'techniques of the self', an effort on the part of writers 'to transform themselves, to change themselves in their singular being, and to make their life into an *oeuvre* that carries certain aesthetic values and meets certain stylistic criteria'.[27] These writers were often, however, also closely concerned with the relationship between self and society. Ruth Livesey has examined the conjunction between Aestheticism and Socialism, their common attachment to a 'productive, communal ideal of art' at the end of the century, while Matthew Potolsky has proposed that Decadence, usually envisioned as a movement of dissolution and radical individualism, also involved the creation of 'a transformatively "modern community"'.[28] The writers I examine here are among those whose work contains a sustained engagement with questions of both the individual's successful aesthetic life in an imperfect world and the potential for the individual aesthetic life to be an active source of good in that world, though their approaches vary from Pater's interest in what the universal and communal can contribute to self-cultivation, to the strict sense of responsibility for the lives of others that motivated Johnson and Lee. At all points these ethical processes were closely concerned with the body; with its physical, moral, and spiritual health, and the effect this had on the health of the social body.

The texts that I look at here, whether or not explicitly involved with ethical argument, were generally received in their time as ethical pronouncements, as statements concerning the most desirable ordering of life, including sexual life. In a society in which new theories of individualism were emerging from all points on the political spectrum, an anxiety emerged, as Regenia Gagnier has shown, concerning 'individual development threatening the functioning of the whole'.[29] Negative responses to Aesthetic and Decadent writing (and writers) broadly focused upon two points: excessive sensuality, and excessive individualism or selfishness, which together were represented as especially detrimental to society. And unsurprisingly this perceived threat was often expressed as a physiological disease or sickness, the threat of the 'morbid and sickly' as a 'source of corruption' that was only partly metaphoric.[30] The connection of these putative failings was commonplace at this point in history, and can arguably be attributed to the residue of the eighteenth-century moral code that has been called 'civic humanism', in which personal moderation was associated with social good, and personal excess with social dissolution – itself deeply rooted in long-standing connections between sexual behaviour and social order.[31] When Robert Buchanan, for example, castigated what he called 'the fleshly school of poetry' – for him exemplified by Baudelaire and Gautier in France, and Swinburne and Dante Gabriel Rossetti in England – for 'its sickliness and effeminacy', he accused its proponents of being 'equally self-indulgent and sensual'. This double disease, of 'animalism' and 'eternal posturing before the mirror', in which the one is readily imaginable as entailing the other, is conceived as a threat to society at large; its writers are 'public offenders, because they are diligently spreading the seeds of disease broadcast wherever they are read and understood'.[32] Five years later, W. H. Mallock also coupled selfish individualism and sensuality in the character of Mr Rose, a parody not only of Pater but also of a particular way of reading his work. We are told of Mr Rose that 'his two topics are self-indulgence and art', but the two themes upon which his talk actually hinges are individualism and sensual love.[33] He soliloquizes on 'the new pleasures that modern culture has made possible for us', especially 'the passion of love, in its distinctly modern form', and also proclaims that he looks 'upon social dissolution as the true condition of the most perfect life. For the centre of life is the individual, and it is only through dissolution that the individual can re-emerge'.[34] By the time of Robert Hichens' *The Green Carnation* (1894), which satirized the Decadence of the 1890s, the parody aesthete was quickly recognizable in his mixture of self-obsessed individualism and sensuality. Of Reggie Hastings, supposedly modelled on Alfred Douglas, Hichens writes both that 'the white flower of a blameless life was much too inartistic to have any attraction for him' and that 'he knew that he was great, and he said so often in Society'.[35] Though these are arguably all attacks aimed at specific individuals, the similarity of their construction reveals a recognizable set of anxieties through which Aestheticism and Decadence were commonly represented.

Some Decadent writers used this association between sensuality and selfishness to construct a socially critical position, affecting a deliberately cultivated sensuality at least in part as a protest against either a particular state of society or the idea of social interference in the world of art in general. For example, Livesey finds this conjunction of values in much aesthetic-socialist writing of the period, such as that of Edward Carpenter and Olive Schreiner; while many Decadent writers – Oscar Wilde, Arthur Symons, and (despite his inclusion in this book) George Moore – frequently engaged in a similar sensual individualism, though these writers as often affected conservative as socialist politics. But another ethical approach is discernible in Decadent writing, in which a productive ideal of sexual continence deflects charges of both sensuality and excessive individualism. Continence has a long history of association with social usefulness; not only in a negative sense in which one's sensuality is suppressed for the greater good of a society built upon family and marriage ties, but also as a constructive behaviour in its own right, imagined as somehow enhancing one's personal potential for sociability or sympathy, as we saw in Pater's Hippolytus.

For some writers, continence also had the ability to connect this sociability with a non-sensual position that nevertheless did not sacrifice intense sense experience. In his *Memoirs* John Addington Symonds remembers that in his youth he thought that he 'had transcended crude sensuality through the aesthetic idealization of erotic instincts'.[36] Though he later came to repudiate this possibility, he represents it as a position that had been plausible enough at the time. In the chapters that follow, I argue that there existed a Decadent tradition which distinguished between sensuousness and sensuality; a subtle distinction but perhaps more plausible to nineteenth-century readers than those of the twenty-first century. The distinction was more one of attitude than behaviour, in the first instance: sensuousness, the intense and pleasurable experience of the external world via the senses, could be separated at least intellectually from sensuality, an approach to such experience in an excessive, selfish, possessive, or lustful manner. It was often represented as an uneasy, unstable distinction, but it was nevertheless integral to much nineteenth-century ethical thinking about art and beauty both within and outside of Decadence, as it had long been crucial in religious agonizing over pleasure and the senses. In emphasizing this distinction a writer could benefit particularly from a productive model of sexual continence, as it could be imagined as allowing and even intensifying sensuousness, without such sense experience becoming sensual and therefore potentially anti-social. Combined with the supposed sociability of continence, an aestheticism could thus be theorized that would be both socially and personally productive.

This formula would not, of course, have held water with all Victorian audiences. Sexual continence had a fraught history in Victorian England. Abstinence was at least superficially expected before marriage, especially among the middle classes (though such expectations were undoubtedly more easily waived in the case of men than women). But continence freely chosen (even temporarily) as an alternative to marriage had been widely held in suspicion since the Reformation as an essentially Catholic sentiment. 'Anti-Catholics', writes D. G. Paz, 'assumed as a given that celibacy, being unnatural, was a front for lascivious behaviour'.[37] Katherine Snyder has shown how deeply entrenched was the ambivalence of Victorian England towards bachelors as 'both admirable and contemptible, enviable and execrable, dangerous and defanged'. She writes that, 'Often seen by their contemporaries as disruptive to domestic life', they often represented all the dangers of prostitution, corruption of the young, and sexually transmitted disease; and yet there was a sense too that their potential sexlessness was itself threatening, undermining the reproductive imperative at the heart of Protestantism, and, especially later in the century, potentially endangering the race.[38] Like Lee Edelman's negative queerness, continence could 'figure the bar to every realization of futurity, the resistance, internal to the social, to every social structure or form'.[39] This was true also for women who deliberately chose to remain unmarried. Though they were less immediately associated with sexual threat, their choice seemed to some to undermine social values, especially later in the century when politically active women often worked sexual continence into 'a complex philosophy of sex, designed to show both how women's subjugation had originated and how women were maintained in subjection to men from day to day'.[40]

This element of compulsory sexuality in Victorian society, however, should not be treated as though it were thoroughly dominant, with all other discourses identifiable as radical or socially dissident. As Lesley Hall has argued, nineteenth-century Britain was 'a complex society containing a plethora of social and economic groups with very different ideologies. Too often historians have given exaggerated attention to a single strand'.[41] Victorian sexual 'normativity' was not limited to Protestant reproductive marriage. Though it was certainly organized around that core, it is gradually coming to be recognized that its borders were wider and more porous than has often been assumed. Pamela K. Gilbert, for instance, has recently argued that sexual representation in Victorian fiction 'was always wilder and woolier than we gave it credit for being', including many forms of extra-marital, non-reproductive existence marked as thoroughly normative.[42] Ideals of sexual continence could be found at all points on the political spectrum in the late nineteenth century, from radical to ultra-conservative, so that the presence of such ideas alone is not enough to diagnose the political orientation of a writer or mode of thought.

Within British Decadence productive ideals of sexual continence were almost always associated with Pater. Pater's legacy within late nineteenth-century Decadence was double-edged. Recent Paterian scholars have almost universally attended to one particular aspect of this legacy, in which his emphasis on sense experience and what could be interpreted as radical individualism ('What is this song or picture [...] to *me*?')[43] were adopted as philosophical supports to an already extant Aestheticism that deliberately ran sensuousness into sensuality, and found in such phrases as 'stirring of the senses' and 'exquisite passion' a justification for what one contemporary essayist called the 'deification of the flesh'.[44] Frank Harris remembered that, as a young man, he had 'met an Oxford graduate' who 'preached Pater, Pater unregenerate, Pater the Pagan. He showed me long passages of Pater's essays on the "Renaissance" and I went down before him'.[45] Readers of Harris' famously explicit autobiographies will have no trouble recognizing the tongue-in-cheek sexual reference in his final phrase here.[46] Edgar Jepson also, reminiscing about his time as an undergraduate at Oxford in the 1880s, remembered:

> I would read Pater, slowly, till I had finished my pipe, then stroll up to the market to buy some flowers, for the Aesthetic Movement was waxing to its height, and I wore my hair rather long and was striving, as Pater prescribed, to become a monochronos hedonist.[47]

Pater himself famously objected (at least outwardly) to this characterization, complaining to Edmund Gosse, 'I wish they wouldn't call me "a hedonist"; it produces such a bad effect on the minds of people who don't know Greek', though his work notably maintains an interpretive space for those so wishing to read it.[48] It was also this Pater that Mallock caricatured in *The New Republic* as the sensual Mr Rose, who 'always seems to talk of everybody as if they had no clothes on'.[49]

There was another Pater. Richard Le Gallienne, in his 1899 novel *Young Lives* – a semi-autobiographical tale of an aesthetic young man coming of age in 1880s Liverpool – has his protagonist, Henry Mesurier, stumble upon Pater's 1885 novel *Marius the Epicurean*. In it he finds 'a beauty at once so sensuous and so spiritual – the beauty of flowering laurel, the beauty of austerity aflower'. 'The whole book was the spiritual story of a young Roman's soul, a priestlike artistic temperament', though 'the theme presented many fascinating analogies to the present time'. Henry's first impulse is to compare the temperament of Marius with his own – he 'found many correspondences with his own nature' – and to recommend it to his sister and friends as an ethical guide: 'what gleaming single phrases, whole counsels of existence in a dozen words! He must copy out some of them for Esther'. And though emphasizing always Pater's 'joy in the sensuous form', yet he is clear also that this is separate entirely from sensuality and sexuality, and he scoffs at an insensitive reader who he remembered had compared it in conversation to Gautier's *Mademoiselle de Maupin*: 'was not the beauty of that masterpiece, in comparison with the beauty of this, as the beauty of a leopard-skin to the beauty of a statue of Minerva, withdrawn in a grove of ilex[?]'. Having read the book in a public house, 'Henry emerged from his tavern-cloister upon the warm brilliancy of the streets. All around him the lights beaconed, and the women called with bright eyes'. But his reading of *Marius* has, at least temporarily, chastened Henry: 'to-night there was no temptation for him in these things. They but recalled another exquisite quotation from his new-found treasure, which he stopped under a lamp to fix in his memory'.[50] Standing under a street-lamp, surrounded by the temptations of Liverpool's nightlife, Henry then re-reads a passage in which Marius, having arrived for the first time in Rome, faces similar temptation and resists, since 'it was to no wasteful and vagrant affections, such as these, that his Epicureanism had committed him'.[51] In imitation of this moral example, Henry heads homewards, having used *Marius* much as one would an advice book for 'young men', a genre that proliferated towards the end of the century, and which invariably recommended an ideal of productive continence for unmarried men.

For some among the generation that followed him, Pater meant not indulgence in sensual pleasure, but rather this strict, austere, disciplined ethical position that extended for many to a particular attitude towards sexuality. T. S. Eliot named *The Renaissance* as Pater's 'more "influential" book', and in general this may be true;[52] yet when Yeats recalled that he and his peers at the end of the century had 'looked consciously to Pater for our philosophy', it was *Marius* rather than the famous 'Conclusion' to *The Renaissance* that he gave as example.[53] Yeats continued, 'Pater had made us learned; and, whatever we might be elsewhere, ceremonious and polite'. He wrote of 'the temperate life Pater had commended'.[54] Along with this outward manner, Yeats associated with Pater an attitude of ethical caution:

> Perhaps it was because of Pater's influence that we, with an affectation of learning, claimed the whole past of literature for our authority, instead of finding it, like the young men in the age of comedy that followed us, in some new, and so still unrefuted authority; that we preferred what seemed still uncrumbled rock to the still unspotted foam; that we were traditional alike in our dress, in our manner, in our opinions, and in our style.[55]

The philosophy he inspired was often one of what Lionel Johnson called 'grave beauty, passionate scholarship, elect restraint'.[56] It was this Pater, the Pater of reserve and restraint, that so many young readers and writers of the next generation – including Lionel Johnson, Vernon Lee, and George Moore – associated not with sexual license, but with a culturally conservative aestheticism to which productive sexual continence was vital. Le Gallienne, in his gossipy memoir *The Romantic '90s* (1925), refers to 'the gospel of beauty and "ecstasy", which Pater taught with hierarchical reserve and with subdued though intense passion and colour of words'. Pater's attitude of 'reserve' in teaching this 'gospel' is compared to that of Wilde, who 'popularized, and indeed somewhat vulgarized, as he perhaps to a degree misunderstood, and certainly dangerously applied' that same creed.[57] This tradition of reading Pater does not ignore what Catherine

Maxwell calls Pater's 'tendency towards embodiment'; rather, it views this tendency as compatible with, and even conducive to, a restrained conduct.[58] The dynamic of 'passion' and restraint emerges again and again in late nineteenth- and early twentieth-century characterizations of Pater. For Arthur Galton 'his world is shown in the dry light of reason, but a reason mellowed by wisdom, though charged and coloured by tense and almost passionate feeling'.[59] Johnson remembered that although 'Mr. Pater was never more characteristically inspired than in writing of the discipline of art, its immense demands, its imperative morality [...] No books are more full than his of gracious loving-kindness; of such tremulous and tender pity as would disgrace the hedonist in his Epicurean calm'.[60] A. C. Benson found in Pater's writing 'a character of curious intensity and depth, within certain defined limits', a 'richness under a severe restraint', and is explicit about the sexual behaviour that such a style implied: 'to be intellectually and perceptively impassioned indeed he desired; but the physical ardours of love, the longing for enamoured possession – with this Pater had nothing in common'.[61] If some of these readers can, like Benson, be found elsewhere professing homosexual desires and even speculating on Pater's own sexual preferences, this only reinforces their association of Pater's work with a discourse of productive sexual continence that, as well as being relatively common in Victorian writing, was actively exploited by early apologists for homosexual identity, as will be seen in Chapter 1.[62]

Whether or not such lack of sexual desire was indeed the case for Pater the man, Benson's was certainly not a controversial opinion. It was common also to find Pater lacking in 'virility' or 'vitality': he was, wrote Benson, 'a man of low physical vitality', while Harris mused that, 'if Pater had had [...] a little more vitality and hotter blood [...] he would have been another Gautier'. Gosse similarly wrote of 'natures like his, in which the tide of physical spirits runs low, in which the vitality is lukewarm'.[63] Occasionally these doubts were expressed as gender disruption, with Gosse describing Pater's manner as that of 'a sort of solemn effeminacy', and Le Gallienne remembering him as 'almost maidenly, if one might use the word of so large and masculine a man'.[64] These phrases recall particularly references, by no means always negative, to the celibate John Henry Newman as having had the manner of a maiden lady, a tendency which, as Oliver Buckton notes, continued into the twentieth century.[65]

Both Newman's and Pater's idealizations of continence have recently been read as expressing a nascent form of homosexuality: in Newman's case, what Frederick Roden has called 'queer virginity', an unconscious 'sublimation' of homosexual desire into religious ardour or feelings of friendship for men; in the case of Pater, as everything from a similar 'unconscious' homoerotic inclination to a conscious and physically active though covert homosexuality.[66] It is clear that proponents of what was quickly beginning to look like modern homosexual identity consciously adopted many of the discourses I outline here as connected with productive sexual continence. Writers such as Wilde, Carpenter, Symonds, and Marc-André Raffalovich drew on many historical sources in common with the discourse of productive sexual continence – Ancient Greek culture, particularly as represented in Plato, the Christian Church Fathers, Catholicism – as well as sometimes finding expression in similar ideals of behaviour, such as sexual restraint within romantic friendship. The discourse of productive sexual continence has, throughout history, overlapped with and allowed covert expression of what we would now term homosexual desires, and has provided a framework for emergent homosexual culture: as Benjamin Kahan writes about celibacy, it can be thought of as 'an additional pattern or model that striates the long history of homosexuality before its emergence as such'.[67] To this extent, the history of sexual continence is inevitably relevant to those writing the history of homosexuality (and vice versa). It is vital, however, that these discourses are also recognized as having distinct existences and histories. As Nunokawa says in his reading of the similar (but more sexualized) ideal of 'sexual self-management' in the work of Wilde, such a position 'may be especially appealing to the homosexual', but 'it is not his or her exclusive property'.[68]

The writers explored in this book may well have recognized sexual feelings that aligned them with the self-conscious cultures that were beginning to emerge around same-sex desire. Long before his death in 1894, rumours were circulating about Walter Pater's appreciation for young male beauty and Ancient Greek idealizations of homosocial bonding. We know that on at least one occasion this appreciation led to the writing of letters that ended in the rustication of an undergraduate and may have seriously impeded Pater's university career.[69] Lionel Johnson also toyed frequently with the gossamer boundary between romantic friendship and sexuality, and cultivated the company of those known to have crossed that boundary. Vernon Lee's series of intense relationships with women like Mary Robinson and Clementina ('Kit') Anstruther-Thompson have often been considered to have had a sexual element, whether this was acknowledged by Lee herself or not. Biographers and critics throughout the present and last centuries have adopted every possible position with regards to the sexual lives of these three, from total denial of all same-sex attraction to the positing of full active engagement in sexual communities, the necessary secrecy of which can account for the dearth of archival survival.[70] Even the aggressively heterosexual George Moore has been described by biographer Adrian Frazier as 'a homosexual man who loved to make love to women', with the rationale that Moore was attracted to non-reproductive forms of sexuality and to Paterian Aestheticism.[71]

It is undoubtedly true, at least in part, that historical discourses of sexual continence such as those expressed in the work of these writers owe something to either the unconscious repression or the conscious coding of homosexuality. Nevertheless, attending to them exclusively as such risks obscuring the place held by such discourses in wider networks of meaning. It could reasonably be claimed, for instance, that it was precisely the wide political potential of continence, its ability to accommodate both radical and conservative positions, normative and non-normative ideals, which made it especially attractive to an emergent homosexual culture interested in both anti-social and socially conciliatory attitudes. 'Coding' – the use of agreed upon generic signs and signals to indicate dissident sexualities – is of little use in a suppressive society if it cannot at once signal disruption and safety. If the sign does not signify, most of the time and to most people, a socially acceptable and therefore innocuous sexual or non-sexual configuration, then it would be useless as a device with which to circumvent majority understanding. Productive sexual continence was occasionally exploited as 'code' for socially deviant sexualities. But for the most part it represented a sexual concept entirely in accord with much historical, and with a significant portion of Victorian, sexual discourse. It is this primary discourse, rather than what it potentially signalled to a minority readership, that this book describes, in the hope of ultimately facilitating better understandings of both. In reading this discourse for its usual rather than unusual meanings, I hope both to demonstrate the centrality of productive sexual continence to Victorian systems of thought and to advocate for the (not exclusive, but nevertheless vital) importance of reading methods that preserve rather than disrupt the delicate tissue of discourse that makes up historical representations of sexuality.

* * *

The late nineteenth-century existence of a Decadent aestheticism built around sexual continence relied heavily on a mode of imagining the sexuality of artists that reaches back to the Romantic period, a mode that itself draws on a much wider means of conceiving of productive sexual continence. Victorian writers, both within and outside of the Decadent

Movement, thought of sexuality as playing various roles in the lives of artists or those to whom art was important. Of these discursive possibilities perhaps the most familiar to us (because they are also most prevalent today) are those in which the aesthetic or artistic life was associated with sexual license, this being often in turn associated with social transgression or liberation and political radicalism.[72] The idea of a close relationship between sexuality and art found expression, for instance, in Grant Allen's 1894 essay 'The New Hedonism', in which he uses the very commonness of the idea to make deliberately incendiary conclusions from the importance that Darwin's evolutionary theory had attributed to sexuality. Having proclaimed (in a manner recognizable from Protestant anti-Catholic rhetoric) that 'the unclean and impure things are celibacy and asceticism', he then pushes this familiar idea to provocative extremes:

> everything high and ennobling in our nature springs directly out of the sexual instinct. [...] To it we owe the evolution of music, of poetry, of romance, of *belles lettres*; the evolution of painting, of sculpture, of decorative art, of dramatic entertainment. To it we owe the entire existence of our aesthetic sense, which is, in the last resort, a secondary sexual attribute.[73]

Despite his reliance on emergent conceptions of sexuality, Allen was able to make such claims in a mainstream (albeit liberal) publication like the *Fortnightly Review* because this aesthetic-sexual discourse had strong roots, though always co-existent with alternative models, in the same romantic conceptions of the artist from which Victorian Aestheticism and Decadence in part developed. Andrew Elfenbein, in his work on eighteenth-century romantic conceptions of genius (particularly artistic genius), has described the 'two models for genius' that had arisen by the beginning of the nineteenth century: the anti-domestic, sexually transgressive genius, and the solitary, ascetic, sexually disinterested genius.[74] The first of these was the more common, and evolved from the notion of the genius as someone who was both entirely original and, in Elfenbein's account, 'sublime', the latter quality being closely associated with excess. The original and sublime geniuses 'refused all boundaries and became laws unto themselves', and 'existed to let the reading public experience vicariously what it would never know in real life'. For them, 'no arena was more open to experiment than sexual desire'.[75] Elfenbein posits this sexually transgressive genius, epitomized in the scandalous Byron, as 'the prehistory of a homosexual role', since the search for the ultimate transgression led Romantic artists to deviant sexuality. This artistic type may also be considered a part of the history of the wider nineteenth-century discourse that presumes a connection between artistic vocations and transgressive sex, as seen in Allen's discussion of art and the poet.

But then there was also the second model of the romantic genius, what Elfenbein calls 'The ascetic image of a poet's Hippolytus-like indifference to women'.[76] Associated more with Wordsworth than Byron, this idea of the continent genius also had a strong influence on nineteenth-century conceptions of the aesthete, as we saw in the case of Pater's Hippolytus. Alongside the Byronic sexual-aesthetic discourse, and often even with reference to the same individual, or indeed the same piece of writing or artwork, there existed throughout the nineteenth century this alternative discursive possibility in which art, and particularly aesthetic living, was associated with a productive ideal of reserve, restraint, and austerity. Within this model, sexual continence was often imagined as more than only an example of self-discipline; it was also a productive practice that contributed either to the creation of artworks or to an aesthetic mode of life. George Bernard Shaw's early novel *Love among the Artists* (written c. 1880, published 1900), for instance, presents a muddle of competing sexual-artistic discourses. For the actress Madge, 'passion and poetry' are 'conditions of her full efficiency as an actress'; and yet she herself 'rather pitied her married colleagues, knowing perfectly well that they were not free to be so fastidious, reserved, and temperate as her instincts told her a great artist should always be'.[77] Though Madge's pity begins with the mutual constraints imposed by marriage, it ends in something more than that, by implying that continence carries its own rewards for the artist quite beyond practical freedom.

In contrast to Shaw's ambivalence and open contradiction, an attempt to reconcile and rationalize these co-existent discourses can be found in Francis Galton's *Hereditary Genius* (1862), in which his efforts to determine whether or not particular kinds of genius were hereditary led him into a taxonomy of types based partly on sexual behaviour. Though poets are, he writes, 'a sensuous, erotic race, exceedingly irregular in their way of life', nonetheless they are 'clearly not founders of families'.[78] Elfenbein finds similar claims in eighteenth-century treatises on genius, where artistry implies a wildness of character not fit for domesticity.[79] For Galton, however, the reason for such incompatibility goes further:

> To be a great artist, requires a rare and, so to speak, unnatural correlation of qualities. A poet, besides his genius, must have the severity and stedfast [*sic*] earnestness of those whose dispositions afford few temptations to pleasure, and he must, at the same time, have the utmost delight in the exercise of his senses and affections.[80]

The successful poet and artist for Galton was not only a sensual character, but one also who must exercise the utmost discipline over himself – and his sensuality – to turn such impulses into artistic form: too much discipline, it is implied, to allow even the erotic expenditures of married life.

For many in the period such restraint and discipline, especially for the 'great artist' or genius, required at least temporary sexual continence. To a certain extent, this continence can be justified as a negative rejection of domesticity, of the everyday, or of the existing social order as an environment uncongenial to artistic creation. But there was also a positive element of this vision, of something to be actively gained from a sexually continent state. And rather than leading to what Frank Kermode famously called the 'necessary isolation or estrangement' of the Romantic artist, the result of which is an inevitably self-destructive suffering, this restraint was often imagined as the means of reconciliation between this artist and the inartistic world of which they were a part.[81] This version of aesthetic sexual ethics was in itself part of a much wider discourse – discoverable in a vast range of writing about sexual health throughout the period – in which sexual continence was associated with intellectual or spiritual gain. In most instances (especially earlier in the nineteenth century but continuing well into the twentieth century) this gain is figured as not in itself sexual – differing in this aspect from pseudo-Freudian sublimation – and as having positive implications either for the individual or for society (in most cases both).

A late example can be found in Robert Bridges' *The Testament of Beauty* (1929). 'Celibat lives', writes Bridges, 'are led/without impoverishment of intellect or will'. In some cases, he continues:

> virginity may seem a virile energy
> in its angelic liberty, prerequisit
> to the perfection of some high personality.[82]

The Testament of Beauty, though written in the early twentieth century, was a culmination of the artistic and sexual sensibility that Bridges spent the latter half of the nineteenth century evolving. Bridges had trained as a physician in the 1860s, and in many ways his conception of the body remained Victorian. Similar survivals can be seen in the work of George Moore and Vernon Lee, who continued to express an arguably outdated, though by no means defunct, idea of bodily function well into the twentieth century.

Comparable statements can be found throughout nineteenth-century literature, and not only from England. In the widely read *Walden* (1854), Henry David Thoreau writes:

The generative energy, which, when we are loose, dissipates and makes us unclean, when we are continent invigorates and inspires us. Chastity is the flowering of man; and what are called Genius, Heroism, Holiness, and the like, are but various fruits which succeed it.[83]

Both Bridges and Thoreau frame their statements with Christian sentiment: the latter continues, 'Man flows at once to God when the channel of purity is open. By turns our purity inspires and our impurity casts us down'.[84] Yet in the same paragraph, and in support of the same argument, Thoreau quotes also from ancient Chinese philosopher Mencius and from the ancient Indian Vedas. This discourse does not originate in nineteenth-century Britain; it is a manner of conceiving the sexual body that can be found in many cultures, as part of widely differing conceptions of the body as a whole, and with an enormous range of associated cultural values and meanings. This ubiquity, with the risk it introduces of too-ready recognition of a coherent historical object, is precisely why methods of reading are needed that can recognize the discourse's importance within specific networks of meaning, such as that of late nineteenth-century Decadence.

The protagonist of Tolstoy's famously pessimistic novella *The Kreutzer Sonata* (1889) also expresses his theories on sexuality in a way that suggests a similar model of productive continence, though corrupted in an excessively sensual world to produce only the 'utter infatuation' of romantic love.[85] In his non-fiction Tolstoy outlined a more positive model of how a more permanent sexual continence, by nullifying sexual desire, could become a positive force in an ideal life. In an 1890 essay entitled 'A Reply to Critics of "The Kreutzer Sonata"', first published in English translation in the short-lived English periodical *The Universal Review*, he promised to offer 'in plain and simple language my own views on the subject handled in the story'. He confirmed his feeling that the obsession with love and sex in Western societies meant that 'the best energies of our men and women are drawn forth and exhausted during the most promising period of life'. In contrast, he recommended an abstemious life combined with strong exercise. 'No one need go far', he wrote, 'in search of proofs that this kind of abstemious living is not merely possible, but far less hurtful to health than excess. Hundreds of instances are known to every one'. Such abstemiousness, he made clear, involved a strict sexual continence both outside and inside of marriage, with sexual relations limited to reproductive acts.[86]

Tolstoy assumes throughout his writing that the majority of people in the societies for which he was writing (middle-class Russian and European) lived a life of excessive sensuality, unaware of the benefits of the austere life he recommended. Yet his theories are based on a model of the sexual body that dominated medical opinion in the nineteenth century throughout Europe and beyond. Systems built upon this model, of which there were many variations, relied on the idea that sexual activity involved a loss of something – physical, mental, or spiritual – the retention of which was beneficial to the rest of the body and even the mind. Some of these more formalized medical theories, and their counterparts in public conceptions of sexuality, will be explored in Chapter 1.

This understanding of how the sexual body works was primarily rooted in the experience of the male rather than female body; but this has not prevented its frequent application to the latter, by women as well as by men. In its more anatomical forms, it pivots upon the sense that semen is a valuable substance which, if lost, may weaken the whole body, but if retained may actively increase one's health or wellbeing. There has, therefore, often been close interaction between these theories and a culture's constructions of gender, especially masculinity. Writing based on a regulative model of the sexual body has often reproduced and reinforced negative ideas concerning female sexuality, both in medical contexts and in the wider cultures to which it has contributed. This interaction can be clearly seen in *The Kreutzer Sonata* in which, though it is implied that the continent life is ideal, one may nevertheless suspect that this ideal is more easily achievable by men than women. Though the protagonist claims that continence is the natural state for men (though they are often early 'debauched' by women), he suggest that women are naturally animal and sexual – and therefore, one may imagine, less able to benefit from continence. 'A woman' he says, 'knows very well that all the talk about elevated subjects is just talk, but that what a man wants is her body and all that presents it in the most deceptive but alluring light; and she acts accordingly'.[87] A similar gendering can be seen in *The Testament of Beauty*, where the quotation given above can be found within a larger section that takes as its subject the sexual difference between men and women. 'The allure of bodily beauty is mutual in mankind', muses Bridges, 'as is the instinct of breed, which tho' it seem i' the male/more activ, is i' the female more predominant'. Therefore, while successful and healthy celibate lives can be lived by both genders, 'this thing is rare in women, whereas in the man/virginity may seem a virile energy', and so on.[88] Far from the common association of virginity and chastity with women, Bridges allows men almost exclusive access to a particular type of productive sexual continence.

The Decadent writers I examine here, both male and female, also tend to gender disciplined control as masculine, and soft looseness as feminine, in a tradition that reaches back to the gender politics of ancient cultures.[89] The attitudes and practices associated with sexual continence played a crucial role in the construction of many styles of nineteenth-century masculinity, including that of the male artist. James Eli Adams in *Dandies and Desert Saints* (1995) has explored the relevance of concepts such as reserve and restraint to the gender performances of nineteenth-century writers, and has found the work of writers as disparate as Carlyle and Pater to 'lay claim to the capacity for self-discipline as a distinctly masculine attribute and in their different ways embody masculinity as a virtuoso asceticism'. And Herbert Sussman's *Victorian Masculinities* (1995) has illustrated the importance of mainstream medical discourse to the understanding of how nineteenth-century artists conceived of their profession both as a sexual practice defined by regulation and a style of masculinity, responding to 'the need to refashion the notion of manliness and of artistic manhood in a world transformed by industrialization and by *embourgoisement*'.[90] Despite this association between the self-control and discipline needed for sexual continence and that demanded by many styles of Victorian masculinity, however, many women drew on similar sexual discourses to theorize their own aesthetic ethics beyond the empty negativity of purity and innocence often attributed to feminine virginity, as is seen in the case of Vernon Lee. Though this book does not focus exclusively upon gender, there is ample scope for expansion in this direction, especially concerning the role of this discourse in thinking about the relationship between reproduction and creativity.

* * *

This book sits on the cusp between intellectual history and literary criticism. The debate about how far sexuality should be considered as a social construct specific to time and place, as opposed to an essential and biological instinct or drive, is of course as old as the study of historical sexuality itself. The historical meanings of sexual restraint in literature remain, however, particularly vulnerable to ahistoricist readings which, while useful in their own right, can nevertheless obscure specific earlier significances. This is at least in part because sexual restraint occupies a space of political and emotive burden in modern thought and cultural discourse. Recent theorists of asexuality have built on Foucault's 'repressive hypothesis' to identify a 'compulsory sexuality' at the heart of modern Western society, in which the rejection of active sexual desire is interpreted as the rejection also of much that such societies value; from family and all the social order represented by such, to the personal pleasure and self-expression that underpins consumer capitalism.[91] Discourses of sexual restraint have been used violently in many modern cultures, especially against groups whose active sexuality has been seen as a threat to existing social orders: women, lower socio-economic classes, those with non-normative desires (especially during and in the wake of the AIDS epidemic). And although there have been recent gains in the recognition of asexuality as a legitimate identity rather than 'a pathology and dysfunction', it remains most common for readers to approach representations of sexual inactivity or absence of sexual desire as negative, repressive, or dishonest, as a violence directed at others or oneself.[92] And while the last fifty years or so have seen great strides in the treatment of sexuality as a serious subject for research in the humanities – due to the work especially of certain branches of Feminist Theory, Gay and Lesbian History, and most recently Queer Studies – even within these disciplines this negative and ahistorical conception of sexual abstention has been until recently all but ubiquitous, and still retains great persuasive force.

How, then, should a study of a specific, unfamiliar historical discourse of sexual restraint shape its relationship with these theoretical approaches, especially Queer Studies, which in its varied, nuanced, and creative approaches to texts has transformed work on sexuality across the humanities? Despite 'its refusal to define its proper field of operation in relation to any fixed content', Queer Studies as it has so far been practiced has developed conventions that make recognition of this book's subject difficult: for instance, the tendency to work via psychoanalytic concepts that take sexual desire (and the pathology of its absence) for granted, and the common equation of queer antinormative agency with active sexuality (whether practiced or actively cultivated as part of one's subjective experience).[93]

This study is not, of course, the first to approach this conundrum. Karli June Cerankowski and Megan Milks, in the introduction to their 2014 edited collection *Asexualities: Feminist and Queer Perspectives*, ask what place asexuality has in the traditions of feminist and queer studies that 'have largely operated with a universal sexual assumption that ignores the possibility of asexuality as a viable lived experience'.[94] And Benjamin Kahan addresses a similar problem in his 2013 *Celibacies*, which examines twentieth-century American attempts to work celibacy into a positive sexual identity. Kahan points to both the 'sex wars' of the 1970s and 1980s and the AIDS crisis as formative events that still broadly determine the approach taken by most Queer theorists to sexual restraint. The former debates, with their focus on an individual's right to sexual expression, established 'a dichotomy (which queer theory inherits) between censorship and conservative politics on the one hand, and expression and oppositional liberal politics on the other', while the latter can be seen as 'heightening the stakes of the sex wars by seeing [sexual] expression not merely as the alternative to censorship but as the alternative to death'. The result is what he calls 'the expressive hypothesis', in which sexual expression is equated with the political Left, while sexual restraint is identified exclusively with the political Right. Under this 'expressive hypothesis' restraint can be rehabilitated only if it is revealed as the result of censorship or repression, and therefore redescribed by the critic as a hidden non-normative sexuality. 'The very real tension between celibate and queer ways of reading is indicative of more than a hermeneutic question', writes Kahan: 'this divergence maps competing and overlapping sexual ideologies and cultures'.[95]

Both *Celibacies* and *Asexualities* reconcile their methodologies with Queer Studies via two routes: by reframing celibacy and asexuality, respectively, as in themselves sexual identities, albeit diverse ones; and by finding common ground in the celebration of the non-normativity of socially marginalized identities. Cerankowski and Milks, while asserting that asexuals 'are diverse in practice, identification, and politics', nevertheless point to the 'relatively "new" [...] formation of communities around the common language of asexuality as it is understood today'. It is these communities, as well as the inherently marginalized position of asexuals in modern societies, that for Cerankowski and Milks lead back to Queer Studies:

> We undoubtedly view this project as a queer one: making sense of the social marginalization and pathologization of bodies based on the preference not to have sex, along with exploring new possibilities in intimacy, desire, and kinship structures – how could that not be queer?[96]

Kahan is less ready to identify celibacy as in itself queer: 'celibate and queer readings overlap', he says, 'without being coextensive'. However, his focus on the sexual content of celibacy and its potential radicalness leads him to linger as close as possible to that point of overlap. While he aims to 'pluralize the realm of the nonsexual' by moving away from flat representations of celibacy that can be found in much recent theory, his project nevertheless involves 'resexualising the nongenital in order to imagine a celibacy animated by sexual currents, desires, identifications, and pleasures'.[97] This resexualization of celibacy allows Kahan to argue for its relevance to ongoing conversations about queer sexualities: his study 'revalues celibacy as possessing special purchase on its putative counterpart "the sexual"'; it 'unsettles the familiar repression/liberation and normal/

queer binaries' and 'exceeds the boundaries of the hetero/homo binary, requiring a rethinking of sexual categories and the concept of sex as such'. Although he admits that 'celibacy is certainly not always connected to progressive politics', it is nevertheless part of his broader purpose to show that celibacy *can* be a productive part of radical politics by focusing on instances in which this has been the case. 'Before we decide to cede celibacy to the Right', he writes, 'we might want to consider reclaiming the radical political potential that nineteenth- and twentieth-century artists and activists found in the practices of celibacy'.[98]

Like Kahan, I acknowledge the overlap between sexual continence and queer sexualities, and trace the relevance of the history of queer sexualities, especially homosexuality, to the history of sexual restraint and vice versa. And like him I treat these as overlapping but distinct categories, and therefore generally avoid broad use of the word 'queer' to refer to the writers who are the focus of this study, to their work or ideas, or to my own reading methods. My own study, however, operates at a further remove from Queer Studies than Kahan's. Unlike Kahan's largely twentieth-century celibacy, the sexual continence explored in this book often relies on a contemporary credulity regarding the possibility of true sexual restraint that the employment of psychoanalytic frameworks risks trivializing. Whether we as readers consider such restraint to be credible is irrelevant to this reading. Furthermore, the many meanings and associations of such a discourse are readily obscured by methods of reading that seek to align it politically, to identify it wholesale with radical or conservative politics (conscious or not), or a normative/antinormative force.

Although the present study owes a great debt to Kahan's work on celibacy, the challenges of approaching productive sexual continence while working with such inheritances from Queer Studies can be seen in Kahan's analysis. Despite his interest in historical sexualities, Kahan is also interested in celibacy as an ahistorical sexual configuration, as a sexual identity that inherently operates against or beyond sexual normativity. Although he acknowledges that celibacy often appears 'to follow the rules of normative sexual life exactly', he argues that this appearance is often, even usually, deceptive: 'Celibacy distorts the intentions of codes of respectability, subverting them from the inside in order to launch a full-scale assault on a deeply inequitable sex/gender system. In short, celibacy forges respectability as revolution'.[99] Annamarie Jagose has written about the almost total identification of Queer Studies with a certain concept of antinormativity, from within as much as from outside of that field. 'These days', she writes, 'it almost goes without saying that queer is conventionally understood to mean "antinormative"', where the normativity involved is characterized as static, hegemonic, easily identifiable, potentially surmountable through individual agency (what she calls 'the sovereign subject's voluntarist assertion of political will against normative power') and, above all, heterosexual. 'This model', Jagose argues, 'is a long way removed from Foucault's articulation of sexual normalization, not least because – with its manifold, dissident genderings flying beneath the radar of heteronormativity – it covertly buys back into the repressive hypothesis so roundly debunked in *The History of Sexuality*, volume 1'.[100] In reducing normativity to a deceptively manageable size, she claims, Queer Studies risks replacing repression with a mythical 'normativity', and in the process continuing normativity's work of promising 'enlightenment, liberation, and manifold pleasures' as a result of sexual proliferation.[101]

In identifying celibacy as *essentially* antinormative, whether or not the subject is conscious of it as such, Kahan follows a pattern of reasoning familiar within Queer Studies. A combination of this finding of antinormativity at the heart of celibacy, and his tendency to reference psychoanalytic theory – even to deny its relevance – rather than historical theories of bodily function in untangling a writer's sexual ideas, leads Kahan to dismiss the relevance of productive sexual continence in his reading of Henry James. The enduring influence of psychoanalysis on Queer Studies means that productive continence is frequently read as coextensive with its most familiar incarnation, Freudian sublimation. This happens in *Celibacies* also, as Kahan distinguishes his radical celibate from the 'nonrevolutionary sublimated subject'. His own celibate, he says, 'poses a threat, entailing a more radical withdrawal and reshaping of the social order than is the case with the recognized and validated sublimated subject'. When it comes to discussing the importance of Henry James's celibacy to his model of artistry, therefore, Kahan argues against the relevance of a mechanism in which 'sexual energy is rechanneled into a socially useful direction such as the creation of art', because 'sublimation is normative at heart [...] and thus does not capture the queer, revolutionary, and socially disprized aspects of modernist celibacy that this study explores'. James cannot be sublimated because his sexuality is antinormative. The potential for James' model of bodily function to differ from Freud's or Kahan's own is not pursued.[102]

The discourse explored in this book cannot be straightforwardly identified, even in its own time, as normative or antinormative. Unlike homosexuality, its expression and representation were never constrained or politicized by legal sanctions. Despite its close relationship with male physiology, it cut across lines of power such as gender, class, and race.

Individuals who engaged with it felt themselves to be positioned very differently from each other towards social norms. If this book prioritizes individual indications of how controversial or otherwise they considered their ideas or opinions to be, or how contemporary readers received their statements, it is not because these individuals are taken for sovereign subjects, or because their indications or receptions are confused with the actual workings of normativity (i.e. with what were believed to be controversial positions being equated with actual antinormative impulses); rather, it is because in such written statements we glimpse the outlines of a discourse. If these indications do not always seem to square with existing narratives of Victorian sexual culture, or indeed preconceptions concerning the politics or affiliations of a given individual, then it is perhaps these narratives or preconceptions that need to be re-examined and complicated.

This book is not an intellectual history of continence; yet a methodology closer to my own can be found in studies that are either explicitly intellectual historical projects or are influenced by such. Peter Cryle and Alison Moore in their 2011 *Frigidity: An Intellectual History* write of the difficulty of identifying historical discourses that bear superficial resemblance to, and indeed have a genealogical relationship with, concepts that have an important place in modern systems of thought. In their case, the attempt to rediscover the varied significances that frigidity has held over time must confront the very negative meanings that female frigidity in particular holds in twentieth-century feminism and psychoanalysis. They address this potential hazard by sharply delineating their own agenda from that of these approaches, though acknowledging shared values. While they 'concur with the impulse to bury frigidity as a model for explaining and pathologizing forms of sexual desire or its lack', they 'are not concerned to ameliorate the happiness, self-acceptance or sexual fulfilment of anyone'. Rather, it is their intention to restore a sense of discursive 'untidiness' and 'complication' to what was in danger of becoming a somewhat shallow concept, to 'show frigidity to be a rather variable object of knowledge without being a particularly inscrutable one'. 'Intellectual history', they claim, 'can reveal the patchiness, the unevenness, the instability of notions that may in fact be too quickly recognized by modern eyes'. Ultimately, this process can only enhance the feminist and psychoanalytic project by enabling more nuanced understandings of how sexual ideas and concepts have operated variously in different 'discursive economies'.[103]

Sexual restraint, like frigidity, has suffered from being 'too quickly recognized by modern eyes': recognized as suppressed homosexuality, as more or less effective sublimation, as asexuality. Recent work, however, has started to reveal a rich and varied genealogy that does not always respond to modern categorizations. For instance, the work of Sharon Marcus and Carolyn Oulton on romantic friendship in the nineteenth century suggests conscious exploitation of the overlapping space between sexuality and friendship that challenges current conceptions of the sexual. Marcus' analysis of female friendship in late nineteenth-century novels and popular writing indicates the conceptual prevalence of a form of relationship that was important in its own right. Reading such friendship always as suppressed or latent homosexuality, Marcus argues, eliminates an important concept from Victorian networks of meaning.[104] Oulton follows a similar method when she calls for greater attention to 'the terms of late nineteenth-century thought'.[105] She contends that romantic friendship was not a space of unusual sexual innocence, but rather one that recognized the area it shared with same-sex sexuality, and thrived on the careful regulation of feeling away from it. Of the deployment of Plato in this context, for instance, she writes that 'this conscious adaptation of Greek ideals can hardly be consistent with a lack of sexual awareness'; circumvention of homosexual content in Plato may be self-aware, and yet not necessarily hypocritical. 'Whatever ambiguities later scholars have identified', she states, 'in the nineteenth century demonstrations of love between friends could escape condemnation from, or even be deployed by, otherwise conservative commentators'.[106]

The productive sexual continence that this book finds in Decadent writing also challenges many binaries that modern readers may be tempted to take for granted: sexual and non-sexual, heterosexual and homosexual, the political Right and the political Left. Like Arnold I. Davidson in his *The Emergence of Sexuality* (2001), I focus less on determining what sexuality actually is, was, or can be, and more on describing 'styles of reasoning': the manner in which sexuality (and its absence) is represented, and the relationships drawn between it and other things, as distinct from the desires, pleasures, eroticism, or affective states that undoubtedly do inform and shape texts.[107] I also follow Davidson in approaching the late nineteenth century as a period of both conceptual disruption and overlap, in which understandings of sexual function and perversion were gradually separated from anatomical thinking to produce modern 'sexuality'.[108] The result was a late nineteenth-century culture in which various models of bodily function co-existed relatively unproblematically, among qualified and practicing medics as much as in lay discourse. The idea that sexual continence was possible, at least potentially healthy, and could positively affect both one's personal experience and one's relationship with others was one which both existed and was considered persuasive in many different strata of this multifarious late nineteenth-century British culture. Recognition of this discourse, and the many different values which were attached to it, can contribute to our understanding not only of how sex (including the choice to avoid sex) has been conceived of and represented, but also of the myriad other areas of thought upon which sexual discourse touches.

I have therefore, though working closely with a Foucauldian notion of 'discourse', followed Davidson (as well as Cryle and Moore, and Kahan) by putting Foucauldian questions of 'power' hypothetically on hold, in order to allow the description of a discourse that, while often converging around points of social and political privilege – male, heterosexual, middle class – also often overlapped categories of gender and sexual orientation.[109] While my relegation of these topics to the borders rather than the centre of my discussion has given room for a single discourse to be described at length, it is my hope that the detail given here will allow and encourage further readings of late nineteenth-century Decadence in its relation to power, particularly as reflected in its treatment of gender and sexual identity, as well as recognition of the importance of a discourse of productive sexual continence to other areas of late nineteenth-century British society.

The book has five chapters. The first chapter attempts to indicate something of the pervasiveness of a productive ideal of sexual continence in late nineteenth-century British culture. The sheer ubiquity of this discourse in the period makes this section necessarily selective; and yet I have sought to preserve an impression of breadth, of multiple potential lines of influence rather than imply a misleading sense of direct causality where none can be conclusively identified. This is followed by four chapters in which a particular branch of late nineteenth-century Decadence, to which productive sexual continence was central, is explored. Chapter 2 examines the alternative tradition of reading Walter Pater described above, which emphasized his advocacy of restraint and reserve as both stylistic and ethical principles. Informed by early readings in this latter tradition, I demonstrate the plausibility of an interpretation of Pater's work as carefully distinguishing between aesthetic sensuousness and sensuality. Pater can viably be read as assessing the ideal aesthetic life in terms of health and love, and representing sexual continence as conducive to both. And although his choice of language never explicitly excludes an eroticized continence, such eroticization is always an interpretive option rather than essential to his reasoning.

Chapter 3 looks at the poet and critic Lionel Johnson, and particularly at his incorporation of this continent ideal into his Christianized cultural humanism. In the poetry, resistance to temptation is described as a process by which potentially sensual experience is made 'safely' sensuous, while in the letters and criticism can be found admiration for various continent states that reconcile individual aesthetic experience with social responsibility. And in Chapter 4, the pre-1900 essays of Vernon Lee are shown to be consistently anti-sensual, though they distinguish this sensuality from a kind of continent sense experience identified as aesthetic, and associated with Pater. Lee also uses this aesthetic sensuousness as a model for 'ideal' – that is, disinterested and unpossessive – relations between people, and between people and things. A fifth chapter then explores the resurfacing of this discourse in the work of George Moore, a writer who combined it with very different and potentially even contradictory sexual systems. Finally, a conclusion indicates the usefulness of this revised understanding of sexuality within Decadence in looking at various other aspects of late nineteenth- and early twentieth-century literature and culture. I hope to show how the discourse of productive sexual continence was worked closely into thinking about the aesthetic life in the late nineteenth century, as well as to demonstrate the sheer abundance of possible sources for such ideas in the wider culture, and the degree to which this discourse can be seen to influence thinking about art in the twentieth and even twenty-first centuries.

CHAPTER I

Loss and Gain
The Victorian Sexual Body

The late nineteenth century saw what Lesley Hall has called 'the beginnings of certain "modern" ways of thinking about sex'.[1] From the 1880s onward the English birth rate dropped dramatically, for which later marriages and a wider employment of contraceptive practices (including abstinence within marriage) have been posited as major causal factors.[2] Gender roles were undergoing very public revision and unconventional sexual desires and behaviours, together with efforts to contain them, were becoming more visible. And although venereal diseases still had no effective cures, their separate aetiologies were becoming better understood.[3]

Such material changes were underpinned by paradigmatic shifts in how sex and sexuality operated discursively. Michel Foucault famously argued that the nineteenth century saw a 'discursive explosion' during which modern 'sexuality' was not only defined, but created: what had been thought of as merely incidental behaviours started, under the aegis of a new many-branched sexual science, to be seen to constitute identities; 'The sodomite', for instance, 'had been a temporary aberration; the homosexual was now a species'.[4] Arnold I. Davidson has built upon this Foucauldian theory of the origins of sexuality to identify a gradual shift from 'anatomical' to 'psychiatric styles of reasoning' about sex. Davidson argues that, whereas medical thinkers at the beginning of the century considered sexual diseases to be diseases of the sexual organs, by mid-century emphasis had shifted to the brain. Despite (or perhaps because of) frequent acknowledgement that too little was known about brain anatomy to accurately locate specific functions, it began to be assumed that such identification would be made as science advanced. The later part of the century saw a further shift away from the specificities of anatomy to allow for the emergence and eventual dominance of what Davidson calls 'a system of psychiatric knowledge that has its own very particular style of reasoning and argumentation', in which 'The appropriate way to understand the sexual instinct is in functional terms, not in anatomical ones'. By parting with anatomy, sex was able to take on a newly central importance to identity: the new psychiatry 'took sexuality to be the way in which the mind is best represented. To know a person's sexuality is to know that person'.[5]

This chapter does not challenge the thesis of transition and change that has been the focus of most studies of nineteenth-century sexuality, and especially those of Decadent sexuality. But, as Hall points out, 'at any given moment in history several discourses may be operating at both the social and the individual level'. Not only is it true that 'people (and indeed societies) are capable of simultaneously holding ideas inconsistent with one another', but it is also the case that sexual discourse at any time is made up of 'the constant interplay of "reactionary", "progressive", and apathetic forces'.[6]

The discourse explored here – in which sexual continence was imagined as positive and productive – was one that, in terms of models of bodily function, tended to point backwards rather than forwards, to continuity with the past rather than the emergent future. Its extensive history made it infinitely adaptable, adjusting to new developments in physiological and sexual science; yet it also had a long memory, and often appeared alongside supposedly outdated theories of bodily function, not least among which was (and still is when similar ideas come up, as they often do) the remarkably persistent idea that semen is an important substance for the health of the male body. Late nineteenth-century productive continence was compatible with radical politics, changing gender roles, and non-normative sexualities. But at the same time, it most often dealt with what was starting to seem like an old-fashioned notion of sex: with behaviours rather than identities, and with an anatomical more than a psychological understanding of sexual health. Resorts to such 'reactionary' models of sexuality are frequently found side by side with the most progressive views and attitudes, including those concerning sex. The reworking of productive continence at the heart of psychoanalysis as sublimation illustrates its deep tenacity.

There are many reasons for this small 'c' conservativism in sexual discourse, not least the fact that sexual ideas have most often been absorbed in the first instance – on the part of intellectuals and artists as much as anyone else – through gossip between peers or serendipitous exposure rather than from doctors (themselves far from universally knowledgeable) or up-to-date medical texts. But it also seems pertinent that productive continence often appeared, in both medical and non-medical writing, hand in hand with a more tenacious discourse: the suspicion that sexual activity could be potentially harmful, could involve some sort of damaging loss. The Victorian period was a time of what Lesley Hall and Roy Porter have called sexual 'polyphony', in which even the seemingly orthodox forces of medicine, law, and religion contained drastic contradiction when it came to sex, without one set of ideas necessarily being identifiable as more mainstream or normative than others.[7] And yet this suspicion of sex – a concern that too much of it *could* be dangerous, whether physically, emotionally, spiritually, or morally – underlay even the most pro-sensual voices, though there was wide disagreement over just how much was too much. This was true regardless of any political or religious affiliation: Michael Mason, for instance, has argued that anti-sensual positions were more common among progressive agnostic groups throughout the period than among regular churchgoers of any denomination.[8]

It was also true despite the co-existent fear that too little sex could also damage the health, causing all sorts of dangerous obstructions and atrophies in both men and women. Herbert Sussman has written of early Victorian sexuality, especially male, as a 'continuum of degrees of self-regulation' in which the goal was a precarious balance between too much and too little. More than health depended on striking the right balance, including 'the assumption that the creative prowess of men depends upon the appropriate regulation of their sexuality'.[9] As the century wore on, however, there was increasingly less consensus on exactly where this sweet spot lay. By the 1890s, as we will see, many voices both medical and non-medical were arguing for the healthiness of at least temporary continence for both men and women, both outside and inside of marriage, while few seemed willing to deny the possibility of sexual excess.

The ubiquity of sexual wariness in late Victorian culture has rarely been allowed for in studies of Decadent sexuality. Suspicion of sex was arguably relieved to some extent as the twentieth century progressed. Anxieties about sexual loss were partly divested of force as sex became less physically dangerous in a way wholly unprecedented – as contraception became more reliable, childbirth less dangerous, and many venereal diseases curable – and gradually gave way to anxiety that too little, rather than too much, sex was the primary danger. Yet even today contexts in which concern again arises that sex may be in some way damaging often produce a hope that continence may prove actively beneficial; in sports, for example, and in certain religious traditions.

It is not the business of this book to construct or uphold a master narrative to account for the increased interest of late Victorian writers in productive continence. Continence, regulation, and self-discipline were valued across the period far beyond the management of the sexual body. The physical and emotional self-control expected within Victorian models of manliness, for instance, is without doubt relevant to each of the examples explored in this book. Sussman, James Eli Adams, and Trev Broughton have detailed the extent to which this varied and tenacious masculine normativity shaped the lives of men intent on creative and intellectual work.[10] And Pamela K. Gilbert has shown how this primarily middle-class white masculine ideal determined styles of living well beyond this group by feeding into the liberal construction of public health discourse, as the body of the good citizen was modelled on that of the gentleman.[11] The saturation of Victorian Britain with metaphors of regulation and restraint has been far from adequately explored, and certainly goes some way towards explaining the persistence of productive sexual continence even when the anatomical models of bodily function that would best explain its popularity became outdated. The very pervasiveness of such metaphors, however, can obscure the ideological differences in their deployment. This chapter argues for the importance of an overlooked discourse without limiting that importance to any one context, though the potential for continence to operate metaphorically is never forgotten.

The texts examined in this chapter are all concerned with how the sexual body should be managed, though their motives for this concern differ widely. Some are more explicitly interested in the transition from boyhood to manhood, dependent child/subject to responsible adult/citizen; others exploit these discourses for commercial gain; still others are primarily concerned with physical health, though undoubtedly underpinned by the norms outlined above. Likewise their perceptions of what is at stake if such management is not achieved vary widely: physical wasting and death, selfishness and cruelty, loss of public respect, non-normative sexual behaviour. Whatever their motives, the shared interest of these texts in physical-ethical regime links them to the Decadent literature explored in this book, even where no direct line of influence can be established. Above all this chapter seeks to establish the commonplace nature of productive sexual continence in Victorian discourse, with a view to expanding and complicating the critical conception of both Victorian sexual normativity and British Decadent sexuality.

This chapter begins by tracing productive sexual continence through nineteenth-century medical writing about the male sexual body as it progressed (slowly, unevenly, messily) from anatomical to psychiatric models of sex and sexuality. This section argues that such continence was at no point attributable to a single model of bodily function that could be superseded or debunked. The long history of this discourse lent it a physiological adaptability that allowed it to co-exist alongside blatantly contradictory theories and ideas with surprising amicability. Although the texts examined focused largely on the male sexual body, their findings were often used to extrapolate concerning female sexuality in a way that makes them relevant to the history of both. Sex was, of course, by no means an uncontroversial topic for Victorian medics: at a time when medicine was striving to professionalize by claiming for itself the disinterestedness and rationality of science, addressing sexuality risked aligning the writer with the fringe or 'quack' doctors who had long exploited public fears on this subject. This section covers both 'professional' medical writers and 'quacks', and yet acknowledges that this distinction was by no means always clear.

A second section looks at non-medical genres which treat sexual health as part of a wider physical, mental, and spiritual system. It begins with two popular genres – advice for young men and 'new women' writing – that were both products of what Hall calls 'the new articulateness about sexual morality' from the 1880s onward, and shared an interest in emphasizing the healthfulness of continence to a much wider audience than did the writing of medical professionals, as a social as much as an individual responsibility.[12] They also shared with British Decadence an interest in lifestyle and regime, advocating sexual practices that were both continent and embodied. This similarity throws light upon both Decadent literature and its reception, as contemporary readers showed themselves eager to receive the same ethical lessons from both genres. The section then looks at two branches of intellectual culture that intersected more explicitly with literary Decadence: Platonism and Tractarianism. The texts examined in this section use sexual continence to theorize a spiritually and morally acceptable (according to their lights) embodiment, an ethical practice that harnesses rather than rejects the body. These texts were highly influential on the intellectual culture of Decadence as it likewise pondered the ethics of embodiment.

The chapters that follow will rarely argue for the direct influence of particular texts on Decadent writing, yet similar 'styles of reasoning' about sexual continence point to significant cultural continuity. Decadent writers may well have frequently thought radically and non-normatively about a range of topics, including sexuality; but many of them were very much of their time when it came to envisioning the sexual and ethical body.

Medicine and the Male Sexual Body

The spermatic fluid [...] is not [...] an excrementitious fluid, and intended, like the urine, to be eliminated from the body; but, on the contrary (except during an occasional act of generation) to be received into the circulation, and thence distributed to every part of the system. It is the presence of the semen in the circulating fluids of the male, and the accumulated influence of the unexhausted ovaria in the system of the female, which gives to the countenances of the continent and chaste the peculiar expression of energy and vigorous health which generally characterise them, and which, though the features themselves should not be fashioned to the lines of beauty, never fails, notwithstanding, to impress the beholder with a sense of admiration, and some feeling of respect.[13]

The above pronouncement by James Richard Smyth, M.D., was published in 1841 in *The Lancet*, in an article titled 'Impotence and Sterility'. Relatively little is known about Smyth. He was born in Ireland and qualified in 1833 in Edinburgh with a thesis on cholera epidemics.[14] After a few years as medical referee for the Clerical, Medical, and General Life Assurance Office in Banbury, and a few more as a physician in London, he sought to build professional credibility by publishing in medical journals on a range of topics: rickets, heart and brain diseases, and impotence.[15] These publications were collected in 1844: a reviewer for *The Medico-Chirurgical Review* found the book 'very interesting', but without 'sufficient stamen to render their collection into an expensive volume, a desirable proceeding'.[16] Smyth was not a venereal specialist, and does not appear to have become particularly notable, successful, or famous. But there seems little reason to suggest, as Michael Mason does, that he was a 'semi-quack' who operated on the 'edge of legitimacy', with a commercial interest in outdated theories.[17]

Smyth claims that most impotence, as well as 'perhaps nine-tenths' of more generalized cases of 'nervousness, mental imbecility, and derangement', can be traced to sexual debility, largely caused by sexual excesses in the patient or an ancestor. He does not specify what constitutes excess but suggests that anything outside of potentially reproductive acts would be suspect, with masturbation being especially dangerous due to additional excitation.[18] Such excesses can, he writes, cause not only physical but also emotional and ethical breakdown, with patients 'always becoming deteriorated, more or less unprincipled and ungenerous, as sexual intemperance or disorder has enfeebled their generative economy'. The invariable result is that the 'sexual sensualist' is not only physically debilitated but also 'separated from the society and sympathy of his species'. Continence, on the other hand, actively encourages both physical health and positive social relationships, as the retention of spermatic fluid in men (and, more mysteriously, the 'unexhausted ovaria' in women) imparted 'energy and vigorous health' and the 'admiration' and 'respect' of others.[19] This productive state of continence, though necessarily involving restraint, is not incompatible with occasional moderate sexual acts; in fact, continence is represented as necessary for correct sexual function.[20]

Smyth is not wholly representative of the early Victorian medical profession's sexual attitudes. Throughout the century the profession was what Mason calls 'pro-sensual in tendency', asserting that sex – within limits that varied widely in strictness – was not only natural but often necessary to physical and mental health. Doctors worried that lack of exercise would render genital organs useless and that unexpelled fluid would poison the system. The hazy category of 'sexual excess' frequently included excessive continence, though this became less common as the century progressed.[21] Belief in the dangerousness of prolonged continence often seems to have led doctors into the uncomfortable position of recommending illicit sexual relations to men not in a position to marry. John Addington Symonds remembers Spencer Wells, surgeon to Queen Victoria, having (much to Symonds' repugnance) 'recommended cohabitation with a hired mistress, or, what was better, matrimony' as a cure for nervous illness resulting (he believed) from involuntary seminal loss.[22] Another surgeon to royalty, James Paget, in his 1870 lecture addressed to doctors on 'sexual hypochondriasis' or psychosomatic sexual illness, warned that 'many of your patients will ask about sexual intercourse and some will expect you to prescribe fornication'. Though Paget does not recommend such prescription, there was evidently sufficient opinion to the contrary for the healthfulness of continence to require justification.[23] Medical prescriptions of extra-marital sex do not seem to have been extended to women, despite the fact that the destructiveness of continence was much more consistently asserted by the medical profession in relation to women (a consistency that did not, however, stop non-medical writers from imagining healthfully continent states for women).[24]

Despite this near-universal medical insistence on the naturalness of sex, however, it would be difficult to find a nineteenth-century medical professional who would deny that sexual excess – whether in quantity or in type – could have severe consequences, especially for men. Likewise, it was common to claim that extended periods of continence were compatible with – and often necessary for – a healthy body and mind, as well as social integration, while some authorities extended this healthfulness to total abstinence. *The Medico-Chirurgical Review*, for instance, complained that Smyth's comments on sexual excess were commonplace: 'all this, which [...] the author seems to announce almost as a novelty, has been long known to, and is continually acted upon, by every well-educated medical man'. And although the 'too great prolixity' with which case studies are presented is objected to (in a dig more at *The Lancet* as original publisher than at Smyth), the paragraph on continence is quoted as a valuable excerpt.[25] It may not have been accepted in all its details by every medical professional, but there was no question of this section being controversial, objectionable, or outdated.

Smyth's productive sexual continence relies upon a dubious physiology in which semen is reabsorbed into the system, giving rise to all manner of benefits. The idea that semen is related to or derived from the blood, and so could be reabsorbed into the circulation if not expended – what Mason calls 'haematic theory' – can be traced to Galenic medicine.[26] The physiological thinking behind this theory was complex. Semen, it was thought, was life-giving, and must therefore contain the substance necessary to all life, 'breath' (the Galenic *pneuma* or *spiritus*). Observing during animal dissection the structural similarity between lungs and heart, researchers supposed that they shared a function, and that *pneuma* must circulate in or with the blood. Semen, it followed, must therefore contain, or even be entirely made up of, blood.[27] From this logic, combined with the observation that men especially felt tired and depressed after ejaculation, followed the deduction that sexual activity in practice drew too readily on the blood of both genders, and that excessive activity exhausted the body's natural process of production, causing it to drain other systems of blood and with it, life-giving *pneuma*. Smyth's belief in spermatic reabsorption directly relates to his pragmatic approach to physiology, which takes older systems to contain truths that must be assimilated alongside modern systems: he claims that humoral pathology, despite containing 'a great many fancies, and what might very properly be denominated *false facts*', nevertheless 'still abounds with many grave and important truths, which, to prescribe with success for many diseases, it is highly necessary to be conversant with'.[28]

But not all Victorian descriptions of productive continence attributed it to the retention of semen. Much has been written about the importance of semen to the nineteenth-century sexual body.[29] In 1972 Ben Barker-Benfield coined the phrase 'spermatic economy' to describe the way in which nineteenth-century doctors (in his case largely American) imagined the male body as an economy in which semen was a coinage to be judiciously spent and saved. Barker-Benfield argues that this physiology was the product of nineteenth-century models of masculinity created under the economic pressures of capitalism.[30] Sussman and Broughton have also related this 'spermatic economy', redescribed as a 'hydraulic' or fluid-management system of masculine sexuality, to early nineteenth-century representations of masculine labour. And Elizabeth Stephens accounts for spermatorrhoea – the notorious nineteenth-century male disease caused by involuntary loss of spermatic fluid – as a medicalization of nineteenth-century anxieties concerning 'the softening and weakening of the male body in contemporary urban environments'.[31]

The cultural shifts in masculinity and economics identified by historians are clearly relevant to many of the texts explored in this chapter. My current purpose, however, is less to identify what cultural shift brought a certain mode of thinking about sexuality into predominance, and more to argue that a common 'style of reasoning' about sexuality made productive continence comprehensible to Victorian men and women even as sexual science changed dramatically. The use of phrases such as 'spermatic economy' to describe Victorian male sexuality disguises the fact that semen itself was only part of this attitude (though an important part), as writers continued to imagine sexuality as a matter of loss and gain, and to credit both the danger of sexual excess and the possibility of productive continence, even where spermatic loss was considered negligible. The variability and idiosyncrasy of the value systems that integrated productive sexual continence throughout the century must be related to a sexual discourse that was itself variable in the physiologies that underpinned it and the metaphors that it used, and was all the more tenacious for this variability.

Productive continence did not rely upon a single medical theory that could be debunked by new discoveries. It related to a constellation of sexual systems, some elaborate and some rudimentary, which worked to a similar logic and were by no means limited to nineteenth-century Britain. Even Galen did not attribute all danger of sexual excess to loss of semen, but also feared that the convulsions of orgasm were harmful to the bodily systems, and that excessive shocks could enervate the whole body, especially the brain.[32] What constituted such 'excess' depended on how well one wished to believe the body naturally adapted to sexual activity. The eighteenth century saw a proliferation of bodily systems, many of which incorporated a sexual logic of loss and gain whether or not they valued semen. For example, Friedrich Hoffman (1660–1742) developed a system of *tonus* or tone (broadly related to muscular tone, tension, or firmness), in which the organism was made up of fibres with the ability to contract and dilate. Hoffman worried about the strain that orgasm and particularly male ejaculation caused to these fibres. 'Hoffman', writes Thomas Laqueur, 'thought that a kind of ether acted through the nervous system on the muscles and kept them, as well as the body's fluids, in motion; it animates life. At times it seems almost as if semen were that ether'.[33] Likewise the Brunonian system of John Brown (1735–1788), in which life-force was measured according to excitability, led to far more anxiety around the exhaustion caused by over-excitation than that caused by excessive inertia. Excessive sexual activity was cited as an example of such over-excitation, a theory that resurfaces in Smyth's 1841 article when he claims that masturbation is the most damaging form of sexual activity because 'the generative organs and the entire nervous system are excited to a degree much beyond what takes place during actual copulation'.[34] The 'loss' in these systems is not necessarily of semen, but rather of some idealized balance or harmony of forces. Theophile de Bordeu (1722–1776), however, who expanded upon 'Brunonianism' with emphasis on the lymphatic glands, saw the secretion of semen as drawing on the body's vital essences, leading ultimately to debility if abused.[35] Eighteenth-century sexual discourse, like that of the nineteenth century, often expressed ideas that were antithetical to concerns about loss, such as the harmfulness of continence and necessity of regular sexual activity to health. These too continued into the nineteenth century, eventually evolving into the psychiatric belief that continence constitutes a dangerous 'repression' of instinct. But the eighteenth-century integration of sexual loss and productive continence into the new medical discourses of 'nerves', 'tone', and 'energy' also had a profound effect upon nineteenth-century thought.[36]

Semen was of central importance to the 'quack' or blatantly commercial specific cures for male 'sexual debility' that multiplied through the eighteenth and nineteenth centuries, reportedly making vast fortunes for many of their promoters.[37] Pamphlets advertising cures insisted on the importance of semen to the general health of the body: 'the greatest part of this seed', one claimed, '*is absorbed into the blood*, and produces on its return surprising changes. *It causes the beard and hair to grow*, and in short, may be looked upon as the *very essence of existence*'.[38] One 'Dr Hammond' even advertised as curative a 'seminal replenisher', which would 'not only create erectile power and brain matter, but likewise replenishes the seminal fluid'. This was handily 'prepared in small phials, which can be carried in the waistcoat-pocket'.[39] But the strength of quack literature lay in its appeal to audiences with varied physiological knowledge and prejudice. A pamphlet advertising 'Sir Astley Cooper's Vital Restorative' (nothing to do with Cooper himself) warned against 'the *immoderate loss* of the system's *most important fluid*': yet it also referred, like other medical writers, to a more balanced bodily economy, stating that 'all parts of the body may fail in their office and true performance of their relative duties, either by a deficiency in their own or deprivation and injury from other parts'. The pamphlet also picks up on the mid-century fashion for 'nerves', lamenting the 'undue excitement affecting the central ganglia of the sympathetic nervous system' caused by sexual excesses.[40] The evident success of peddlers of such wares suggests a widespread comprehension of a loss-and-gain understanding of sexual health like that expressed in professional medical literature among the men at whom such advertising was primarily aimed.

Medical professionals were almost certain, after about 1850, to state explicitly that semen itself was negligible to health, despite the continued and widespread credence given to the disease of spermatorrhoea. These statements were occasionally followed by references in the same texts to semen as a 'vital fluid' or 'precious substance', or to sexual excess as a 'drain' on vitality: an inconsistency suggestive of either lingering ideas, the strength of residual public opinion that doctors were loath to alienate, or reluctance to abandon any persuasive argument in what could be considered a moral as well as medical cause. But even where semen was consistently claimed to be negligible, or not mentioned at all, texts often contained forms of description – most often multiple forms – that suggested that the logic of sexual loss and continent gain continued to make sense throughout the period, to doctors as much as to their patients, though the nature of and reasons for that loss become less obvious or remain unstated as emphasis moved towards the nervous system. Paget's 'Sexual Hypochondriasis' bemoans the erroneous importance given to spermatic loss by men who attribute to this loss a complete breakdown in health. Referring to patients who expected to be prescribed extra-marital sexual intercourse to prevent more solitary losses, he admits that sometimes, in theory, 'a patient's health would be better for the wrong-doing'. In practice, however, he has 'never heard one say that he was better or happier after it; several have said that they were worse: and many, having failed, have been made much worse'. Sexual excess is evidently a danger for Paget even if not attributable to seminal loss. He claims that excessive sexual activity of all kinds could cause 'exhaustion, effeminacy, over-sensitiveness and nervousness', though not the insanity and death which many attributed to it. He does not say why sexual excess is harmful if seminal loss is natural and unremarkable, but the nervous system is evidently involved, as allowable quantity depends on 'the power of the nervous system'. Continence, on the other hand, he describes as both physically salutary and morally desirable. Unlike sex, 'chastity does no harm to mind or body; its discipline is excellent: marriage can be safely waited for'.[41]

More inconsistency concerning semen and sexual loss, as well as a clearer statement of the productive potential of continence, can be seen in what is likely the most widely referenced text of Victorian sexual medicine: William

Acton's *Functions and Disorders of the Reproductive Organs* (1857). Acton was a venereal specialist who had trained partly in France and built a career around importation of French treatments for sexual diseases. He also took an interest in public health, especially prostitution, and presented to the Select Committee investigating the Contagious Diseases Act in 1868. *Functions and Disorders* was enormously popular throughout the century and across the world; Havelock Ellis in 1910 wrote that it 'sets forth the traditional English view' on sexuality, and Robert Darby has written about its influence in Australia.[42] The extent to which Acton's work, and particularly his opinions on female sexuality, have been taken as typical of the period has rightly been questioned. However, as Ivan Crozier and Lesley Hall have argued, Acton's writing on male sexuality was representative of a central branch of thinking, and his preoccupations are a likely match for popular ideas.[43] *Functions and Disorders* is addressed at least partly to a male lay audience (apart from the odd sentence it treated only male sexuality) and Acton was well known as a practitioner dealing primarily with male sexual dysfunctions. Symonds reports in his *Memoirs* that, before being advised to co-habit or marry by Spencer Wells, he 'went to Acton and allowed him to cauterize me through the urethra': a common though extremely painful treatment for seminal disorders.[44]

Functions and Disorders firmly states that continence is conducive to physical and mental wellbeing but vacillates in rationalization. Acton claimed that 'the continuance of a high degree of bodily vigour is inconsistent with more than a very moderate indulgence in sexual intercourse' (a maximum of every seven to ten days for a healthy middle-aged man, and significantly less for the young, old, or otherwise weak). He is nevertheless scornful of the idea that semen is literally reabsorbed into the body. 'It is', he reports, 'a generally received impression that semen once secreted can be reabsorbed into the circulation, giving buoyancy to the feelings, and that manly vigour which characterizes the male', but continues, 'My experience goes counter to this theory, and I cannot bring myself to its adoption, notwithstanding the weight of authority in its favour'.[45] Acton does not, however, abandon the idea that something vital is lost during sex, and something valuable gained from continence. Having dismissed semen's health-giving qualities, Acton must account for why ejaculation damages the system. That it *is* damaging he never questions: he not only ascribed the worst possible consequences to sexual excesses, but also built much of his career upon the introduction of intrusive French treatments for spermatorrhoea.[46]

He refers to 'the importance of the fluid semen, which young men would thus lavishly expend'. But this economic metaphor of spending does not necessarily imply that continence is a productive saving. Acton does believe that loss of semen beyond a certain amount is damaging, but it is the secretion of excessive semen into the testes, from which it must be expelled either in sexual excesses or involuntarily in excessive nocturnal emissions or in the urine and faeces, that is problematic. Male sexual desire, for Acton, is largely created or at least activated by the collection of semen in the testes, and this collection can be consciously controlled. 'Semen is secreted sometimes slowly, sometimes quickly; and very frequently under the influence of the will'. He does not deny that some find continence difficult but claims that this 'sexual suffering' is caused by either occasional incontinence or dwelling on sexual subjects. Those who were physically continent but did not control their thoughts – what he calls 'half-continence' – produced a state of constant unfulfilled desire.

The successfully continent man, however, will secrete semen only at an untroublesome rate, with moderate nocturnal emission acting as a 'safety-valve'. His secretion will be controlled by refraining from excessive sexual acts or sexual thoughts; by redirecting blood from the sexual organs to other bodily muscles through exercise; or by expending energy in intellectual pursuits:

> In the weak scarcely any semen is secreted; the little that is formed lies in the vessels of the testes. This likewise occurs in the chaste. If there is no semen, there is no ejaculation; the nervous system is therefore not excited, and all the vigour of that powerful stimulus is centred on the well-being of the individual. Hence the power of the athlete of old, and of those who do not exert their sexual organs, or only very moderately.

This rationalization, though focusing on secretion, also draws on a model of bodily economy in which the driving force is nervous energy rather than semen.[47] 'In accordance with natural laws', he says, 'the expenditure of vital force in one direction diverts it from others'.[48] This emphasis on limited force suggests an analogy with nineteenth-century laws of thermodynamics, which identified the limited nature of physical energy and its tendency to entropy.[49] Despite the reference to 'expenditure', it is a reminder that not all economic metaphors in this period were financial.

Another reason given by Acton for the dangers of incontinence was the damage done by orgasm to the nervous system. As we have seen, belief in the intimate connection between sex and the brain is at least as old as that of the importance of semen. In the second edition of *Functions and Disorders* Acton grumbled over the way in which 'long exploded scientific opinions linger in the public mind', particularly sexual ideas. It was not haematic theory or spermatic economy he complained of, but the notion that male emission involved 'the actual passage of brain down the spinal cord'. He reports that he had overheard 'one man of the world informing another' about 'a noted old libertine' who had 'long since ceased to emit semen', but in whom 'under unnatural excitement, the substance of the brain was now passing away in the venereal orgasm, as was proved by the great nervous depression which followed each sexual effort'.[50] As Davidson notes, however, Acton was writing at a time when 'anatomical' models of sexuality were coming to focus with unprecedented force upon the brain.[51] It is unsurprising, therefore, that Acton also turns to the nerves when rationalizing sexual excess, and considers himself up-to-date in doing so. 'I think', he writes, 'with many modern writers, that there is a good deal of evidence now existing which shows that shocks constantly received and frequently repeated on the great ganglionic centres may produce irritation in them, thus causing many of the obscure forms of disease to which we have hitherto failed in discovering a key'.[52] Moderate shocks should, he says, be safe for the healthy adult male but were dangerous for all others, while excessive shock was universally inadvisable. Again, the boundaries of 'excessive' are pliable, and rely on individual constitution.

Acton's continence relies on the possibility and necessity of a genuine restraint of sexual desire as well as action. He writes that 'the sex-passion, strong as it is, can be, and ought to be, kept within bounds. This abstinence and self-denial is better for the individual [...]; it is absolutely necessary for the well-being of society, and is in conformity with the laws of natural and revealed religion'.[53] Further, the 'power' that he imagines continence giving to men is fuelled by a 'nervous force' that is not in itself sexual; although it can be 'expended' in that way, the same force fuels digestion, intellect, and muscular exertion. Continence, for Acton as for most early and mid-century writers, is the boundary of the sexual. As the century entered its final quarter, sex took on new importance and expanded significance in the emergent field of evolutionary psychology. The combined influence of Darwin's *Descent of Man* (1871) and continental sexology led to the 'sexual instinct' being imagined as the unconscious motivation behind apparently non-sexual emotions and actions.[54] Henry Maudsley, a leading British proponent of evolutionary materialism in psychology, wrote in *The Physiology of the Mind* (1876) that 'The appetites for food and drink and the sexual appetite are the strongest motives of action, as they are the fundamental and urgent appetites of the organic being'. Maudsley's conception of sexual instinct as an unconscious and primary psychological force leads him to posit the sexual origin of all higher emotions, especially altruism and 'the moral sense' due to the bringing of people together in communities. 'If we were to go on to follow the development of the sexual instinct to its highest reach', he writes, 'we should not fail to discover a great range of operation; for we might trace its influence in the highest feelings of mankind, social, moral, and religious'.[55]

Evolutionary theory, however, involves Maudsley in some degree of irony in his conception of man's progress. The growth of civilization, which for Maudsley entails increase in moral sensibility, also produces a more elaborate and delicate nervous organization which if abused can cause degeneration of both the individual and the race. Despite the sexual origin of all moral feeling and noble endeavour, sexual activity is rife with dangers for this fragile nervous system. In *The Pathology of the Mind* (1879) sexual excess, as a form of 'sensual indulgence and the exhaustion consequent thereupon', is among the most common causes of mental illness and insanity, with Maudsley insisting on such excesses as a major cause of general paralysis long after venereologists had attributed this to tertiary syphilis.[56] And although his emphasis is on stress to the nervous system and semen is not mentioned, yet economic and fluid metaphors are found only in cases involving male sexual excess: he describes the 'fatal drain upon the vitality of the higher nervous centres' after sex, and writes of a suffering businessman 'the work of his life might have been done without strain if he had not exhausted his capital by the steady drain of habitual slight excesses, and so made a great burden of his daily duty'.[57] When it comes to women, especially unmarried or young women, Maudsley often attributes insanity to 'unsatisfied or wrongly satisfied sexual feelings'. Yet he claims that 'privation of sexual function is more injurious to women than to men', the only explanation being that this instinct in women has no 'vicarious diversion of its energies in a busy life of work and interests'.[58] Maudsley implies that individual men as well as the race at large can redirect originally sexual instinct into non-sexual activities.

The late nineteenth century saw this broadened concept of sexual instinct – which influenced Maudsley but was for him still rooted firmly in the materiality of the brain – develop into the 'psychiatric style of reasoning' that Davidson argues gave birth to what we today call sexuality: 'Sexual identity is no longer exclusively linked to the anatomical structure of the internal and external genital organs. It is now a matter of impulses, tastes, aptitudes, satisfactions, and psychic traits'.[59] If earlier medical writers had conceived of sex as the key to the body (of which the mind was a part), sexologists and later psychiatrists figured sexuality as key to mind, personality, and identity. Despite the importance that anatomical thinkers such as Smyth, Paget, Acton, and Maudsley attribute to sexual excess, the very comprehensiveness of this category makes it unlikely that they would have appreciated the psychological importance that sexologists gave to minute differentiations between types of sexual behaviour, desire, and perversion.

This 'epistemological break', however, did not make productive continence unthinkable. Davidson allows that his 'three-stage structural partition does not precisely coincide with historical chronology; the three forms of explanation are often mixed together'.[60] The new sexuality integrated a sexualized version of productive continence, suggesting that excessive sexual activity was still considered to constitute a loss even if the substance of that loss became less tangible. Continence therefore entered a complicated phase. Although it ostensibly became a part of sexual experience rather than its border, both anatomical and psychological approaches to sexuality remained in play, while the terms in which even psychological texts described continence often implied the persistence of anatomical models of bodily function. As the new psychology of sexuality spread beyond specialist medical texts, productive continence was described in similar terms whether the containment was understood as sexual or not, despite this question constituting the distinction between dramatically opposed approaches to sexuality. This co-existence of sexualized and non-sexualized continence, though often confusing, nevertheless produced a discursive fuzziness that was utilized by those who sought to recategorize homosexuality as a legitimate sexual state.

The persistence of productive continence, as well as the tenacity of anatomical modes of description, can be seen in the work of a writer who dominated early twentieth-century sexual discourse in England. At the turn of the century, as Hall writes, 'Acton as approved expert was succeeded by Havelock Ellis, greeted as a sound English voice on a subject largely identified with Continentals'.[61] Unlike other medical authors examined in this section, Ellis's interest in sexuality was not shaped by the need to build and maintain a successful medical practice; although he trained at St Thomas's Hospital in London for seven years, became a licentiate of the Society of Apothecaries, and held several assistant medical posts as a young man, his career was mainly literary. His published work ranged between medical, philosophical, anthropological, and literary critical, and his social circles were similarly eclectic, including close connections with the British Decadent Movement. Arthur Symons, his close friend, brought him to meetings of the Rhymers' Club; his primary influence as a critic was Pater; and he co-authored with John Addington Symonds the first English monograph on 'sexual inversion' or homosexuality. His work on sexuality, especially *Studies in the Psychology of Sex* (1897–1910, with a supplementary volume in 1928), found a wide audience in the early twentieth century and had earlier influence in intellectual and artistic circles.

As Ellis's biographer puts it, 'the message of all his books was that sex was a mysterious gift to mankind which should be embraced with ardour and attention'.[62] Ellis was less concerned with how much sex one had than with the way one conducted one's sexual life, continent or otherwise. He despised 'all the unnatural and empty forms of chastity', blindly followed as convention or religious rule and at odds with one's temperament.[63] This pro-sensual attitude did not, however, prevent Ellis from advocating what he called 'a return to the older and sounder conception of chastity', a practice that is 'a virtue because it is a discipline of self-control, because it helps to fortify the character and will'.[64] Ellis imagines sexuality as a psychological as well as a physical category, and so doubts the possibility of total abstinence, which would mean rendering 'the whole psychic field a *tabula rasa* so far as sexual activity is concerned'.[65] Instead, 'chastity' involves a deliberate cultivation and concentration of the sexual impulse, in order to experience not only intensification of physical sensation, but also an integration of body and soul that constitutes Ellis's moral-sexual ideal. Erotic gratification, he says:

> can only be attained by placing impediments in the way of the swift and direct gratification of sexual desire, by compelling it to increase its force, to take long circuits, to charge the whole organism so highly that the final climax of gratified love is not the trivial detumescence of a petty desire but the immense consummation of a longing in which the whole soul as well as the whole body has its part.

He references H. G. Wells and Edward Carpenter as expressing similar ideals of what he calls 'erotic chastity'; a theme that was also developed by George Moore, who like Ellis belonged to the community of literary men living in the Temple in the 1890s. Ellis quotes Carpenter's *Love's Coming of Age* (1896):

> He only gets the full glory who holds himself back a little, and truly possesses, who is willing, if need be, not to possess. He is indeed a master of life who, accepting the gross desires as they come to his body, and not refusing them, knows how to transform them at will into the most rare and fragrant flowers of human emotion.[66]

Full sexual function for Ellis and Carpenter relies on restraint as much as it did for Smyth and Acton, though the underlying model of bodily function is different (*Love's Coming of Age* also references older models: 'what a loss', complains Carpenter, 'on the merest grounds of prudence and the economy of pleasure is its unbridled waste along physical channels!').[67]

Carpenter was one of many non-medical writers to elaborate such a theory in reference to homosexual desire. Early homosexual literature had a complex relationship with continence. Continental sexology of the 1880s and '90s had given homosexuality, or 'sexual inversion', new importance but had categorized it as a disease or degenerative state, often either the cause or symptom of sexual excess in the patient or an ancestor.[68] Non-medical writers responded that inversion could not be understood within this dichotomy of health/disease, but must be reimagined as an alternative sexual mode or harmless congenital abnormality. This was a radical innovation in sexual categorization that relied upon newer conceptualizations of sexuality, including the re-evaluation of continence. A concept of 'psychic' sexuality that existed beyond physical continence was crucial for the decriminalization as well as depathologization of inversion, as it allowed its congenital nature to be discussed without implying that individuals were therefore impelled uncontrollably towards criminal sexual acts.

Those arguing for the recategorization of inversion denied that troublesome sexual urges could easily be eradicated. The concept of erotic continence, however, allowed the sexual invert to experience their sexuality within the law, and gave them an object to discuss that was difficult to legislate against. The extension of this into an eroticized *productive* continence – a continence in which sexual energy was put towards non-sexual ends without losing its sexual character – allowed inverts to be imagined as useful members of society without pathologizing, criminalizing, or eradicating their desires. Although most writers went further to argue that some sexual acts should be allowed (stopping short, usually, at sodomy), and although actual practice in writers who were themselves homosexual undoubtedly departed from this standard, yet in print at least writers such as Carpenter, Symonds, and Ellis used erotic productive continence to normalize sexual inversion within Victorian sexual ethics.[69] The increasingly messy overlap between sexualized and non-sexualized continence was fertile ground for this endeavour.

Symonds argued in his privately printed *A Problem in Modern Ethics* (1891) that inverted sexuality should stand in equal relation to health and the law as 'normal' sexuality. Instead of representing inversion as a type of sexual excess, he described it as subject to the same excesses and restrictions as 'normal' sexuality: 'indulgence of inverted sexual instincts within due limits, cannot be proved to be especially pernicious' he writes, although 'Excess in any venereal pleasure will produce diseases of nervous exhaustion and imperfect nutrition'.[70] He makes room for healthy though moderate inversion within Victorian medical orthodoxy, with the mention of 'imperfect nutrition' especially suggesting an economic model of bodily function. When he writes of inverted love relationships, however, he uses a 'psychic' theory of sexuality to collapse the divide that Victorian discourse had erected between romantic friendship and same-sex love. While insisting, as Carolyn Oulton describes Victorian writers on friendship doing, that continence was important to these relationships (though Symonds was unconcerned that this continence remain perfect), he nevertheless asserts that the emotion remaining is sexual and therefore still inverted in character.[71]

As well as the common example of Plato – of which more in the third section of this chapter – Symonds finds a means by which 'abnormal instincts may be moralised and raised to higher value' in Walt Whitman's ideal of male comradeship as outlined in the 'Calamus' section of *Leaves of Grass* (1855). Whitman was alive and vulnerable to sexual scandal when *A Problem in Modern Ethics* was first printed. Symonds therefore exploits the similarity between older, non-sexual productive continence and emergent eroticized continence to claim the relevance of Whitman's male love to inverted relationships, without necessarily identifying Whitman as inverted. Whitman had written about male love that went beyond 'merely personal possession' to 'cement society and to render commonwealths inviolable'.[72] Symonds reports, however, that Whitman had responded to his queries about the relevance of this love to sexual inversion that this was 'disavowed by me and seem damnable'. He concludes that *Leaves of Grass* was consciously written within a recognizable heterosexual discourse of romantic friendship and productive continence:

> an impartial critic will, I think, be drawn to the conclusion that what he calls the 'adhesiveness' of comradeship is meant to have no interblending with the 'amativeness' of sexual love. Personally, it is undeniable that Whitman possesses a specially keen sense of the fine restraint and continence, the cleanliness and chastity, that are inseparable from the perfectly virile and physically complete nature of healthy manhood.

While allowing Whitman his avowed intentions, however, psychic sexuality allows Symonds to doubt that this boundary can be maintained in practice. 'Human nature being what it is, we cannot expect to eliminate all sexual alloy from emotions raised to a high pitch of passionate intensity'. Readers may find the 'inevitable points of contact between sexual inversion and [Whitman's] doctrine of comradeship' whether that contact was intended or not. And Whitman himself, Symonds writes, surely allows his readers this interpretive space whatever he may say in his correspondence: 'Whitman never suggests that comradeship may occasion the development of physical desires. But then he does not in set terms condemn these desires, or warn his disciples against them.'[73] The co-existence of psychic and anatomical sexuality allows Symonds to establish a cultural context for inversion far beyond its explicit or even conscious manifestation, without implicating individuals as capable of what were then criminal acts. His treatment of 'Calamus' illustrates the complex co-existence of sexualized and non-sexualized discourses of productive continence at the turn of the century, and the space that this co-existence created for the development of a new homosexual identity.

Symonds had been collaborating with Havelock Ellis on *Sexual Inversion*, the first full-length study of homosexuality to be published in English, when he died in 1893. Ellis claimed to have eliminated Symonds' contributions when the work was published as the first volume of his *Studies in the Psychology of Sex*, but the collaboration evidently shaped his thinking. Like Symonds, Ellis argued that inversion was congenital, involuntary and ineradicable, and that neither punishment nor cure were appropriate responses. In seeking to eradicate homosexual desires, he writes, we potentially rob society of the good that homosexual continence may produce: 'in so doing we may, perhaps, destroy also those children of the spirit which possess sometimes a greater worth than the children of the flesh'. His alternative, however, is not toleration of homosexual acts, but rather an 'ideal of chastity' that sounds like productive continence. 'The method of self-restraint and self-culture, without self-repression, seems to be the most rational method of dealing with sexual inversion when that condition is really organic and deeply rooted.'[74] Ellis believed that inversion had an inevitable relationship with such restraint, as what he called the 'feminine' element in male inverts and the 'masculine' in female inverts meant that their desire was for heterosexual bodies, producing an 'almost absolute lack of any genuine satisfaction either in the way of affections or desires'. Ellis's melancholy invert is forever burdened with an unsatisfied desire which the 'intellectual aristocracy' among them will convert into art, philanthropy, and continent affection.[75]

Although the insistence on continence in early writing about homosexuality was necessitated by the conditions of social suppression, it did much to ensure productive continence a place in emergent sexual schemas. Inverted continence looked forward to a twentieth-century mode of considering all continence simply as a psychological elaboration of sexual instinct – what Benjamin Kahan calls 'the sexiness of no sex' – rather than the genuinely non-sexual ideal of most Victorian thinking on the subject (however difficult that ideal was to actualize).[76] Yet outside of these texts, turn-of-the-century writing about productive continence continued to look back to anatomical models of the sexual body. Havelock Ellis's physiology comes much closer to the older discourse of productive sexual continence when he treats the sexuality of artists or intellectuals, despite his emphasis on 'erotic chastity' even when writing about non-inverted sexuality. 'Chastity' he writes, 'has a more special value for those who cultivate the arts', and 'The masters of all the more intensely emotional arts have frequently cultivated a high degree of chastity'. In justifying this observation, he turns to a physiology of energy regulation based in the relation between the brain and the sexual function: 'We do well to remember that, while the auto-erotic manifestations through the brain are of infinite variety and importance, the brain and the sexual organs are yet the great rivals in using up bodily energy.' Ellis approaches the artist's continence as a condition of extraordinary achievement, concluding that 'a high degree of energy, whether in athletics or in intellect or in sexual activity, is unfavourable to the display of energy in other directions. Every high degree of potency has its related impotencies'. And although he goes on to claim that chastity 'only has its value when it is brought within the erotic sphere', he does not attempt to reconcile the conflicting models of bodily function in which this subject involves him.[77] It is worth mentioning that Ellis also claimed in an earlier volume of *Studies* that 'the seminal fluid is not a waste material, and its retention is, to some extent perhaps, rather an advantage than a disadvantage to the organism', though he did not elaborate either on the physiology or nature of this advantage.[78]

The gradual move away from anatomical sexuality gave rise to a new and now familiar metaphor for productive continence, already seen in Symonds' reference to 'sexual alloy': sublimation. Referencing chemistry rather than physics – the process by which a solid substance is converted directly to vapour – this metaphor arguably had closer relation to theological discourses of fleshly and spiritual love than Victorian economical metaphors, and perhaps reflects the moral anxiety that accompanied early attempts to redefine sexuality. Ellis wrote of inverted love that it was often 'more or less finely sublimated from any gross physical manifestation'.[79] The twentieth-century use of 'sublimation', however, often described a process of redistributing or husbanding resources that is not present in the chemical process. Anson Rabinbach, in his study of 'energy' in nineteenth-century Europe, claims that Freud was among those who 'transposed the energetic model of nature to sexuality', rebranding 'nervous' energy, with its stubborn cleaving to anatomy, as 'psychic' or 'sexual' energy. He viewed this 'sexual energy' as having a close relationship with the impulse to all action, and in his later writings sexuality often seems coextensive with this impulse.[80] And yet even for the later Freud 'psychic energy' is, like physical energy, a limited quality, with the difference that man's replenishment of such energy is by no means so certain as that of physical energy. 'Since a man does not have unlimited quantities of psychical energy at his disposal, he has to accomplish his tasks by making an expedient distribution of his libido.' This need for 'distribution' is central to Freud's concept of sublimation, in which excess psychic-sexual energy is redirected towards non-sexual tasks such as building stable societies and creating art. Neurosis takes the place of seminal loss as Freud laments the prevalence of imperfect distribution, and therefore the 'useless waste of a large quota of energy which might have been employed for the improvement of the human lot'.[81] Elsewhere he directly relates his doubts about the general practicability of sublimation to the thermodynamic law of entropy: 'A conversion of psychical instinctual force into various forms of activity can perhaps no more be achieved without loss than a conversion of physical forces.'[82]

In Freud's later work, sexuality occupies an opposite position from that it had taken in nineteenth-century discourse. Rather than sexual activity taking energy from other bodily processes, the non-sexual activity of civilization requires that 'a large amount of the psychical energy which it uses for its own purposes [...] be withdrawn from sexuality'.[83] This line of thinking becomes misogynistic in a manner reminiscent of Maudsley, as Freud claims that 'women are little capable' of the sublimations necessary for civilization, and so remain 'hostile' to large-scale communal living, representing instead 'the interests of the family and of sexual life'.[84] Freud seems to understand 'psychic energy' to work similarly to physical energy.

The ideal of productive continence – especially for those considered to be otherwise unfit for sexual activity, such as the invert and the artist – lingered far beyond the physiology that made sense of it, forcing those who sought at the beginning of the twentieth century to classify and explain a newly psychologized sexuality to incorporate this idea even if it meant integrating seemingly contrary sexual models and metaphors. At the same time older anatomical models persisted in both medical practice and the public sphere, especially where writers sought to embrace embodied sensuousness without necessarily eroticizing this experience. The remainder of this chapter looks at some of the places in which non-medical writers throughout the period integrated the idea of productive sexual continence into their various efforts to theorize – and in many cases prescribe – a nonsensual embodiment.

Sexual Health Beyond Medicine

Young Men and New Women

Sexual health was a crucial part of two seemingly very different late nineteenth-century genres: that of advice for young men, and that of first-wave feminism. Beginning with widespread anxiety about the move of single young men from the country to rapidly industrializing towns at the beginning of the Victorian period, advice for young men was a readily recognizable genre by the middle of the century. It was initially characterized by the swift expansion of the Young Man's Christian Association (YMCA), and was originally Low Church and Evangelical in tone; but by the 1880s it had expanded into an industry in its own right, with dedicated books, journals, newspaper columns, clubs, and lecture halls that pedalled 'a breezy practical morality without oppressively religious connotations'.[85] Such texts varied from earnest attempts to intervene in what was perceived as a genuine moral crisis, to blatantly commercial attempts to exploit a growing market.

Although religion was often not far from the guidance on offer, yet the medical discourse of sexual self-discipline acted within these texts as a seemingly disinterested means of addressing issues that bound together physical and moral health, with the authority of science superseding (and yet conveniently echoing) that of the Church. Among other things, the claim was frequently made that sexual continence outside of (and to a certain extent within) marriage was not only conducive, but even necessary to health, productivity, sociability and happiness. 'Young men' culture intersected closely with the campaigns for male purity that followed the controversy surrounding the Contagious Diseases Acts (these Acts, which legalized the forcible medical examination of women in certain towns suspected of being prostitutes, introduced the issue of male sexual responsibility to public discussion), and formed a large part of organizations such as the Social Purity Alliance and the White Cross League, though it was by no means limited to these groups. And although the genre of 'young men' literature may initially seem very far from Decadence – a great many of these works contain warnings about 'unhealthy' aesthetic or French-inspired modern literature – yet the mutual employment of the *bildungsroman* format, with its focus on the 'young person' making his or her way in the world, as well as their concern with offering ethical guidance concerning everyday conduct, creates a significant discursive overlap between the texts examined here and something like Walter Pater's *Marius* the *Epicurean* (1885), or Vernon Lee's *Miss Brown* (1884). These texts certainly worked with a similar understanding of sexual health, and of the relation of sexuality to other areas of ethical deportment. As we saw in the Introduction, the protagonist of Richard Le Gallienne's *Young Lives* is portrayed using *Marius* very much in the way that readers were invited to use, for instance, Frederick Atkins's *Moral Muscle and How to Use it* (1890), as a guide to 'all the difficulties and dangers that attend the outset of life'.[86]

The texts associated with this culture were generally repetitive and formulaic, advising the presumed young reader on the attainment of mental, physical, and moral excellence. Almost all of them addressed the importance of avoiding sexual encounters before marriage – either with women or with oneself through 'self-abuse' – and of limiting sex even within marriage; and placed this continence within a wider physical and moral regime. In the medically conscious Victorian period this required some degree of physiological justification. The sexual discussion in these pamphlets and magazines was less melodramatic and less medically detailed than that of quack literature, at least in England (the American equivalents, many of which had wide circulation in Britain, came much closer to quack rhetoric). But young men of the period reading both would have received a consistent message that any sexual activity involved a dangerous loss, and that continence could yield increased mental and physical strength.

One such young man, Charles Sayle – later writer of idealized homoerotic poetry, friend to Lionel Johnson, and librarian of the University Library, Cambridge – records in his diary that he was given at the age of fourteen (1878) by an elder brother, John Stuart Blackie's *On Self-Culture: Intellectual, Physical, and Moral*, which describes itself as 'a *vade mecum* [handbook or guide] for young men and students'.[87] This book, like so many others, presented a model of the body as a delicately balanced system, in which the over-use of one system depleted others. Within this rule, Blackie states that young men must 'learn to recognise the great truth that those are the strongest men, not who the most wantonly indulge, but who the most carefully curb their activities'. 'All debauch', he writes, 'is incipient suicide; it is the unseen current beneath the house which sooner or later washes away the foundations'.[88] It is not difficult to see how the medical discourse of spermatic retention could match up easily with the Christian discourse of life as a battle between what another such advice book calls 'animal nature' and 'spiritual nature'.[89]

Others were more explicit in addressing sexual behaviour. Hugh Sinclair Paterson, a Glasgow-educated doctor and nonconformist minister, produced the popular *Life, Function, Health: Studies for Young Men* (1885). In

the section on health – also sold separately as *Health Studies* – he outlines
a theory of bodily regulation in which one manages the balance between
intake and output of energy. But although, when speaking of the muscles, he stresses that 'we cannot be too frequently renewing ourselves', his
logic differs when speaking of sexuality. This he treats as an appetite rather
than a muscular activity, the satisfaction of which is both unnecessary and
potentially very harmful. 'A man may live all his days celibate', he says,
'and not suffer in the slightest degree in health [...]. We may maintain the
utmost vigour, and engage in all the work that is needful, and reach a ripe
old age without the slightest indulgence of this appetite'. On the other
hand, sexual activity is an 'expenditure of energy', in which 'the expenditure is large in proportion to the excitement'. Paterson does not explicitly
mention semen, and does not need to; his theory of a body regulated by
energy is sufficient to rationalize the danger of sexual excess, though he
gives no reason why this activity wastes more energy than any other. He is
vague about what constitutes excess, but firm that all activity followed by
'a feeling of weakness and vapidness' is excessive. Such excess, he claims,
damages the entire body, as 'it withdraws power from the different functions that might be otherwise needfully used'. This withdrawal, he claims,
'is often to be blamed for weakness of the digestive organs; very frequently
it is to be blamed for weakness of judgement and weakness of the brain'.
Further, 'it tells very injuriously on the whole frame, and it tells most
injuriously on the most vital and important part – the nervous system'.[90]

This element of 'young men' culture found its most emphatic expression in the many organizations associated with the late nineteenth-century
'social purity' movement, particularly the White Cross Army or League,
founded in 1883 and dedicated to persuading young men to take vows
of chastity; and the YMCA, founded in 1844 and by the end of the century much more about secular self-cultivation and physical education than
prayer. A large part of this culture consisted of lectures, given by men and
women who were often also or originally nonconformist preachers, taken
on tour around the country and indeed the world, and often published in
the form of pamphlets that attracted huge international sales. Paterson's
book, for example, was originally a series of lectures given to YMCA audiences.[91] Along with threats of the dangers of sexual excesses that rivalled
the similar lectures given by quack doctors at anatomical museums, these
lectures often included promises of the felicity and strength to be gained
through sexual continence. In 1883, the social purity journal *The Sentinel*
reported a lecture by Dr Edward Wood Forster to the North East District
Union of YMCAs, in which he spoke 'strongly not only of the moral

obligation of continence and self-restraint, but of their benefit alike to body and intellect'.[92] Another lecturer, Henry Varley, spoke of how 'the strength of the brain, the richness of the blood, the brilliance of the eye, the vigour of the mind, the hardness of the muscle and the firmness of the flesh' were all 'mainly dependent on the seed'.[93] Varley's *Lecture to Men Only* toured internationally, and the related pamphlet is said to have sold 90,000 copies.[94] The same discourse of positive continence was still present in the literature of the Scouting Movement, established in 1907. As late as 1922, Baden-Powell was writing in his *Rovering to Success* that a man's retained semen 'gives the vigour of manhood to his frame, and it builds up his nerves and courage'.[95] This publication served as the handbook for the Rover Scout section of the Scout Association until 1966, and was distributed in this version to 200,000 scouts.[96] It is not quite true, then, as Edward Bristow has claimed, that social purity discourse was 'entirely negative': though it may well have understood sexuality as, as Bristow has it, 'a nasty appetite to be curbed by faith, cold water and lessons in good citizenship',[97] its conception of continence was more than simple negative suppression, as those involved hoped to gain health and happiness from its practice.

Much work has been done on the connections between such organizations, and the promotion of empire, eugenics, and racism, as well as their role in the middle-class 'reformation' of working-class lifestyles.[98] These are certainly some of the political purposes to which the discourse of productive sexual continence was put in the late nineteenth and early twentieth centuries. But this was a contingent, rather than necessary connection. Already by the mid-nineteenth century the discourse was pervasive and multifarious enough to prevent this association from becoming necessary, as is seen in the formation of a different set of associations in Decadent literature. Mason has written of the 'difficulty in defining the clinical equivalent of the politically – or even the medico-politically – "progressive"', as 'different medical dogmas about sexual function cannot readily be correlated with conservative or reforming elements in the medical profession'.[99] The same can be said of medical theory outside of the medical profession, as clear correspondence cannot always be found between specific ideas and political orientation.

Another genre with significant overlap with that of advice to young men, not least because of a similar association with the social purity movement (along with eugenics, empire, and race), was the literature of late nineteenth-century first-wave feminism. Unlike advice for young men, the literature of this movement had close relations with Aesthetic and

Decadent writing in the last quarter of the century, as has been shown by critics such as Sally Ledger, Talia Schaffer, and Ruth Livesey, and as will be seen particularly in Chapter 4.[100] The early feminist approach to sexuality was anything but homogenous, with much disagreement about fundamental sexual physiology. Some deployed various sexual models as the situation demanded. Some argued for what was called 'free love', though in England this usually represented the right to long-term unmarried unions rather than general promiscuity. The majority, however, advocated sexual continence outside of and occasionally within marriage, often subscribing like writers of 'young men' literature to the widespread discourse of 'higher' and 'lower' selves, in which the 'lower' represented sensual feelings and behaviour.[101] A significant portion found strength in periodic or lifelong continence, which they associated with individual happiness and social usefulness. Writing about this positive continence often uses rhetoric reminiscent of that of male productive continence.

In advocating sexual continence, particularly voluntary lifelong celibacy, women were going against dominant medical discourse. The nineteenth-century medical profession was more unanimous on the question of the damage done to health by female continence than they were on the male equivalent. Some feminists, such as Olive Schreiner and Jane Hume Clapperton, were inclined to agree that continence endangered women: Schreiner said that 'a person might stifle their sexual desire by diverting their energy into other channels and yet suffer in health', while Clapperton claimed first that continence was harmful only if not freely chosen, and later that it was universally harmful, leading to 'hysteria, chlorosis, love melancholy and other unhappy ailments'.[102] But the majority of late nineteenth-century feminists strongly disagreed with this physiological model, asserting instead that continence was perfectly possible for both sexes. Some even argued that for women, at least, it could be an exalted state. This situation is demonstrated in Lucy Bland's analysis of an incident in the Men and Women's Club, a select intellectual society set up by Karl Pearson in the mid-1880s with the aim of encouraging debate between the sexes on sexual matters. 'The relationship of chastity to health' was of great concern to the club; most of the women were eager both to escape the imperative for women to marry, and to discourage men from claiming a right to sexual relationships on health grounds. In 1885 Dr Reginald Ryle addressed the club, according to the secretary's notes, upon 'some physiological facts which bear upon the relations of the sexes', including 'the relation of activity or inactivity of sex relations to general health of individual'. Ryle denied that there was any relationship between the two;

but two doctors present, Dr Louisa Atkins and Dr Bryan Donkin, disagreed. The discussion that followed focused almost entirely on female continence. The group was split, with the women (apart from Schreiner) and some of the men agreeing with Ryle, despite the fact that the weight of medical opinion in the room pointed in the opposite direction. It is likely that this lay bias, regardless of medical opinion, reflected at least upper-middle-class progressive opinion in the latter half of the nineteenth century.[103]

Given the associated male medical discourse, it was perhaps inevitable that of those feminists who asserted the viability of healthy prolonged continence for both men and women, some would go further to claim that for women at least, it could be a state even more healthy, and more conducive to personal happiness and social usefulness, than the married state. Some, like practising doctor Elizabeth Blackwell, found wider social potential in the female maternal instinct, imagined as the main force behind female sexual desire. Blackwell argued that women had the same force of sexual desire as men, but greater powers of self-control and sexual discipline. Female superiority did not rely on actual motherhood, but the potential for what she termed 'spiritual motherhood', described by Bland as 'an altruistic approach towards humanity in which a whole nation represented a woman's progeny'.[104]

Many feminist writers and activists, such as Margaret Shurmer Sibthorp, Frances Swiney, and Elizabeth Clarke Wolstenholme Elmy, while disagreeing upon other points such as the origins of male dominance and the degree to which women were superior to men, nevertheless agreed that sex should be limited to the purposes of reproduction, and that avoiding it could lead to what they all called the 'higher life'.[105] Some were more equivocal, or admitted the healthiness of sexual continence only in certain situations. For the novelist and self-described 'new woman' Sarah Grand, for instance, some sexual activity is generally requisite for a healthy life, though she evidently considered too much or the wrong sort to be more damaging than not enough. But Grand also allows that the unhealthiness of continence can be mitigated by intellectual activity. In *The Heavenly Twins* (1894), it is said of Evadne, a woman who spends much of her life in a celibate marriage, that:

> She had owed her force of character to her incessant intellectual activity, which had also kept her mind pure, and her body in excellent condition. Had she not found an outlet for her superfluous vitality as a girl in her condition of mind, she must have become morbid and hysterical, as is the case with both sexes when they remain in the unnatural state of celibacy with mental energy unapplied.[106]

Grand's 'superfluous vitality' interestingly appears to be employed either in sexual or intellectual activity, much like Acton's regulation of 'energy'. There seems little reason to assume that this vitality is originally sexual, as it would be in a Freudian model of sublimation.

This idea of redirected and transformed energy was drawn upon and expanded by Henrietta Müller to outline an ideal of female productive continence. Müller was very active in progressive movements: she had been an executive member of the National Vigilance Association, one of the country's more extreme 'social purity' organizations – although she resigned when the Association described a contraceptive pamphlet as obscene – and was active in support of the temperance and women's suffrage movements. Müller claimed that a new type of 'single woman', whose attention was given to personal cultivation and public work rather than family, could be imagined as 'rejecting the personal or the grosser form of love' in order to make herself 'more free to give a larger, holier and deeper love to those who need it most'. In describing the personal benefits that allow such public-spiritedness Müller echoes the discourse of masculine productive continence familiar from medical, quack, and 'young men' literature. 'Her physical life', she writes, 'is healthy and active, she retains her buoyancy and increases her nervous power if she knows how to take care of herself, and this lesson she is rapidly learning'.[107] There is, of course, a long tradition of the communal usefulness of sexually inexperienced women informing Müller's elaboration of sociable continence. Yet the terms 'buoyancy' and 'nervous power' are particularly reminiscent of the rhetoric of spermatic retention. Reasons other than bodily regulation are given for the lack of this in non-continent women (child-birth, inactivity); but what allows this recycling of language is a lingering sense that physical health may be lost through sexual activity. Müller speaks of the envy of such women felt by 'those men whose past has been for ever robbed of the bloom which is life's sweetest gift', again taking advantage of the emotional discourse surrounding male continence in order to describe a female equivalent.[108] A similar kind of borrowing and echoing will be found in the work of Vernon Lee in Chapter 4.

An idea of sexual, though not necessarily spermatic economy therefore permeated the period, being co-opted and adapted by many different groups or individuals, who had a wide range of ideological, political, religious, or commercial motivations. This surely reflected a situation in which most men, and some women, gave at least some credence to the idea that their body worked in a way compatible with such logic; in which it was, above all, plausible, whatever significance one gave that fact. This idea of continence, however, was in itself amoral, and was therefore worked into various incompatible moral and political systems, some of which were similar to that of the branch of Decadence described here, and some different. The next two sections will explore some less medicalized potential sources in which Decadent writers would nevertheless have found models for a sexual continence that was not only personally productive and conducive to health and wellbeing, but also formed an essential connection between the individual and society.

Nineteenth-Century Platonism

The reading of Greek and Roman texts heavily influenced Victorian British literary culture. Of the writers examined in this book, two (Pater and Johnson) were trained at Oxford and maintained close links with that institution throughout their lives, while the others displayed a sustained fascination with classical literature. A great deal of recent scholarship has outlined the use that Decadent writers made of the classics in their thinking about sexuality in particular, with a focus on responses to Greek and Roman pederasty in the formulation of a modern homosexual identity.[109] However, many central branches of Ancient Greek and Roman philosophy – Platonism, Epicureanism, Stoicism – also imagined sexual continence as a creative state, whether the desires involved were heterosexual or homosexual in object, and in doing so heavily influenced the development of sexual ethics in the West.[110] Philosophers in these traditions brought upper-class ideals of deportment and conduct, such as those 'techniques of the self' explored by Foucault in the second and third volumes of his *History of Sexuality*, together with Eastern ascetic traditions to form ideals of sexual continence with both mundane and transcendent significance.[111] This classical emphasis on continence was arguably of even more wide-reaching importance in Victorian culture than ancient pederasty, and was concurrently influential upon Decadent writing.

Such idealization of continence does not, of course, constitute all Greek and Roman sexuality any more than a similar idealization constituted all Victorian sexuality. Nevertheless, for many branches of ancient philosophy – particularly Epicureanism and Stoicism, against which Pater tested a form of aestheticism in *Marius the Epicurean* – sexual continence was essential not only to individual health, but also to a healthy relationship between individual and community.[112] Plato, however, was by far the most important Greek philosopher for nineteenth-century Decadence. The nature of that influence varied between writers, with many using Plato's explicit references to pederasty in order to form a homosexual identity.[113] It was also possible, however, for nineteenth-century writers to find in Plato a theory of beauty to which sexual continence was essential, regardless of the gender towards which desire had been initially directed. The Platonic management of desire, away from sexual activity and towards an intellectual or spiritual beauty, mapped easily onto the Victorian medical discourse in which energy was channelled away from sexuality in the service of non-sexual activity. It was undoubtedly this productively continent interpretation – usually involving a conscious bypassing, rather than ignoring, of Plato's homosexual content – that was favoured by the majority of Victorian readers, and it remained important even for many (though by no means all) writers who accepted and approved of Plato's emphasis on same-sex desire.

Further, this continent Plato could be made to echo the Victorian distinction between sensuous and sensual embodiment that was so crucial for Pater, Johnson, and Lee; the nineteenth-century secular concept of sensuality having its roots in a Christian tradition that was itself heavily influenced by Platonic philosophy. Pre-Socratic Pythagorean philosophy had pulled together Orphic religious culture, Indian and Persian ascetic traditions, and the latest medical and philosophic thinking into a cultic life-model, within which sexuality was usually viewed as a weakening activity best preserved for the purpose of reproduction. This philosophy, with its parallel divisions between the worldly and unworldly, body and soul, was developed and refined upon in the writing of Plato.

Plato's influence on Victorian British intellectual life was wide reaching and various to the point of direct contradiction: much as it had been throughout Europe for the past nineteen centuries.[114] One notable point of departure between different Platonic traditions was the extent to which Plato was understood as entirely rejecting or merely disciplining the desires of the body. John Dillon, writing of the adoption of Plato into the Christian Church, remarks that there are

> two significant strands in that tradition, both stemming from Plato himself, but developing separate histories in later times: that of straightforward rejection of the body, or at least of the soul's association with it, which involves what I would identify as a negative attitude to the world; and that of the disciplining and refining of the body, to make it a worthy, or at least noninjurious receptacle of the soul, which might be seen, I think, as essentially world-affirming.[115]

The former, world-denying Platonism is traced by Dillon to the *Phaedo*, in which Socrates counsels to 'consort with the body as little as possible, and do not commune with it, except in so far as we must, and do not infect ourselves with its nature, but remain pure from it'.[116] But while the *Phaedo* argues for a dualistic and antagonistic body/soul division, *The Republic*, as Dillon shows, introduces a tripartite division, in which rational and irrational parts of the soul must together work with the potentially destructive body to produce a stable, harmonious life. Instead of the extirpation of troublesome elements, including sexuality, it recommends that earthly desires be disciplined and channelled into more useful activity, so that (in Dillon's words) 'the ensouled body' becomes 'an organism that gains greatly by being finely tuned'.[117]

Similar concerns with bodily discipline are found in places where Plato writes most directly about physical love: the *Phaedrus* and the *Symposium*. The emphasis of these dialogues on sexual continence meant that they could be – and frequently were – read as compatible with Victorian sexual orthodoxy, regardless of their explicitly same-sex content, in what Carolyn Oulton calls 'a deliberate consensus to extract certain elements and not others'.[118] In the *Phaedrus*, Socrates and Phaedrus debate upon the nature of love, during which Socrates argues that the soul has an innate desire for beauty. This beauty is conceived as one of Plato's Ideal Forms and in a sense is representative of the Ideal as a category. The soul, Socrates claims, was once able to see this Ideal beauty, but that ability was lost when it became embodied. It nevertheless remembers what it had seen, and strives towards it. The sight of earthly beauty reminds the soul of the Ideal Beauty that it saw before it was body-bound, inspiring it to mount to heaven in order to look once again at the sphere of Ideal Forms. But it can only do this if it disciplines the earthly nature that it inevitably takes from the body. Just as in the *Republic* the tripartite model is introduced, with the soul compared to a charioteer controlling two horses, one of which is easily controlled, the other less so and requiring strict training. 'For the horse of evil nature weighs the chariot down, making it heavy and pulling toward the earth the charioteer whose horse is not well trained.'[119] The body is not absent from this model – the troublesome horse cannot simply be unhitched. But it must be controlled if Ideal beauty is to be perceived: a message not dissimilar from much Victorian discourse on bodily discipline.

A similar distinction between desire for earthly and Ideal beauty is made in the *Symposium*, where again the subject of discussion is love. This time Plato introduces his famous 'ladder of love', in which desire for a beautiful body inspires one to strive towards knowledge of abstract, Ideal beauty:

> Beginning from obvious beauties he must for the sake of that highest beauty be ever climbing aloft, as on the rungs of a ladder, from one to two, and from two to all beautiful bodies; from personal beauty he proceeds to beautiful observances, from observances to beautiful learning, and from learning at last to that particular study which is concerned with the beautiful itself and that alone: so that in the end he comes to know the very essence of beauty.[120]

It is possible to interpret this theory of love as glorifying sexual desire and potentially even activity, particularly between a man and a young boy, as a gateway to knowledge of the Ideal. This was the approach (to varying degrees) taken by late nineteenth-century apologists for same-sex love. Symonds described Plato's writings as 'the most electrical literature of the world', recording the night when he discovered the *Phaedrus* and the *Symposium* as 'one of the most important nights of my life', while A. C. Benson, who maintained a continent ideal while recognizing his own homosexual inclinations, queried in 1913, 'Isn't it really rather dangerous to let boys read Plato, if one is desirous that they should accept conventional moralities?'[121] As Stefano Evangelista has written, 'It is hard to overstate the role played by Plato in the formation of private or public homosexual identities in the society of Victorian Britain, in which public expressions and representations of homosexuality were effectively censored'.[122]

But it was also possible to interpret Plato as emphasizing a strict distinction between a chaste love originating in sensuous perception of beauty, and the sensuality that such love could become: that is, love which appreciates the sensuous beauty of a lover as indicative of Ideal beauty, as opposed to love which only appreciates physical beauty as an end in itself. This is a fine distinction, but one that was essential to many a Victorian writer's relationship with the body and its senses. The place of actual sexual activity within it was complex, no doubt because it drew upon categories that predated the very idea of 'sexuality'. Sensuous love, for instance, potentially included sexual activity between heterosexual partners within Christian marriage, though even that must be undertaken in a particular way in order not to become a more worldly and problematic sensual love. For the married and unmarried alike, sensuous love – whether of a wife or husband, of friends, or of beautiful objects or nature – involved a strict appreciation of sensuous beauty only insofar as it represented and indicated the existence of a further, less worldly beauty, whether of God or some higher spiritual ideal of which Plato's Ideal beauty could be considered an equivalent. It was this relatively continent Platonic ideal – the ideal which gave rise to the term 'Platonic love' as signifying a love that remains determinedly and consciously non-sexual – that the majority of Victorian readers chose to emphasize in Plato's theory of love.

Many homosexual writers used the haziness between sensuous and sensual readings of Plato to discuss same-sex love relatively openly without committing to a potentially criminal discourse: much as we saw them use the discursive similarities between non-sexualized and sexualized continence. Symonds, for instance, 'formulated an ethical theory of modern homosexual conduct which is closely modelled on Pausanias's distinction, in the *Symposium*, between a celestial (chaste and ennobling) and a vulgar (sexual and polluting) form of male love'.[123] Symonds's Plato utilizes 'the passion which grovels in the filth of sensual grossness' so that it is 'transformed into a glorious enthusiasm, a winged splendour, capable of soaring to the contemplation of eternal verities'. Yet just as Symonds himself advocated a thoroughly sexualized continence that made space for limited expression, he portrays the Plato of the *Symposium* (though not the *Laws*) as having pragmatic sympathy with the occasional sexual act that his philosophy facilitated if not encouraged: he 'condoned a lapse through warmth of feeling into self-indulgence'.[124] Oscar Wilde likewise took advantage of overlapping interpretations of Plato when he declared, at his 1895 trial for gross indecency, that the 'Love that dare not speak its name' was 'such as Plato made the very basis of his philosophy [...] that deep, spiritual affection that is as pure as it is perfect'.[125]

Symonds also acknowledged, however, that 'Plato's name is still connected with the ideal of passion purged from sensuality', and that 'Few modern writers, when they speak with admiration or contempt of Platonic love, reflect that in its origin this phrase denoted an absorbing passion for young men'.[126] If such writers did not reflect it was not from lack of knowledge. George Ridding, for instance, headmaster of Winchester College and an early mentor of Lionel Johnson, argued in an address to the 1883 Reading Church Congress that no sane reader would 'make Greek genius justify Greek vice any more than Greek slavery'.[127] For the majority of readers, the important contention was whether Plato's continence was world-affirming or world-denying, embodied or disembodied, with any references to homosexuality excusable as a cultural quirk.

The most famous proponent of a continent Plato, whose chastity was so beyond doubt as to neutralize any question of sexual object, was Benjamin Jowett. As Oxford fellow and Master of Balliol College, Jowett played a central role in the early Victorian overhaul of the Oxford curriculum that not only saw Plato take the place of Aristotle as foundational text, but also established a generously interpreted Plato 'as a metaphysical basis for the liberalism of the Oxford reformers', as Linda Dowling has demonstrated.[128] Further, Jowett's translations of Plato's texts, together with his introductions to the same, were widely used as educational texts at Oxford and elsewhere well into the twentieth century, to the extent that the vast majority of late Victorian readers – including Decadent writers – first encountered Plato through Jowett's translation and commentary.

Jowett's purpose in reading and interpreting Plato's comments on sexuality was in part to account for, and neutralize, their homosexual sentiment, in order to 'discursively reflect and reproduce culturally sanctioned gender and sexual systems'.[129] Linda Dowling has shown how Jowett's translation practice was informed by both an 'ethically centered providentialism and an ethically relativizing historicism', so that although he was anxious to 'naturalize and make vitally relevant the unfamiliar or alien turns of Platonic thought by presenting them in terms of Christian and English parallels', yet his grounding in German historicism required him to acknowledge Plato's references to sex between men and boys.[130] Jowett's commentary, therefore, explains away Plato's homoeroticism rather than eliding it entirely, though his translations did also creatively downplay this aspect of the *Dialogues*, as Lesley Higgins has demonstrated.[131] This was increasingly the case in later editions, as conversations with Symonds (a former pupil) persuaded him that the homoeroticism of Plato's texts risked alienating young readers from the ethical codes of their society.[132]

Homoeroticism was not, however, the only sexual difficulty with which Jowett contended in interpreting Plato's dialogues for a broad audience. He was also keenly aware that Plato had historically been used to justify a world-denying – and sex-denying – asceticism that, in the largely Protestant Victorian England, could sound uncomfortably like a Roman Catholic apology for celibacy. As an unmarried college fellow at Oxford, he was as vulnerable to the charge of idealizing celibacy as he was to that of excusing homosexuality. And yet he also evidently wished to interpret Plato in a way that allowed space for continence, both within and outside of marriage. As a compromise between these demands, Jowett appeals to a model of productive sexual continence that would have been familiar, and relatively unobjectionable, to many of his readers.

In navigating this problem, Jowett interpreted Plato in a manner that would bear many similarities with Walter Pater's reading in *Plato and Platonism* (1893). Higgins and Evangelista have both persuasively outlined the extent to which Pater differed from Jowett in his reaction to Plato's homoeroticism, typical of the 'well-documented homophobia' that also led him to stage disciplinary intervention into a possible developing relationship between Pater and a Balliol undergraduate in 1874.[133] But this does not mean that Pater would have rejected Jowett's interpretation of Plato entirely. Higgins has argued that 'at the heart of Pater's enterprise is that which Jowett finds unspeakable: the body'.[134] Yet both Jowett and Pater interpreted Plato as spurning certain kinds of sexual expression while retaining a disciplined yet sensuous embodiment, though their parameters of acceptable experience may have differed. They both, therefore, argued that Plato's theory of ideal love can be understood as a channelling of an undesirable sexual passion towards different ends, in a manner that involves not the total rejection, but rather the disciplining of the body: what Pater calls Plato's 'acquired asceticism'. In general, Jowett portrays this ideal love as married sexuality, while Pater – as will be seen in the next chapter – represents the desired ends as largely artistic and sensuously intellectual (Plato is, for Pater, 'a seer who has a sort of sensuous love of the unseen').[135] But even Jowett eventually allows that Plato can be used to justify a productive continence for those few who, like himself, were not destined for marriage.

Jowett's interpretation of Plato's asceticism again vacillates between his need for historical accuracy, and a desire to fit Plato to an English Protestant moral framework, producing a back-and-forth swing observable even within the same paragraph or sentence. Jowett evidently considered the historical Plato to be world-denying, but this does not fit the Protestant interpretation that he wishes to communicate. In order to combat the argument that Plato is overly ascetic, Jowett forwards several stages of not necessarily compatible argument. At first he allows that Plato *is* ascetic, but claims that Victorian readers may recognize the limits of this pagan philosophy. In his introduction to the *Symposium* he used a similar argument to claim that, although Plato was indeed talking about male-male sexuality, yet Victorian British readers will realize that 'there is a great gulf fixed between Greek and Christian Ethics'.[136] In the context of the *Phaedrus* he represents Plato as so caught up in his desire for abstract ideals that he failed to make a proper distinction between the sensory and the sensual, between innocent and immoral sense experience. 'In the attempt to regain this "saving" knowledge of the ideas, the sense was found to be as great an enemy as the desires; and hence two things which to us seem quite distinct' – that is, desires and the senses – 'are inextricably blended in the representation of Plato'.[137] Plato's asceticism, then, errs in throwing out the sensuous baby with the sensual bathwater.

And yet elsewhere Jowett is not content that his readers should think that Plato was preaching celibacy for all. Plato, he argues, never intended this harsh anti-sensory doctrine to apply to everyone. 'In the end something is conceded to the desires, after they have been finally humbled and overpowered.' That something for Jowett is, of course, applicable to Christian marriage rather than a sexual relationship with a boy, though it is to the latter that Plato undoubtedly refers. 'It is unnecessary', he claims, 'to enquire whether the love of which Plato speaks is the love of men or of women. It is really a general idea which includes both, and in which the sensual element, though not wholly eradicated, is reduced to order and measure'.[138] But having so fitted Plato to a Christian framework, Jowett's historicism kicks in to acknowledge the very secondary nature of this solution in Plato's eyes. 'And yet the way of philosophy', he continues, 'or perfect love of the unseen, is total abstinence from bodily delights'. He continues by again attempting to fit this to a Christian framework: '"But all men cannot receive this saying"'.[139] In quoting Matthew 19:11 ('But he said unto them, All men cannot receive this saying, save they to whom it is given') Jowett turns Plato's continent love of philosophy to a love of God.

Jowett must have known that this text was commonly used by Catholics and (as we will see below) Oxford Tractarians like Newman to justify priestly celibacy. He attempts to bring this distinction between disciplined sensual love and the continent love of philosophy back towards marriage, at least for the many. During his analogy between Plato's theory of love and Christian matrimony, he writes, 'when they have attained to this exalted state, let them marry (something too may be conceded to the animal nature of man): or live together in holy and innocent friendship'.[140] However much Jowett may valorize Christian marriage, however, his own life, and that of many of his Oxford colleagues, was deliberately celibate. Though conceding enough sexuality to Plato to make him compatible with a Protestant marriage imperative, he nevertheless returns again to a model, not of chaste love within Christian marriage, but of productive continence outside of that institution.

Plato, he says in his introduction to the *Symposium*, 'is conscious that the highest and noblest things in the world are not easily severed from the sensual desires, or may even be regarded as a spiritualized form of them'. And yet his example of Plato's awareness of the importance of sexuality is the productive continence of Socrates: 'We may observe that Socrates himself is not represented as originally unimpassioned, but as one who has overcome his passions; the secret of his power over others partly lies in his passionate but self-controlled nature.'[141] This conception of Socrates as one whose control of his passionate nature produces a heightened power was common in Victorian England. A popular 'advice for young men' text entitled *Chastity: Physical, Intellectual, and Moral Advantages* (1894), written by the American pseudo-medical writer M. L. Holbrook but widely circulated in England, cites 'A Lesson From Socrates' in illustration of 'The Great Advantages of Chastity': 'Socrates, with his passional [*sic*] nature quite as strong as any sensualist, became one of the greatest men of antiquity, simply because he used his tremendous bodily resources for other ends.'[142] This sentiment stands in direct opposition to Symonds' description of Socrates as 'the mystagogue of amorous philosophy', to whom the more erotic content of Plato's work should probably be prescribed, and shows once again the discursive overlap of sexualized and non-sexualized continence.[143]

It may be thought that Jowett uses the example of Socrates purely because Plato affords no positive model of married chastity. But Jowett is more emphatic in his description of this productively continent state than this would necessitate. In the context of the undesirability of a too-exclusive love of an intellectual ideal to the detriment of marriage, he nevertheless writes:

> there is a probability that there may be some few – perhaps one or two in a whole generation – in whom the light of truth may not lack the warmth of desire. And if there be such natures, no one will be disposed to deny that 'from them flow most of the benefits of individuals and states;' and even from imperfect combinations of the two elements in teachers or statesmen great good may often arise.[144]

For these few, Jowett makes the argument that Platonic continence is not incompatible with social duty, and might even be conducive to it. This form of argument would become important to Decadent writers eager to integrate sexual continence into an individually productive and socially responsible aesthetic mode of life.

The Oxford Movement

It is difficult to make sense of the nineteenth-century currency of productive continence without acknowledging the great influence, both religious and secular, of Anglo-Catholicism, through which the unfashionably Catholic notion of priestly celibacy found a relatively wide audience in Victorian Britain. The Oxford Movement, or Tractarianism, emerged in the 1830s. Its influence on Aestheticism and Decadence has long been acknowledged, with David DeLaura going so far as to say that 'the substance of dogmatic Christianity was transformed, within one or two generations, into the fabric of aestheticism'.[145] This influence included but was by no means limited to the Decadent Catholic revival, the character of which was greatly determined by famous Anglo-Catholic conversions such as that of John Henry Newman.[146] Tractarianism was, as Owen Chadwick observes, 'more a movement of the heart than of the head'; there were, of course, certain doctrinal constants, as well as many focused doctrinal debates, but what really made Newman, Keble, Pusey, Faber and others the founders of a movement was a shared mode of feeling, a renewed attention to tradition and ritual and an attitude of reverence and awe in religious observance.[147] These spread, as the century progressed, far beyond the movement's original geographical and doctrinal boundaries.

Anglo-Catholicism was itself highly influenced by artistic culture. 'It is', remarks Hilary Fraser, 'a critical commonplace that the Oxford Movement was, in some important respects, a late theological flowering of Romanticism'.[148] Many of its originators were highly successful poets, with Keble's *The Christian Year* (1827), 'the outward sign of the new sensibility in the piety of high churchmen', selling over 10,000 copies a year for at least 50 years, surpassing the sales of the then Poet Laureate William Wordsworth.[149] 'Aesthetic sensibility', Fraser writes, 'defined the special character of the Victorian Anglo-Catholic revival', and can be found at every level of Tractarian debate.[150] This religious appropriation of Romantic sensibility made it easy for Romanticism's literary inheritors, including those associated with Pre-Raphaelitism, Aestheticism, and Decadence, to appropriate Tractarian ideas and modes in turn. Among these was an ideal of austere beauty in everyday life that could include, among other behaviours, sexual continence. Decadent writers adopted this ideal in varying degrees. To some, such as Le Gallienne, Symons, and Wilde, it was revered as one beautiful attitude among many, but did not hold an exclusive place in their representations of sexuality. For others, particularly Pater and Johnson, the values that Tractarians attached to continence, as well as their conception of it as a productive state, significantly influenced the manner in which sexuality was incorporated into their ethical thinking, and continued to act as a primary source of religious affect even for those who, like Johnson, converted to Catholicism.

Like Aestheticism and Decadence, Tractarianism was criticized as both overly selfish and overly sensual. This was particularly true of Tractarians who valued sexual continence highly, and advocated priestly celibacy. As Vance has observed, 'it was a common objection that mortification of the flesh and other religious observances were often ultimately selfish will-worship', while Tractarian celibacy was read in the anti-Catholic tradition as hypocritical, and the congregations of celibate priests represented as 'the deluded dupes of men who lusted for sex, money, and power'.[151] Anglo-Catholicism was commonly perceived as both a dangerous deviation from ideal manliness, and a sexual perversion characterized alternately as hetero- and homosexual. And by the end of the century at least, the association with homosexuality was not always unjustified, as Anglo-Catholicism, like Hellenism, was utilized in attempts to define an emergent homosexual identity.[152] But the Tractarian advocation of celibacy should not be read entirely through what Dominic Janes has called 'the Protestant sexualisation of rival forms of religious expression'.[153] To do so risks obscuring a discrete discourse within which Tractarians associated distinct values with celibacy. Tractarian discussion of celibacy did not explicitly worry about seminal loss, or express the attendant idea of the positive effects of seminal retention. But it did consistently follow the historical Christian tradition of representing continence as a productive state that has positive value both for the continent individual, and for the society of which they form a part. In doing so it frequently employed language reminiscent of that associated with seminal retention. The many resonances between the manner in which continence is described and utilized within Decadence (including Catholic Decadence) and Tractarianism suggests direct influence, such as that identified by David DeLaura between Newman and Pater.[154] But they also imply a shared common culture in which productive continence was a plausible product of many sexual discourses.

R. W. Church in 1891 described the Tractarian celibate ideal as 'in the highest degree a religious and romantic one'. 'To shrink from it', he writes, 'was a mark of want of strength or intelligence, of an unmanly preference for English home life, of insensibility to the generous devotion and purity of the saints'.[155] Where Tractarian celibacy has recently attracted critical attention, it has largely been treated as a Victorian cover for homosexuality. The first to make such an argument was Geoffrey Faber, who in his 1933 account of the main figures of the Oxford Movement proposed repressed homosexuality as the psychological origin for the continence of Richard Hurrell Froude and Newman in particular. 'Psychology', he wrote, 'had not yet taught men to look for the roots of spiritual ideals in their animal nature', but 'psychology lies between us and them. We cannot help looking for those animal roots'.[156] Faber assumes sexuality to be, at least to a certain extent, historically constant. More recent readings of Tractarian continence have also interpreted it – no doubt often correctly – as conscious or unconscious homosexuality.[157]

Whatever its 'animal roots', continence was imagined by many in the movement as the consequence of much that they valued: a general attitude of awe and reverence towards the divine, including the divine in the world; a practice of discipline and restraint in everyday life; and a sense of spiritual intensity. This was especially true of Newman and those who were close to him. Moreover, it is in this nexus of values that it is possible to find strong echoes of that particular branch of continent Decadence that is the focus of this book. Tractarian continence was closely associated with the doctrine of reserve. In its simplest form, reserve is the principle that God is hidden: the incapability of our minds fully to comprehend the divine is caused by our finite nature, and is thus an inevitable result of our fallen state. In practice, 'reserve' referred both to this principle, and to a range of practices and beliefs that it implied or generated. Primarily it led to emphasis upon the principle of gradual revelation, the idea that the divine is revealed to us slowly, in proportion to our capacity to receive such apprehension or knowledge. This conception of revelation informed much of the Tractarian approach to divinity; it cautioned awe and reverence in the treatment of sacred things, inspired attention to ritual in church services and prayer, and recommended gradual communication of religious knowledge to those without it, according to their relative capacity to receive it, rather than wholesale preaching of church doctrine. Above all, it imposed the close consideration of one's own capacity to receive divine knowledge, and improvement of that state. In this way, doctrinal reserve made contact with more generic connotations of the word, indicating a manner towards others and towards the world.[158] Duc Dau and Kirstie Blair have both explored the manner in which this reserve, for Dau expanded to include all 'deferral, concealment, self-containment, discipline, the veil, and the lack of touch', can be used to reveal the extent to which Tractarians, at least in their poetry, tied continence to their foundational religious beliefs.[159]

Tractarian continence was in some ways rather alien from that of Decadence, particularly in its close association with asceticism and penance. Emphasis upon sense experience and beauty is ultimately difficult to reconcile with an ascetic denial of worldly good, however much one may aesthetically admire ascetic figures such as St Francis or Thomas à Kempis. But there was another side to Tractarian continence, especially as expressed by Newman, in which the personal and social benefits of continence were stressed beyond their doctrinal basis. Tractarian reserve saw the convergence of Christian attention to the ethics of lifestyle, to the details of everyday behaviour, with a high valuation of both discipline and beauty. This furnished some Decadent writers – Pater and Johnson in particular – with an example of an aesthetically inclined ethics that engaged with many ideas dear to them, including a conception of sexual continence that was both individually productive and socially useful.

Newman frequently described his own continence as a matter of personal feeling, preceding his intellectual investigation of the subject.[160] He claimed in his *Apologia Pro Vita Sua* (1864) to have been convinced from the age of 15 that he would not marry, anticipating therefore his first religious conversion from his family's Evangelicalism to Anglicanism.[161] In his comments upon clerical celibacy in particular, at least before his eventual conversion to Roman Catholicism, he was careful always to draw a line between personal conviction and church doctrine. 'I consider it [...] as a more holy state', he wrote to Frederick William Faber, 'but could not urge this strongly on another, this view being so much a matter of feeling'. Earlier he had written to a correspondent: 'for years I have made up my *mind* to remain in single blessedness — but whether my *heart* be equally made up, time alone can tell'. The emphasis was thus placed variously on intellectual choice and feeling.[162] This individualist continence, more life-mode than dogma, closely echoes the Decadent sexual continence that appears later in the century. Continence was frequently associated with the necessity for discipline (definable both as rigour and ritual) in religious life that falls just short of penitential asceticism. Such discipline could feature as both end and means, as the process by which an ideal mode of life was achieved, and the visible evidence of that achievement.

The conception of a spiritual few whose journey toward God will be swifter than the many meant a great deal to some Tractarians, particularly Newman, who evidently saw these few as ideally continent. 'The celibate', he wrote to Ryder, 'is a high state of life, to which the multitude of men cannot aspire — I do not say, that they who adopt it are necessarily better than others, though the noblest ἦθος [ethos] is situated in that state'.[163] The idea that continence was suited only to a few drew on 1 Corinthians 7:9 – 'But if they cannot contain, let them marry; for it is better to marry than to burn' – as well as on Matthew 19:12: 'For there are some eunuchs that were so born from their mother's womb: and there are some eunuchs, which were made eunuchs of men: and there be eunuchs which have made themselves eunuchs for the kingdom of heaven's sake. He that is able to receive it, let him receive it.' The preceding verse links this directly to the scriptural argument for reserve in communication of religious knowledge: 'But he said unto them, All men cannot receive this saying, save they to whom it is given' (the same verse, we may remember, that Jowett quoted in defence of Platonic continence). Such elitist continence was not limited to Newman; many Tractarians wrote of it as a higher state to which they feared they were not called. Faber in 1840 writes:

> I honour the celibate so highly, and regard it so eminently the fittest way of life for a priest, that if Christ would graciously enable me to learn to live alone, I should prefer much, even with great selfdenials [*sic*], to live a virgin life, and to die a virgin, as God has kept me so hitherto. But I am under no vow, and distrust myself too much to make one.

He also wonders whether there is not a '*moral* continence, [...] the power of living alone so far as visible things to lean on are concerned; but I fear I have it not'.[164] Faber seems to recognize here that continence is not, for Newman among others, simply a physical state, but rather a temperament or mode of being in its own right.

The Tractarian celibate, especially the celibate priest, also borrowed the Catholic conception of celibacy's connection with social usefulness and disinterest. In 1832 Newman wrote to Henry Wilberforce, 'You mistake me, if you think I consider clergymen, as such, should not marry, I only think there should be among the clergy enough unmarried, to give a character of strength to the whole — and that therefore, every one should ask himself whether he is called to the celibate'.[165] This argument for the special communal usefulness and power of the celibate also comes out of and feeds into the secular nineteenth-century humanistic discourse of the few among the many that Jowett utilized in his introductions to Plato's dialogues. As DeLaura notes, although 'the idea of a "clerisy" or an intellectual elite was a commonplace in nineteenth-century England', it is particularly evident in the intellectual line that leads from German Romanticism through Newman and Arnold to Pater. One might well add, as DeLaura suggests, such inheritors of Paterian Aestheticism as Johnson and Wilde; and it would be possible to continue the list with Lee, and (sometimes) Moore.[166] DeLaura shows the great influence of Newman's sermon on the text 'Many Called, Few Chosen', and especially the words 'the few can never mean the many', on Arnold's conception of a society, bringing out of Newman's words 'the theory of a spiritual and intellectual elite who are alone the privileged bearers of truth'. Pater, he argues, read Newman in conjunction with Arnold.[167] But Pater does get something from Newman's idea of 'the few' that Arnold does not. With Pater, and subsequently with those Decadent writers who most closely followed this line of his thinking, Newman's original close association of 'the few' with 'the celibate', a group who exercised both an individual discipline and communal usefulness, is restored. Newman's useful, strong continence also occasionally carried, as Frank Turner has pointed out, a misogynistic tone, as continence is figured as a masculine state threatened by close relation with women.[168] 'The Church wants expeditos milites', he writes, 'not a whole camp of women at its heels, forbye brats'.[169] Decadent writers, as we will see, also occasionally perpetuated this masculine prejudice.

Late nineteenth-century Decadence was the product of a culture to which the idea that sexual continence could form part of an individual cultivation of health and wellbeing, while also enabling that individual to turn that cultivation into communal usefulness, was familiar and commonplace. The aesthete who faced charges of selfishness and sensuality could find in this already well-worked discourse a way in which to explore new ways of being, while never stepping irreversibly outside socially acceptable sexual modes. Whether or not these writers actually practised sexual continence, and whatever the gender of the potential objects of their sexual desires, it remains the case that when writing about or representing sexuality they frequently returned to a discourse of productive sexual continence, the roots of which can be found (and were frequently found by Victorian readers) to stretch back through historical Christianity to the ancient pagan world, as well as through a significant portion of Victorian representations of bodily function. The chapters that follow outline this less familiar Decadence in the work of three writers, connected by their manner of elaborating the idea of the aesthetic life: Walter Pater, Lionel Johnson, and Vernon Lee. A fourth chapter presents, in contrast, a case in which this sexual discourse is combined with other, more positively sensual discourses of the period – George Moore.

CHAPTER 2

'A Passionate Coldness'
Walter Pater

We began with Walter Pater's essay 'Hippolytus Veiled', and his representation of that exemplary celibate as healthy, happy, and social. In Pater's retelling, Hippolytus' death results from the utter inability of his stepmother, Phaedra, to understand his sexual state, and of her subsequent interpretation of this continence as childlike under-development, manipulative trickery, and finally, as a sexual violence in its own right. The last thirty years of Pater scholarship has largely focused on the homoeroticism of his texts, and 'Hippolytus Veiled' certainly bears this interpretation.[1] Hippolytus' resistance can be read as coded reference to a desire placed elsewhere. But this interpretation does not account for Pater's pointed direction of his readers' attention towards the positive nature of Hippolytus' celibacy – his sensuous appreciation of nature, his passionate engagement with scholarship, his mysterious attractiveness for others – and the destructiveness of the foiled effort to attribute meaning to it from without. What if such modern decoding were to repeat Phaedra's refusal to take Hippolytus at face value? This chapter asks what elucidation can be brought to Pater's work by considering his treatment of sexuality as the product of a different manner of conceiving sexual continence; not as the indication of something missing or unsaid, but as an active and productive state in its own right.

Alternative readings of continence in Pater's writing are not rare, but they are rarely followed through. Linda Dowling, while evaluating Pater's intellectual (rather than personal) position in the homosocial-homoerotic continuum that she traces in nineteenth-century Oxford Platonism, has located him at what she calls the 'non-genital' end of the scale, preferring 'a mode of spiritual and emotional attachment that was, at some ultimate level, innocent or asexual'.[2] Both Gerald Monsman and Adam Lee have discussed Pater's idealized, physically restrained 'Platonic Eros'.[3] William Shuter argues that Pater's writing frequently returns to 'a condition not of sterility or impotence but of reserved potency', emphasizing this condition's 'cultural and artistic fertility',[4] and Kate Hext has drawn attention to 'reserve' as Pater's answer to an otherwise irresolvable tension between the liberating potential of sensuous experience and its destructive possibilities. 'Restrained expression', Hext writes, 'is *essential* to Paterian desire', regardless of the object of that desire.[5] Most importantly for current purposes, Herbert Sussman has foregrounded the historical context that can be given to Pater's sexual reserve. Sussman places Pater at the end of his study of the manner in which early nineteenth-century writers related the regulation of male sexuality to the production of art. But the discourse that Sussman examines – present in Victorian culture alongside that explored here – emphasized the equal dangers of both too much and too little sexual activity, rather than the positive construction of continence.

This chapter builds upon Sussman's work, placing Pater at the beginning rather than the end of a genealogy. Although it does not dispute his claim that Pater's 'aesthetic regimen of mind' pushes beyond regulation to a productive retention because his 'desire takes the form of a forbidden homoeroticism', it nevertheless asks what can be gained from shifting focus from the male/female continuum to that of active sexuality/continence.[6] Quite aside from Pater's own evident homoerotic sympathies, his theory of aesthetic self-discipline certainly was incorporated into homosexual culture within late nineteenth-century Decadence, as found in the work of Wilde, Carpenter, and Symonds. But this is not the only aspect of sexual culture that defined meaning in Pater's work and characterized its reception. This chapter looks to the degree of sexual activity or continence, rather than to the object of sexual desire, to broaden our understanding of the place of sexuality in Pater's aestheticism.

Productive continence arises in Pater's texts at crucial points, and exemplifies much that those texts value. It can be found, particularly, in places where Pater distinguishes between the embodied sensuous experience that was always at the heart of his aesthetic practice, and the tipping over of this sensuous pleasure into sensuality, the well-worn Christian category – frequently secularized by Victorian thinkers – that encompasses not only the abuse of the body's capacity for pleasure (including sexual pleasure), but also the inevitable transience, corruption, and death of worldly things. Attending to Pater's use of this nexus of association reveals a tendency to prefer sexual continence, especially for the aesthete, whose susceptibility to sensuous pleasure acts both as a danger and an opportunity. This limitation is not imagined negatively as an absence, but as a positive, productive state that is frequently described in language reminiscent of late nineteenth-century medical writing about sexual health. Most importantly, it does not exclude sensuous aesthetic pleasure, but is rather imagined as conducive to that experience. How far that restrained sensuousness can include a form of auto-eroticism is largely left to the reader to determine, as Pater lingers (consciously or not) over areas of linguistic ambiguity heightened by changing conceptions of sexuality.

Hext has written on Pater's ambivalence about sense experience, and anxiety to moderate its destructive potential. But although Hext recognizes the connections that Pater habitually drew between sex, transience, and death, her twenty-first-century use of the word 'sensual' to refer to both positive and negative aspects of sense experience, as well as her contention that 'Pater realises that the emergence of sensuality as a problem is distinctly modern', underestimates the extent to which Pater's problematization of sense experience utilizes much longer-established categories, familiar to his readers regardless of religious affiliation.[7] This is not to say that Pater entirely scorned transience: the absolute temporality of things, the principle of 'perpetual motion', was the basis for his infamous 'Conclusion' to *The Renaissance* (1873).[8] He often admired the beauty given to things by their very susceptibility to time, to decay. And yet, as Hext puts it, 'Pater hankers still after some [...] unifying essence', a permanence and stability beyond even what Whitney Davis has called 'the dialectic of the delicate pause', the enshrinement of the 'moment' as eternal in its very changeability.[9] Hext (like many others) does not see Pater extending his search for 'unifying principles' to ethics: 'He did not believe in objectivity, eternal truths or philosophical systems, nor did he believe that rational discourse can ascertain moral values.'[10] Attending to sexual continence in Pater's work reveals how semi-stable ethical values and preferences, if not absolute rules, might have been found there by the nineteenth-century readers who attempted to use his work as a guide to living, despite Pater's own perpetual qualifications and equivocations.

One measure of (relative) ethical objectivity throughout Pater's work, though gaining particular emphasis in *Marius the Epicurean* (1885), is health. Productive continence appears where Pater emphasizes the healthiness of sensuousness properly exercised, and unhealthiness of sensuality, of the body misused. But it is also often present when he casts doubt upon the easy separation of health from disease, of sensuousness from sensuality. This is especially the case when he worries about the transitory nature of all pleasure, especially bodily pleasure. Though he frequently celebrated ephemerality as heightening aesthetic experience, such impermanence nevertheless often threatens to connect all sensation, whether sensuous or sensual, with death. 'How often', reflects the protagonist of *Marius*, 'had the thought of their brevity spoiled for him the most natural pleasures of life, confusing even his present sense of them by the suggestion of disease, of death, of a coming end, in everything!'[11] This threat was particularly apparent to a secularist who, like so many Victorian secularists, renounced Christian metaphysics but in many respects wished to retain what they considered to be Christian moral standards. Continence figures as evidence not only of the personal discipline, the 'marvellous discretion'[12] and 'passionate coldness' (*Renaissance*, 183) – a combination of enthusiasm and detachment – needed for such fine distinctions, but also as both the indication and requirement of a temperament that makes one especially effective at filtering the good from the bad, the healthy from the unhealthy, in specific objects or periods or people; as he put it in *Marius,* to make 'use of the flower, when the fruit perhaps was useless or poisonous' (vol. 1, 194); though this did not mean, it must be said, that Pater did not consider *anything* to be purely poisonous: 'Surely evil was a real thing', he has Marius reflect, 'and the wise man wanting in the sense of it, where, not to have been, by instinctive election, on the right side, was to have failed in life' (vol. 1, 243). There is surely something in this of St Paul's statement, so often appropriated by Victorian writers, that 'To the pure all things are pure' (2 Corinthians 8:15). In this way Pater not only reconciles productive continence with the widened experience, or at least intellectual independence, that was as morally necessary to him as was the avoidance of sensuality, but also represents continence as actively facilitative of such independence. Pater strongly implies that this temperamental faculty is proper to the aesthete, and so generates a tenacious association between the aesthetic life that he idealizes and the productive sexual continence that he admires. However, health was not the only measure of ethical success in Pater's work. His later writing particularly finds in the presence (or absence) of a widened 'sympathy' or 'love' the potential for emotional connection with and consideration for others, a similar marker of effective filtering, and again the continent aesthete very literally embodies this ethical success.

The privileging of these points of association undeniably leaves many aspects of the works hanging as loose threads, particularly aspects that require interpretation or gesture in opposite directions to what is said elsewhere. This continent, somewhat preachy Pater would nevertheless have been familiar to many late nineteenth-century readers, as we saw in the Introduction. For all that he was lauded by many among the generation that followed him as, in the words of Frank Harris, an 'apologist of strange sins', for others (and indeed for Harris himself) Pater meant not sensual indulgence, but rather a strict, austere, disciplined (and yet sensuous) ethical position that extended to a particular attitude towards conduct in general, and sexuality in particular.[13] It was this Pater, as much as Pater the hedonist, who shaped the course of late nineteenth-century literary culture. Regardless of one's opinion concerning Pater's own meanings and intentions, ignoring this important element of his reception leaves a noticeable gap in the study of Aestheticism and Decadence in the late nineteenth and early twentieth centuries.

To read Pater's work almost as if it were an advice book for young men like those examined in the previous chapter, and to emphasize that which in Pater's depiction of sexuality corresponds to depictions found in so much late nineteenth-century writing about sexual health, will be the task of this chapter. And as this involves emphasizing that which can be interpreted as guiding the reader towards a certain conduct of life, it will also find a coincidence there with what may for nineteenth-century readers, as for the protagonist of Le Gallienne's *Young Lives*, have 'presented many fascinating analogies to the present time'.[14] For Pater, 'modernity' was a recurring state of culture and state of mind as much as a specific period of time, observable as much in Antoinine Rome and late Renaissance France as in nineteenth-century England (though the latter may have been, for him, particularly characterized by what was essentially 'modern', the most modern of modernities). One's own time, particularly as observed when young, presented for Pater an excellent opportunity to demonstrate that gymnastic of filtering, of selection and discrimination, which was necessary to the aesthetic temperament. Modernity, Pater suggests, while offering some of the most exciting opportunities to the aesthete, is also dedicated to the present moment, and so has an inevitable relationship with death and decay that one must come to terms with. Carolyn Williams has shown how Pater's characterization of 'modern thought' was essentially destructive in spirit, though containing an element of truth that must be acknowledged. Rather than adopting a radical relativism himself, she argues, Pater responded to the problems of modern thought 'by fully acknowledging them, confronting them, and regulating their effects'. This final step of regulation involved the construction of what Williams calls a 'provisional objectivity', an assertion of a severely limited, and yet no less emphatic, objective knowledge.[15] This attitude resembles Pater's approach to aesthetic ethics, as a process of acknowledgement, discrimination, and filtering of desirable from undesirable elements in a given object.

This chapter attends to the ethical rather than epistemological implications of Pater's 'modernity'. Though always fascinating, one's own period has not yet been subject to the filtering of time, and so is also full of much that is objectionable (an accusation to which no age is immune), whether sexual licence, ugliness, physical corruption, or selfishness. Hext quite rightly claims that 'enlisting the arts as part of a crusade for moral improvement was not Pater's way'; he is rarely didactic.[16] But Pater's habit of representing his theories in concrete form, through the lives of historical or fictional figures, means that this coming to terms with and eventual transcending of death by identifying what is eternal and permanent in the world is often represented as a practical process in which an individual must either learn to sort sensuous from sensual experience, or fail to learn this to their detriment. The Paterian aesthetic hero, however much he (it is always he) may resort to history for his finer pleasures, must also find in the modern world the necessarily fleeting sensuous pleasure, the 'ecstasy' that Pater so valued, without finding too much else besides. Modernity, then, presented Pater with the perfect opportunity to evolve a secular ethics, an ethics with no standard beyond direct experience. The potently continent aesthete functioned as a symbol of success for this ethics.

I begin, as is traditional, with *Studies in the History of the Renaissance*, especially its 'Conclusion' (Pater's most famous attempt to develop his aestheticism into an ethics for a sceptical modern age) and the essay 'Winckelmann'. However, I read these alongside the unpublished manuscript 'The Aesthetic Life', usually assumed to date from the period immediately preceding Pater's death in 1894. In this unfinished essay he arguably attempted to re-write the 'Conclusion' by emphasizing the selection and distinction, based in aesthetic discretion, necessary to modern, sceptical ethics. Teasing out from *The Renaissance* those passages in which a similar emphasis is made brings out also, I argue, a fine hierarchy of experiences, at least for the aesthete. I then turn to the novels – *Marius the Epicurean* and *Gaston de Latour* – where Pater can most obviously be read as making a case for a secular and aesthetic ethical practice that draws certain tentative lines around desirable behaviour, at least for those of an aesthetic temperament. Again, we find sexual activity, with the possible exception of reproduction within marriage (never, however, undertaken by Pater's aesthete-heroes themselves), to constitute the strongest and most frequent indication that these lines have been crossed, while productive continence (potentially, but not necessarily, eroticized) is discernible as an alternative ideal.[17]

The Renaissance and 'The Aesthetic Life'

When *The Renaissance* was published in 1873 it met with both enthusiasm and fierce condemnation, with both camps pointing particularly to its 'Conclusion'. This essay offered a somewhat equivocal introduction to a question that Pater would spend so much of his career attempting to answer: can an aesthetic ethics be extrapolated from a sceptical epistemology? Modernity was central to his thinking, as it had been from his earliest published essays.[18] The essay begins on a hypothetical note, by identifying Heraclitan flux as the defining feature of 'modern thought' (186). Starting with physical science, he finds that modern thinking about 'our physical life' implies that 'it is but the concurrence, renewed from moment to moment, of forces parting sooner or later on their ways'. He passes to epistemological philosophy and psychology, or 'the inward world of thought and feeling' (187), and finds again a 'continual vanishing away, that strange, perpetual weaving and unweaving of ourselves' (188). Having conducted this survey of 'modern thought', which had not explicitly denied God, but had not mentioned him either, he changes to a more direct mode to derive, not only a more satisfactory epistemology, but also an ethics without religious justification: as Sara Lyons puts it, 'an ideal of human flourishing that is conceived without reference to the transcendent, or to anything beyond or higher than the human and the natural'.[19] 'Not the fruit of experience', he says, 'but experience itself, is the end' (188). In a world in which 'we are all under a sentence of death but with a sort of indefinite reprieve' (190), the question is how to spend the interval so as to 'be present always at the focus where the greatest number of vital forces unite in their purest energy', to 'burn always with this hard, gem-like flame, to maintain this ecstasy'; in short, to extract the utmost from life under modern, secular conditions (188–9).[20]

Lyons, in her study of secularism in Victorian Aestheticism, has argued that 'Pater's *The Renaissance* caused a scandal in part because it pushed the established discourses of religious doubt to their limits'; but that the power of this outrage derived from an 'old (and very Victorian) association of atheism with unfettered sexuality' not thoroughly anticipated by Pater himself.[21] Those who claimed that the 'Conclusion' could potentially lead young readers astray by failing to explicitly proscribe sexual license undoubtedly, however, had a point. Pater's 'Conclusion' was not a prescriptive morality, a list of behaviours that must or must not be indulged in, but was rather an ethics, a set of general rules of life adaptable to different temperaments. John Morley recognized this distinction, and the problematic tendency of readers to elide it, in his 1873 review – Pater, Morley wrote, had 'no design of interfering with the minor or major morals of the world, but only of dealing with what we may perhaps call the accentuating portion of life [...], what remains for a man seriously to do or feel, over and above earning his living and respecting the laws'. In a letter to Morley,

Pater gave thanks for his 'explanation of my ethical point of view, to which I fancy some readers have given a prominence I did not mean it to have'.[22] But Pater's reluctance in the 'Conclusion' to provide practical guidance concerning conduct facilitated divergent readings, particularly in light of what sounded like an imperative to infinite experimentation: 'What we have to do is to be for ever curiously testing new opinions and courting new impressions, never acquiescing in a facile orthodoxy' (189). For 'facile orthodoxy', many read (and still do read) 'conventional morality'.

Contemporary readers agonized over Pater's use of certain phrases at the climax to a book which detailed the necessity of 'pleasure', 'passion', and the 'sensuous' to aesthetic experience. What did Pater mean when he wrote that 'Great passions may give us this quickened sense of life', and that one of these passions might be 'ecstasy and sorrow of love' (190)?[23] What did this mean as part of a 'desperate effort to see and touch', and as part of a rejection of 'facile orthodoxy' (189)? Sidney Colvin, while accepting Pater's ethic as appropriate for artists and critics – for those, that is, who were practiced in the sensuous discrimination that he professed to believe Pater really intended – wrote in his review, 'but do not tell everybody that refined pleasure is the one end of life. By refined, they will understand the most refined they know, and the most refined they know are gross; and the result will be not general refinement but general indulgence'.[24] Colvin recognized that much of the text's divisive power derived less from its tolerance than from the inherently euphemistic nature of sexual description, in which the language of pleasure and embodiment can refer equally to sexual or non-sexual experience. It remained, and will always remain, for individual readers to decide how far Pater consciously cultivated this ambiguity.

Pater's only exclusionary moment in the 'Conclusion' is the warning that one must 'be sure it is passion – that it does yield you this fruit of a quickened, multiplied consciousness' (190). He leaves actual behaviour to the individual conscience and temperament. Readers keen to interpret 'passion' as sexual license could well read back to the opening essay of the collection, where Pater's use of the figures of Abelard and Heloïse to represent the twelfth-century awakening of the secular embodiment of the Renaissance came close to suggesting that the sexual nature of their relationship was crucial to the awakening of that spirit. But he does also, in the 'Conclusion', provide a clear hierarchy of passionate experiences. We are told that some spend that interval before death 'in listlessness, some in high passions, the wisest, at least among "the children of this world," in art and song'.[25] And 'Of such wisdom, the poetic passion, the desire of beauty, the love of art for its own sake, has most', because 'art comes to you pro-posing frankly to give nothing but the highest quality to your moments as they pass, and simply for those moments' sake' (190).[26] It is surely this preference of art over other modes of life, one of which was 'high passions', which led Symonds to describe Pater as 'careless of maintaining at any cost a vital connection with the universal instincts of humanity'. Elsewhere Symonds was clear that his objection was sexual, writing: 'I cannot sym-pathize with Pater's theory of life […]. I have always thought it the theory of one who has not lived & loved – of a Pagan, not a Papal soprano [cas-trato]'.[27] Although Pater does not exclude love (and its possible reading as euphemism for sex) as a route to 'quickened, multiplied consciousness', he asserts that poetry, art, and beauty constitute a higher road. Art, not sex, is the most rational response to secular modernity.

The 'Conclusion' was excised from the second edition of *The Renaissance* (1877), but returned to the third (1888), with the disclaimer that, though it had been removed because he 'conceived it might possibly mislead some of those young men into whose hands it might fall', he had now 'dealt more fully in *Marius the Epicurean* with the thoughts suggested by it' (186 n.1).[28] *Marius* was not, however, the only text to explore similar ideas. Second edition copies of *The Renaissance* ended with what in other editions was the penultimate essay, an extended discussion of the eighteenth-century art historian Winckelmann. This essay addresses similar questions concern-ing modern and secular ethics as the 'Conclusion', but with specific refer-ence to the aesthetic temperament, asking how the sensuously inclined aesthete was to live an ideal life of self-culture in the modern world. Here the question of sexuality is approached more directly. Winckelmann was already known for what Pater calls 'his romantic, fervent friendships with young men'.[29] Rather than circumvent these friendships, Pater makes their potentially sexual nature both evident and central to Winckelmann's affin-ity with the Hellenic spirit. 'These friendships', he asserts, 'bringing him in contact with the pride of human form, and staining his thoughts with its bloom, perfected his reconciliation with the spirit of Greek sculpture' (152). As Pater argues in this essay that sculpture is an expression of what is typically Hellenic in Greek art, and that the Hellenic represents an ideal spirit of culture, this is tantamount to claiming that homosexual desire allows Winckelmann to access true self-culture. Whereas the 'Conclusion' presented an unconnected hierarchy of experiences, 'Winckelmann' sets sexuality and art in a Platonic structure of progression whereby 'romantic, fervent friendships' can lead to an enhanced aesthetic understanding. As Stefano Evangelista and Katherine Harloe put it, 'his argument might be read as normalizing Winckelmann's homosexual leanings or, even, as an elevation of homoeroticism into a marker of intellectual distinction – the foundation of Winckelmann's ability to achieve a privileged insight into the ancient world'.[30]

'Winckelmann' has, since the 1990s, become the central text for critical readings that seek to establish the crucial importance of homosexuality to Pater's aestheticism. Richard Dellamora described the essay as 'a humanist polemic for sexual tolerance', while Evangelista has argued that 'Winckelmann' is not only 'a pioneering psychological study of how sexual preferences colour artistic taste and intellectual life more generally', but also 'one of the earliest attempts to define a modern gay sensibility'.[31] More recently, Dustin Friedman has read 'Winckelmann' as Pater's clearest explication of a pseudo-Hegelian dialectic, in which aesthetic experience allows one to see beyond the normative determinations of one's own sociopolitical setting and therefore feel something like subjective freedom. Aesthetes, he writes, 'use their faculty of aesthetic perception to facilitate the acquisition of sexual self-knowledge and, in turn, allow their erotic desire to catalyze the development of a new mode of seeing themselves and their relationship to the world'. Although admitting that such experience is available to all readers, Friedman claims that late nineteenth-century aesthetes such as Pater perceived that in a homophobic society, the realization of their socially proscribed desires gave queer aesthetes privileged access to this dialectic. 'Once one realizes it is possible to embrace desires that society has declared verboten, it becomes possible for one to question all the truths society presents as absolute and unquestionable'.[32] 'Winckelmann' is, for Friedman, the place where Pater shows that art facilitates such realization of one's forbidden desires, and in doing so gives queer aesthetes access to an autonomy and progressive potential beyond that of non-queer subjects: the 'sense of freedom' Pater states the modern spirit is so in need of (184).

Certainly 'Winckelmann' is the closest that Pater comes to asserting that sexual desire is a valuable, even necessary, part of aesthetic experience. This is particularly the case if one reads all references to touch, sensuous pleasure, and the body as inevitably erotic, as is common practice in critical work on Pater and sexuality. 'Winckelmann' also, however, clearly delineates between degrees of sensuous experience in a manner that would become habitual in Pater's later work, and which echoes nineteenth-century discourse concerning sexual continence and excess. The relevant paragraphs are rarely referenced in modern criticism despite the frequent attention given to this essay. Pater does not simply describe Winckelmann's relationships with young men; he also emphasizes the limit that was (he asserts) set to these relationships. While their *potential* eroticism is not denied, they are nevertheless explicitly depicted as sexually continent: 'Of passion, of physical excitement, they contain only just so much as stimulates the eye to the finest delicacies of colour and form' (154). The first publication of the essay in the *Westminster Review* (1867) put as much emphasis on the necessary presence of 'passion' in these relationships as on its necessary limitation: 'Of passion, of physical stir, they contain just so much as stimulates the eye to the last lurking delicacies of colour and form'.[33] By the second edition of *The Renaissance*, however – that is, the edition from which the 'Conclusion' was withdrawn – the addition of the word 'only' shifts the emphasis to limitation, suggesting an anxiety to further highlight continence and to play down the necessary part played by a particular form of 'physical excitement'.

This later equivocating may well be a concession to homophobia that initiated readers were intended to ignore, though as Friedman points out it was not unusual to refer to Winckelmann's homosexuality in scholarly work.[34] What matters for the present analysis, however, is not whether Winckelmann's friendships actually were continent, or even whether Pater actually believed them to be or intended his readers to believe so, but only that he claims that they were in a manner that lays the groundwork for explication of a productively continent sensuous practice. Furthermore, at least some contemporary readers evidently felt this distinction to be of importance to Pater's aesthetic theory. A. C. Benson references Pater's emphasis on continence when he writes that 'in Winckelmann he found one who could devote himself to the passionate contemplation of beauty, without any taint or grossness of sense'.[35] Even Harris, notorious for his (occasionally imaginative) outing of *fin-de-siècle* sexuality, and persuaded of Pater's inclination to, though not practice of, 'strange sins', cites the above passage as among all his writing the most 'soul-revealing', showing that 'his physical hold on life was so slight that his desire merely led him to a finer appreciation of the beauties of art'.[36] These two readings notably differ in the degree to which they interpret the importance of sexual desire to Pater's productive continence; Benson assumes an effective divorce between sensual and sensuous experience, while Harris takes for granted the rooting of the latter in the former.

However one reads them, taking Pater's comments about continence in 'Winckelmann' literally does not conflict with the rest of the essay. He admits, no doubt controversially and with no small risk, that the nature of these friendships with young men is erotic. Yet the fact that they are not actively sexual, that the sensuousness integral to these relationships does not go beyond the stimulation of the eye (rather than any other body part), is an important, though subtle, distinction, and essential to his thinking. Evangelista describes how the homoerotic content of 'Winckelmann' resides not only in open reference to romantic friendships with youths, but also in the use of Plato's *Symposium* and *Phaedrus* to outline a progression from homoerotic to intellectual experience. 'In "Winckelmann", he writes, 'Pater borrows from the *Phaedrus* to construct a modern intellectual type in which erotic and aesthetic impulses are collapsed'.[37] This collapse, however, is performed as much by the reader as by Pater himself, who while potentially leaving this option open nevertheless makes great efforts to write about sensuous, embodied aestheticism without *necessarily* collapsing it into the erotic. Moreover, he made a similar distinction at the end of his career with regard to Plato. In *Plato and Platonism* (1893), he acknowledges that 'Plato himself had not been always a mere Platonic lover', knowing 'all the ways of lovers, in the literal sense'. Yet he attributes Plato's genius to his control and redirection of this erotic potential; what he calls his 'acquired asceticism'.[38] Adam Lee has outlined the importance of this potentially continent reading of Plato's writing on love in the *Phaedrus* and the *Symposium* to Pater's later work, especially *Gaston de Latour*.[39] Plato was, Pater writes, 'from first to last unalterably a lover'. Yet he assures us that, in terms of sexual passion, 'he was glad when in the mere natural course of years he was become at all events less ardent a lover'. Instead he learned to apply 'the discipline of sensuous love' to 'the world of intellectual abstractions', to climb the ladder of love described in the *Symposium* as leading from sensuous (and possibly, but not necessarily, sexual) love to a higher apprehension of perfection in things. In this way, Pater claims, Plato's early 'amorous temper' is compatible with his being, 'with a kind of unimpassioned passion [...], a lover in particular of temperance'.[40] This distinction between destructive sensuality and disciplined sensuousness becomes pertinent to the reader concerned with Pater's ethics, whether or not that reader was attending to the homosexual context of these passions.

But why is this distinction so important to Pater? In his discussion of Greek sculpture in 'Winckelmann', Pater also introduces his concern with the temporal and the universal. Having stated, with reference to Hegel, that the 'spirit' of every age contains both contingent (the circumstances of the day) and permanent (to be found potentially in all phases of humanity) elements, he wonders of the more permanent spirit of Greek art, 'Can we bring down that ideal into the gaudy, perplexed light of modern life?'

(181–2). The answer is, with qualifications, yes; and success in doing so will result in the aesthetic life. Pater's modern Hellenism is one of self-culture, in which one's life is treated in the manner of art; it is also contingent modernity tempered by reference to an already filtered ideal. That this mode of living, described, in Arnoldian manner, as 'culture', is possible in modernity had been (Pater claims) demonstrated by Goethe, who uses Hellenism's 'balance [and] unity with one's self' as a corrective to the 'perplexed currents of modern thought' (182).[41] Despite Pater having claimed that every age combined transient and permanent elements, 'modern life' is clearly associated with a preponderance of transience. As such, modern Hellenism, and the aesthetic realization of Pater's ethic, which itself was formed in response to the perpetual flux of an epistemologically sceptical philosophy, become virtually indistinguishable. The ethical work of the 'Conclusion', all that grasping, discriminating, and selecting of pulsations, is here expanded upon for the aesthete specifically, whose temperament allows access to all that is most permanent in past ages.

In accordance with Winckelmann's adoption of Hegelian terms, Pater attributes two characteristics to the aesthetic ethic of Hellenism: 'Heiterkeit – blitheness or repose, and Allgemeinheit – generality or breadth' (170). Having introduced these terms, he specifies that 'breadth' should not be understood as indiscriminate expansion or, when applied to life, a kind of license:

> But that generality or breadth has nothing in common with the lax observation, the unlearned thought, the flaccid execution, which have sometimes claimed superiority in art, on the plea of being 'broad' or 'general.' Hellenic breadth and generality come of a culture minute, severe, constantly renewed, rectifying and concentrating its impressions into certain pregnant types (170).

The acquisition of Hellenic breadth is to be associated with discipline. This note is struck repeatedly throughout Pater's work, and became a defining characteristic for many contemporary readers.[42] 'The duty of absolute discipline', wrote Lionel Johnson, 'appealed to him as a thing of price'.[43] Pater himself, when writing of this discipline as an element of style rather than living, described it as 'the male conscience in that matter, as we must think it under a system of education which still to so large an extent limits real scholarship to men'.[44] Though this gendering seems contingent on cultural conditions, and to regret that present order, Pater does elsewhere present it in a more essentialist manner, as Megan Becker-Lackrone has shown.[45] This gendering did not, however, prevent all female readers from incorporating Pater's disciplined breadth into their own lives, as we will see in Chapter 4.

When applied to life, disciplined 'breadth', Pater says, will include a constant renewing of experience, the refusal to be limited by dogma (as outlined in the 'Conclusion'). But such wide experience is required only to the end that each new thing be tested against the ideal, a quality which will become slightly different for every person based on innate temperament: 'the proper instinct of self-culture cares not so much to reap all that those various forms of genius can give, as to find in them its own strength' (183). And then, 'In every direction it is a law of restraint', he says. 'It keeps passion always below that degree of intensity at which it must necessarily be transitory' (172).[46] Here we have a clear association of excessive passion with the perpetual flux that is the mark of Pater's modernity, while a low heat like that of Winckelmann (in Pater's representation) in his relations with young men is associated with a Hellenic permanence. It is not impossible to imagine a limited sexual relationship that would allow such self-culture, as we saw outlined by Symonds in *A Problem in Greek Ethics*; but such an interpretation is again difficult. It is true, again, that the essay does linger over the physical element of Hellenism, its tactility, in which the intellectual and the sensuous are fused: Winckelmann is famously dubbed, like Plato, 'lover and philosopher at once', though critics have disagreed about whether or not the word 'lover' is intended sexually.[47] Winckelmann 'apprehended the subtlest principles of the Hellenic manner, not through the understanding, but by instinct or touch' (154). Although such relation with the concrete and sensuously apprehendable is essential to Pater's understanding of Hellenism, he is nevertheless eager to impose upon it a limit, a restraint that Pater's earlier mention of Winckelmann's 'friendships' with young men urges us to connect to sexual restraint. Whether or not we consider this limitation to imply a sexualized or genuinely non-sexual continence depends very much on what we as readers believe sex to be.

In this spirit Pater describes the ideal attitude of the aesthete engaged in self-culture as 'a kind of passionate coldness' (183), as he engages with all kinds of culture, including 'sensuousness', only to weigh their worth against their ongoing development of the intellect (not the body) before moving on to other experiences. Arthur Symons echoes this phrase, describing Pater as characterized by his 'gift and cultivation of a passionate temperance': both 'gift' and 'cultivation' because based in temperament *and* actively fostered.[48] And in this essay more than any other in *The Renaissance*, that temperance can be read as extending to sexual continence. Even when again emphasizing (as if this were the element likely to be missed) the embodied sensuousness of all aesthetic experience, Pater is careful to detach such sensuousness from an essential relationship with sexuality. 'He may live, as Keats lived, a pure life; but his soul, like that of Plato's false astronomer, becomes more and more immersed in sense, until nothing which lacks the appeal to sense has interest for him' (176–7). Sexual experience is not, Pater implies at this point, necessary to this sensuousness, though it may play a larger part for some than for others, for a Winckelmann than for a Keats. This argument harmonizes with Pater's assertion that the beauty of Greek sculpture was 'a sexless beauty: the statues of the gods had the least traces of sex. Here there is a moral sexlessness, a kind of ineffectual wholeness of nature, yet with a true beauty and significance of its own' (176). The first two published versions included the phrase 'a kind of impotence'. In an earlier essay, 'Diaphaneitè' (of which more later), Pater used the same words to describe an ideal character, described by Benson as 'narrow and potent'.[49] It has become common, following Richard Dellamora's analysis of this passage, to read the word 'sexless' as implying primarily gender ambiguity, and this is certainly part of Pater's meaning here.[50] But reading the words 'impotence' and 'sexlessness' to also indicate sexual continence is wholly in keeping with the rest of the essay.

Such potent narrowness, the cultivated heat that results from careful restriction or limitation and therefore escapes the transience of an indiscriminate burning, is especially stressed in the 'Winckelmann' essay, and may have acted for some as a corrective to the 'Conclusion' (in editions where they were presented together). Pater himself appears to have been ambivalent about such intensifying narrowness, often admiring it, but becoming suspicious when it becomes an end in its own right rather than a means to general cultivation. He often admires the potency that comes from restraint, but with reservations that were stated less strongly as his career progressed. In the 1866 essay 'Poems by William Morris', for instance, he describes the idealized love of medieval poetry in similar terms. 'A passion of which the outlets are sealed', he writes, 'begets a tension of nerve, in which the sensible world comes to one with a reinforced brilliance and relief'. This tense restraint is attractive but unhealthy: it is 'but a beautiful disease or disorder of the senses'.[51] In 'Winckelmann' Pater sometimes seems apologetic for the praise he appears to heap upon this necessary restraint. 'There have been instances', he says, 'of culture developed by every high motive in turn, and yet intense at every point; and the aim of our culture should be to attain not only as intense but as complete a life as possible'. And yet, 'often the higher life is only possible at all, on condition of the selection of that in which one's motive is native and strong;

and this selection involves the renunciation of a crown reserved for others' (149–50). Less apology is evident when he says of Winckelmann that 'Other interests, practical or intellectual, those slighter talents and motives not supreme, which in most men are the waste part of nature, and drain away their vitality, he plucked out and cast from him' (147–8).[52] Such seminal metaphors of waste and drainage of vitality could not but be familiar to his nineteenth-century readers, as would be the idea that without such drainage, an intense potency in another direction may be possible. Though 'Doubtless Winckelmann's perfection is a narrow perfection [...] within its severe limits his enthusiasm burns like lava' (148). Pater uses this narrow potency to connect Winckelmann's personal temperament to his beloved Hellenism and to sculpture, all of which work within a 'happy limit' (164).

'Winckelmann' ends by asking how the Hellenic ideal can be brought into modern life specifically. 'Certainly, for us of the modern world', he says, 'with its conflicting claims, its entangled interests, distracted by so many sorrows, with many preoccupations, so bewildering an experience, the problem of unity with ourselves, in blitheness and repose, is far harder than it was for the Greek within the simple terms of antique life'. And yet humanity's needs remain constant: 'not less than ever, the intellect demands completeness, centrality' (182). He uses Goethe as an example of the modern aesthete who does not accept the 'narrowness' of Winckelmann, but who, by practicing a 'passionate coldness' in his dealing with 'various forms of genius' (183) – the sensuous, the metaphysical, the spiritual – develops a proper self-culture.[53] This is breadth, or *Allgemeinheit*, tempered and increased by blitheness or repose, *Heiterkeit*. It is not entirely clear in this essay why Pater thinks that modernity is particularly complex, or exactly in what this complexity consists. But science, and the determinism that science seems to imply, has a great deal to do with it, and the role of art is to alleviate the emotional implications of scientific modernity so as to 'satisfy the spirit' (184). 'The chief factor in the thoughts of the modern mind concerning itself is the intricacy, the universality of natural law, even in the moral order' he says, a state of things that must be responded to 'with blitheness and repose' (184–5). 'Natural laws we shall never modify, embarrass us as they may; but there is still something in the nobler or less noble attitude with which we watch their fatal combinations' (185). Modernity here is a threat as much as an opportunity, to be approached, like sense experience, in a particular manner: with discipline, reserve, and control. Benjamin Morgan has written of 'Winckelmann' as an effort to come to terms with the lack of freedom imposed by modernity's determinism without resorting to a Hegelian (and Kantian) rejection of the body and retreat into 'ever higher universality', by accepting the sensuous pleasure that can be found in unfreedom: 'for Pater aesthetic sensitivity is important precisely because it allows us to experience and reconcile ourselves to a world in which we lack the autonomy we desire'.[54] Pater likewise uses productive continence to find a middle ground between embodied contingency and intellectual universality, whereby a disciplined sensuousness means that the latter actually facilitates experience of the former. As we will see in the following section, he used his novels to explore how the implications of this situation could unfold in specific circumstances.

The 'Winckelmann' essay, then, suggests that a sexually austere practice may align with the aesthete's habitual approach to all experience. It becomes associated with an attitude in which embodied sensuousness is brought to bear on all experience and all assessment of that experience, but in a way that is restrained, disciplined, observant, and inactive, a 'passionate coldness'. Passion, in this reading, is to be fostered within oneself, rather than necessitating sexual interaction with others, and thus never becomes destructively sensual. As Benson puts it, 'to the serious student, pleasure and joy must always have a certain bracing austerity; might be sipped, perhaps, held up to the light, dwelt upon, but not plunged into nor rioted upon'.[55] This in turn is presented as a way of enjoying transience while avoiding extreme contingency, the perpetual flux of sceptical modernity as figured in the 'Conclusion'. And though it is likely that this continent mode of life may have been particularly attractive to readers attempting to control or suppress same-sex desires in a society that disallowed the expression of such – Benson himself is likely an example of such continence – this very appeal relies upon its conformity to a mode of productive continence that would have been readily recognizable and acceptable within wider Victorian society.

Benson complained that 'the peril of such a creed' is that, 'stated in the form of abstract principles, it affords no bulwark against the temptation to sink from a pure and passionate beauty of perception into a grosser indulgence'.[56] Pater's early model of self-culture was remarkably generous, either in the behaviours that it allowed (if they could be squared with individual temperament), or in the faith that a proper 'education' would develop an ethical as well as an aesthetic filter. There is little in *The Renaissance* to suggest such an all-round filter: continence in 'Winckelmann' is represented as conducive to self-culture, but not as more morally or socially desirable than sexually active practices. Most studies of sexuality in Pater's writing attend primarily to these earlier texts, with the rationale that later texts are coloured by personal experience of homophobia and therefore present a more closeted or coded – and consequently less radical – outlook. While that may well be the case, the later texts are certainly interesting for elaborating the ethical consequences of his productively continent aesthetic practice in a way that would correspond to the social implications given to continence in much late nineteenth-century writing.

When Pater died in 1894, he left another unfinished attempt to rewrite the above sentiments in the form of a manuscript entitled 'The Aesthetic Life'. This text outlines how an aesthetic self-culture may also entail an ethical practice that is not far divorced from Christian morals, despite its lack of metaphysical underpinning. It begins, like the 'Conclusion', with modernity, but this time turns immediately to ethics. 'In a generation like our own, as much as, perhaps more than, in any past one, there will be those who say "Let us eat and drink, for tomorrow we die"'.[57] This phrase, often misattributed to Epicurus, is biblical and refers (in Isaiah 22.13 and 1 Corinthians 15) to the conduct of those who are without God. Pater's continuation of this sentence – 'and among them some who will eat and drink finely – so finely that they may seem to be sitting at a heavenly banquet' – can be read as a claim that not only is an ethics without God indeed possible, but this ethics could satisfy the most stringent with regard to conduct (1). He expressed a similar sentiment in *Marius*. For some, he writes, the infamous phrase

> may come to be identical with – 'My meat is to do what is just and kind;' while the soul, which can make no sincere claim to have apprehended anything beyond the veil of immediate experience, yet never loses a sense of happiness in conforming to the highest moral ideal it can clearly define for itself; and actually, though but with so faint hope, does the 'Father's business' (*Marius*, vol. 1, 145).

Though this is supposedly paraphrasing the Cyreniacism of Arristipus, Pater nevertheless returns to Christianity when it comes to conduct, 'the "Father's business"' (quoting Luke 2:49). He had earlier described this philosophy as having an 'inward atmosphere of temperance which did but further enhance the brilliancy of human life' (*Marius*, vol. 1, 134), one of many instances in which Pater suggests restrained conduct can intensify aesthetic experience.

Materialism, he goes on in 'The Aesthetic Life', has failed to provide a satisfactory guide to living, as it ignores the emotional needs of the individual. 'Space and time, if infinite, are still drearily mechanical space and time, with their hard successing of phenomena, and leave the conscious individual, the personal organism, a somewhat hopeless being' (2–3). At

best this modern, scientific individual, irremediably aware of their insig-
nificance in a tedious and suffering world, faces life as 'a hopeless catas-
trophe, or an incurable disease' (3–4). While modern thinkers may assert
that 'a doctrine of the unchangeable there cannot be' (1), nevertheless there
is, he insists, an unchangeable something in the world: human need and
suffering. And 'in a world from which science will never quite expel pain',
this calls forth humane feeling, 'a wholly human charity', which continues
to exist in a world without God, 'the course of natural development having so greatly enlarged, if the capacity of pain, so also of sympathy with
it' (4–5). Pater establishes not only a personal ethics without religion, but
a model of sociability too, based on the enduring emotional and physical
needs of humanity.

'And of those who say "Let us eat and drink for tomorrow we die," a
certain number at least will be found no vulgar gluttons' (6). Having established the need for a modern, secular mode of conduct based on individual
need but not selfishness (for those who achieve it, 'It will be their triumph
to enjoy the pleasures of others more than their own' (5)) he demonstrates
that aestheticism can provide such a 'law or idea, a new "ethick" [*sic*]'. 'The
life of sensation', he says, 'suggests its own moral code, has its own conscience'. And his emphasis when outlining the practicalities of this conscience is always on restraint and selection. 'The true business of his life', he
writes of the aesthete, 'will seem to be the conservation, the enlarging, the
refinement, of the energy of ear and eye' (9). Though it is unclear in physiological terms what the 'energy of ear and eye' is, and no specific behaviour
is indicated, the stipulation to conserve, and through such conservation to
enlarge and refine an energy of any kind, would have sounded familiar to
readers of nineteenth-century literature about sexual health.[58] While not
in itself referring to sexuality, this phrasing makes the accommodation of
sexual license within this 'ethick' seem unlikely to a contemporary readership. It is a scheme 'from the practical point of view costly perhaps as being
somewhat exclusive or disqualifying' (11). Choices must be made.

To illustrate, Pater asks how 'this supposed son of the age' is to live the aesthetic life in the 'unlovely age' of Victorian Britain (11, 13). 'Certainly with a
soul conformable to modern London, as a visible fact one would be nowhere
aesthetically' (15). Judicious, informed selection is again the key. 'Does not
the aim of all art lie in the establishment of an ideal depending partly on
negative qualifications culture in its most general sense being in large measure
negative or renunciant a fine habit of ignoring or forgetting' (14). The aesthete
must cultivate himself as a filter, to take his aesthetic sense, that 'supreme
authority within' that is 'illuminated by an artistic ideal or type generalised

from a large comparative survey of the beautiful things of the past', as a guide to selection and rejection (19). With this generalized type in mind, 'he goes on his way about London, plethoric complicated indiscriminate, for the most part visibly ostentatiously sordid – not always with a painful sense of contrast but with an eye for touches of a kindred charm even there: a hundred delicate beauties the like of which no one ever valued before' (19). Not only is 'sordid' London – Symons remembered of Pater that he disliked 'whatever seemed to him either morbid or sordid, two words which he often used to express his distaste for things and people' – able to furnish beauty for the careful observer, but this modern landscape can yield a *new* beauty.[59] Friedman writes that Pater 'presents art as the preeminent vehicle through which powerful yet socially proscribed desire can transform into something more than itself': a similar Hegalian transformation seems to take place in this manuscript, though it would require a very expanded model of sexuality to identify homoeroticism as the basis for aesthetic feeling here.[60] This novel beauty, however, is only identifiable because study of past beauty has made the aesthete able to properly filter the sordid from the beautiful, 'by a process of gradual correction & assimilation to the/our ideal' (33). Beauty emerges for the aesthete only because he will 'carry about with him in self-defence through a vulgar age a habit of reserve' (31). London's physical ugliness is a prime example of the need for such selection, but the behaviour of others offers a similar opportunity. 'Were there not even in Athens as Plato knew vulgar young men with vulgar songs and the like "abounding in their own sense?"' (15). The Hellenism of Plato, it is suggested (and one may conclude, his idealized homoeroticism) also required such an 'ignoring or forgetting'.

Had he finished the manuscript, Pater would possibly have been more explicit about the application of this process of discrimination to conduct. In its later, more fragmented, stages, he asks whether 'such a temper' may 'extend itself/be extended further still & by modifying practice generally, present itself as a theory or prin[ciple] of service to other men's lives' (37). 'In morals', he noted, 'always, there are 2 aims – art in itself supplies the age figures of temperance, & for charity, for unselfishness' (38). Pater evidently considers, at least at this point in his life, that morals and aesthetics, if both properly trained, would come at least in principle into accord. But is his point that morality would be entirely *produced* by the aesthetic 'conscience', and potentially depart radically from convention? Or rather, does he mean that such a conscience would naturally produce something resembling a conventional conduct? '"Duties" towards others', he writes, 'will come to bear on [the aesthete] too as susceptible of a like development. Who knows? He may find them a truer guide regarding such matters than might seem probable at first sight'. The syntax suggests that it is the 'duties', readable at the very least as what one owes to one's immediate circle and easily extendable to society more broadly, that can act as a guide to the aesthetic sense, not the other way around. Though it may be true, as Freidman says, that Pater's aesthetic experience makes it 'possible for one to question all the truths society presents as absolute and unquestionable', such questioning does not necessarily lead to wholesale rejection.[61] 'His apprehension of moral fact', Pater continues, 'will identify itself with his native and acquired appreciation of the sensible charm in things' (10). However this identification comes about, this 'apprehension of moral fact' is not only separate from the aesthetic sense, but constitutes an *innate* sense of duties towards others that in his fiction he would frequently associate with sexual restraint. Though again no specific behaviours are mentioned, this is far in spirit from Evangelista's reading of this text as 'explicitly conceived in opposition to conventional (old) moral teachings'.[62] In Hext's words, 'it is all terribly conventional'.[63]

As in the 'Conclusion', nothing in 'The Aesthetic Life' indicates the limiting of any specific behaviour, never mind sexual activity. But it would be difficult to conclude that license in that, as in any other area, was considered prudent, or that the process of 'curiously testing new opinions and courting new impressions' would entail serious breach of conventional conduct. *The Renaissance* and 'The Aesthetic Life' both, from the two poles of Pater's career, associate sceptical modernity with an ethics of selection, discrimination, and discipline, at which the aesthete is considered to be adept. 'Winckelmann' explicitly extends this practice to sexual conduct. And although homoerotic feeling is evidently part of aesthetic practice in that essay, it is an allowable rather than necessary part, and is tempered by continence. His novels, *Marius the Epicurean* and the unfinished *Gaston de Latour*, can be read as demonstrations that these ethical principles spring from innate human needs as urgent in Antonine Rome and late Renaissance France as in nineteenth-century Britain. Their aesthete-heroes both come to realize that while sex is an important part of the world and, within certain limits, of the lives of most people, their aesthetic temperaments make continence the more comfortable and productive choice.

Marius the Epicurean and *Gaston de Latour*

Pater's earliest known essay, 'Diaphaneitè', was read to the Old Morality Society at Oxford in 1864, and published posthumously in 1896. The essay outlines an ideal character type that has often been identified with the aesthete-heroes that populate Pater's writings. This 'unworldly' type resembles the aesthete as described in *The Renaissance*, especially in its ability to act as a cultural filter. 'Its ethical result', Pater says, 'is an intellectual guilelessness, or integrity, that instinctively prefers what it direct and clear, lest one's own confusion and intransparency should hinder the transmission from without of light that is not yet inward'.[64] Though not motivated by moral principle in the strictest sense, this type recognizes by instinct not only what is worth preserving both in his own culture and in those of the past, but also what in specific objects is valuable: the type 'seeks to value everything at its eternal worth'. The terms in which Pater describes this lasting element are those with which he also habitually describes health – 'direct', 'clear', 'simple'. The character 'lets through unconsciously all that is really lifegiving in the established order of things; it detects without difficulty all sorts of affinities between its own elements, and the nobler elements in that order'.[65] The essay, like the 'Conclusion', leaves its reader (or auditor) to decide what manner of things would be considered 'nobler' or 'lifegiving'.

Pater describes the unconscious effortlessness of this ideal character in exercising its privileged function. 'The character we mean to indicate achieves this perfect life by a happy gift of nature, without any struggle at all'. However, just as individual objects may be composed of a mixture of life-giving and death-like qualities, so character is not, by the end of this essay, as absolute as this sentence suggests. 'Perhaps', he suggests, 'there are flushes of it in all of us; recurring moments of it in every period of life. Certainly this is so with every man of genius'.[66] The diaphanous type is closely related to the aesthete-heroes of *Marius the Epicurean* and *Gaston de Latour*. Yet as Williams points out, these narratives present the type not in the abstract, but in the process of growth and under specific historical circumstances, in Antoinine Rome and late Renaissance France, respectively.[67] The effect of this method is not only an embodiment of aesthetic and historical theory, but also an active indication of the kind of elements in any period that may be selected as worthwhile and lasting, and the principles along which such a selection may be made. For readers inclined to consider themselves as aesthetic in temperament, it is plausible to interpret Pater as asserting that sexual continence is appropriate, healthy, and productive for the aesthete.

The novels have similar narrative trajectories. Both protagonists, after a sheltered childhood, enter a wider social sphere. They experience excitement and anxiety as they observe both the attractions and the 'corruption', particularly sexual corruption, of their respective modernities. This is their first opportunity to filter the good from the bad in specific things. They must learn to benefit from the influence of certain beloved friends in whom the modern spirit is embodied, without being corrupted by their worldliness. This process is repeated throughout the novels, as the protagonists extract what is valuable from the people that they meet without being permanently tainted by their less valuable attributes. Extra-marital sexuality can be read throughout as indicating unworthiness, though it is usually mixed with beauty or attractiveness that must be extracted, cultivated, and learnt from. And throughout both novels – and this is where the novels differ from the essays – this filtering takes place against a background not only of the protagonist's aesthetic temperament, but also what David DeLaura calls the 'complex vision of man's permanent moral and aesthetic needs' that Pater shared with Arnold and Newman, and with many of his contemporaries.[68] If the aesthetic temperament, at once sensuous and idealistic, acts as an impulse to filtration, it is an instinct for wider human need that guides this selection. In both novels these needs are identified as health and love, the demands of the body and the spirit, with extra-marital sexuality the most common and obvious indication of infringement of either or both requirements.

Marius the Epicurean

As a boy, Marius is profoundly influenced by Apuleius' story of Cupid and Psyche, inserted into the text in Pater's own translation. This story can be read as an allegory of the aesthetic filtration process, of learning to distinguish between worldly and unworldly, sensuous and sensual experience even within a sexual relationship (the story was, the narrator tells us, 'full also of a gentle idealism, so that you might take it, if you chose, for an allegory' (vol. 1, 61)). Psyche resides in a beautiful house, 'a place fashioned for the conversation of gods with men' (66), and enjoys at night a pleasurably sexual relationship with a lover whom she never sees. Her jealous sisters eventually persuade her that her lover is a terrible monster. In her terror she exposes him as Cupid himself, whereupon he immediately abandons her.

Like Eve, Psyche loses her felicitous state through desire for knowledge. But, unlike Eve, she is eventually restored to happiness and marries Cupid: 'It seems good to me', says Jupiter, 'that his youthful heats should by some means be restrained' (90). The child of this marriage is named Voluptas, or pleasure. It is possible to read the story (in Pater's telling) as an allegory of successful aesthetic filtration. The hidden lover does not change: rather, it is Psyche's attitude that makes of him either a god or a monster, just as the aesthete may approach experience in a worldly or unworldly manner. Having lowered the tone, as it were, Psyche must endure a long journey and many difficult tasks before she can again be united with her lover, this time as her husband. If this is a Platonic tale of lost ideal innocence (of which sexuality was plausibly a part), it is also one of the processes by which some of that innocence may be regained. The narrator of *Marius* explains that the tale is about 'the fatality which seems to haunt any signal beauty, whether moral or physical, as if it were in itself something illicit and isolating' (93). The aesthete must avoid this fatality, this deathliness (and learning to enjoy aesthetically is a form of such avoidance) if he is to experience sensuous pleasure in a post-lapsarian world in which innocence is no longer an option. Marius himself applies the lesson of the story not by seeking sexual relationships himself, but by using its 'ideal of a perfect imaginative love' (92) to approach non-sexual experience. 'In contrast with that ideal', he reflects, 'men's actual loves [...] might appear to him, like the general tenor of their lives, to be somewhat mean and sordid' (93). His Epicureanism manifests 'not as the longing for love – to be with Cynthia, or Aspasia – but as a thirst for existence in exquisite places' (157).

Marius reads this tale with his boyhood friend, Flavian. This friendship can be read as an encounter with sensual modernity, Marius' first opportunity to extract what is best from something potentially 'sordid' without being unduly influenced by it. He first encounters Flavian when he attends school in Pisa, and is so fascinated by the sensuous opportunities and 'graceful follies' (47) of the busy town that 'he was ready to boast in the very fact that it was modern'. He begins to question the disciplined, traditional religion of his childhood. 'Could its so limited probabilities be worth taking into account in any practical question as to the rejecting or receiving of what was indeed so real, and, on the face of it, so desirable?' (48–9). Flavian too is beautiful but, as has frequently been pointed out, symbolizes sensual excess.[69] He had 'certainly yielded himself, though still with untouched health, in a world where manhood comes early, to the seductions of that luxurious town' (52–3), and 'Marius wondered [...] at the extent of his early corruption'. Flavian's beautiful sensuality embodies that of the pagan world: 'To Marius, at a later time, he counted for as it were an epitome of the whole pagan world, the depth of its corruption, and its perfection of form'. Yet 'in his mobility, his animation, in his eager capacity for various life', he is also an 'epitome' of transient modernity (53). 'Flavian indeed was a creature who changed much with the changes of the passing light and shade about him' (49). It is Flavian who first introduces

Marius to religious scepticism and moral relativity: he 'believed only in himself, in the brilliant, and mainly sensuous gifts, he had, or meant to acquire' (52).

Marius first sees in Flavian 'a tone of reserve or gravity there, amid perfectly disciplined health' (49). But the assertion that Flavian has yielded himself 'with still untouched health' may generate a suspicion that corruption and health are generally not found together, and that this healthiness may not last. The reference to health harks back to the preceding chapter, in which Marius had visited a temple-hospital of Aesculapius, god of medicine, among the 'official ministers' of which we are told is Galen himself, 'whom Marius saw often in later days at Rome' (35) (we saw in Chapter 1 that Galen was often referenced in the nineteenth century to justify a sexually continent health regime). The prevailing philosophy of this temple is that 'all the maladies of the soul might be reached through the subtle gateways of the body' (27), resulting in an ideal of 'bodily sanity [...] the body becoming truly, in that case, but a quiet handmaid to the soul' (28). During his time there Marius meets a doctor-priest (Monsman comments, 'the celibacy of this priest is patent') who explains his aesthetic temperament to him.[70] He wakes from a nightmare about snakes, an animal that he had hated since accidentally observing them breeding. This experience had been 'like a peep into the lower side of the real world [...] for the face of a great serpent [...] has a sort of humanity of aspect in its spotted and clouded nakedness. There was a humanity, dusty and sordid and as if far gone in corruption' (23–4). The doctor-priest tells him that his aesthetic temperament means that he must avoid that 'lower side' by trying 'to keep the eye clear by a sort of exquisite personal alacrity and cleanliness'. 'If thou wouldst have all about thee like the colours of some fresh picture, in a clear light', the attendant says, 'be temperate in thy religious notions, in love, in wine, in all things, and of a peaceful heart with thy fellows' (32–3). Temperate conduct, Marius learns, is essential to both aesthetic experience and health.

Has Flavian's body become more than 'a quiet handmaid to the soul'? Readers of late nineteenth-century advice books for young men would not have been surprised to see this youthful excess end in illness and early death. Flavian does not die of anything so obvious as spermatorrhoea or syphilis, but his final illness and his sexuality are described in such close conjunction as to allow symbolic inference. He contracts plague, 'the terrible new disease' (110), said to have been brought from a military campaign 'in the East' by the co-emperor Lucius Verus who, like Flavian, is an amiable sensualist with a 'constitutional freshness of aspect which may defy for a long time extravagant or erring habits of life', but is nevertheless 'healthy-looking' rather than actually healthy (194, 195). Lucius Verus eventually dies of the same plague. Flavian falls ill during a ceremony dedicated to Isis, 'that new rival, or "double," of ancient Venus' (105), readable as representative of modern worldly beauty. Marius remains healthy, despite also attending the ceremony and nursing Flavian devoutly, even sharing his bed 'to lend him his own warmth, undeterred by the fear of contagion which had kept other people from passing near the house' (119). His personal temperance allows an exercise of compassion not available to other people, while some readers may find significance in the conjunction of such compassion with homosocial and potentially homoerotic affection.

Matthew Potolsky has complained that the traditional reading of Flavian's death as punishment for his pagan sensuality – and especially the common identification of this sensuality with the form of aestheticism outlined in the 'Conclusion', from which it is argued that Pater was attempting to distance himself – is over-simplistic and fails to account for Pater's extensive admiration of Flavian's 'euphuism' or aesthetic literary style. 'Flavian does not die because he is an aesthete', Potolsky argues; 'Pater's implicit argument suggests, in fact, that Flavian is not enough of an aesthete, not sufficiently attentive to the formal qualities of his art'.[71] Friedman has built upon this argument to claim that the homoerotic nature of the relationship between Marius and Flavian is crucial to the knowledge that he gains from him, the 'unaware, lustful physical desire he felt for Flavian' acting as a catalyst to the revelation that there are right and wrong ways of living aesthetically.[72] As in my own reading, Flavian's sensual modernity and its consequences are a learning opportunity, but one which offers a lesson in what and how to appreciate as well as what to avoid.

Both Potolsky and Friedman focus on Pater's lingering over Flavian's poetic style, and especially his act of writing on his death bed. Potolsky particularly reads this 'reciprocal relationship between Flavian and his text' to indicate that the symbolism of the death should be sought in Flavian's aesthetic selfishness, his use of literature to dominate others, rather than in his sensual corruption: 'Flavian quite clearly falls as a result of an implicit interference between his pedagogical aims and methods, and not as a result of his seductive persona or his aestheticist doctrine'.[73] However, neither Potolsky nor Friedman mention the overtly sexual subject of this text, described as 'a kind of nuptial hymn, which, taking its start from the thought of nature as the universal mother, celebrated the preliminary pairing and mating together of all fresh things' (113). While reading Flavian's death as a punishment for sexual corruption is certainly unhelpfully simplistic, it is equally reductive to elide the clear connections that Pater draws here between sexual corruption, unhealthiness, selfishness, a certain aesthetic naivety, and an unsatisfying death. Flavian's dying hymn to sexuality is a further filtering opportunity for Marius. The style, he sees, is new and valuable, 'the foretaste of an entirely novel world of poetic beauty to come' (114) (a quotation reveals the poem to be the anonymous *Pervigilium Veneris*, or Vigil of Venus, commonly seen as representing a transition from Roman to medieval poetry). But faced with bodily death, Marius is 'haunted by a feeling of the triviality of such work just then' (115). The poem quickly comes to represent the transience of all worldly things as Flavian snatches final stanzas like the fleeting moments of the 'Conclusion': 'in hard-set determination, defiant of pain, to arrest this or that little drop at least from the river of sensuous imagery rushing so quickly past him' (117).

Flavian's eventual 'dying passively, like some dumb creature' (118) is a warning to Marius that the pagan scepticism that he represents is ultimately unsatisfactory; not wrong exactly but limited and perhaps inhumane.[74] But this episode also establishes extra-marital sexuality as a marker of the intersections of modernity, transience, and death, of the dangers of the present moment as opposed to its genuine attractions (also fully acknowledged). Marius' version of Epicureanism is formed in reaction to his horror of this hopeless, animal death. Taking as its goal 'Not pleasure, but fulness [*sic*] of life, and "insight" as conducting to that fulness' (151), the narrator acknowledges that this philosophy may occasionally be found 'breaking beyond the limits of the actual moral order': a potential danger for those (he quotes Pascal on Montaigne) 'who have any natural tendency to impiety or vice' but not the 'strong and in health' (150). On Marius' arrival in Rome – full of 'curiously vivid modern traits' (153) – it is made clear that in practical terms this philosophy excludes sexual indulgence. Hearing, at nightfall, 'the lively, reckless call to "play," from the sons and daughters of foolishness', Marius, 'slight as was the burden of positive moral obligation with which he had entered Rome', decides that 'it was to no wasteful and vagrant affections, such as these, that his Epicureanism had committed him' (187). The word 'wasteful' reminds readers of the transience of sensuality, while also invoking the economic rhetoric of loss so often associated with nineteenth-century male sexuality. It was this sentence, we may remember, from which Le Gallienne describes his young protagonist taking council in *Young Lives*.

Marius' career follows a repeated pattern of exposure to a philosophic influence embodied in a person; appreciation of how that philosophy or person can expand his current store of wisdom; and identification of where that influence should stop. Lucius Verus is physically attractive but extravagant, while Marcus Aurelius is disciplined and kindly, but unhealthily ascetic and overly tolerant, whether of the cruelty of the Coliseum or of his wife's adultery. But throughout Marius' observation of Marcus Aurelius we are invited to compare those valuable elements with similar traits in another friend, the Christian knight Cornelius. As with Flavian, recent critical analysis of *Marius* focuses on the homoeroticism of this relationship. Friedman, for instance, reads Pater's account of the influence of Cornelius being 'more physical than moral' as indicating that 'Marius is motivated to follow Cornelius' example not because his Christian worldview offers a superior moral philosophy but because he desires his body'; a desire that is 'more self-conscious and "disinterested"' than his attraction to Flavian 'yet still markedly erotic'.[75] Once again, the identification of eroticism depends upon where one is willing to draw the boundaries of the sexual, and Pater allows both readings. Although he does emphasize the embodied nature of the relationship, the initial effect is one of a moral and physical discipline more exclusive, and less tolerant, than that of Marcus Aurelius. Marius' restraint on his arrival in Rome comes not only from his Epicureanism: he 'could hardly doubt how Cornelius would have taken the call' (187). The rationale behind Cornelius' discipline – his Christian faith – is withheld until Marius is able to understand it, but the influence is no less potent, a move that is readable as a version of Tractarian reserve.

In a chapter entitled 'Second Thoughts', Marius, 'anxious to try the lastingness of his own Epicurean rose-garden', asks 'What really were its claims as a theory of practice[?]' (vol. 2, 14). Here, rather than with Marius' initial development of his Epicureanism, the narrator directly draws parallels with the spiritual needs of the nineteenth century. 'That age and ours have much in common – many difficulties and hopes. Let the reader pardon me if here and there I seem to be passing from Marius to his modern representatives – from Rome, to Paris or London' (14). The result of these second thoughts is an 'assent' (the word is Pater's, though it will be familiar to readers of Newman's *Grammar of Assent* as acquiescence without rational comprehension) to moral convention based not only on beauty, but also 'lastingness', the accumulated knowledge of each moral system in its 'more nobly developed phases' (21).[76] Convention is:

> a system, which, like some other great products of the conjoint efforts of human mind through many generations, is rich in the world's experience; so that, in attaching oneself to it, one lets in a great tide of that experience, and makes, as it were with a single step, a great experience of one's own (26).

Pater suggests that this assent will have the same result in any period of time. 'Perhaps all theories of practice', he says, 'tend, as they rise to their best, as understood by their worthiest representatives, to identification with each other' (20). Further, this 'best' is identifiable by a 'savour of unworldliness' (21), 'a single ideal of temperance or moderation' (20). Assent to moral authority, he implies, will mean accepting moderation as a guiding principle. For Marius himself, this is 'not so much a change of practice, as of sympathy – a new departure, an expansion, of sympathy' (27). Is such assent, and acceptance of both temperance and sympathy, what is needed in the nineteenth century as well as in Marius' own life?

Of course, the word 'moderation' is, like 'excess', open to interpretation based on one's own requirements. Further, assent to 'convention' does not necessarily imply wholesale acceptance of one's own social norms, which Pater would be the first to point out are themselves made up of both contingent and lasting elements. The 'Second Thoughts' chapter, however, is followed by an example of both temperance and sympathy in action, though a sympathy that, unlike that of Marcus Aurelius, does not tolerate in others that which undermines its own principles. Reproductive sexuality, restrained within marriage, is shown to be essential to this way of life, though not for every individual participant. On visiting the Christian household of Cecilia, Marius finds 'the vision of a natural, a scrupulously natural, love, transforming, by some new gift of insight into the truth of human relationships, and under the urgency of some new motive by him so far unfathomable, all the conditions of life' (109). Christianity, in basing its doctrine in a high valuation of compassion and love, has discovered a way of life more satisfying in this respect than Epicureanism.

In practice, this is characterized by subordination of selfish desires to the needs of others weaker than oneself: a principle manifested, among other things, in familial domesticity as a source of self-sustaining community. But it is also manifested in what Pater calls 'chastity':

> Chastity, – as he seemed to understand – the chastity of men and women, amid all the conditions, and with the results, proper to such chastity, is the most beautiful thing in the world and the truest conservation of that creative energy by which men and women were first brought into it (110).

As Monsman notes, Pater is here echoing Renan's 1882 *Marc Aurèle et la fin du monde antique*: 'La femme chaste est la plus belle chose du monde, le plus parfait souvenir de la création primitive de Dieu'.[77] Renan, in the relevant passage, is summarizing from the *Clementine Homilies*, dated by him to the reign of Marcus Aurelius. But Pater adds to Renan's phrasing, extending the sentiment to men, and also changing the passively reflective, potentially Platonic 'souvenir' to a more physical and active 'conservation', suggesting that 'creative energy' is a quality over which men and women might exercise active control: to conserve or not to conserve. Pater's version of chastity is therefore closer to a sexually regulative discourse than that of Renan. It also suggests a model of 'energy' like that found in the work of William Acton, whereby sexuality derives from a source of energy that, if conserved, can be put towards other non-sexual ends, unlike the unstable sexual energy of Freud.

In *Marius* this Christian chastity within marriage leads not only to the birth of children and creation of families, but also, in a manner identified by Sussman as Carlylean, to a redeployment of spare energy towards labour. 'Chastity, in turn, realised in the whole scope of its conditions, fortified that rehabilitation of peaceful labour, after the mind, the pattern, of the workman of Galilee' (114).[78] And the use of the phrase 'creative energy' in *Marius* may well make one wonder if artistic production or even aesthetic living could perhaps be contained within this labour, particularly as Pater makes explicit connection between this Christian spirit of chaste love, and the humane spirit that arises in the artistic culture of Renaissance Italy, likening it to 'that regenerate type of humanity, which, centuries later, Giotto and his successors [...] working under conditions very friendly to the imagination, were to conceive as an artistic ideal' (110). We have here an echo of the 'conservation, the enlarging, the refinement, of the energy of ear and eye' that played such an important part in the manuscript of 'The Aesthetic Life', though with more overtly sexual significance.

It has become common for critics to follow Dellamora in reading the persecuted Christian community in *Marius* as a representation of Pater's own Victorian experience of homosexual persecution.[79] It is true that the present reading does not do justice to the violence that Pater's early Christians face, though much may be made of his fascination with the effect that an altered relationship with futurity has on the community's approach to death, even violent death. Heather Love has written of Pater's admiration of the childless beauty of Greek female statuary as indicative of his place in 'a queer tradition of the refusal of reproduction and of the future-oriented temporality of the family'.[80] In *Marius*, however, the affections and sympathies of Christian family life are praised as a pre-eminent response to the universal human need for sympathy and love. But if the domestic sexuality necessary to such family life is sanctioned, the enjoyment of the affections it creates is not limited to those engaged in marriage. Marius himself is unmarried – he considers marriage to Cecilia, but soon withdraws in favour of Cornelius. On his deathbed, Marius recognizes that children, as a kind of permanent residence or legacy in the world, could have comforted his dying soul; but even in his

unmarried state, his affection for those who are to survive him, and his hope
that such domestic affections will spread as Christianity expands, provide
a comparable solace. And although this could be read as setting up queer
'alternative forms of sociability', at this point at least it is hard to escape
the dependence on heterosexual familial structures.[81] The community, the
family in which Marius has, through his self-sacrifice for Cornelius (during
false imprisonment for practice of Christianity, he had allowed his guiltier
friend, instead of himself, to be released), found a place, survives him. 'It
was thus too, surprised, delighted, that Marius, under the power of that new
hope among men, could think of the generations to come after him' (222).
As Potolsky points out, Marius dies of the same plague that killed Flavian:
but this does not necessarily indicate a similar fall as Potolsky claims; rather,
it may highlight the different way in which the same material is treated.[82]
Whereas Flavian died like an animal, Marius' aesthetic practice finally reconciles him even to death itself.

Sensuous continence is portrayed in *Marius* as the inevitable outcome of
the successful adaptation of circumstances, both environmental and temperamental, to humanity's permanent physical and spiritual needs, while
sensuality (rather than sexuality) acts as an indication that these needs have
been violated. As in earlier work, Pater allows for this continence to be as
sexualized, and therefore potentially as homoerotic, as his readers wished it
to be, though this eroticized content is never portrayed as essential; readers
are free to make connections between the narrator's emphasis on embodied
pleasure and the protagonist's close emotional relationships with boys and
men, but the physical continence of these relationships is difficult to avoid.
Further, modernity – with its relation to sense experience (and its potential
abuse as sensuality), transience, and isolated death – is used as an opportunity for Marius to exercise his aesthetic system of filtration in order to be 'on
the right side' (vol. 1, 243) of history, to select that element that in its very
permanence is ironically an indication of progress. But Marius achieves this
process (if he indeed ever thoroughly achieves it) like the diaphanous type,
rather effortlessly. In *Gaston de Latour*, a similar young man takes a more difficult journey. And though the manuscript of this novel is incomplete, there
are indications that a similar ending would have been reached.

Gaston de Latour

Gaston de Latour was never finished, though the first five chapters appeared
in *Macmillan's Magazine* in 1888 and a version of the seventh chapter in
the *Fortnightly Review* in 1889. Seven complete chapters were published

together after Pater's death; but six more exist in incomplete manuscript form.[83] *Gaston* has received relatively little critical attention and even less from critics focusing on sexuality, possibly because its unfinished state leaves Pater's intentions uncertain. But the published sections were eagerly awaited by readers – in September 1888, Lionel Johnson wrote to a friend, 'Are you keeping up with Gaston de Latour? it is wondrous fine' – and Pater is known to have discussed his work in progress with close friends like Johnson and Vernon Lee.[84] Johnson also assisted in the sorting of Pater's literary manuscripts, including the unfinished sections of *Gaston*, after his death in 1894.

Gaston is of a similarly aesthetic temperament to Marius; he is 'a creature of the eye' (66). But in *Gaston* a greater distance is maintained between narration and protagonist, so that the narrator often calls attention to the negative side of what Gaston nevertheless uneasily accepts. In comparison to Marius, Gaston is slow in learning how to filter the valuable elements from what he sees. Pater here both gives to the alluring beauty of sensuality an acknowledgement taken for granted in *Marius*, and points even more emphatically to the worm hidden in that bud, in the shape of destructive violence, extra-marital sexuality, and an excess of transience. As Monsman says, 'in *Gaston* Pater faced the crisis of art's practical influence'.[85] But the unfinished manuscripts for later chapters indicate a potential source for more positive guidance, from which Gaston may have formed a more effective – not only personally less distressing and unhealthy, but also less selfish – mode of living.

The third chapter of *Gaston*, entitled 'Modernity', relates Gaston's introduction to the poetry of Ronsard, and then to the poet himself. The poetry is explicitly described as dealing both with sense experience and with love specifically, and is said to represent 'the power of "modernity", as renewed in every successive age for genial youth' (65). Like Flavian's poetry, Ronsard and his school are characterized by a renewed attention to 'the visible' (64), and by a fitting of style to substance that allows it to express the original spirit of its time. But more explicitly than with Flavian's efforts, this poetry asserts 'the latent poetic rights of the transitory, the fugitive, the contingent'. Habitual readers of Pater may have found this emphasis on the transitory consistent with Ronsard's focus on sexuality. His verse is not only a confession of 'his love-secrets especially, how love and nothing else filled his mind' (65), but also an application of sexual feeling to everything: he lends 'a poetic and always amorous interest to everything around him' (66). 'Yes!' the narrator cries, voicing Gaston's feeling, 'that was the reason why visible, audible, sensible things glowed so brightly, why there was such luxury in

sounds, words, rhythms, of the new light come of the world, of that wonderful freshness' (65). We might recognize here that 'passion of which the
outlets are sealed' which, in 'Poems by William Morris' (to be reprinted,
the year after the first appearance of the 'Modernity' chapter, as 'Aesthetic
Poetry' in the collection *Appreciations*), produced an unhealthy 'tension of
nerve, in which the sensible world comes to one with a reinforced brilliance
and relief' (though the period here is later). But here the tension results
from the expression of an overwrought sexuality at least sometimes reflected
in the poet's real-life experience.

Gaston is even more attracted to this poetry than Marius was to
that of Flavian. 'The gifted poet seemed but to have spoken what was
already in Gaston's own mind, what he had longed to say, had been
just going to say' (65): he accepts it 'faults and all' (64). But doubts
arise (they may already have occurred to readers who noticed that this
poetry was said to have 'the sickliness of all spring flowers' (62)) as
Gaston and his friends journey to the house of Ronsard himself. The
message of universal amorousness sours as Gaston observes the marks
of war, 'the spectacle of the increased hardness of human life' (66). On
arrival they find Ronsard not an amorous young man, but 'a gaunt figure, hook-nosed, like a wizard' with 'a face, all nerve, distressed nerve'
(67). Though Ronsard does not die like Flavian, nevertheless 'this evo-
cator of "the eternally youthful" was visibly old before his time' (71).
And though Gaston finds some of those poetical loves to have been 'a
somewhat artificial and for the most part unrequited love' (69), the
poet's reminiscences reveal enough 'cruder youthful vanities' (70) to
account for his untimely withering. Again this may have reminded
nineteenth-century readers of the premature weakness that was said to
result from sexual excess.

While Flavian's death shocked Marius into a temperate Cyreniacism,
Ronsard's decline is not enough to deter Gaston. The chapter ends with
his 'consciousness, no longer of mere bad-neighbourship between what
was old and what was new in his life, but of incompatibility between two
rival claimants upon him, of two ideals'. He ponders, 'Might that new religion, so to term it, be a religion not altogether of goodness, a *profane* religion, in spite of its poetic fervours?' (36). This sensuousness tipping into
sensuality leads to a philosophy of moral relativity: 'Rather, good and evil
were distinctions inapplicable in proportion as these new interests made
themselves felt' (72–3). But Gaston does not desire to filter the eternal element from this new 'religion' so much as to be told that his concerns are
unfounded:

Might there be perhaps, somewhere, in some penetrative mind in this age of novelties, some scheme of truth, some science of men and things, which could harmonise for him his earlier and later preference, 'the sacred and profane loves', or, failing that, establish, to his pacification, the exclusive supremacy of the latter? (73)

He finds that justification for 'general license' (a 'dubious lesson', the narrator assures us) (96) in the morally relative philosophy of Montaigne. Adam Lee has shown how Pater employs the rationale of Platonic communion to describe the more positive elements of Montaigne's influence upon Gaston, in which he draws him away from the cruder sensuousness of Ronsard.[86] But Lee does not describe the explicit tracing of everything that is portrayed negatively in *Gaston* to a mindset that Montaigne shares, in which moral relativity leads to tolerance of a damaging sensuality. 'Might one enjoy? Might one eat of all the trees?' that generation is portrayed as asking, while the narrator comments that some 'had already eaten and needed, retrospectively, a theoretic justification, a sanction of their actual liberties [...] that justification was furnished by the Essays of Montaigne' (80). Montaigne's theory of life as summarized here does sound very like that of the 'Conclusion': it begins from the instability and flux in all things, and finds a temporary stability only in the individual, 'Whatever truth there might be must come for each one from within, not from without' (92). But its practical result is an excessive tolerance like that of Marcus Aurelius, a 'moderation' that is a little of everything rather than the selection of the best. 'Was that why his conversation was sometimes coarse?' (94), wonders Gaston, while the narrator reflects that 'In truth, he led the way to the immodesty of French literature' (95).

Furnished with this moral 'license', Gaston moves to Paris. There, unlike Marius, he engages in an explicitly sexual relationship. Pater makes Gaston's half-accidental relationship with Colombe readable as the outcome of the over-tolerant 'moderation' of Montaigne's philosophy, which takes all things as equally deserving of consideration. 'Was the "undulant" philosophy of Monsieur de Montaigne, in collusion with this dislocating time, at work upon him', the narrator asks, so that 'he found himself more than he could have thought possible the toy of external accident?' The Huguenot Colombe is attracted by Gaston's sensuous beauty, through her yearning 'for those harmless forbidden graces towards which she has a natural aptitude'. He, however, responds because she seemed 'to have some claim upon him – a right to consideration – to an effort on his part: he finds a sister to encourage'. But this half-hearted encounter is evidently sexual: Colombe's brothers 'interfere just in time to save her from the consequence of what to another than Gaston might have counted as only a passing fondness to be soon forgotten'. The marriage, because celebrated under Huguenot rather than Catholic rites, seemed to Gaston (though not Colombe) 'under its actual conditions no binding sacrament', so that 'for his own conscience at the moment, the transaction seemed to have but the transitoriness, as also the guilt of a vagrant love' (103–4).

Gaston is stung to remorse for this episode by its tragic and symbolic end. Thinking herself abandoned by her Catholic husband during the St Bartholomew's Day massacre, the pregnant Colombe flees 'already in labour it was thought' (106), and Gaston finds only vague reports of her death. 'His recoil from that damaging theory of his conduct' – that he, as a Catholic, deserted his Huguenot wife, but perhaps also that she was more of a mistress than a wife to him – 'brought home to a sensitive conscience the fact that there had indeed been a measure of self-indulgent weakness in his acts, and made him the creature for the rest of his days of something like remorse' (101). That self-indulgence, the egotism also indigenous to Montaigne's philosophy and to the period in general, is as important here as the weakness. He recognizes now that Colombe could have been more than a mistress, as he thinks of 'the delicate creature whose vain longings had been perhaps but a rudimentary aptitude for the really high things himself had represented to her fancy, the refined happiness to which he might have helped her' (105). Adam Lee shows that, when Pater later quotes the *Song of Songs* to describe Gaston's sense of spiritual influences calling to him in the midst of 'a world of corruption in flower' – '*Open unto me! Open unto me! My sister, my love, my dove, my undefiled!*' – the repeated 'sister' and 'dove' recalls the lost wife ('colombe' is French for dove) (108).[87] But the name 'Colombe' is also reminiscent of Columbina, the mistress of Harlequin in the Italian *commedia dell'Arte*. Now realizing that their relationship could have been a true Christian marriage, in which husband and wife mimic the relationship between God and the soul, Gaston finds that he has instead played a crude comedy ending in tragedy. His philosophy has ended in not only sensuality, but also cruelty to another quite aside from potential abandonment, and no less cruel for having resulted from indolence rather than malice.

Cruelty and sensuality are also the qualities that Pater represents, in the persons of the Catholic court and in the culture of Paris itself ('the latent ferocities of a corrupt though dainty civilisation' (104)), as leading to the massacre. This relation is only partly symbolic, as Gaston is portrayed as a product of the same cultural forces that produce those circumstances. Gaston himself makes this connection: 'not the cruelty only but the obscurity, the accidental character, yet, alas! also the treachery, of the public event seemed to identify themselves tragically with his own personal action' (105). In part Gaston's failed marriage embodies historical forces. But the violence of the massacre also embodies and reveals a violence and cruelty in Gaston's affair that would otherwise not have been obvious either to him or to readers.

This incident serves to make Gaston suspicious of the cruelty and transience attendant on sexual indulgence but does not provide him with an alternative ethic. Attending a lecture by Giordano Bruno, he is influenced afresh by a philosophy of 'indifference' (this element was enhanced as Pater revised the essay for the novel) that leads in practical terms to moral relativity (110). Pater uses the term 'borrowed fire and wings' (114), highly suggestive of productive continence, to describe the relationship that Bruno sees between Plato's suppressed sexuality and his intellectual achievements, yet Bruno's emphasis on 'indifference' still leads to an amorality that itself leads back to sensuality. The narrator comments that some listeners 'would hardly fail to find in Bruno's doctrines a method of turning poison into food', and connects this through reference to Dante with sexual license: 'how would Paolo and Francesca have read this lesson?' (121). Gaston himself can firmly object only in terms of aesthetics, 'the "opposed points" of which, to Gaston for one, could never by any possibility become "indifferent" – the distinction, namely, between the precious and the base, aesthetically; between what was right and wrong in the matter of art' (83). Would the narrative, if finished, have found in aestheticism a basis for moral certainty, as in the 'The Aesthetic Life'?

The surviving manuscripts suggest that this would have been the case. Gaston is seen exploring the fashionably aesthetic house of a friend who was later to die as a consequence of his affair with the notorious Queen Margaret. Again there are echoes of the 'Conclusion', as he finds there 'the exhibition of every day life as a fine art' (126). But this is not the ethical aestheticism described in *Marius*; rather, it is one from which, as Adam Lee has it, 'the real soul of art is absent'.[88] Again the narration criticizes a mode of life that Gaston himself would reluctantly follow. 'Did this novel mode of receiving, of reflecting the visible aspects of life', Gaston wonders, 'commit one to an intellectual scheme, a *theory* about it, the remoter *practical* alliances of which one could not precisely ascertain at present, but would inevitably be led to in due course?' (128). Readers could perhaps ascertain these alliances more firmly than Gaston, especially while reading chapters in which Gaston is drawn into the sensual court of Queen Margaret and King Henry. Margaret herself, to whom Gaston acts as secretary, is described as 'the genius of cruel or unkindly, as opposed to kindly, love' (99), and this distinction is expanded upon in a chapter titled 'Anteros'.[89] Here the important distinction is not between a low or high heat as it was in 'Winckelmann', but between 'the Love which must needs please another' and 'that which can only please itself' (100). The latter, 'the carnal, consuming, and essentially wolfish love' (145), 'love for love's sake as a doctrine and a discipline' (146), characterizes not only Margaret, but also the prevailing spirit of late Renaissance Paris: 'in such an age, we might perhaps trace the steps by which the desire of physical, of carnal beauty, becomes a sort of religion, a profane and cruel religion' (145). Pater is careful to keep Gaston from corruption by this 'selfish love'. He is 'Enthralled constantly by the spectacle before him [...] yet chilled to the heart by a wretched sense of brevity, of decay and hasting in it' (148), and is 'himself certainly uncontaminated as if invisibly shielded' (166). His task is always to appreciate the beauty of what he sees, to find 'those saving inconsistencies in evil' (167), without becoming unduly influenced by it, though he only partly succeeds: 'The reader sees him, it is to be hoped, pleased or at least interested, yet regretful, sorrowfully puzzled for himself and others, curious, indulgent, not however very self-indulgent, and certainly not with a made-up mind' (159).

An indication of what may have eventually led to a better ethic can be found at the end of a manuscript headed 'Book iii, Chapter XIII', that was possibly therefore intended as a decisive turning point in the narrative.[90] Gaston is taken by a friend to see the art collection of Francis I, and sees for the first time the work of the Italian Renaissance, including Leonardo da Vinci. This is not, like the art of the French court, simply a 'worship of the body' (146). 'Here', the narrator tells us, 'art, according to its proper ministry, had been at once the interpretation and an idealisation of life', fostering in Gaston 'that increasing preoccupation with the greater unchangeable interests of life with which he entered upon the coming new and later phase of his own maturer manhood' (183). In these paintings he finds 'the genius not of an unkindly – as we call barren earth unkindly – but of a kindly love, a manifestation of nature and man, as if under the genial light of God's immediate presence' (182). This kindly love is, like unkindly love, also potentially sexual – reminiscent of the 'creative energy' of *Marius* – but is characteristically reproductive both in the literal sense of creating children and more metaphorically, in reproducing its own 'genial' spirit. Plato's *Phaedrus*, in which the nobler men are said to be those who produce intellectual and spiritual rather than physical children, was surely in Pater's mind, suggesting that reproduction and creative production, though related, may also to a certain extent be mutually exclusive (though there is no suggestion this time of a Platonic hierarchy for Pater, wherein art is inherently better than babies).[91] 'Kindness [...] forgetting itself in the love of visible beauty, the eyes, the lips kindled to the reproduction of its like, renewing the world, handing on, as a ground of love and kindness forever, the beauty which had kindled it [...] linking paternally, filially, age to age, the young to the old, marriage, maternity, childhood and youth' (182–3). Nothing explicitly excludes non-reproductive sexual activity, but the emphasis on procreation and generation makes it unlikely (the ideal is, however, far less necessarily reliant on actual heterosexual reproduction here than in *Marius*). But just as Christian chaste love in *Marius* did not exclude the unmarried, so this kindly love 'looks favourably also on the virginity, the restraint which in fact secures the purity, the ardency therefore, of the creative flame' (183). Restraint here is no passive state, but an active cultivation and intensification of creative power. This productive restraint is the marker of effective filtering of eternal from transient elements of life.

Adam Lee expresses surprise at the 'rather cynical' tone of *Gaston de Latour*, given that Pater 'characteristically eschewed negative criticism'.[92] Attending to sexual continence in Pater's work does reveal an exclusionary habit, in which the attraction to transitory beauty so often considered to characterize his thought is problematized. This is not only the Pater of restraint, renunciation, and discipline, but also a Pater increasingly willing to indicate where those renunciations should fall, where precisely that discipline should be exercised. It is, notably, a relatively conservative rather than radical Pater, willing to value convention and moral conformity in theory though remaining pragmatically cagey about details. But isolating these elements to describe them does, inevitably, exaggerate such criticism far beyond the experience of reading Pater's work. This ideal was, crucially, not merely negative, and discipline was never an end in itself. Paterian continence was part of a process of aesthetic self-cultivation, of constant adjustment to those elements of experience that had, he insists, always troubled those of aesthetic temperament, but which now seemed particularly to press upon aesthetes of the secular and scientific nineteenth century: relativity, transitoriness, selfishness, sensuality, and death. The aim of such cultivation was often the safely aesthetic enjoyment of precisely those things: of the beauty of transience, the vitality of sensuality, the pathos of death. And not only this ideal of productive continence, but also the language in which Pater describes it, would have reminded many readers of other nineteenth-century writing about sexual health.

CHAPTER 3

'A Holy Indifference and Tolerant Favour'
Lionel Johnson

In 1891, his busiest year, Lionel Johnson was a promising young poet and critic just out of Oxford: already known as a scholarly 'traditionalist of traditionalists', as a convert to Catholicism, and as a friend to Walter Pater.[1] By 1902 he had collapsed, at the age of thirty-five, in a public house and died without regaining consciousness. Reports were even more dramatic – he had, it was said, been found unconscious in Fleet Street, or pulled out of a gutter having drunkenly dashed under the hooves of a cab horse – testifying to an early impulse to mythologize this seemingly ascetic yet undeniably alcoholic Decadent writer.[2]

Those remembering Johnson from a twentieth-century vantage often sought to account for apparent contradictions in his life, or between his life and work, with a post-Freudian narrative of repression – generally sexual – and violent outbreak, especially as Johnson's own work contained a persistent idealization of sexual continence.[3] W. B. Yeats wrote of Johnson that 'now that I know his end, I see him creating, to use a favourite adjective of his, "marmorean" verse, and believing in the most terrible doctrines to keep down his own turbulence'. Yeats used Johnson's celibate alcoholism, painted somewhat luridly, to illustrate his narrative of a 'tragic generation' that suffered from an excess of unworldly idealism, leading to a reaction of destructive debauchery: 'What portion in the world can the artist have/Who has awakened from the common dream/But dissipation and despair?'[4] For Johnson this unworldliness had, in Yeats' account, a physical equivalent in the supposedly undeveloped state of his sexual organs. 'Johnson had', Yeats writes, 'refused rather than failed to live, and when an autopsy followed his accidental death during intoxication it was found that in him the man's brain was united to a body where the other organs were undeveloped, the body of a child'.[5] Johnson's physical childishness – he was said to resemble a fifteen-year-old, though the actual postmortem report mentions nothing of underdevelopment – is combined with deliberate withdrawal.[6] With Yeats' *Autobiographies*, Johnson's biography – and his sexuality – became inextricably tied to the twentieth-century effort to understand the near past. This interpretive pattern was referred to by Ezra Pound in 'Huge Selwyn Moberly', in which an 1890s poet (Johnson's close friend Victor Plarr), 'out of step with the decade':

> Told me how Johnson (Lionel) died
> By falling from a high stool in a pub [...]
>
> But showed no trace of alcohol
> At the autopsy, privately performed –
> Tissue preserved – the pure mind
> Arose toward Newman as the whiskey warmed.[7]

Since the 1950s Johnson's suppressed 'turbulence' has been read as homosexuality. Otherwise the narrative has changed little. The suppression has continued to be associated with Johnson's supposed retreat, as 'traditionalist of traditionalists', from the modern world, and this withdrawn Johnson used to symbolize the Decadent Movement as a whole. Barbara Charlesworth claimed that Johnson and his friends lived in a 'realm of dream' that inevitably led to tragedy, but that Johnson especially escaped into 'daydreams which eventually destroyed what had been a clear mind'.[8] For Ian Fletcher, 'in a sense his life *was* a literary device'.[9] R. K. R. Thornton has said of Johnson that though his habitual asceticism was inimical to most forms of Decadent excess, 'his traditionalism is an equally typical Decadent turning away from life to the inspiration of art', while Murray Pittock has written of 'Johnson's rejection of life' and 'his fear of existence'.[10] More recently Alex Murray, in dealing with Johnson's frequent appeal to the past, has referred to his 'hatred of the modern age'.[11]

Did Johnson hate the modern age? And did he himself relate this 'hatred' to sexual abstinence, as a like refusal 'to live'? This chapter argues that a new understanding of Johnson's idealization of sexual continence is needed in order to answer this question in full. Johnson as a writer (I make no claims about his personal life) certainly emphasized the authority of tradition and custom, in style as much as in morals. He found his ideals in the courtesy of the seventeenth-century cavalier, in eighteenth-century humour and manners, in the loving-kindness of the Catholic Church. In contrast he occasionally found the nineteenth century to be rowdy, hasty, and egotistical, admitting no authority but the individual's undisciplined mind. And just as Pater associated excessive transience with non-reproductive sex, so Johnson often associated these failings with sexual excess. But also like Pater, and like Pater's aesthete-heroes, Johnson was exhilarated by his own time, and found himself in need of a means by which to benefit from what was worthy in it, without being tainted by its problematic elements. An 1891 article celebrates the crowded nineteenth-century city. 'The enormous energies of London' he writes, 'call up answering emotions in the hearts of spectators: it is the summons to a fuller life, the inspiration of a fuller understanding'. And this widened sympathy – sympathy not only with individuals but across time and space – is crucial to the artist: 'the more abundant and varied life be, the better for the man of letters: it educates him'.[12] This reaching beyond oneself to principles of continuity was central to Johnson's theories of both art and life, as (like Pater) he found in history not a retreat, but an example of filtering that could act as a means by which to test the lastingness of the present.

Johnson repeatedly associates sexual continence both with widened sympathy and effective artistry, which for him is indistinguishable from ethics: 'an artist', he wrote, 'is forbidden, by the facts of his natural structure, to dissociate his ethics from his aesthetics'.[13] And he frequently describes this successful aesthetic continence as a productive retention, a restraint that, like that seen in medical writing about sexual health in the period, results in renewed potency and intensification. In social terms this practice produced for Johnson a transcendence of egotism and sympathy with all humanity: a 'holy indifference and tolerant favour'.[14] In art it meant the combination of this spirit with perfection of form and style. Johnson converted to Catholicism in 1891 and differs from Pater in the consistency with which he uses sexual continence as a point of contact between religious and secular culture. His thinking was profoundly influenced by the many Victorian attempts to reconcile these means of knowing the world, particularly those of Newman and Arnold. Specifically, Johnson developed a cultural humanism that gave full consideration to both nineteenth-century Aestheticism and Catholic theology. He did this through a re-Christianized Paterianism, shorn of Pater's religious ambivalence.

This chapter examines the place of productive sexual continence in Johnson's work, and considers the extent to which it can be read as part of a coherent Paterian heritage. There is an unevenness in Johnson's archive – the mid-twentieth-century loss of the majority of his papers means that his extant correspondence is heavily weighted towards the early years, while much of his critical output (largely unsigned newspaper reviews) remains uncollected.[15] But while reliance on the early letters for biography would give a skewed picture of Johnson's life, they are valuable for their explicit experimentation with ideas that would later become important, but less explicit, in Johnson's poetry and criticism. The first section looks at these letters for the insight they offer into the way in which Johnson drew together a wide range of disparate influences and experimented with the synthesis of this material into an ethic both personally and socially plausible. The second section shows how Pater was integrated into this process, and shaped it as Johnson matured. The third finds in his poetry indications of an ethic that is both religious and aesthetic, while the fourth sees this extended into a theory of sociability in the modern world, in which Paterian aestheticism is reconciled to the Catholic convention of priestly indifference.

The *Winchester Letters*

Some Winchester Letters of Lionel Johnson was published anonymously in 1919. The editor was Frank Russell, Johnson's schoolfellow and lifelong friend.[16] Written while still at Winchester College (1883–85), the letters were addressed to Russell and Charles Sayle at Oxford, and John Badley at Rugby and Cambridge. It has been said that the transcriptions contain 'extensive bowdlerization';[17] in fact the originals show Russell's excision mostly of references to his own rustication from Oxford for writing a 'scandalous' letter to another undergraduate (a charge that he strongly denied).[18]

The collection shows Johnson in only one of his epistolary incarnations: in another slightly later correspondence, to his cousin Oswald Carnagy Johnson, he writes 'I am always all things to all men, if by any means I may suit some one's taste. I carefully consider yours, when I write'.[19] But if the *Winchester Letters* are at least part pose, nevertheless this particular pose is often (unlike that of the letters to Oswald) an early version of his mature critical voice. These letters contain his first efforts – at the demand of his more earnest friends – towards the formation of a coherent ethic, and involve a remarkable range of reference and level of articulation, though in tandem with a seventeen-year-old's experiments with self-representation and toying with the sensitivities of his correspondents. They take a broad selection of nineteenth-century philosophical and religious systems and go through several stages of synthesizing these into a workable ethic. And even if these early experiments in ethical theory bore no relation to the work of the mature Johnson, they show how an intellectually inclined young man of the 1880s could combine available discourses in a way that suggested productive continence as a desirable practice, not for everyone, but for certain aesthetically sensitive temperaments. To Russell he describes their position as that of 'two of young England's rising generation in search of a creed' (23).

For Johnson this search requires the balancing of various claims, the achievement of which process he variously describes as 'light', 'love', or 'warmth'. His letters express two focal conflicts. The most overt is between one's duty to self and towards one's community. On the one hand, Johnson needs a personally satisfying spiritual experience requiring isolation, while on the other hand he is painfully aware that no spiritual system can be ultimately satisfying that cannot potentially be extended to all, or at least integrate the isolated individual within some wider system of common good. Murray has shown how a similar concern animated Johnson's later Catholicism; the *Winchester Letters* show this conflict to be fundamental to his thinking even preceding conversion.[20] Johnson in these letters is far more interested than Pater in community for its own sake, as a duty or responsibility, rather than in its capacity for contributing to the richness of the aesthetic life. Sexuality plays a large part in these vacillations, although not initially in the way that might be expected at a time when sexuality was so often associated with selfish individualism. Johnson most frequently associates continence with the ideal isolation of the individual, and active sexuality with the community into which he must integrate. He assumes, rather than interrogates, the obvious desirability of continence (at least in these letters).

The second conflict is between the religious element he requires – a satisfactory 'creed' for him must allow worship of a transcendental being or ideal – and the secular culture he admires. Pittock has recognized this tension as central in Johnson's work: 'conflict [...] arises from a wish both to elevate the role of the artist and at the same time remain conscious of his own faith and its demands'. Pittock uses this conflict to explain Johnson's alcoholism. 'Hence his asceticism and his passion', he says, 'the drink beside his bed, the Mass an unsteady walk away'. And this personality is again used to establish Johnson as a symbol of his period: 'Johnson is thus the decadent simultaneously participating in and sitting in judgement on his own values'.[21] Pittock supposes that Aestheticism and religion are mutually exclusive, and thus does not adequately allow for the possibility that an idiosyncratic yet effective reconciliation *could* be achieved, via what Mark Knight and Emma Mason call the 'capacity of the Christian faith for renewal, reform, and even revolution'.[22] Such reconciliation had been effected by members of the Oxford Movement, many of whom regarded aesthetic beauty as crucial to their spirituality.[23]

The *Winchester Letters* begin in 1883 with Russell's introduction of his friend to Buddhism. Johnson tests Buddhism against the above criteria. At first (and in hindsight ironically) he writes, 'it repels me, chills me. I would rather be a Roman Catholic [...] it has not enough warmth and light and love to satisfy me' (19, 20). But he is soon seduced by the personal intensity of Buddhist spirituality, and particularly values Buddhism as a personal ethic, a system that, like Pater's aestheticism, guides and beautifies all aspects of life:

> Its special nobility seems to me to be this: that whereas orthodox Christians can go on in a slip-shod way, trusting to deathbed repentance and priestly absolution, in Buddhism [...] every act is a cause: every step in life, every thought and word and deed is of the utmost importance. This strikes me as the supreme height of moral grandeur (31).

His social conscience, however, is troubled. He asks, 'But is it at all practical?' (21). He finds it a creed that is, to him, personally satisfying – 'Were I alone in the world such a life of abnegation and purity and absorption of self into deity would be the ideal for me' – but without an adequate communal provision: 'think of the people you meet every day, and then of that system!' (19). Pater does not worry so explicitly about the social application of his ethic.

Johnson's anxiety about Buddhism's social potential is manifest also in worry about its sexual dimension. 'Do Buddhists practice celibacy?' he asks, continuing, 'If so, it entails difficulties, and confirms what I said as to the impossibility of the religion of Buddha ever really spreading' (22). He is informed that they do, and is greatly perturbed, though not because he personally dislikes the idea. Celibacy prevents Buddhism from being a universal creed because reproductive necessity requires that ideal to be unachieved, and Johnson will have nothing to do with a creed from which even a small section of humanity is necessarily excluded. His qualms, however, are soothed when he learns of reincarnation. 'The successive incarnations we undergo is perhaps meant to explain the apparent injustice I supposed with regard to the entire purity enjoined on us' (29). Reincarnation allows everyone to achieve celibate perfection, though not all at the same time, as each life is reincarnated into a higher form; one might marry in this life, and remain celibate in the next. Throughout this discussion, the innate value of celibacy above marriage is taken for granted, and only its practicality questioned.

Johnson did not become a Buddhist. But his sense of the conflicting values of personal spirituality and humane community remained throughout the letters, as did his ambition to reconcile them. He doubts the attainability of absolute truth as a basis for living – 'I have come more or less to the conclusion that there is no absolute, universal Truth – that each of us has to struggle on, and make his Truth for himself' (23) – and resolves to settle for a cultural humanism. 'In the meantime, what Matthew Arnold calls "morality" and "conduct" will be a half guide' (24). Increasingly this sounds like the adoption of art as an ideal, providing the basis for his later Paterianism. He writes, 'I feel, as all must feel who believe in spirituality, an intense love of beauty in all its forms: I realize to myself an infinity of love in listening to true music, in seeing true paintings, reading true poetry'. But again, he worries about egotism:

> but, in the midst of all this delight, I feel an impatient longing to crash discords into the music, to burn and destroy the poetry and painting with their memories, to be up and doing or suffering (55).

This Carlylean desire to 'be up and doing' runs counter to the critical commonplace that stresses Johnson's contemptuous withdrawal from the world. But it accords with Johnson's subsequent life, with his involvement with Christian Socialist projects at school and university, his teaching at 'a sort of Catholic Toynbee Hall' in London (at Newman House, Southwark), and lecturing in the Irish cause in both London and Ireland.[24]

The letters go through several phases in their efforts to integrate personal spirituality with social values. He quotes approvingly from Elizabeth Barrett Browning, 'What's the best thing in the world? Something out of it, I think', only to agonize again over the isolation and exclusivity this implies: 'but how can I get the "something" into the world? I can get myself out, but I can't take my brothers' (68). He worries particularly about his moral squeamishness compared to his peers' tendency to discuss sex freely. In November 1883 he asks Russell to send him a copy of a paper entitled *Purity* by George Ridding, headmaster of Winchester (33). As a member of College (his 'house' at Winchester) Johnson was taught by Ridding, and reported personal discussions with him on topics such as religion and happiness. When Ridding left Winchester in 1884, Johnson complained: 'Ridding's leaving is an inconsolable grief to me: he is the only person here who (I am not speaking conceitedly) understands me at all' (61). Ridding's *Purity* argues that 'Purity is, after all, true to nature; and to the great majority it is an element not of conventional restraint, but of general comfort and happiness'; in other words, a question not only of morality, but also of health. He continues that 'premature waste of vital force is profligate bankruptcy for maturity', and 'intemperance has not more victims of extreme excess in gaols and asylums than unchastity; nor has it ruined more careers of promise in public and intellectual life'. We can recognize here the repetition of the medicalized sexual discourse that so often in the period produced an ideal of productive continence.[25]

There is little in these letters to suggest that Johnson deviated from Ridding's views on sexuality, though they suggest that he struggled to reconcile what he knew about his peers with his desire for 'brotherhood'. Following Ridding's departure from Winchester, the problem of other people's sensuality looms large, and is combated through a theory of personal detachment and disinterestedness. An April 1884 letter responds to rumours in Oxford of some immorality on Johnson's part. The details of this episode are hazy, but as his defence turns on his refusal, not to renounce sensuality in his own case, but to condemn it in others – 'no one can excite my loathing nor my indignation' (75–6) – it seems likely that he had deliberately failed to report or hinder, in his role as prefect, homosexual behaviour among his peers.[26] A similar tolerance can be found in his letters to Oswald, where he boasts of time spent with 'Russian sodomites' (by whom he meant Count Stenbock and friends), and flirtation with Simeon Solomon, albeit with much exaggerated anxiety afterwards: 'I can never see him again', he writes to Oswald, 'without a police escort for protection'.[27] These letters also contain the only record of a sexual relationship on Johnson's part, with a women at the London Alhambra nicknamed 'Aspasia' ('she lies like anything' he writes, 'in as many senses of the word as you may please').[28] But in 1884 the question was whether Johnson could tolerate sensuality in others without himself becoming corrupted. He remembers telling Ridding of his reluctance to judge others. 'He told me', he writes, 'that he did not expect me [...] to keep myself (from my own point of view) unspotted from the world, and to have any friends in the world' (77).

This conversation suggests that Johnson's purported amorality at this point, with which he distresses the morally earnest Russell and Sayle, did not extend to himself. He elaborates this theory, 'a gospel of toleration, a proclamation of no sin' (104), by combining priestly and Decadent poses. 'After reading *Thomas à Kempis*', he writes, 'I can listen with no disgust to sensual conversation: I can return freely to walk over the downs' (76, italics in original). Johnson is likely drawing here on a chapter of *The Imitation of Christ* entitled 'On Bearing Other Men's Infirmities and Faults', which advises 'Such things as a man may not amend in himself and in others he ought to suffer patiently'.[29] Johnson forms from this a strategy of personal immunity from unhealthy influence similar to (though simpler than) that attributed by Pater to the aesthete, and combines it with a Decadent amorality. He writes, 'I do not love sensuality: I do not hate it; I do not love purity; I do not hate it; I regard both as artistic aspects of life' (76). Eventually he placates the outraged Sayle by tempering this amorality again into Thomas à Kempis' calm, tolerant comradeship: 'I do not say to the drunkard "drink if you will, I don't know why you drink: I won't presume to dictate: I love you," but "Brother, can I help you?"' (137). He also outlines a less Decadent aestheticism:

By the way, I protest against your petty denunciation of 'aestheticism': in the vulgar sense I mostly agree with you: but so far as it means the gospel of emotion waking as an artistic morality it is a high hope for mankind: true, never eat lotus, lotus is poison, and, in truth, an insidious and unknown one (87).

A separate letter to Edgar Jepson (also an Oxford undergraduate) elaborates the Decadent pose further, but ends again by weaving it into a theory of personal withdrawal and disinterestedness, in which unpleasant sensations are regarded critically and aesthetically rather than directly and painfully experienced. Channelling Baudelaire through a Decadent variety of Paterianism, quite unlike that which he would later express (and that explored in the previous chapter), but popular in Jepson's Oxford, he writes, 'the flowers of evil are more beautiful than the sensitive plants of purity – and tears and protestations have an ugliness about them', and 'exquisite emotions and desires and pangs – these are the spirit of the best life possible'. It soon becomes clear that Johnson believes himself immune from such 'flowers of evil': 'this refinement in beautiful evil, this scrupulous precision of choice, precludes all really insane and unhealthy infection'. His attitude does not, he insists, result in 'immoral' behaviour. 'My theory and practice', he continues, 'have the merit of utility: they do not lead me into harsh situations and practice'.[30] Further, the 'evil' he is concerned with here is not sensuality, but loneliness. 'Convert Despair into an observant tolerance', he counsels, 'and you find yourself sufficient for all your desires'. He advises Jepson to practice disinterested withdrawal as a process of transformation that sounds, in its logic of gain from restraint, very like Pater's productive retention: 'a complacent power of spiritual alchemy, whereby the dross of vulgar life is transmuted to the subjects of cultured experiment'.[31]

Two other lines of argument in the *Winchester Letters* foreshadow his later work: his determination to be a priest, and his apparent belief in a cultural sainthood. Early on he had expressed his intention to 'combine the position of a man of letters with that of a quasi-religious lecturer' (16). In May 1884 he declares, 'I will be a priest of the Church of England, as I have so often dreamed of being' (85). When Pater describes Marius as 'something of a priest', he refers to personal discipline, 'that devotion of his days to the contemplation of what is beautiful, a sort of perpetual religious service'.[32] Johnson sees priesthood as a convenient compromise between this and social duty. 'I do long with all the energies of hope to be an influence' (85), he says; 'Only think of the chances which the priesthood offers: the countless influences of the pulpit and the altar, all potent against the devil in even feeble hands' (86). But his ideal of priesthood, while centred around contribution to the world, a determination to 'make men who are immoral, trivial, careless, believe that the world is holy by their human presence' (138), is nevertheless physically detached: 'I won't have a parish, but try and get the loaves and fishes by literature. I will be all things to a few men' (92). Like John Keble, he imagines taking the world by storm from a rural curacy, though the idea of preaching to the few rather than the many is also reminiscent of Newman. And again, this religious position blends into his aestheticism; at one point he directly compares the role of critic to that of the priest, writing that 'When I absorb the soul and love of a picture, I worship: when I bring another to it, I have done the priest's office' (136). In this exploration of priestly influence in detachment, he finds a compromise between continent individualism and social duty reminiscent of the Catholic doctrine of priestly indifference.

Johnson also keeps returning to the idea of a community of like minds, both dead and alive, encompassing both religious and secular figures, and accessible to all through literature:

> Christ lives! lo, he is alive for evermore [...] and Shelley is with him, and Plato, and Dante hand in hand with Beatrice: they are Spirits: with identity of love and goodness: not themselves, but each his brother! (97)

These 'Spirits, numberless, aureoled with love, garmented with compassion, scientifically exact' are represented not as metaphors, but as reality: 'Why do you persist', he writes to Sayle, 'in thinking of these things as mere fantasies, beautiful imaginings? I tell you, they are actualities' (99). Eventually they are resolved into a pseudo-angelic hierarchy, made up, on one level, of earthly priests like himself, and on the other by those deceased who have embodied its spiritual/humane ideal. He bids Sayle:

> Compare my hierarchy with Comte's. What do you think of a few souls, elect, precious, mere memories and records beside my spiritual spheres filled with all dead things, where Christ and Cicero and tortured animals are together glorified: all equal in glory and majesty? (101)

The reference to Comte shows Johnson's awareness that he is modifying a common tendency towards hierarchical systems in modern thought, though with some juvenile excess (the inclusion, for example, of 'tortured animals', a reference to vivisection). It was a theory that he was to expand and refine, rather than reject, on conversion to Roman Catholicism with its Communion of Saints, as this passage suggests:

> My Catholic Saints and seraphs [...], Browning, Blake, Swinburne, Ros-
> setti, Hugo, Whitman, Pater, Catullus, Chopin, and so many more: all pass
> through the world with holy indifference and tolerant favour on their lips,
> the sun of Righteousness in their eyes, for the healing of the nations (190–1).

The phrase 'holy indifference and tolerant favour' is particularly notewor-
thy; its combination of sympathy and separation would come to epitomize
much of what Johnson valued.

Pater

From the outset of his intellectual career, then, Johnson worried about
how to best interact with the world around him, and how to reconcile
religious and secular influences. Sex played a large part in his thinking on
these themes as, assuming his own desire (in the *Winchester Letters*) for
relatively isolated continence, he sought to integrate this via a discourse of
productive continence with both his social conscience and desire for companionship. The poems, letters, and criticism of Johnson's Oxford and
London periods continue these preoccupations.

The *Winchester Letters* also express a further struggle, not unrelated,
between the pleasures of sense experience and the pleasures of spirituality.
In 1883 he writes:

> I have always been trying to find a philosophy of soul and sense which
> should unite the two, the result always being the subjection of the former:
> now, of course, I see how utterly mistaken I was, and how infinitely harder I
> have made it to break the ties of the latter and free my spirit altogether (46).

He continues to be occupied by this conundrum, especially as his amorality brings, as we have seen, charges of potential sensuality from his recipi-
ents. At first he is willing to admit some truth in this conclusion, writing,
'Sensuality: what is it unless the expression of the *mind* instead of the
spirit? [...] it leads to ruin of body and grossness of spirit: alas, yes! but not
till Morality has spurned it and trampled on it' (81–2). Later he introduces
a Paterian separation between sensuality and sensuousness, referring to
'sensuality or rather vulgar indifference to the spirit of the senses' (135).
'Beauty', he says, 'means the fusion of spirit and sense' (130).

On his eighteenth birthday Johnson read *Marius the Epicurean*, recently
published. He wrote to Russell, 'I am revelling in Pater's book: full of
the most perfect literary quality, and infinitely wise and true and beautiful' (180). Though his Decadent pose incorporated Paterian vocabulary,
this is his first mention of Pater, and the beginning of a very different

Paterianism. A month later, he refers to 'the perfection of beautiful literature, Pater's *Marius*: a revelation of wonderful beauty and delight: a
book to love and worship: a good book' (183). Johnson's Oxford career
corresponded with Pater's move to London, but he nevertheless made his
acquaintance. His university letters contain many references to time spent
with Pater and his sisters in London. In 1889 he writes: 'I lunched with
Pater, dined with Pater, smoked with Pater, walked with Pater, went to
Mass with Pater, and fell in love with Pater'.[33] By 1891, by which time
Johnson was also living in London, his letters suggest intimate terms with
the Pater family, and discussion of the unfinished *Gaston de Latour*. 'Pater,
I see frequently: he is bringing Gaston to a conclusion. It is marvellous!'[34]
On Pater's death in 1894 Johnson was involved in organizing his papers.
He writes: 'I have been at Oxford, going through the whole of Pater's
manuscripts: a wonderful experience and [privilege]'.[35]

In his published studies of Pater, Johnson combines the 'fusion of spirit
and sense' with his earlier preoccupations. 'A perpetual wondering joy in
the messages brought by beautiful things, through their visible forms', he
claims, 'was a kind of worship to him'.[36] He was eager to defend the sensuousness of Pater's work against those who portrayed him as 'stiff and
stately in his jewelled vestments'.[37] But he is careful also to distinguish
sensuousness from the sensuality as which it was also widely read. 'It is
possible', he says,

> that to his congenital distaste for what has no colour, form, warmth, play
> of life, is due a certain misconstruction of his 'philosophy' [...]. Assuredly,
> Mr. Pater held the power of recognising and of loving beauty in the world
> to be a possession past praise, and a passionate constancy of concern for it
> to be no mean state of mind; but assuredly in no ignoble way.[38]

This final clause is clarified in a letter dated a month after Pater's death.
Claiming that 'Pater was perceptibly more gentle and retiring and serious,
in a semi-monastic sort of spirit, for the last two or three years', Johnson
continues:

> Not that he ever came to the point of undervaluing 'culture': but that ever-
> lasting Greek delusion, of the Symonds sort, certainly attracted him less,
> and a kind of religiousness, Catholic Puritanism, more.[39]

The 'Greek delusion' may refer to a general idealization of Greek culture;
and yet Johnson's reference to Symonds – whose *A Problem in Greek Ethics*,
an account of homosexuality in Greek culture, had been privately printed
and circulated in Oxford in 1883, and whose own homosexual inclination
was an open secret – surely concedes that Pater may have been attracted

to the idea that romantic, potentially sexual relationships between men and boys was either permissible or ennobling. Johnson occasionally refers in letters to the physical beauty and homosexuality of his male peers, and wrote a handful of unpublished poems while a schoolboy in which this sensuous admiration is evidently erotic.[40] His willingness to publicly acknowledge awareness of the idea of Greek love is evidenced by the tongue-in-cheek poem 'In Praise of Youth' (1891), later rewritten as the more earnest and critical 'A Dream of Youth' and dedicated in the 1895 *Poems* to his Oxford friend Alfred Douglas. It is very likely that his poem 'Destroyer of a Soul', beginning 'I hate you with a necessary hate' and dedicated 'To ———', is addressed to Oscar Wilde, to whom he had introduced Douglas in 1891.

In his published work Johnson both chastened and Christianized Pater, though only insofar as was compatible with full acknowledgment of his friend's emphasis on sense experience. In doing so he repeats the Tractarian process of co-opting cultural products for religious ends; he can be seen as doing for Pater what many of those of the last generation had done for the Romantic poets, while some of the ease with which he does this can be assigned to Pater's initial secularization of Tractarian ideas such as reserve and assent.[41] In the process Johnson elaborates a Catholic aestheticism that can be traced through both his poetry and criticism, in which intense spirituality is reconciled to community, imagined variously as involvement in 'the world', modernity, social duty, and companionship. That he remains close to Pater's work rather than proceeding through biographical speculation, taking liberties only in drawing religious intimations where they are not explicit, further illustrates that work's responsiveness to such reading.

In his 1893 reviews of Pater's *Plato and Platonism* Johnson Christianizes Pater's Plato, and in the process Pater himself. David DeLaura has argued that in *Plato and Platonism*, 'Plato is made to sound like an aestheticized Newman'.[42] Johnson draws out the residue of Newman in Pater's Plato, and then reads Pater himself through his own moral-aesthetic composite. But he does so by emphasizing the importance of *both* sensuous pleasure and self-restraint to Pater, Plato, and Newmanite Christianity alike. He suggests both that Plato can be read as a pseudo-Christian author, and that Pater's reading of Plato, and incorporation of his ideas into his own philosophy, is also of this nature. But his starting point is Pater's emphasis on Plato's sensuousness. 'Once more', he says 'Mr. Pater has shown us how fruitful of good things is this visible world, with its garniture and furniture for every sense', especially in his portrayal of Plato's having 'used the eyes, together with the mind, of an artist'. But he then qualifies this sensuousness; 'yet Plato is not of Cyrene', he reminds us, alluding not only to Plato's position in Greek philosophy, but also both Pater's description of Marius' initial Epicureanism as the 'New Cyreniacism', and the adoption of this term by those of Pater's critics who wished to represent him as an amoral hedonist. Having brought Plato and Pater together in this way, Johnson then poses a series of questions in which this modulation of Plato's (and Pater's) sensuousness becomes a Christianization:

> just where and how does Plato's high philosophy join hands with his delight in visible life? What harmony was that he would effect among the multitudinous sounds, the many colours, of this world? Can life become a fair service of God, by any disciplined care for the best things in life, the worthiest and the finest of them all?

Comparing Plato's desire for high, spiritual beauty to Augustine's desire for the beauty of God, he says, 'There was no such outbreak from the soul of Plato; but, from the first a lover, he also passed into a knower of an unoriginate beauty and of a very light'. The word 'unoriginate', a theological term referring to God's position as first cause, suggests that Plato's idealism can be read as an intuition of the divinity, while perhaps hinting also at the unreproductive nature of this ideal. And both Plato and Augustine are interpreted as inhabiting a kind of Paterian aestheticism through their perception of 'beauty'. Just as in the *Winchester Letters* Johnson was eager to find similarities between philosophical systems and faiths, so now, having committed to the actual truth of Catholicism, he interprets all similar sentiments as intuitions of this truth: Plato's 'intuition was much that of Augustine'. His next sentence suggests that Pater himself deliberately makes this elision between Plato's 'high philosophy' and Christian morality: 'Mr. Pater, in his first lectures, traces the growth of Plato's mind upon these matters'.[43]

Essential to this portrait is Pater's lingering over Plato's potentially sensual nature. But also essential is the curtailment of sensuality through self-restraint. Pater characterizes Plato, says Johnson, as having 'A love of love, sensuous certainly, by virtue, or vice, of a passionate temperament; but tempered by an austere love of temperance, restraint, and order'. Johnson, more than Pater, is careful to concede – in order to disarm – the possible interpretations of this temperate passion. Like Pater's followers, Plato's 'lovers, not always wise, have been something too apt to take him, literally, "at his word"'. This is not only dangerous; it is also, according to Johnson, to misinterpret Plato. 'In ethics, his ultimate aim [...] was a "faire music and divine concent", body obeying soul'.[44] The phrase 'divine concent' suggests the early modern use of the word 'concent' to indicate the harmonious relationship of voices, and more specifically the ethical application of such harmony.[45] He expands upon this Christianization in his description of Plato's 'Dorian self-restraint': 'It is, if you consider it, a scholar's vision: away with the vulgarity of excess! And a saint's vision: away with the iniquity of lawlessness!'[46] This scholar-saint is evidently as much Johnson's vision of Pater as of Plato; in the poem 'Walter Pater' (1902), one of the last poems that Johnson wrote, he calls Pater 'Scholarship's constant saint'.[47]

A similar impression is gained in 'The Work of Mr. Pater' (1894), published only a month after Pater's death. In describing *Marius*, Johnson says its success arises from a 'keeping close to life, a sensitiveness almost in excess', yet also that 'A marvellous self-discipline has made the book'. Unsurprisingly, Johnson interprets *Marius* as an essentially Christian book, in which, though Marius is not actually converted, 'the sweetness and the greatness of Christianity steal over him, as over the reader'.[48] Marius himself he describes, like Pater and Plato, as exercising a restraint that not only intensifies an inner passion, but also turns this passion towards a yearning for an ideal: 'this questioner of the oracles, with so much fire beneath his dainty and deliberate bearing, so much wistful anger and hunger of heart; amorous of nothing else, unable to be at peace with less, than the *Deus absconditus* of his desire'. Again, the introduction of the phrase *Deus absconditus* (hidden God), most famously associated with Thomas Aquinas, interprets Marius's life as a Christian search for divine truth, a 'pilgrim's progress'.[49] He also is a scholar-saint.

Johnson traces the Christian spirit of *Marius* not only to the events of the book, but also its style. Its austere control of sensuous pleasure is for Johnson a specifically Christian impulse. The influence this style exercises over the reader at first seems, he says, 'as though the writer "willed" it almost without words', but in reality 'it is through his austere delicacy in using them that the miracle is worked upon us'.[50] It is entirely open to us to take Johnson's use of the word 'miracle' here seriously; Pater's style very likely did appear to him as the working of the divinity in the world. In the poem 'Walter Pater' he describes Pater as:

> [...] he who toiled so well
> Secrets of grace to tell
> Graciously; as the awed rejoicing priest
> Officiates at the feast,
> Knowing, how deep within the liturgies
> Lie hid the mysteries.[51]

Again both the mysteries of God and culture are hidden, requiring in both cases the intermission of and interpretation of a priest-critic. 'Grace', too, was an important concept for Johnson. Elsewhere, he posits 'grace' as the essential link between stylistic beauty and divine favour. 'Grace!' he says, 'the word sums up theology; and it is no less the secret soul of literature'.[52] Stephen Cheeke finds a similar, though secularized, use of the term 'grace' in the work of Pater, as 'simultaneously a formal beauty, and a moral value; a sign of order and harmony that betokens moral goodness'.[53] That Johnson connects literary grace with the role of the priest, as arbiter between worshippers and those 'mysteries' of the liturgy, is reminiscent of his association in the *Winchester Letters* of a priest's position with an ideal reconciliation of individual withdrawal with social duty and influence. The roles of scholar-saint and priest are combined in Pater's style, which is both passionate in restraint and able to communicate this restrained passion to others.

Poetry

In his poetry Johnson often describes a Paterian, but thoroughly Christianized, process of self-restraint; not as a denial of sensuous pleasure, but as the productive containment and transformation of potential sensuality. His most anthologized poem, 'The Dark Angel' (1894), describes temptation as a necessary process for the attainment of holiness, since it provokes one to make a conscious separation of sensuous from sensual experience. The 'dark angel' of temptation is imagined literally as Satan, who must be acknowledged to have been appointed to his role by God in order to provoke one from the passive state of indifference to an active holiness:

> I fight thee, in the Holy Name!
> Yet, what thou dost, is what God saith:
> Tempter! should I escape thy flame,
> Thou wilt have helped my soul from Death[.][54]

The utility of temptation is outlined by Thomas à Kempis in his *Imitation of Christ*. 'Temptations', he says, 'are ofttimes right profitable to men, though they be heavy and grievous; for in them a man is meekened, purged and sharply taught'.[55] Johnson follows this poem, in the roughly thematical arrangement of his poems in the original volume, with another entitled 'A Friend', also dated 1894, in which he prays that a seemingly happy but secular friend be sent a dark angel like his own, that he may be turned toward God:

> But in the lonely hours I learn,
> How I can serve him and thank him best:
> *God! trouble him: that he may turn*
> *Through sorrow to the only rest.*[56]

Critical response to 'The Dark Angel' has generally treated the poem as what Ian Fletcher calls 'lyric autobiography', and has been concerned with the identification of the specific temptation that the poem describes, often in order to find in it an expression of violent inner conflict that could explain Johnson's alcoholism and sudden death.[57] Early attempts generally read it as either a confession of struggle with alcohol, or of the vague, unspecific unhappiness responsible for addiction.[58] Since the 1970s it has been more common to read it as revelation of repressed homosexuality. Brian Reade describes it as a 'homosexual poem' that can 'barely be read correctly if the anguish expressed in it is not grasped as a fantasy of starved affection', and Ellis Hanson as a 'recognition of the sadness and the loneliness of the Victorian homosexual in his efforts at sublimation'.[59] A handful of critics have circumvented this search for specific temptation, reading 'The Dark Angel' as a more general meditation on conflict between spiritual and worldly experience. Thornton describes the poem as an expression of 'finely grandiloquent ascetic idealism […] balancing the fear of worldly corruption', Ronald Schuchard as the epitome of the 'sensual-spiritual malaise' passed by the 1890s to the modernist period.[60] And Pittock spiritualizes the entire conflict, seeing it as 'a battle between two kinds of transcendent reality', namely Aestheticism and Christianity.[61]

Pittock is right, I think, to identify Aestheticism as part of the poem's immediate context, and there is nothing in the poem itself to disprove either alcoholism or homosexuality as the described temptation. But given Johnson's emphasis elsewhere on the importance of sense experience, it seems more fruitful to read the conflict of 'The Dark Angel' not as between two kinds of transcendent reality, but rather between two kinds of relationship with the physical world. The particular function of the angel is to turn a potentially innocent experience into a sensual one:

> When sunlight glows upon the flowers,
> Or ripples down the dancing sea:
> Thou, with thy troop of passionate powers,
> Beleaguerest, bewilderest, me.[62]

The temptation of the poem is not limited to sense experience. 'Because of thee, no thought, no thing,/Abides for me undesecrate.' But its examples generally are sensuous, and the experience of beauty is particularly picked out: 'all the things of beauty burn/With flames of evil ecstasy'.[63] Again this is a common feature of Tractarian religious experience, especially later in the century, when the Movement's intense focus on sense experience as revealing God's immanence, especially through art and nature, led them also to agonize over the fine line between sacred and profane sensuous pleasure.[64] It is likely that Johnson, having collated such writings with his reading of Pater, took it with him on his conversion to Catholicism.

Johnson's underscoring in 'The Dark Angel' and elsewhere of the *use* to which this contest can be put, especially within the context of beauty, sounds like a Christianized version of Pater's lingering over the borders between sensuous and sensual experience. Its mechanism of reserve and transformation is also reminiscent of the medical logic associated with productive retention. Another set of poems written around the same time and entitled 'To Passions' (1893–94) elaborates on the process of this transformation. Having complained of 'Passion, imperious, insolent', the poet cries:

> Thou fool! For if thou have thy way with me,
> Thou wilt be still the same: but victor, I
> Should make some fair perfection out of thee,
> And reach the starry Heaven of Heavens thereby.[65]

As in 'The Dark Angel', the business of overcoming temptation is not an act of renunciation so much as transformation, the logic of which resembles that of Pater's productive continence.

From 'The Dark Angel' a possibility arises, despite its protracted fretting over temptation, of what a triumph over that temptation would look like, a world in which nature and art can be enjoyed without fear of 'The hinting tone, the haunting laugh'.[66] Such a regenerate world would not, it must be noted, be one of calm detachment from sensuous experience. Johnson's poetry generally reserves 'calm' as a description of the height of pagan virtue, the furthest towards virtue that one can get without God. 'A Friend' represents the friend as 'A classic saint, in self-control,/And comeliness, and quiet mirth', yet prays for the disturbing of that calm.[67] In contrast holiness is always for Johnson an impassioned state. An early poem, 'An Ideal' (1888), also represents the drama of temptation: '*Come!* sigh the shrouding airs of earth:/*Be with the burning night*'. The poet resists – 'I come not. Off, odorous airs!' – but, though the temptation itself is named 'passion' (he scoffs 'let passion garnish her wild lairs/Hold her fierce holiday'), yet the 'ideal' of the title is not calm, but an alternative passion:

> Mine be all proud and lonely scorn,
> Keeping the crystal law
> And pure air of the eternal morn:
> And passion, but of awe.[68]

It is likely this impassioned state, rather than cold calmness, that we are to imagine in the final lines of 'The Dark Angel': '*Lonely, unto the Lone I go;/Divine, to the Divinity*'.[69]

Yet despite the passionate, sensuous nature of Johnson's religiosity, resistance to temptation is for him always associated with singleness. It is this singleness (which should not be automatically interpreted as a negative state) that suggests that the 'passion' resisted might be specifically sexual; that giving in to it would yield something other than loneness, a sinful connection with another person. But if this sexual interpretation is admitted, homosexual orientation is not the only possible frame of reference (though it may well be a relevant one) for this contained sexuality. '*Lonely, unto the Lone I go*' closely echoes many Tractarian vows of celibacy, so often imagined as a sacrifice of the intimate companionship of marriage, only imperfectly replaced by intimate same-sex friendship.

Johnson's poems often describe an impassioned single state as, if not ideal for all, at least necessary to some in a world less than perfect. 'Magic' (1887–88) first describes the magician as embodying a Newmanite rejection of reason – 'I work not, as logicians work,/Who but to ranked and marshalled reason yield' – before going on to repudiate those who misunderstand the life of the scholar: 'They wrong with ignorance a royal choice,/Who cavil at my loneliness and labour'. 'I choose laborious loneliness' he continues, scorning those who 'Lead Love in triumph through the dancing city'. Again, an attitude to the world is outlined with which 'Love' is incompatible, but which produces a different kind of passion: 'Ah! light imaginations, that discern/No passion in the citadel of passion'.[70]

A more overtly Christian example is 'Our Lady of the Snows' (1887), written in defence of the monastic spirit against R. L. Stevenson's poem of the same name, which had described the 'unfraternal brothers' as 'aloof, unhelpful, and unkind'.[71] Written in the first person, and therefore exploring the epistemology of the monk from his own point of view rather than another's, the poem protests: 'You are the happier for our prayer;/The guerdon of our souls, you share'. The monk is not anti-world, but rather sacrifices his own potential for worldly pleasure to facilitate the innocent pleasure of others: 'Our spirits with your tempters fight'. The monks are themselves represented as enjoying no worldly pleasure themselves, sensuous or sensual; 'we live alone,/Where no joy comes'.[72] After Johnson's death many friends remembered having heard that he was about to enter a monastery, and his letters suggest that a vocation for monasticism and the ministry were ideas that he liked to play with, or have people believe of him. But his poetic treatment of monks and nuns implies that while he saw their lives as impassioned rather than cold, nonetheless their denial of sensuous as well as sensual experience was a sticking point when he tried to imagine himself in such a role. In 'To a Belgian Friend' (1898), addressing Olivier Georges Destrée, who had entered a Benedictine order in October 1898, he says, while offering 'praise', that 'The nothingness, which you have flung away,/To me seems full of fond delightful cares'. He ends by putting himself in the position of those prayed for by the religious: 'Give me your prayers'.[73] The cloistered monastic role is admitted to be holiest, though by no means suited for all, while sensuous continence in the world may be imagined as an allowable compromise.

A more melancholy note is struck in another of his most commonly anthologized poems, 'Mystic and Cavalier' (1889), in which the cerebral mystic bewails the distance between himself and the world. Again, this poem is almost universally interpreted as autobiographical, with the famous line 'Go from me: I am one of those, who fall' often used to refer to his drunkenness and even the fall that killed him; 'Johnson fell quite often, both symbolically and physically' reads his entry in the *Oxford Dictionary of National Biography*.[74] The poem can be read, however, as an experiment with the splitting of experience into the entirely worldly and the entirely spiritual, with the latter particularly coming in for negative representation. This is, as we have seen, by no means in conflict with Johnson's religious orientation. Knight and Mason have highlighted the anxiety of Catholic writers in particular to distinguish between mysticism and religion in the period, and have warned against critical confusion of the terms.[75] Johnson's poem displays a similar anxiety. As in Pater's treatment of medieval mysticism in 'Poems by William Morris', the mystic's excessive focus on the unworldly causes a spiritual malaise. But this malaise does not produce the 'tension of nerve, in which the sensible world comes to one with a reinforced brilliance and relief', as it did for Pater's mystic; such tension is reserved by Johnson for the properly sensuous religious.[76] Instead it causes an excessive preoccupation with death that is every bit as bad as, if not worse than, the irreligious state of the cavalier, and is described in similar terms to a desire for 'calm': 'Who ever sought that sudden calm, if I/Sought not?'[77] Another poem commonly read as autobiographical, 'Nihilism' (1888), dramatizes a similar excessive abstraction, this time resulting from obsession with self. Again there is a preoccupation with death and calm:

> Where silent things, and unimpassioned things,
> Where things of nought, and things decaying, are:
> I shall be calm soon, with the calm, death brings.

It is in this context that Johnson writes the words, so often read autobiographically, 'of life I am afraid'.[78] This spiritual position is entirely different from that professed in the majority of his poetry, in his letters, and in much of his criticism.

Johnson's poetry, then, develops an individualist spirituality that is not an alienation from the world, but rather an ongoing process in which the sensuous is separated from the sensual. When applied, as it often is, to the experience of art and beauty, this method reproduces the logic of the productive continence that Johnson in his criticism attributed to Pater, though it also has clear roots in Tractarian attitudes towards both sensuous experience and art. In his criticism, written almost entirely after he moved to London in 1890, Johnson builds upon this ideal spiritual position, combining his Paterianism with his reading of Newman and others to create a Catholic aestheticism that is both sexually continent, and firmly engaged with the modern social world, however unappealing that world may occasionally seem.

Criticism

Johnson's mature critical career began when he moved to London in 1890. He soon began to write an impressive number of reviews, a practice that faltered only in the last few years of his life, when for months at a time his hands were swollen enough with gout to prevent his writing.[79] In 1891 he joined the staff of the short-lived *Anti-Jacobin* under the editorship of Frederick Greenwood (a journal that, according to the Waterloo Directory, was 'conservative' but 'agitates for just reform').[80] As well as acting as general reviewer, he also provided a series of articles on mostly literary topics, in which he outlined the beginnings of a coherent literary theory. This section looks at the *Anti-Jacobin* articles, before showing the development of their main themes in Johnson's only critical monograph, *The Art of Thomas Hardy*, as well as in his general reviewing practice. Among these may be traced a recurrent insistence on an intellectual and spiritual sociability that connects what is best in the past to what is worthwhile in the present, which he associates closely with sense as distinct from sensuality, and with the mechanism of productive restraint referenced in his poetry. Far from hating modernity, Johnson can be seen to follow Pater in learning how to filter from his own time what will and should be 'lasting'.

Johnson's critical stance is heavily influenced by his reading of Newman, Arnold, and of course Pater. It is difficult to allocate some aspects of this thinking to any one of these rather than the others, partly because, as DeLaura has shown, Newman had a profound influence on Arnold, and both Newman and Arnold deeply shaped the thinking of Pater.[81] But it is also true that Johnson deliberately selects aspects of nineteenth-century cultural humanism that can be found in all three, or at least two of the three, and uses this synthesis to claim for humanism a universal interest that transcends all time and place. He then follows Newman in identifying this cultural humanism as essentially Christian, though his doing so via Arnold and Pater results in his humanism's encompassing a much wider range than Newman's. Whereas Newman worried that art could become an end in itself, a distraction from rather than help to religion, this is almost impossible for Johnson, for whom the ends of good art *are* those of religion.[82]

Much of what Johnson valued in both literature and life can, as Gary Paterson has noted, be summed up in the words 'human' and 'humane'.[83] But he meant far more by it than might at first be thought, referring to a nexus of values – tradition, obedience, community, and self-denial, but also sensuous experience and spiritual ecstasy – that can be traced as points of overlap between Tractarian and Catholic theology. For Tractarians as for Catholics, the doctrines of tradition and of the Church as a communal body both on earth and in Heaven were intimately connected. One of the main tenets of the Oxford Movement was that the Church had to be considered not as a mere earthly institution that could be separated from the individual conscience, but as a body encompassing both space and time, making religion a community into which the individual was initiated rather than a matter of individual reading of Scripture. To this end, tradition was valued as the lifeblood of the Christian community, connecting any newcomer both to the Church of the past and that of the present; to ignore tradition was to cut oneself off from true religious understanding.[84]

Arnold secularized these twin concerns into an opposition to what he called 'provincialism', and an ideal of 'disinterestedness' that emphasized both community in the form of social duty and a tradition of elite learning that extended through time and space. Johnson, rather than returning to the Tractarians' theologically dense position, effectively re-Christianizes the Arnoldian position, traces of which he knew could also be found in Pater (particularly late Pater). He also uses the similarity between Pater's and Newman's rhetoric of the 'personal' to reinvigorate both, giving to Newman's concessions towards art a newly sensuous warmth, while Pater's 'kindly love' gains an element of social duty that he never fully elaborated (though there are, as we saw, hints of such a focus in the manuscript of 'The Aesthetic Life'). The thread with which Johnson connects these three humanistic positions is sexual continence. With this ideal he strings together Pater's discipline, Arnold's Hellenism, and Newman's 'reserve' to create a recognizably humanist temper that could be at once a style and an ethic, and within which artistic and Christian morals were at one.

Richard Le Gallienne described Johnson as 'a literary Catholic believing devoutly in the apostolic succession of all really great writers'.[85] An *Anti-Jacobin* article entitled 'Inspirers and Teachers' posits a theory of sociability very similar to that expressed as a semi-secular Communion of Saints in the *Winchester Letters*. 'The inspirers of the world', he writes, 'form a company of gracious or commanding men, champions by their very names and memories against degrading views of life'. The examples he gives are a mixture of Christian and secular, as well as alive and dead: Thomas à Kempis, Carlyle, Arnold, and Ruskin; 'each is human and humane'.[86] But most conspicuous in the piece is Newman. Newman had called for feeling over reason in matters of faith; for example in 'The Tamworth Reading Room' (1841): 'after all, man is *not* a reasoning animal; he is a seeing, feeling, contemplating, acting animal'.[87] Johnson extends this line of thought, writing: 'it may be a pitiful confession, but it is true, that they are the world's spiritual masters who tell us of things irreducible to forms of logic'. He continues, 'after all, it is by the affections that men become powerful and become loveable: by the humanity of their spirit more than by the strength of their intellect'. Belief in the ultimate ascendency of faith over reason was common to all Tractarians, but Johnson connects his communion of love with Newman specifically. In quoting his heraldic motto, 'Cor ad cor loquitur: heart to heart speaketh', Johnson connects the word 'humanity' with a particular type of religious spirit, relieving it of any potentially secularist associations. He reminds readers that Newman also believed in a spiritual elite connected by love, though not as open to secular membership as Johnson's.

Though not named, the spirit of Pater hovers behind Johnson's adoption of a Platonic title for this piece. 'Inspirers' clearly echoes the Platonic relationship of inspirers and hearers that Johnson associated with Pater, but which he interpreted in 'Mr. Pater Upon Plato' in a thoroughly Christianized, and sexually chastened, sense. He combined this Paterian Platonism seamlessly with Newmanite Catholicism: 'the inspirers of the world are not they who impose laws, but they who win hearts: it was the secret of Newman'. It is possible, though perhaps unlikely, that Johnson is deliberately compiling a homosexual network here, as recent queer readings of Pater and Newman would suggest; this is a point at which emerging homosexual discourse and that of sexual continence overlap. He is deliberately widening his cultural sainthood by focusing on points of agreement between Tractarian and Aesthetic thought, creating the impression of a continuous set of beliefs that can be understood as a universal truth that transcends time and place. 'The "spectators of all time and of all existence", as Plato calls them, have nothing of [...] parochial and circumscribed authority; they are men who would be at home in any country and at any time'.[88] This is a humanism that is *both* religious and secular, or rather can, from Johnson's point of view, be split into its conscious and unconscious religious elements.

The interdependence of tradition and community is stressed in an article entitled 'The Way of Writing', and both are made to rely upon Paterian stylistic discipline. The 'ways' of writing are the stylistic 'high traditions' once recognized by all writing men, amounting to 'literary morals', and consisting in 'those fascinating qualities, of stateliness, of moderation, of *grace*'. Moreover they are the ways of the 'great dead Kings of literature', connecting a writer to a large literary community. These ways are achieved only through a dedicated discipline which, it is heavily implied, connects these literary morals with personal ones. 'Composure, then, a composition, must have certain qualities of law and order, qualities of such a nature that they produce grace and beauty through obedience to wise rule'. This principle of stylistic 'obedience to wise rule' is surely similar to that of Catholic as opposed to Anglican obedience. It is also here that he explicitly equates stylistic with theological grace: as quoted above, 'Grace! the word sums up theology; and it is no less the secret soul of literature'.[89] He ends the piece with the words 'Dead! you and I and our works, because ours is not "the way of writing"' (though it seems unlikely that Johnson would always be willing to include himself in this category).[90] The word 'dead' brackets together exclusion from community, and from a literary immortality that verges upon the literal afterlife, a fate reminiscent of the 'Second death, that never dies' of 'The Dark Angel'.

But such obedience and discipline, while reminiscent of Arnoldian 'disinterestedness', are more like Pater's 'style' in that they produce not cold detachment, but rather a warm personal element, an unselfish 'kindly love' rooted in community rather than ego, and thus approximating also to what Newman meant by the 'personal'. It should be remembered at this point that Johnson implied that he had been read to from or shown manuscripts of *Gaston de Latour* in 1891, the same year in which these

articles were written. 'There are certain writers', says Johnson, 'who share
this charm: writers full of energy and life; but writers, too, of dignity, of
meditation'.[91] 'Grace' for Johnson is a link between literary style and the
humane spirit outlined in 'Inspirers and Teachers'. This is demonstrated
in the article 'Of the Spirit of Books': 'books, either redolent of mellow
age, or full of a writer's kindliness and grace: these we prize, and these we
love'.[92] To the would-be writer he says: 'give yourself, your personal force,
or grace, your spirit and your very heart, and we will welcome your book
and you through it'.[93] Johnson's discipline and disinterestedness is less that
of a philosopher king and more that embodied by the ideal Catholic priest,
a restraint that floods the world with warmth and passion.

Johnson is aware that this 'personal' element is in danger of being mis-
taken for a cult of 'personality', a principle of ego rather than kindliness. It
was a danger that the Tractarians faced also, while it had been the source
of much of what Johnson, among others, saw as the misinterpretation of
Pater, who confronted the problem in the essay 'Style'.[94] He is far more
explicit than Pater about the difference between the personal and the
egotistical, and makes this distinction with reference to sexuality, relying
as Pater had done on the traditional association of sexuality with selfishness, like Pater also associating these qualities with transience. In an article entitled 'Criticism in Corruption', he castigates critics who value the
open expression of sexuality in literature, reading this preoccupation as an
expression also of all that is selfish, egotistical, and more importantly transient and 'dead' in literature and life. Referring to one critic's claim that
''tis the nature and degree of his sense for love that give the truest measure
to the poet', he writes that 'by love we must understand sensuality, animalism, quite as much as the higher passion'. And as evidence against this
claim that the artist is sexual, he appeals to the great traditions of literature,
identifiable both in past and present work: 'Now, this is false to the verdict
of all great poets and critics, from ancient to modern times.' Of course
this is only true for Johnson because his own criteria for whether a poet or
critic is 'great' not only does not involve their 'sense of love', but actively
excludes it. Throughout this article, attraction to sexuality for its own sake
is treated as a disease, a deviation from the normal and healthy state of
things. 'These men seem to delight in disease, distortion, in deformity' he
says, 'it is time to protest against this; for there is a vast deal too much of
it [...] Why are we asked to follow with delighted eyes the aberrations of
sexual maniacs, and not equally those of a kleptomaniac?' Referring to the
same critic, he says that 'after reading him, we want to wash our hands,
take a walk into the country, and come back to Homer or Addison'.[95] We

may remember his earlier boast, on having listened to the sexual gossip of his school friends, that he could 'return freely to walk over the downs' (*Winchester Letters*, 76). And yet it is important to remember that Johnson included writers in 'modern times' in his category of 'all great poets and critics'; that he is objecting to an aspect of modern writing, rather than modernity in itself.

'Criticism in Corruption' takes its illustrations from the work of Edward Delille – an American critic of modern French literature and of Paul Verlaine in particular. Johnson's objection to the wider cultural response to late nineteenth-century Decadence is also expressed in 'The Cultured Faun', the only one of the *Anti-Jacobin* articles to have received sustained scholarly attention. Reading it alongside his other productions for the same journal reveals the extent of Johnson's criticism of fashionable Decadence in this piece. 'You breed it this way', he begins:

> Take a young man, who had brains as a boy, and teach him to disbelieve everything that his elders believe in matters of thought, and to reject everything that seems true to himself in matters of sentiment [...]. He will then, since he is intelligent and bright, want something to replace his early notions.

The 'cultured faun', in other words, is the product of a rejection of both tradition and personal conscience, the two cornerstones of the Oxford Movement and Johnson's own religious orientation. The result is a parodic version or travesty of Johnson's cultural humanism, a matter of the right behaviours for the wrong reasons. 'Externally, our hero should cultivate a reassuring sobriety of habit, with just a dash of dandy', and 'internally, a catholic sympathy with all that exists, and "therefore" suffers, for art's sake'.[96]

Among the preoccupations of this 'creature' is 'a tender patronage of Catholicism', in which 'these refined persons cherish a double "passion": the sentiment of repentant yearning and the sentiment of rebellious sin'.[97] This is the arguably superficial and fashionable Decadent Catholicism described by Ellis Hanson.[98] Alongside this pseudo-Catholicism are found 'occasional doses of "Hellenism": by which we mean the Ideal of the Cultured Faun. That is to say, a flowery Paganism, such as no "Pagan" ever had'. Within this Johnson mentions the Decadent fashion for what he has elsewhere called 'the Greek delusion', referring to 'the elegant languors and favourite vices of (let us parade our "decadent" learning) the *Stratonis Epigrammata*', the homoerotic Greek epigrams, known as the *Musa Puerilis*, or The Boyish Muse, of Straton of Sardis.[99] But he is careful not to have his criticisms include all sense experience: 'now art, at present, is not a question of the senses so much as of the nerves'.[100]

It must be acknowledged here that Johnson does not always criticize Decadent literature, or the literature of his own time, wholesale. In an article for *The Century Guild Hobby Horse*, entitled 'A Note upon the Practice and Theory of Verse at the Present Time Obtaining in France' (1891), he finds in 'the modern poetry of France' a 'spirit of excellent curiosity'. And he particularly praises French Decadent and Symbolist literature, including Verlaine, as productions of 'infinite pains, and of singular attention'; as 'universal, not parochial'. This has been possible, he says, because the French are especially sensitive to what the past can teach them: 'it is, for the poets of France, a matter of scholarship, a mark of nobility, that poetry should be in touch with some high tradition; or, that it should go forth upon untried paths, with an anxiety and a discretion, in themselves traditional'. In other words, this poetic Decadence is a literary success because its 'sordid' subject matter is tempered by stylistic discipline and reverence.[101] 'The Cultured Faun' criticizes Decadence as a cultural phenomenon rather than a literary aesthetic, acknowledging that while it produces, at its best, excellent poetry, its more mediocre productions are often antithetical to the values that Johnson elsewhere professes. Again, it is not modernity itself that Johnson objects to, but to a certain lazy spirit within it.

These values, at once literary and ethical, are boldly stated in Johnson's only full-length critical book, where they are also more explicitly voiced as a reaction to what he saw as the problems of the modern spirit. Commissioned by John Lane and written in 1892, *The Art of Thomas Hardy* was not published until 1894. In the opening and closing chapters of the book, Johnson outlines the philosophical underpinnings of this 'spiritual temperament'. 'I wish to declare my loyalty to the broad and high traditions of literature', he writes; 'to those humanities, which inform with the breath of life the labours of the servants, and the achievements of the masters, in that fine art' (4). These traditions of literature are, as always for Johnson, also ethical traditions. Though he had, in dealing with French Decadent verse, implied that ethical failure can still produce good poetry, here he insists on the absolute unity of a writer's ethics and aesthetics: 'it is tempting to cut the knot', he says, 'by declaring that art and morals have nothing in common: or that one must give way to the other. These theories might be rational in Utopia, and lucid in a Land of the Fourth Dimension: they are inexpressibly meaningless, here and now' (225). This identification of aesthetics with ethics is crucial to the vision that Johnson elaborates here of a literary sainthood promoting a humane spirit through perfect art. He begins the opening chapter with the following statement:

> Literature has commonly been called humane, by way of precept and of praise: if that fact be well taken to heart, it rebukes our solitary pride in our own works, and it calms our feverish concern for our own times: it fills the mind with a cheering sense of security and of companionship (1).

Again, 'humane' means for Johnson an ideal state of companionate detachment.

And again, he finds the antithesis to this ideal state in the literature produced by a problematic element in the modern spirit. In 'our century', he complains, 'We "refine upon our pleasures," as Congreve has it; and our refinement takes the form of that paradoxical humour, which confounds pleasure with pain, and vice with virtue' (2). This refinement matches the description that Johnson gives in the *Hobby Horse* of Decadent literature, in which 'passion, or romance, or tragedy, or sorrow, or any other form of activity or of emotion, must be refined upon, and curiously considered, for literary treatment'.[102] In *The Art of Thomas Hardy*, he finds that this attitude generally produces 'a sick and haggard literature', one 'of throbbing nerves and of subtile [sic] sensations' (2). Though he had earlier praised the best of what Decadence produced in France, here he finds it to be antithetical to his brand of humanism. 'Literature, under such auspices, must lose half its beauty, by losing all its humanity: it ceases to continue the great tradition of polite, of humane letters: it becomes the private toy of its betrayers' (3). It is interesting that Johnson's sexual metaphor here also implies selfishness, the private as opposed to the public.

But if Johnson is harsher in his assessment of Decadent literature here than in earlier writings, he still does not equate it with all modern literature. Against it he poses a classicism in style and manners that is jealous of a certain standard but is nevertheless widely inclusive both in the past and in the present. 'The classics, of all ages and in all tongues, are a catholic company: in their fellowship is room for comers from the four winds, laden with infinitely various gifts and treasures.' Yet 'as the Church Catholic', though 'embracing Tauler and Saint Teresa, excludes Swedenborg and Behmen: so too acts the catholic company of the classics' (3). He continues, 'diversity is admirable: perversity is detestable' (3–4). He goes on to describe the difficult process of the artist in distinguishing diversity from perversity as an ethical dilemma solvable only by appealing to tradition, to the literary sainthood: 'in the old, great masters, and even in the excellent, old writers of less excellence, we have our test, a test of the widest

application, whereby to assay ourselves and others' (6). He very deliberately makes the analogy between this community of classics and the communion of saints: in appealing to them, he says, we should 'Call it rather,
not a debt due, but a grace sought and received' (7). 'The humanists', he
goes on, 'in any liberal sense of that term, are the catholics of art' (12).

The Art of Thomas Hardy, then, evolves a philosophical position in
which aesthetics and ethics are conflated, and the passionately restrained
scholar-saint is multiplied into a humanist community that transcends
time and place. Johnson compared the quality of Hardy's work, rather
than his moral principles, with that of Wordsworth. The terms in which
he describes both are strongly reminiscent of his portrait of the Paterian
scholar-saint. 'The works of each bring before our minds the presence of a
mind burning with passion, but strong to restrain it', he writes, continuing to describe their work as having 'that beauty of restrained art, which
enchaunts [*sic*] us beyond all the charms of an art ever prodigal and gorgeous' (180). And, characteristically, he blends what begins as a description
of style into one of temperament, while also using this type to define a
community of scholar-saints. Though 'The conclusions of the two men
are far apart [...] in both there is this concentration, this intensity, signs
of a certain spiritual temperament, to be seen in a large class of strenuous
minds' (184).

In the many critical reviews that Johnson wrote throughout his life,
he celebrated over and again this scholar-saint temperament. He also frequently described its most successful manifestations as celibate, virginal,
or cloistered, identifying its restrained disinterestedness with a wider network of values that often included productive sexual continence. Always
he tests an individual or group against his conception of 'humanity', a
kind of warm, passionate, communal sympathy that involves an initial
renunciation, restraint, or discipline. Thus he criticizes Lucian as having
'no humanity' because he has 'no reserves of silence, no secret sanctities
that he respects', and Francis Bacon because, despite having a 'haughty
reticence and restraint', his lack of humour and sympathy 'make him an
oppressive companion'.[103] Failures of restraint he, like Pater, treats less
often, but when he does an excessive sexuality is often involved. Of Marie
Bashkirtseff, described as 'a mind touched by all our modern influences',
he writes that 'the most unpleasant things in the book are her accounts of
men and of her interest in them [...]. They disgust us'.[104] Though it is true
that it is particularly female sexuality that Johnson reacts to here, still it is
difficult to feel in the context of his wider writings that a change of gender
would be of much significance.

Others, however, he praises as combining impassioned restraint with humane sympathy. He calls Saint Francis 'a saint so divinely human', with 'no sign of disease upon him'. 'His spirit', he says, 'lives wherever men and women have learned that perfect suffering, for sake of love human and divine, is perfect joy; that renunciation is enrichment'.[105] A similar enriched, joyful renunciation is found in Thomas à Kempis. His 'common-sense' and 'sense of humour' combine with his asceticism, so that he 'makes world-wide appeal with his doctrine of joy in self-denial'. He is careful always to insist that this withdrawal, this religious asceticism, is no alienation from the world, but rather a particular relationship with it. Again he quotes from Robert Louis Stevenson's 'Our Lady of the Snows', on the monastic life being 'Aloof, unhelpful, and unkind', but now uses Thomas à Kempis as a counter-example. Instead, 'A gentle beauty, with an essential sternness as its secret, belongs to the man', a manner that has endeared him to rather than alienated him from his readers.[106]

This ideal is far from limited to religious figures, though they may as religious celibates embody it with the greatest ease. He writes of Charlotte Brontë's 'intellectual and imaginative virginity', characterizing this quality not as an entire withdrawal from sensuous or communal life, but instead a special relationship with it. 'She was no "woman of the world"', he writes, 'but she was a woman of her own world, her world of the flesh as of the spirit'. Nevertheless, this 'shy, strong woman', he says, 'we might almost call the nun of English literature', though he means by this not withdrawal but discipline; she has 'vowed obedience to the precepts of her art, faithful in the letter and in the spirit, resigned to her own inspiration'.[107] The connection of the scholar-saint with virginity (though not literal in this case) is consistent with Johnson's representations elsewhere of productive continence. When writing of Virgil, therefore, it is not surprising to find him quoting Bacon's description of him as 'the chastest poet and royalest that to the memory of man is known', or elaborating on this by saying Virgil 'has a note of universality, a kinship with all the race of man'.[108] Continent sexuality and universality, or humanity, are clearly connected in Johnson's criticism, just as continent sexuality and sensuous passion were connected in his poetry, through a valuation of restraint, reserve, and discipline that often seem to stretch to include sexual behaviour.

Lionel Johnson, then, did not exactly hate the modern age. Rather, he expressed concerns about its tendency to break with the past entirely, instead of learning from that which time had shown to be most worthwhile in past eras. Johnson can, therefore, be read through his own portrait of Erasmus: 'To fling to the winds the heirlooms and rich heritage of the past because of its rusty incrustations or fungous excrescences', he wrote, 'was to him an intolerable lunacy, an exasperating frenzy, of devastation'. Instead, he advised, 'purify, elevate, restore, but do not destroy'.[109] It seems likely that Johnson would have applied this process as much to the modern age as to those of the past. And throughout his work, his understanding of problematic modernity as selfishly narrow and sensual leads also to a gentle but persistent association of his ideal of widened sympathy and artistic felicity with a vision of productive sexual continence.

CHAPTER 4

'An Ascetic Epicureanism'
Vernon Lee

'You thought poetry morally below you: are you certain that you are morally up to its level?'[1] The question is addressed by Baldwin – the fictitious interlocutor who became the star of many of Vernon Lee's dialogue essays – to a young poet, Cyril, whose views echoed those of Lee's friend and possible lover, the poet Mary Robinson.[2] Cyril doubts the moral justification of spending time writing poetry in a suffering modern world. Baldwin asserts that the poet not only occupies a morally worthwhile position, but also carries grave moral responsibility. In the discussion that follows, Baldwin introduces what he calls 'the ethics of the indecent' (257), in illustration of the moral influence that art can wield. Baldwin assumes that Cyril – and any other incidental eavesdroppers – will inevitably agree that repulsion towards non-reproductive sexuality separates 'mankind' from 'brutekind'. Literature of the past, he argues, included sex not because literature *should* include sex, but because people were 'infinitely less self-conscious, less responsible than now' (258). Their undeveloped intellects can be likened to 'a very primitive system of sewerage', poorly equipped to sift the good from bad, healthy from unhealthy. In contrast, modern readers will find that 'in our wanderings through the literature of the past, our feet are for ever stumbling into pools of filth, while our eyes are seeking for the splendid traceries, the gorgeous colours above' (259).

Baldwin can hardly be taken as an uncomplicated avatar for Lee.[3] He is a tool for the working out of hypotheses, deployed in order to test opinions for which, under her own name or even pseudonym, she may have felt compelled to acknowledge caveats and mediations. Though she admits in the preface to *Baldwin: Being Dialogues on Views and Aspirations* (1886) that 'If I am pushed into a logical corner and compelled to confess the truth, I have to admit the identity between my own ideas and Baldwin's', yet she also describes him as 'better far than I and wiser, but perhaps a little less human'.[4] Nevertheless, much of what Baldwin says about sex is repeated elsewhere in her published work. Statements concerning sexuality are common in her early (pre-1900) writing, perhaps surprisingly so for a writer who, though publishing under a male pseudonym, was widely known to be a relatively young (she was twenty-five when the above dialogue was published) and unmarried woman (though, as we saw in Chapter 1, she was certainly not alone in her feminine outspokenness at this time). Her comments on sex are also, compared with her thinking on other subjects, relatively unchanging, amounting to a clear, though not always thoroughly consistent, intellectual position on the *limited* role that sex should play in life. And throughout her work, this severely limited sexuality is closely associated with her thinking about art, especially the role that art should play in modern society.

Perhaps Lee's most infamous expression of such sentiments is to be found in *Miss Brown*, the 1884 novel in which she uses the sexual failings of 1880s British Aestheticism, as viewed by the morally and sexually pure Anne Brown, to explore a complex set of preoccupations surrounding gender, sexuality, and social duty. *Miss Brown* was, if anything, read by contemporaries as being far more thoroughly about sex (and indeed, about the Aesthetic Movement) than Lee seems to have intended, as she complained in an 1885 letter to her friend the feminist and anti-vivisection campaigner Frances Power Cobbe, who had admired the book intensely. Though she writes that 'The book has been almost universally stigmatised as a scandalous production, unfit for decent readers, & showing a most corrupt mind in the writer', readers had found in the book 'innuendoes which I never dreamed of, about things which were so much Arabic to me, often'.[5] I do not look at *Miss Brown* in detail in this chapter, because approaching the novel as pure polemic, as contemporary readers did (even, one suspects, Cobbe), does not do justice to its complexity as a literary work. Rather, in focusing on her non-fictional writing I make a case for why Lee chose to write as she did.

Sex has featured a great deal in the revival of critical interest in Vernon Lee. Following Burdett Gardner's psychoanalytical reading of Lee's 'lesbian imagination' (1987), critics both amenable and hostile towards Gardner's thesis have found both Lee's life and work to be fraught with sexual desire.[6] Her life has been portrayed as a tale of dissident, but frustrated passion for women, and her writing as the covert expression of this passion. As Jo Briggs put it in 2006, 'recent secondary literature on Lee's writing on aesthetics could be said to function as an ever more elaborate and complex "outing" of Lee's lesbian sexuality'.[7] 'The most striking thing about extant representations of Lee's sexuality', writes Sally Newman, 'is the consistency with which they describe her as a "failed lesbian"'.[8]

Criticism in the last decade has focused less on sex (though interest has certainly not disappeared altogether), with most attention going to her post-1900 psychological aesthetics and her political engagement during World War I.[9] An uneasy consensus has been reached concerning the sexual yet 'inactive' nature of Lee's relationships with women, particularly Robinson and Clementina (Kit) Anstruther-Thompson, though how far Lee herself was aware of the sexual nature of these relationships remains contentious.[10]

This supposed inactivity has not prevented critics from characterizing her writing as an expression of her sexuality. Kathy Psomiades, for example, writes of Lee having 'produced a sexually dissident lesbian aesthetics', and Stefano Evangelista has described her as both engaging with and, as a woman, reacting against a predominantly masculine and sexually dissident Aestheticism and Decadence 'in which the aesthetic ideal was created through a process of cultural-erotic negotiation between men'.[11] Whether represented as intentional on her part or not, 'sex' in Lee's work has commonly been characterized as working obliquely, needing to be carefully teased out of and detangled from her voluminous writings, or even read into that excess itself, while close attention has predominately lingered on her richly sensuous though relatively sparse fiction, rather than her extensive non-fictional writings.[12] Her explicit preoccupation with sexual morality, in contrast, has generally been attributed to early psychological damage. Vineta Colby (Lee's most recent biographer) writes of 'the burden of Puritanism that Vernon Lee carried with her'.[13] Included in this secular 'Puritanism' is Lee's assumption not only that non-reproductive sex is bad – bad for health, for social relationships, for the future of humanity – but that this badness is rationally evident. Like Gardner, Colby accounts for this anti-sex stance as a result of her childhood, though placing the emphasis less on sexual repression and more on the influence of an alternately neglectful and over-bearing mother, who 'indoctrinated' her precocious daughter with 'a rigorous personal morality that permitted of no deviations or compromise'.[14]

Lee's initial attraction to sexual continence may well owe something to her upbringing. Yet these explanations are not essential to understand the part that continence played in her work. Lee's idealizing of sexual continence is central to her theorizing about life, social ethics, and art. Her thinking on these topics is difficult to understand without a sense of their connection to her thinking about sexuality. Further, Lee's use of the idea of sexual continence to reconcile aesthetics and ethics lies comfortably within late nineteenth-century discourses. It bears evident relation to the Decadent tradition of sensuous continence, based on a practice of filtering good from bad, healthy from unhealthy embodiment. As Evangelista argues with regard to a different sexual discourse, Lee can be read as adapting a predominantly masculine aestheticism to her own ends, and so applying to her own case a tradition that often explicitly or implicitly excluded women. And the manner in which she goes about this adaptation is similar to that of the many feminist writers who reworked sexual ideas initially based on male physiology, as shown in Chapter 1. It is to this central part played by sex in Lee's overt theory, rather than the details of her life or the between-the-lines of her writing, that this chapter will attend.

After the turn of the nineteenth century a shift can be seen in Lee's work from a negative to a positive treatment of the ethics of sex and love. Lee is more interested in exploring the complex nature of love relationships (whether between people, or between people are things, nature, artwork, etc.) than Pater and Johnson. Whereas the early work most commonly uses sexual indulgence, and occasionally even romantic love, simply to illustrate ethical failure – as the most extreme case of the larger category of sensuality or abuse of the senses – later work strives to theorize what a good love relationship, incorporating the body but not what she calls 'lust', might look like. In this chapter, therefore, I give most attention to the early work, briefly indicating how its themes can be understood as developing in Lee's mature, post-1900 thinking. I begin by establishing the properties that Lee constantly associates with sexuality and love, and their place in her wider thinking, before going on to trace some of the evolutions that take place in her theories about the relationship between sexual continence and art.

Sex

The dialogue between Baldwin and Cyril, entitled 'A Dialogue on Poetic Morality' and first published in 1881, took for granted that nineteenth-century readers would consider sexual content in past literature to be 'filth'. Lee's letters evince her willingness to express similar sentiments without the protection of either dialogue-persona or pseudonym, at least at this early point in her life. In 1887 she wrote to her mother to discuss the engagement between Robinson and James Darmesteter, a Frenchman whose physical disability, despite having been acquired after birth, led the Paget family to oppose the marriage on eugenic grounds.[15] Darmesteter had agreed that the marriage was to be celibate, a point upon which Lee's brother, the poet Eugene Lee-Hamilton, was cynical. Lee-Hamilton had suggested that a Frenchman would probably intend to use contraception, inspiring Lee to write the following:

> I have long made up my mind (when reading Miss Clapperton's book I discussed it with Bella Duffy) that the common instinct which rejects all such means of indulging passion without accepting its natural consequences and burdens is perfectly correct. I consider all the French and Mrs. Besant's practices as an abomination, bringing marriage to the level of prostitution and only opening the door to unnatural wickedness (as indeed is almost statistically proven) of all kinds.[16]

All deliberately non-reproductive sex is not only to be considered as similar to 'prostitution', but also imagined as a gateway drug, leading to more 'unnatural wickedness'.[17] This was a repeat, in stronger terms, of her review of Clapperton's *Scientific Meliorism and the Evolution of Happiness* (1885), in which she claimed that 'a certain instinct that in such matters the instinct of reprobation is as healthy as it is superficially unreasonable may make one sicken at the suggestions of neo-Malthusianism'.[18]

Lee had also expressed similar sentiments a year earlier, in a letter to eugenicist Karl Pearson, who had openly encouraged inter-gender debate on questions of sexuality in his co-running of the Men and Women's Club. In objecting to his having 'not actually recommended, but at all events not blamed' proposals that contraception would control population growth, she insists on the 'instinctive' nature of what she calls 'repugnance' for such practices. 'I plead guilty', she writes, 'to extreme conservation whenever it is a question of roughly touching certain instinctive repugnances of our nature'. This time her objection is the morally corrupting effect of teaching people that they 'may eat their cake & keep it'. 'Surely', she continues, 'chastity is a virtue not merely because it prevents the earth from being over populated (or under populated, as the case may be) but because it leaves the mind freer for such feelings and enjoyments as can further, and cannot do anything except further, the happiness of the world at large'.[19]

Lee can hardly be thought to be innocent of human sexuality, as Colby has claimed.[20] In the late 1880s she was evidently reading about and openly discussing sexual questions with her friends, as well as being happy to introduce them in conversation with her family. 'Miss Clapperton' and 'Mrs Besant' are Jane Hume Clapperton and Annie Besant, both of whom were heavily involved in pro-contraception campaigning in the late nineteenth century. In the letter to Pearson she refers to 'my friend Miss Clapperton', though stating that she was 'very much opposed' to her on sexual questions, and in July 1887 she visited Clapperton in Coventry.[21] It is unlikely that Lee's reading on sexuality was confined to Clapperton and Besant: her phrase 'as indeed is almost statistically proven' suggests an acquaintance, at least, with the other side of the contraception question. Another friend involved in 'progressive' activities, but with a leaning toward continent sexuality, was Cobbe. Lee turned to Cobbe to introduce her to 'people who represent more practical interests than the aesthetes' after the scandal following the publication of *Miss Brown*.[22] To Pearson, Lee complains of 'the universal indecent prudery' of women; but by prudery she means the unwillingness of women to talk openly about sexual topics. 'I cannot but think', she asserts, 'that a great step will be gained by women becoming doctors: it will familiarise women with certain questions which they have utterly blinked [at], and it will bring to the fore a mass of information which very natural repugnances have hitherto kept back'.[23]

Lee's opinions on contraception and the rhetoric in which they are expressed closely match those of many feminist or otherwise 'progressive' writers and sympathizers in late nineteenth-century Britain, most of whom were opposed to contraception, many for the reasons that Lee puts forward. Lucy Bland has shown how women like Maria Sharpe, Lina Eckenstein, and Florence Balgarnie feared that contraception 'would push men and women back to an earlier evolutionary stage of "brute" existence in which sexual intercourse was devoid of the higher feelings of love and monogamous emotional commitment'.[24] Lee must have been very familiar with such 'progressive' discourses, whether through reading, attending lectures, or in conversation, all of which she would have had plenty of opportunity for during her visits to England in the 1880s. She would almost certainly, in the process, have been exposed to the controversy over the healthiness and productivity of sexual continence that also often animated such discussions, as shown in Chapter 1. Her comments on sexuality throughout her career contain little that was not widely stated in these contexts.

'Poetic Morality' assumes that most of its readers will concur with these opinions. Those who do not agree – Baldwin gives the example of Walt Whitman and 'men who uphold his abominations' – will be doing so, he claims, not because they really *feel* differently, but because of faulty reasoning, a 'simple logical misconception'; in this case, the false belief that whatever is inevitable, such as sexuality, is natural and therefore desirable (258). This naturalistic fallacy was certainly used by proponents of liberal sexuality against advocates for continence in the period.[25] In response, Baldwin uses evolutionary morality to argue that, on the contrary, what is natural and what is desirable are by no means the same thing; rather, mankind has not only advanced from the primitive state in which regular sexual indulgence was necessary to ensure racial survival, but must be actively encouraged to develop further:

> There is in Nature a great deal which is foul: in that which men are pleased to call unnatural, because Nature herself chastises it after having produced it: there is in Nature an infinite amount of abominable necessity and abominable possibility, which we have reason and conscience to separate from that which within Nature itself is innocent or holy (265–6).

This reasoning about Nature is a result of what Colby calls Lee's 'melioristic faith'; her belief that mankind of today has not only evolved but also progressed from mankind of the past, and can and will, with human effort, evolve into an even more perfect mankind of the future.[26] 'I believe', Lee has Baldwin say:

> that mankind as it exists, with whatever noble qualities it possesses, has been gradually evolved out of a very inferior sort of mankind or brutekind, and will, I hope, be evolved into a very superior sort of mankind. [...] I believe, in short, that we can improve only by becoming more and more different from the original brutes that we were (267).

Lee often echoes this sentiment in her non-dialectic essays. This model of development was found extensively in progressive and particularly feminist discourse, as Bland and Sheila Jeffreys have shown.[27] It was particularly championed by Clapperton, whose *Scientific Meliorism* described 'the progressive civilization to which humanity tends', though Lee disagreed with the sexual freedom that Clapperton saw this civilization including.[28] Such faith in progress, however, was not incompatible, for Lee at least, with concern that individual or collective actions may stall this otherwise inevitable movement forward.

In 'Poetic Morality', Lee is so eager to establish the current universality of what she called the 'instinct' *against* sexual indulgence that she introduces an argument that could be considered discordant with the theory that what is natural is not necessarily desirable. Reversing the common argument of the naturalness of sexual instinct, Baldwin claims that anti-sexual feeling is *itself* natural, is itself an instinct, as evinced by its having been felt by all civilized people. 'The world at large', he claims, 'ever since it has had any ideas of good and evil, has had an instinct of immorality in talking of that without which not one of us would exist, that which society sanctions and the church blesses' (261–2). Sheer continuity, he says, shows that this 'instinct' is natural and trustworthy. Havelock Ellis would make a similar argument in 1910: 'the fact that chastity, or asceticism, is a real virtue, with fine uses, becomes evident when we realize that it has flourished at all times, in connection with all kinds of religions and the most various moral codes' (though his use of 'chastity' was very different from that of Lee).[29] And Walter Pater made the same argument, in *Marius the Epicurean*, with regard to 'moderation'. Lee frequently appealed to convention, as in the above letters ('I have long made up my mind [...] that the common instinct [...] is perfectly correct'). In *Belcaro*, however, the argument from nature seems to clash with Baldwin's contention that sexuality in the past is *not* proof of its universal desirability. If the ubiquity of sexual feeling is not evidence of its desirability, how is it that ubiquitous approval for sexual continence *is* taken to constitute such evidence?

Lee recognizes this problem, and attempts reconciliation based on what she takes to be the obvious physical dangers of sexuality. *Both* sexuality and continence can, Baldwin contends, be understood as the result of instinct. But the latter can be imagined as having been developed by civilized humanity to check the effects of the former, left over from primitive mankind. This was a common argument even for those who valued sex highly: Krafft-Ebing, though claiming that 'sexual feeling is really the root of all ethics, and no doubt of aestheticism and religion', nevertheless asserted that civilization was identifiable for its 'high appreciation of virginity, chastity, modesty, and sexual fidelity', and Freud would associate civilization and sexual discipline in *Civilization and Its Discontents* (1930).[30] In making this argument, Baldwin reveals more detailed assumptions about the inherent dangerousness of sexuality both to the individual and society:

> exactly because certain instincts are so essential and indispensable, Nature has made them so powerful and excitable; there is no fear of their being too dormant, but there is fear of their being too active, and the consequences of their excess are so hideously dangerous to Nature herself, so destructive of the higher powers, of all the institutions of humanity; the over-activity of the impulses to which we owe our birth is so ruinous of all that for which we are born, social, domestic, and intellectual good, nay, to physical existence itself, that Nature even has found it necessary to restrain them by a counter-instinct – purity, chastity – such as has not been given us to counteract the other physical instincts, as that of eating, which can at most injure the individual glutton, but not affect the general social order (262).

In Baldwin's opinion (disagreement with which he assumes to be deviation either from logic or health) excessive sexuality is clearly dangerous, even 'ruinous', to physical health to the point of risking death. This individual danger is, in some unspecified but emphatic way, translated into threat to the whole social fabric.

This anxiety concerning the social threat to be feared from sexuality draws on the preoccupation of feminist writers of the period with venereal disease, from the Contagious Diseases Acts onwards, which produced many arguments for particularly male continence (most notoriously expressed in Christabel Pankhurst's *The Great Scourge and How to End It* (1913)). But Lee's language is also reminiscent of the conventional idiom of nineteenth-century sexual health literature as described in Chapter 1, and resembles, in its vague predictions of destruction, not only the melodramatic pamphlets of both purity campaigners and quacks, but also the advice of a significant portion of the mainstream medical profession. Baldwin goes on to say that 'the old intuition, now called conventionalism, which connects indecency with immorality', has been 'entirely justified' by modern science (262). Lee only uses this medical idiom, so often found in literature addressed to a male audience, when speaking through a male mouthpiece, as though she were uncomfortable with the gendered bias of a discourse developed out of a particularly *male* physiology (though it had historically been applied to female health too, as we saw in Chapter 1). Elsewhere she avoids explicitly medical language, instead formulating less embodied, and so less potentially gendered, ways of understanding the relationship between the individual and society to which the dangers of excessive sexuality are central.

The specific threat that Lee may have seen sexuality posing to 'the general social order' can be understood with reference to her larger ethics, especially her evolutionary morality. In a later dialogue, 'Honour and Evolution' (a dialogue addressing vivisection and heavily influenced by Cobbe), Baldwin explains the concept to another young friend:

> For as our physical nature has been evolved by the selection and survival of those physical forms which are in harmony with the greatest number of physical circumstances; so also has our moral nature been evolved by the more and more conscious choice of the motives including consideration for the greatest number of results from our actions, of the motives which, instead of merely enlarging the shapeless and functionless moral polyp-jelly of *ego*, work out, diversify and unify, lick into shape, the complicated moral organism of society, with all its innumerable and wondrously co-ordinated limbs and functions (*Baldwin*, 165–6).

Lee's language here combines the discourse of inevitable evolution, 'selection' and 'diversify', with that of individual volition, 'conscious choice' and 'lick into shape'. Evolutionary morality, in this definition, not only involves evolution to a more moral state, but also defines this progress as a movement from the privileging of what is good merely for the individual, to what is good for society at large.

This was also a common intellectual move. As Regenia Gagnier points out, 'Darwin himself increasingly favoured social cooperation over individualistic struggle, as the means by which *groups* achieved mastery over their habitat'. Rob Boddice has recently described how the first generation of Darwinists sought to incorporate this evolutionary approach to morality into practical life, while Bland has shown that the majority of feminists combined Darwinian morality with a discourse of 'higher' and 'lower' selves.[31] Lee, like so many others, differed from Darwin in emphasizing the active principle in this process, and therefore each individual's responsibility. In the 1894 dialogue 'The Use of the Soul', Althea – like Baldwin a dialectic pawn, supposedly representing Anstruther-Thompson, but often echoing Lee's non-dialectic writing – envisions an ideal and perfectly evolved future, in which societies consist of 'communities of individual souls', and each individual 'shall recognize duties towards our soul and body, our happiness; because our soul, and body, and happiness do not belong merely to ourselves'.[32] This responsibility resembles the eugenic duty of those reproducing to ensure their fitness: the point on which Lee and her family saw Darmesteter potentially failing. But there is an essential difference: moral health is represented as being transferred, not through sexual reproduction, but in all social interactions. 'There is no life a man may lead with one or two others which does not spread and affect the life of all and every one', Althea says in another dialogue entitled 'The Spiritual Life', 'nay, not even the life he leads with his own thoughts' (234).[33] The extension of responsibility from action to thought suggests an even wider remit for 'the ethics of the indecent'.

Lee expresses similar sentiments more directly in the preface to *Juvenilia* (1887), another collection of non-dialectic aesthetic essays. This time, instead of the meliorist progression towards perfection, Lee represents history as constant change, not always for the better. Mankind, she argues, has the power to influence the direction of this change, and ideally to push it constantly towards progression: 'For the whole of all things is ever moving, changing plan and form; and we, its infinitesimal atoms, are determining its movements. The question therefore is, in which direction shall our grain of dust's weight be thrown?'[34] For Lee, the desired direction is towards what she calls 'the ideal', an image of perfection that, though unrealizable in the present at least, she nevertheless in neo-Platonic fashion claimed to be resident in everyone, an elaboration of her previous reliance on a core of moral 'instinct' in all healthy, civilized people. In this she secularizes the morality famously voiced by George Eliot's Dorothea: 'by desiring what is perfectly good, even when we don't quite know what it is and cannot do what we would, we are part of the divine power against evil – widening the skirts of light and making the struggle with darkness narrower'.[35] In the *Belcaro* essay 'Ruskinism' Lee says:

> In the soul of all of us exists, oftenest fragmentary and blurred, a plan of harmony and perfection which must serve us as guide in our workings, in our altering and rebuilding of things[.]

This native idealism must not, she warns, fool us into thinking that any such ideal is to be found in the world: 'we must not expect that with this plan should coincide the actual arrangements of nature'. 'We must beware', she warns, 'lest we use as a map of the earth into which we have been created the map of the heaven which we seek to create' (*Belcaro* 206).[36] The distinction proper is between a 'map' of something that exists, and a 'plan' for something that should exist (though the use of the word 'map' for heaven also reminds us, Platonic fashion, that the ideal does also exist, though not in the same way as the real). But that impossibility must not stand in the way of aspiration, a word that figured prominently in the subtitles to both *Baldwin* and *Althea*.

The result of confusing the real and ideal can be seen in a letter to Robinson, in which she rebukes her friend for having called a tragic novel 'morbid'. Robinson has, says Lee, thought that her (laudable) ideals can be found in the world (literature here seems to be involved in this category), and mistakenly shuns all else. Such exaggerated idealism, she argues, produces precisely the morbidity that it seeks to avoid. 'I am more & more persuaded that we are too morally delicate, liable to catch cold, to get fever & eruptions, to bear any real tragedy now-a-days', she complains. 'We are dreadfully open to the suggestion of evil: our pores seem wondrously absorbent of it: hence our fear of a certain school of writers.'[37] In *Belcaro*, Ruskin is presented as suffering from a similar fear in relation to all art. Fear, for Lee, was never an appropriate aesthetic response, though disgust may be. Like Pater, she believed that evil must be approached boldly, in order that it might be filtered from what was good.

Given this stance on the moral responsibility of the individual and the dire effects of shirkers on society, it is unsurprising that Lee considered the individual dangers of sexuality to be translatable into social threat. Non-reproductive sexuality is therefore not only portrayed as undesirable in Lee's early work, but this undesirability is thoroughly worked into a general theory of individual and social morality that would inform her entire corpus.

Love

Sexuality beyond reproduction has no place in Lee's 'ideal' life. Love, however, occupies a central position. Her explorations of the separation of the 'ideal' from the sensual mark the beginning of Lee's efforts to theorize non-sensual love, an idea that many feminist writers valued. This alliance of sexually continent love with the ideal is expanded upon in the essay 'Medieval Love', published in *Euphorion* (1884). In 'Ruskinism' she had implored her readers to recognize both the need for the ideal, and the impurity of the actual world, so that the gap between the two might be acknowledged and human effort be enlisted in the great task of closing it. 'Medieval Love' enacts this imperative. She acknowledges the part that adultery played in the development of chivalric poetry, and the difficulty of sifting the dross left by such a heritage from the beauty it produced, before going on to trace the emergence from this genre of a poetry of ideal love typified by Dante's *Vita Nuova*. In the process she makes it clear that the two are, like humans and animals, of common origin yet estranged.

'Adultery' she calls 'a very ugly word, which must strike almost like a handful of mud in the face whosoever has approached this subject of medieval love in admiration of its strange delicacy and enthusiasm'.[38] This is the 'filth' that readers must face in exploring past literature, and even some of the beautiful sentiments in present work: 'the very feeling which constitutes the virtuous love of modern poets is derived from the illegitimate loves of the Middle Ages' (374). In contrast to this impure poetry based in adultery, she describes a genre of chivalric poetry stylistically based upon the former but born of different social conditions in which civic involvement has bred stricter sexual morality. This is, she claims, the society of Dante, who inherits the poetic forms of immoral feudal society and renders them moral, separating the vulgar from the beautiful, which happens also to be the morally ideal.

This coincidence between beauty and morality is an uneasy point for Lee. In 'Ruskinism' she argues that the two were not, as Ruskin believed, necessarily connected:

> A pure state of soul is like a pure state of body: a morbid craving is like a disease; a noble moral attitude is like a noble physical attitude; moral excellence and physical beauty are both the healthy, the perfect; but they are the healthy, the perfect, in two totally different halves of nature, and we perceive and judge them by totally different organisms (*Belcaro*, 208).

Yet she ends by admitting that while the beautiful was not necessarily good and the good not necessarily beautiful, the *similarity* in which both operated in human lives often produced apparent correspondence:

> as the moral sense hallows the otherwise egotistic relations of man to man, so also the aesthetic sense hallows the otherwise brutish relations of man to matter; that separately but in harmony, equally but differently, these two faculties make our lives pure and noble (227).

It is this 'pure and noble' ideal that Dante, in 'Medieval Love', is portrayed as filtering from the soiled poetry of chivalric love:

> to prevent such waste of what in itself is pure and precious, is the mission of another country, of another civilization […] who, receiving the new element of medieval love after it has passed through and been sifted by a number of hands shall cleanse and recreate it in the fire of intellectual and almost abstract passion, producing that wonderful essence of love which, as the juices squeezed by alchemists out of jewels purified the body from all its ills, shall purify away all the diseases of the human soul (*Euphorion*, 389–90).

The word 'pure' particularly links Lee's Platonic 'ideal' to sexual continence, though it does not refer *only* to this. Continent love is represented as both an area in which the ideal can be achieved and a catalyst for other ideal-making efforts:

> if the old lust-fattened evil of the world is to diminish rather than to increase, why then every love of man for woman and of woman for man should tend, to the utmost possibility, to resemble that love of the 'Vita Nuova' (419).

Such plainly continent love, 'a veritable platonic passion' (397), is referred to by Lee as 'ideal love', 'ideal passion', which 'has, in the noblest of our literature, made the desire of man for woman and of woman for man burn clear towards heaven, leaving behind the noisome ashes and soul-enervating vapours of earthly lust' (339). Although having been recognized in recent criticism as herself homosexual, Lee is careful here to avoid association with what she most likely knew to be an Oxford tradition of using Plato to justify and idealize male homosexuality. 'Also does there exist', she writes, 'no passion (and Phaedrus is there to prove it) so vile and loathsome as to be unable to weave about itself a glamour of ideal sentiment' (369). Referring to the *Phaedrus*, in which Plato connects his theory of idealized beauty with homosexual desire, as 'vile and loathsome', she disassociates herself from 'fleshly' interpretations of Plato, clarifying that hers is the selective idealism of the Platonic tradition favoured, for instance, by Jowett, and which admits sexual relationships only within strictly curtailed limits.[39] Of course this does not eliminate romantic relationships between women that may now be recognized as 'lesbian' despite not being sexually active.

Lee's comments on ideal love, as opposed to 'earthly lust', in 'Medieval Love' anticipate a change of emphasis in her work, from the dangers of sex to the need for love. Ideal love is described as that 'which craves for no union with its object; which seeks merely to see, nay, which is satisfied with mere thinking on the beloved one' (338). She contends that 'love should increase, instead, like that which oftenest profanes love's name, of diminishing, the power of aspiration, of self-direction, of self-restraint, which may exist within us' (420). This sounds like Pater's distinction, in the unpublished sections of *Gaston de Latour* – which he may have discussed with Lee in the 1880s, plausibly taking from the exchange as much as or more than she did, though he did not begin to write it till late in that decade – between destructive and 'kindly' love, as well as his explicit connection of the latter with sensuous continence.

Lee's later work increasingly focused on the need for a love both of people and things, which appreciates in a disinterested fashion and does not seek possession. This new emphasis begins in *Renaissance Fancies and Studies* (1895), with the essay 'Love of the Saints', in which she reconsiders the historical and aesthetic developments explored in 'Medieval Love'. Where the earlier essay had focused on the 'evil' lineage of spiritual love in adultery, the latter attends to the good created by the new insistence on love, recognizing but downplaying the attendant immorality. The distinction is instead between different kinds of continence, one positive and the other negative. The primary antecedent is eleventh-century Christian asceticism rather than courtly adultery. This asceticism, in valuing virginity for its own sake rather than for the spirituality it fosters, is shown to waste the human affection and love that can be found mixed with lust in worldly, sensual poetry. It is as if she feared that her previous essay could be read as an advocacy of continence as a good in its own right, rather than as part of a good life. She complains of eleventh-century asceticism:

> Chastity [...] becomes in this fashion that mere guarding of virginity which, for some occult reason, is highly prized in Heaven; as to clean living being indispensible for bearable human relations, which even the unascetic ancients recognised so clearly, there is never an inkling of that.[40]

The justification of 'clean living' as that which is 'indispensible for bearable human relations' is vital to Lee's thinking about social relationships. Throughout her early work she scorns monks and nuns whose celibacy is (she opines) part of a general refusal to contend with worldly evil. This selfish withdrawal ignores the inevitability of sociability: as Althea says in the dialogue 'The Use of the Soul', 'the spiritual life is no remote region of existence, it is a mode of living' (*Althea*, 281). Yet that mode of living necessitates that individuals look after their own health, both of body and soul, and neither is compatible with sexual excess. The 'clean living' that Lee advocates is the *only* condition in which civilized social relations can exist. This sociable continence is not only compatible with but also necessary to a general humane love:

> O love of human creatures, of man for woman, parents and children, of brethren, love of friends; fuel and food, which keeps the soul alive, balm curing its wounds, or, if they be incurable, helps the poor dying thing to die at last in peace (*Renaissance*, 17).

Though she includes heterosexual love here, it is for what it shares with what she more often calls 'loving-kindness'. In her subsequent work, such as *Limbo* (1897), *Laurus Nobilis* (1909), *Hortus Vitae* (1903), and *The Handling of Words* (1925), the word 'love' refers almost exclusively to an ideal attitude of disinterested appreciation of anything, from people and animals to objects, places, and art works.

Love for Lee, when it has its base in sensuality, and especially sexuality, is understood as possessive and destructive. But sexually continent love is idealized as disinterested, pure, spiritual, and – as we shall see in the next section – ironically more productive even than reproductive sex. With this understanding of sex and love, we can explore the connections that Lee draws between continence and art.

Art

Lee does not explicitly theorize the connection between sexual continence and art; but her work frequently approaches or assumes such a relationship. Like the dangers of sexuality, Lee treats this relation as a condition of any successful theory of life. One need not resort to her personal history to account for this. Lee was steeped in literature that habitually made this connection, from Carlyle, Thoreau, Emerson, and Pater to the scientific and political literature which she read throughout her life. In this section I consider her early understanding of how sense experience related to aesthetic pleasure, before examining how the same logic is used to separate sexuality from continent love. Lee associates this type of love with art, and both love and art with radical social reform, via her concept of 'the ideal'.

The influence of Pater can be seen in Lee's concern, when considering aesthetic pleasure in *Belcaro*, to separate the sensuous from the sensual. 'The artistic emotions, for instance', says Baldwin in 'The Use of the Soul', 'are incalculably complex compared with the sensual' (*Althea*, 290). In 'Ruskinism', she portrays Ruskin as weighed down by the potential immorality of seeking aesthetic experience: 'the question', as she puts it, 'of the legitimacy not of one kind of artistic enjoyment more than another, but of the enjoyment of art at all' (*Belcaro*, 199). She anticipated her reader's dismissal of this nicety: 'many of us may answer with contempt that the thinking men and women of to-day are not ascetics of the Middle Ages, nor utilitarians of the eighteenth century, nor Scotch Calvinists, that they should require to be taught that beauty is neither sinful nor useless'. But she disagrees that such teaching is unnecessary in the nineteenth century, and depicts Ruskin's preoccupation with this question as the inevitable product of his secularized society, circumstances that one could argue applied more to the sceptic Lee than the Christian Ruskin:

> For, just in proportion as the old religious faith is dying out, we are feeling the necessity to create a new; as the old vocations of belief are becoming fewer and further between, the new vocations of duty are becoming commoner; as the old restrictions of the written law are melting away, so there appears the new restriction of the unwritten law, the law of our emancipated conscience; and the less we go to our priests, the more do we go to our own inner selves to know what we may do and what we should sacrifice: with our daily growing liberty, grows and must grow, to all the nobler among us, our responsibility (199–200).

It is Ruskin's conclusion that moral good can be equated with aesthetic good that she scorns, not the questions that he asks about the potential morality or even immorality of art, questions with which she herself was preoccupied throughout her career.

These questions are asked throughout *Belcaro*, though the thinking of that collection is, as Evangelista has pointed out, Paterian rather than Ruskinian. I have argued in Chapter 2 that Pater can be (and was) read as systematically separating sensuous from sensual experience. Evangelista has described 'Ruskinism' as the point at which Lee first 'picks up the oblique revision of Ruskin made by Pater in *The Renaissance* and voices it with characteristic boldness'.[41] This can also be said of another *Belcaro* essay, 'Chapelmaster Kreisler: A Study of Musical Romanticists', though here Lee arguably adapts Pater's argument to explore the relationship of intellect to aesthetic pleasure. Lee outlines more explicitly than Pater the difference between sensuous and sensual pleasure within aesthetic experience. Whereas Pater had suggested that sensuous experience should be restrained to prevent it from becoming sensual, Lee argues that more must happen for sensuousness to become aesthetic experience. 'Art begins only where the physical elements are subjected to an intellectual process, and it exists completely only where they abdicate their independence and become subservient to an intellectual design' (*Belcaro*, 117).[42] This does not mean that sensual pleasure cannot be got from art, but merely that such pleasure is not aesthetic. Again, she distinguishes between worthwhile and sordid elements in an object and theorizes a filtering process. Though she admits that 'music owes its power over the heart to its sensuous elements as given by nature', she says that 'music exists as an art, that is to say, as an elaboration of the human mind, only insomuch as those sensuous brute elements are held in check and measure, are made the slaves of an intellectual conception' (117). Art can only be enjoyed *as art* if sensuousness is restrained and intellectualized. This intellectualization entails control rather than rejection of the body. Similar logic is used morally in the dialogue 'The Spiritual Life', where Baldwin argues that the cultivation of the soul, though 'an aim in itself', is 'a thing for whose perfection the body must be used' (*Althea*, 250). Body and senses are not rejected but controlled and utilized.

As well as drawing on a Paterian separation of the sensuous from the sensual, Lee's intellectualization of the senses through art not only renders sensuous pleasure safe, but also makes it productive. Her descriptions often approach the language of productive retention used by Pater, and by the sort of scientific and political literature that she read. As we have seen, Pater had said in 'Poems by William Morris' that 'a passion of which the outlets are sealed, begets a tension of nerve, in which the sensible world comes to one with a reinforced brilliance and relief'.[43] A similar mechanism is suggested in Lee's contention that, in enjoying art, 'it is as we should perceive the power of a tiger chained up behind a grating' (*Belcaro*, 124). Pater is writing explicitly about sex, while Lee is writing about art's relation to all sensuousness. For him the result of retention is a 'tension of nerve' that is by no means healthy, though he returned to a productively retentive mechanism more positively elsewhere. Lee's transformation of sense experience by the intellect through art, conversely, results not in agitation but serenity, the state that she frequently considered indicative of mental health. 'Nature has submitted to man, and has abdicated her power into his hands', she says of successful transformation. 'The stormy reign of instinctive feeling has come to an end; the serene reign of art has begun' (122). Lee's metaphor of the chained tiger, with its restless power, is more suggestive of Paterian retention than her general argument, which resembles Johnson's transformational mechanism, in which art allows the pleasures of sense experience to be legitimately enjoyed, though his ideal was impassioned rather than calm. Lee's gender may have meant that while a mechanism of productive retention was attractive to her, its similarity to a masculine understanding of bodily health led her to develop a transformational mechanism instead.

'Chapelmaster Kreisler' does not directly refer to sex. But its division between harmful sensual indulgence and the regenerative experience of intellectualized sensuousness is developed in 'Medieval Love', where its logic is mapped on to the division between sex and love. Lee is revising Pater's comments about chivalric literature, given in 'Poems by William Morris' and the first chapter of *The Renaissance*, 'Two Early French Stories' (in the first edition 'Aucassin and Nicolette' (1873)). Pater had, in the earlier essay, focused on the importation, from religious into secular poetry, of a love directed towards an unattainable object, thus becoming 'a passion of which the outlets are sealed'.[44] In 'Two Early French Stories', however, he had suggested that 'profane' medieval poetry did express physical sexuality, describing its spirit as embodied in the love of Abelard for Heloïse. Lee combines these approaches by splitting chivalric poetry into two generations, characterized, respectively, by sexual and continent love. The first consists 'in a certain sentimental, romantic, idealistic attitude towards women, not by any means incompatible however with the grossest animalism' (*Euphorion*, 341–2). This is consistent with her insistence on one's responsibility to acknowledge evil and ugliness, especially when it is troublingly mixed with the beautiful. To the first generation of chivalrous poets she attaches the unhealthiness that Pater (somewhat more ambiguously) attributed to the whole, though it is the unhealthiness, not of over-refinement, but of atavism, 'the grossest animalism'.

To Dante's generation, however, she allocates an ideal refinement described in a Paterian language of concentration, reminiscent both of that 'tension of nerve' and the 'hard, gem-like flame' of the 'Conclusion'. Dante's love for Beatrice is described as a 'white flame of love' that 'burned [...] strangely concentrated and pure' (339). As quoted above, she claims that these newer poets 'shall cleanse and recreate [medieval love] in the fire of intellectual and almost abstract passion, producing that wonderful essence of love which, as the juices squeezed by alchemists out of jewels purified the body from all its ills, shall purify away all the diseases of the human soul' (389). Lee again seems to be approaching a mechanism of productive retention, in which what is retained is intensified, but avoiding a masculine spermatic idiom.

Lee describes this refinement as healthy because it is idealizing. She anticipates that her readers will view such rarefied love with suspicion:

> The thought will arise that this purely intellectual love of a scarce-noticed youth for a scarce-known woman is a thing which does not belong to life, neither sweetening nor ennobling any of its real relations; that it is, in its dazzling purity and whiteness, in fact a mere strange and sterile death light, such as could not and should not, in this world of ours, exist twice over (338–39).

Yet she denies that it is either unhealthy or unreal, allowing it to symbolize the ideal as described in 'Ruskinism', the unnaturalness that is *better* than nature, created by man:

> But could such love as this exist, could it be genuine? To my mind, indubitably. For there is, in all our perceptions and desires of physical and moral beauty, an element of passion which is akin to love; and there is, in all love that is not mere lust, a perception of, a craving for, beauty, real or imaginary, which is identical with our merely aesthetic perceptions and cravings (*Euphorion*, 397).

It is possible, Lee argues, to extract this element of 'passion which is akin to love', to refine it from the sensuality with which it is so often combined and use what remains to improve (in her opinion) upon nature.

In justifying the possibility of continent 'love', therefore, Lee connects spiritual 'passion' with aesthetic experience, though her phrase 'merely aesthetic perceptions' indicates her increasing tendency to subjugate art to 'love'. In true Platonic fashion, love 'that is not mere lust' is understood as both 'a perception of' and 'a craving for' beauty that makes it 'identical with our merely aesthetic perceptions and cravings'. But she is careful to prevent this identification from being read as a necessary relationship, specifying that desire for beauty contains only 'an element of passion *which is akin* to love' (my italics). Love and art are not necessary to each other; one needn't have loved to appreciate art, though one may doubt whether one may, in Lee's formulation, really love without an aesthetic sense. But Lee then describes this ideal love as originating from art: it was, in her account, during the sifting of beautiful from profane love poetry in the twelfth century that the concept of ideal love was initially created: 'Platonic love was possible, doubly possible in souls tense with poetic wants; it became a reality through the strength of the wish for it' (399). This linking of idealism and aesthetic creative impulse suggests a radical connection between art and social reform that would be articulated in *Laurus Nobilis* (1909).

Meanwhile, the connection between continent love and art is reworked, more than a decade later than 'Medieval Love', in 'Love of the Saints'. This essay, as we have seen, reassesses material from the earlier work, but emphasizes the barren asceticism from which spiritual love emerges. Again, in reaction to Pater, she uses the story of Abelard and Heloïse to illustrate her point, representing Abelard not as the conduit of the renaissance spirit to the world, but as a cold ascetic ignorant of the new kind of love that he had inspired in Heloïse. This love, referred to, as it was with Johnson, as 'loving-kindness', potentially coexists with sensuality (though Lee is always ambivalent about this possibility, liable as she is to consider all lust to be destructive). But it is also separable from it, being what sensual love has in common with love between friends or family members, and even the love of people for animals or artworks, a theme later explored in *Hortus Vitae*. This love is more general than that of 'Medieval Love', and is explicitly said to produce art:

> Justice preached by Hebrew prophets, charity and purity taught by Jesus of Nazareth, fortitude recommended by Epictetus and Aurelius, none of these great messages to men necessarily produce that special response which we call Art. But the message of loving joyfulness, of happiness in the world and the world's creatures, whether men or birds, or sun or moon, – this message, which was that of St. Francis, sets the soul singing; and just such singing of the soul makes art (*Renaissance Fancies and Studies*, 30).

This still does not mean that all art is produced by love, though love can result in art. Lee rehearses here an assertion that she would make more explicitly in the 'Valedictory' to *Renaissance Fancies and Studies*, that art is the produce of 'surplus energy' both in societies and individuals:

> art is the outcome of a surplus of human energy, the expression of a state of vital harmony, striving for and partly realising a yet greater energy, a more complete harmony in one sphere or another of man's relations with the universe (253).[45]

She describes love as produced by similar excess. Love, she claims in 'Love of the Saints', 'gave to mankind a plenitude of happiness such as is necessary, whether reasonable or unreasonable, for mankind to continue living at all; art, poetry, freedom' (25).

'Energy' is a mysterious quantity in Lee's later work, as it was for many of her contemporaries. In 'Valedictory' she seems to be working with a Victorian idea of health as a balanced distribution of energy, a 'vital harmony', but applied, also in Victorian style, to the social rather than individual body. In 'Love of the Saints' she refines this analogy, replacing energy and harmony with 'happiness'. 'Energy' becomes important in her work following the introduction of a vitalist discourse of 'universal life', first emerging in *Althea*, expanded upon in 'Valedictory', and repeated frequently in her twentieth-century essays. It represents all intellectual and creative work, as well as spiritualized (not only continent, but disinterested and unpossessive) love, as offering access to 'the life and joy of the universe' (*Althea*, 251). She often conceptualized this interconnectedness through analogies to a bodily energy system that occasionally slip towards literalism. In the final two dialogues of *Althea*, both Baldwin and Althea represent participation in this universal 'life' as a moral imperative:

> We must direct the bulk of our vital sap upon such parts of us as transcend the mere necessities of our physical continuance, or our half-physical social comfort; on that which is over and above, which needs to grow, and whose complete development is a sort of ideal of perfection for us all, the something in which alone there is room and shelter for the greatest happiness of all (*Althea*, 249).

This rhetoric of philosophic vitalism and development suggests the philosophy of Henri Bergson. Lee's library at the British Institute at Florence contains several of Bergson's works annotated throughout.[46] But vitalist rhetoric was too common at the turn of the century to be traceable to Bergson alone. As Anne Fernihough notes, 'vitalism was such a powerful discourse amongst Edwardian radicals that it impacted upon almost every topic'. It was often combined with a liberatory sexual politics, with sex described as a connection between all life in the universe.[47] This theory was shared by George Moore (as we shall see in the next chapter) and would be seen later in D. H. Lawrence among others. Yet for Lee, as for Pater and Johnson, contact with a wider life is necessarily continent, as she increasingly connects sensuality with the individual ego and 'spirit', a quantity that includes but transcends what she earlier called 'intellect', with universal 'life'. Much as Pater in *Marius* had grouped together selfishness, sensuality, and worldliness, so Baldwin denigrates 'great minds who systematically cultivate their ego, and decline responsibilities towards other egos', regretting, 'their very gratuitous assumption that [the world] was created solely for their individual delectation; or, rather, for the delectation solely of their individual nerves, palate, sex, eyes, ears and vanity' (*Althea*, 241). Rather, he says, 'by the spirit only, by thought and feeling, can the life of one individual be welded with that of others; and only such real union as this can be fruitful of good' (257). Such union can be achieved in true friendship, but it is also 'the special, the essential use of all art and all poetry' (241).

For Lee, then, art is closely bound with sexual continence: firstly by a conception of 'the ideal' that only values a spiritualized body, though it is no less the body (this persistent embodiment, for example, allowed her to develop an embodied psychological aesthetics along with Anstruther-Thompson); and secondly by a moral system and concept of the universe that makes this 'ideal' crucial to human happiness and progress. In a later essay, 'The Use of Beauty' (1909), aesthetic pleasure would be described as 'a mysteriously ennobling quality', an ethical force providing mental and moral discipline in which lower pleasures are gradually eschewed for higher: a process which she claims Pater taught in *Marius* and *Plato and Platonism*.[48]

So far, however, this relationship between art and continence has been strangely divorced from the artist. Art is found to function in social and general 'life' in a similar way to sexual continence, and both become part of the cultivation of one's relationship with oneself that is also integral to one's relationship with others; but we have seen little about actual artistic production. The next section addresses the difficulties that Lee had with the artist's own morality, and her attempts to overcome these by redefining 'art' and, consequently, what it means to be an 'artist'.

The Artist

In the epilogue to *Euphorion*, Lee declares that each of her essays has 'its lesson of seeking certainty in our moral opinions, beauty in all and whatever our forms of art, spirituality in our love' (441).[49] But at this point in her career Lee refrains from allowing the relationship between 'beauty' and 'spirituality' to become essential, especially when located in the individual. Though the same person may be found to seek 'beauty in all and whatever our forms of art' and 'spirituality in our love', the one does not, at this point at least, necessarily imply the other. This discrepancy is particularly evident in artists. An artist, Lee reluctantly admits, can be sexually profligate and her art nevertheless beautiful.

In earlier work Lee refuses to idealize artists, a point that is made in the *Belcaro* essay 'In Umbria: A Study in Artistic Personality'. 'What', she asks, 'are the relations between the character of a work of art and the character of the artist who creates it? To what extent may we infer from the peculiar nature of the one the peculiar nature of the other?' She concludes, 'The artist and the man are not the same: the artist is only part of the man; how much of him, depends upon the art in which he is a worker' (*Belcaro*,

176–7).[50] This rejection of idealized relations between the life and art of an artist, in which the one is reflected in the other, constitutes her greatest departure from Pater in her early work.

This conception of the artist changes as Lee's conception of 'art' changes from a very limited portion even of the artwork, to a nebulous quality made up of all products of the aesthetic impulse. From *Belcaro* to *Renaissance Fancies and Studies* it constitutes part of her radical identification of 'art' with pure form. Most of *Belcaro* is dedicated to identifying what is and is not 'art', a question that she claims is dealt with unsatisfactorily by contemporary critics. 'I gradually took in the fact that most writers on art were simply substituting psychological or mystic or poetic enjoyment, due to their own literary activities, for the simple artistic enjoyment which was alone and solely afforded by art itself' (*Belcaro*, 11–2). The aesthetic, she insists, is a separate category from the psychological, social, or moral, and this insistence leads her, in 'Ruskinism', to assert the need for the aesthetic and the moral to be considered as similar, but essentially unrelated, categories. In 'In Umbria', she applies this logic to the artist's life, finding that 'the artist is only part of the man' (177). In this model, what she later has Baldwin call 'domestic arrangements', as belonging to the man rather than the artist, can have limited impact on their production of beautiful line and colour (*Baldwin*, 268).

But her determination to separate the artist's life and art breaks down whenever she considers literature. 'The artist is only part of the man', but 'how much of him, depends upon the art in which he is a worker' (*Belcaro*, 177). While 'there are some arts in which the work is produced by a very small number of faculties', there are 'others where it requires a very complex machine, which we call a whole individuality' (179). The most complex art is literary: 'this universal artist, this artistic organism which contains the whole intensified individual, is the poet' (187). Of this poet (potentially any literary artist) she admits that 'if he be impure his writings cannot be actively pure' (192).

In 'Poetic Morality' Baldwin argues that the artist plays an important social role:

> In this world there are two things to be done, and two distinct sets of people to do them: the one work is the destruction of evil, the other the creation of good [...]. And this creator of good, as distinguished from destroyer of evil, is, above all other men, the artist (241–2).

The upshot is that 'a man endowed to be an artist [...] is simply failing in his duty by becoming a practical worker' (243). The way in which the poet specifically must create good differs, however, from that of the painter, sculptor, or musician, because the poet's medium is human life, rather than line, colour, or sound:

> a sense of moral right or wrong is required in his art, as a sense of colour is required in painting. [...] as soon as a poet deals with human beings, and their feelings and doings, he must have a correct sense of what, in such feelings and doings, is right and what is wrong (250).

It is with this in mind that Baldwin launches into his illustration of the treatment in poetry of 'the ethics of the indecent', and the greater risk in indecent literature than any other indecent art. Addressed to the reader's moral sense, rather than ear or eye, sexually immoral literature can act as 'filthy narcotics, which leave the moral eyes dim, and the moral nerves tremulous, and the moral muscles unstrung' (269). The poet 'is the artist who, if he blunders, does not merely fatigue a nerve, or paralyze for a moment a physical sense, but injures the whole texture of our sympathies and deafens our conscience' (274).

Lee does have Baldwin clarify that 'I do not think that the poet's object is to moralize mankind'. He says, 'I think that the materials with which he must work are such that, while practising his art, he may unconsciously do more mischief than all the professed moralists in Christendom can consciously do good'. The poet carries 'in his moral arms the soul of the reader' across the 'soft, sinking soil (soft with filthy bogs)' of the human soul (273), a metaphor that resembles one in *Marius*, where Marius' mother bids him consider his soul as 'a white bird [...] which he must carry in his bosom across a crowded public place' (Lee's dialogue was published four years before *Marius*, and several months before Lee first met Pater).[51] But still she refrains from addressing the effect of a poet's actual conduct or sexual practice (as opposed to their inherent moral character) on their art, never mind whether the poet need be sexually continent outside the functions of procreation. Lee does not, here or elsewhere, describe the bodily functioning of the individual artist, whether imagined as working to a mechanism of productive retention or otherwise; where that mechanism is employed, it always remains abstract, and does not necessitate a bodily practice on the part of the artist. Again, it seems likely that Lee's gender made application of this logic to specific sexual bodily practice less attractive. It is therefore unclear whether the moral implications of art, and especially literary art, mean that the artist herself must be moral, and among other things sexually continent.

The question of the moral efficacy of literary art is next confronted in the dialogue 'Of Novels' (1885). Again, she avoids asking whether a literary artist has a responsibility to live in a certain way, but Baldwin does expand further on the moral responsibility of the author, again with reference to sexual morality. Here he asserts that literary arts are, because of their moral content, 'only half-arts' (205), but are not therefore valued less:

> while fiction – let us say at once, the novel – falls short of absolute achievement on one side, it is able to achieve much more, something quite unknown to the rest of the arts, on the other; and while it evades some of the laws of the merely aesthetical, it becomes liable to another set of necessities, the necessities of ethics (207).[52]

Her reassessment of the relative importance of art and morality anticipates the preface to *Juvenilia* (1887). There she distinguishes between 'the serious interests of the soul' and 'its mere pleasant pastimes', claiming to have realized, in the process of maturing, 'the relative values of these things' (5). And, as has been noticed by Evangelista and by Laurel Brake, she does so with reference to Pater, and especially *Marius*. But this preface need not be read, as by Brake, as 'hostile' to Pater.[53] Though Lee describes *Marius* as 'sunny, serene, bracing, like those first spring days' with 'its principal figure, harmonious and strong and chaste like the statue of some high-born boy priest', constituting 'the morality of the youth of such of us as are best' (unlike Pater himself, who associates youth with sexual license), she also describes later re-reading: 'Unfortunately, it is delusive, and when we come to read "Marius" a second time we feel a certain sadness, of which the book is the seemingly serene result' (8, 9). Though she is gently critical of what in *Marius* echoes *The Renaissance*, with its 'bracing', art-centric philosophy, she suggests that Pater wrote *Marius* as a conscious reassessment of this limited aestheticism (this runs counter to Pater's own account of having written *Marius* merely to explain himself better). She therefore portrays herself as following rather than overtaking Pater, though she does, characteristically, state explicitly a principle that Pater approached tentatively: namely, that social morality is ultimately more important than individual aesthetic satisfaction. Where Johnson assigned equal weight to these concerns, Lee explicitly values social responsibility above art. The question of the novel's non-aesthetic and yet highly valued content would continue to form the crux of her thinking on that genre, especially in *The Handling of Words*.[54]

The issue of the artist's personal morality reaches uneasy resolution in 'Valedictory'. There she begins to alter her concept of 'art' from pure form to something much wider. Impersonality is again stressed: 'Art is a much greater and more cosmic thing than the mere expression of man's thoughts or opinions on any one subject'. But instead of interpreting this impersonality as preserving a separate, aesthetic sphere, she posits art as a connection between the individual and 'the universal life': 'Art is the expression of man's life, of his mode of being, of his relations with the universe, since it is, in fact, man's inarticulate answer to the universe's unspoken message' (253).

The exact relationship between art, the individual, and 'the universe', and whether this 'universe' is to be understood as entirely human or containing the inhuman, is unclear. But this vitalist idiom allows her finally to justify an ideal morality in the life of the artist, without the need of firm logic. And she does so, again, through Pater. 'Thoughts such as these', she says:

> bring with them the memory of the master we have recently lost, of the master who, in the midst of aesthetical anarchy, taught us once more, and with subtle and solemn efficacy, the old Platonic and Goethian doctrine of the affinity between artistic beauty and human worthiness (255).

Goethean 'affinity' neatly implies relationship without committing to causality or necessity. She then describes Pater's career in Platonic and melioristic terms:

> By faithful and self-restraining cultivation of the sense of harmony, he appears to have risen from the perception of visible beauty to the knowledge of beauty of the spiritual kind, both being expressions of the same perfect fittingness to an ever more intense and various and congruous life (255–6).

Vitalism allows her to move beyond the coincidental, rather than essential, relationship that, in 'Ruskinism', she had drawn between physical and moral beauty, to something approaching a necessary connection based in the 'universal' quality of 'harmony'. This word reminds one that she had, a couple of pages previously, defined art as 'the expression of a state of vital harmony, striving for and partly realising a yet greater energy, a more complete harmony in one sphere or another of man's relations with the universe' (253).

She next finds in *The Renaissance*, which she values less than Pater's later work, 'a sense of caducity and barrenness, due to the intuition of all sane persons that only an active synthesis of preferences and repulsions, what we imply in the terms *character* and *moral*, can have real importance in life, affinity with life – be, in short, vital' (256). *The Renaissance* failed because it did not clearly enough recognize the 'affinity' between moral and physical beauty; though she does admit that 'even in this earliest book, examined retrospectively, it is easy to find the characteristic germ of what will develop' (257): a view of Pater's work that has more recently been developed by William Shuter.[55] Pater transcended this initial narrowness, she claims, because he realized the value of moral as well as physical beauty, and subsequently treated life in the manner of art:

his conception of art, being the outcome of his whole personal mode of existence, was inevitably one of art, not for art's sake, but of art for the sake of life – art as one of the harmonious functions of existence (259).

She refers to this 'harmony' between the physical and spiritual as the 'functional unity' of 'life' and the 'universe', a fact of which she supposes Pater was aware:

> Surely to the intuition of this artist and thinker, the fundamental unity – the unity between man's relations with external nature, with his own thoughts and with others' feelings – stood revealed as the secret of the highest aesthetics. [...] For art and thought arise from life; and to life, as principle of harmony, they must return (259–60).

And though it is still unclear how 'harmony' functions, she can now suggest a more meaningful relationship between physical and moral health and beauty than that of coincidental similarity outlined in 'Ruskinism'; in particular, 'the connection which we all feel between physical sanity and purity and the moral qualities called by the same names' (257). Weight can finally be given to the feeling, again theorized as 'intuition', that sexual continence – if we assume, in view of her other statements on similar subjects, that moral 'purity' would include this – is actually related to, rather than simply similar to, aesthetic beauty.

In the volumes of essays that followed *Renaissance Fancies and Studies – Limbo, Hortus Vitae,* and *Laurus Nobilis* – Lee embraces what she sees as Pater's conception of art as the 'outcome' of a 'whole personal mode of existence', whether or not an artwork is produced. She can therefore demand 'spirituality' in life on aesthetic as well as moral grounds. It is still possible, within this expanded system, to imagine a profligate artist producing beautiful art: but increasingly a moral life and successful art are tied together, becoming part of a unified effort towards the ideal in which there is ever less room for the sexual artist.

Miss Brown

It is less difficult than many critics suggest to read Lee's fiction as the product of similar thinking about sexuality and aesthetics as her non-fiction. In 1884 she explored, in *Miss Brown*, the physical and moral unhealthiness of English Aesthetic culture.[56] The relatively simple plot of *Miss Brown* conceals a surprisingly complex survey of gender, aesthetics, social morality, and sexuality. In the process Lee forcibly identified what she deemed the Aesthetic Movement's failure (not, it must be asserted, that of aestheticism in general) with sexual immorality. This aspect of the novel attracted outraged attention on publication and has continued to dominate readings since. She described this sexual immorality, and Anne Brown's reactions of disgust, so luridly – Henry James referred to her 'intellectual rowdyism of style' – that a reviewer described her as:

> a strong writer overloaded with knowledge, who exaggerates the area of the sexual question in life and who, in long study of early Italian literature and the history of the Renaissance, has lost touch with English feeling, and does not always know what is good to say or leave unsaid.[57]

James also questioned the space she had dedicated in her novel to sex:

> you take the aesthetic business too seriously, too tragically, and above all with too great an implication of sexual motives ... you have impregnated all those people too much with the sexual, the basely erotic preoccupation [...], perhaps you have been too much in a moral passion! That has put certain exaggerations, overstatements, *grossissements*, insistences wanting in tact, into your head.[58]

Others repeated these criticisms. In a journal entry Lee wrote:

> 'I will show fight', I said yesterday or the day before when it came home to me from the letter of Monkhouse, the talk of Benn, etc., that the anonymous reviewer in the *Spectator* was not alone in accusing me of having written what Monkhouse calls a 'nasty' book.

Lee's 'moral passion' had, these reviews suggest, been responsible for inventing the very immorality that she objected to. She herself wondered if her disgust indicated some impurity in herself. She wrote in the journal 'Benn says that I am *obsessed* by the sense of the impurity of the world ... May this be true? [...] Is my imagination corrupt?'[59] As we saw at the beginning of this chapter, however, her self-doubt did not last long.

Kathy Psomiades, in her reading of *Miss Brown* as a 'lesbian' and 'perverse aestheticist text', preserves this attentiveness to Lee's sexual disgust, as well as the logic that Lee's obsession with 'the sexual question in life' can itself be read as an 'erotic preoccupation'. Going further than James and the reviewers, Psomiades finds in Lee's very stridency a covert expression of dissident sexual desire. 'Purity' in this novel, she argues, is not continence, but a means by which female sexual dissidence can be expressed in a hostile society. Lee protested (possibly deliberately and theatrically) too much: 'The prude', Psomiades says, 'is just a pervert who refuses to admit it'. The novel's 'purity ethos', she continues, 'is both a sign of the violence performed by sexism and homophobia, and a sign of resistance to that violence, as it allows the novel to tell its shocking story anyway'.

This reading of sexual continence as sexual dissidence, in which disgust, because it is a *bodily* reaction, indicates desire (giving Anne Brown what Psomiades calls a 'Swinburnean body'), is justified for Psomiades by Lee's relationship with Pater. Picking up on Lee's description of Anne as 'sexless', she writes: 'in the context of Aestheticism, "sexless" refers not merely to the absence of sex, but to the presence of idealized same-sex desire, as in Walter Pater's essay on Winckelmann'.[60] As I argue in Chapter 2, this need not be the primary significance of Pater's use of the word 'sexless' in the Winckelmann essay, and was certainly not universally taken as such by contemporary readers.

Psomiades assumes that all bodily contact or interaction, and all embodiment of affect, is readable as sexual. This method not only allows no room for sexual continence as a legitimate signifier, but also ignores Lee's careful efforts in her non-fiction to distinguish between sexual and nonsexual embodiment in aesthetic experience. Read alongside the non-fiction, 'purity' in *Miss Brown* aligns with Lee's thinking on sexuality and aesthetics. Anne's physical disgust at the embrace of the sensual Sacha Elaguine, for example, would in Lee's own terms indicate her integral healthiness, her intuitive, physical repulsion from what may infect her both morally and physically, rather than covert expression of dissident sexual desire. This is not to say that the 'sex' identified by Psomiades is not present, but that employment of a modern understanding of sex obscures the value that the text itself attributes to sexual categories.

It is frequently claimed that the style of Lee's fiction, particularly the supernatural tales, contains an expression of sexuality that is at odds with her voiced disgust. Lee's attempts in the former to create a gorgeous, sensuous aesthetic prose in conjunction with exotic settings and blood-curdling narratives have, as we saw at the beginning of this chapter, inspired many to find in them an outlet for the sexuality that she expurgated from her life, while others see a confession of covertly liberated sexuality that has left few traces in the archive. But these tales too can be read as consistent with the theorizing of sexuality in her non-fiction, as attempts to establish a sensuous, embodied, but non-sensual aestheticism, and to push the sensuous to the limits without its tipping quite into the sensual aestheticism that she repudiates so strongly in *Miss Brown*. And as Pater disliked any limits to be put onto aesthetic experience other than those of health and love (though setting that particular bar rather higher than we would today), so Lee, though arguably expressing a far stronger sense of moral duty towards oneself and others, nevertheless harboured a sense also of the responsibility of the really moral individual to be able to deal with all subjects without being tainted by them. There is something in this of the old ideal of the incorruptible virgin, as someone whose personal cleanliness protects her during contact with the immoral: just as, in *Miss Brown*, Anne is able to keep herself 'pure' despite close contact, even marriage, with the weak and corrupt Walter Hamlin. Again, the phrase 'To the pure all things are pure' (2 Corinthians 8:15) hovers in the background.

This method of proceeding is of course not the only way to read sexuality in literary texts. But it is important to acknowledge the possibility of reading Lee's statements on 'purity', 'chastity', and the non-sensual as a network of sustained thinking about the connection between sexual continence and aesthetics: not least because such reading places Lee firmly in a particular Decadent tradition. Throughout her work she continued to integrate continence ever more closely and meaningfully with aesthetic beauty and everything that, for her, came under the heading of 'the ideal'. And she did so by engaging with a variety of late nineteenth-century discourses to each of which sexual continence was central, including a particular brand of Paterian aestheticism.

CHAPTER 5

'Men Have Died of Love'

George Moore

George Moore, unlike Walter Pater, Lionel Johnson, and Vernon Lee, spent much of his career writing joyously about sex. Although he moved in similar circles, and shared with them many aesthetic and intellectual interests, his work was notoriously sexually explicit. As a young writer in London he created a Decadent persona close to that of the narrator of his *Confessions of a Young Man* (1888), and wrote novels on such themes as adultery, alcoholism, single motherhood, and inter-class marriage. Like that of fellow Irish author Oscar Wilde, Moore's literary career was carried out at dinner tables and in drawing rooms as much as in the study. He created what Elizabeth Grubgeld has called 'a self formulated for public consumption, to be understood and "read" just as one would read his written word', and developed this persona in tandem with periodically published autobiographies.[1] His posing included frequent bragging, on and off the page, about sexual affairs, the truth of which was widely doubted. George Bernard Shaw claimed of the young Moore:

> He was always telling stories about himself and women. In every story there was a room full of mirrors and chandeliers, and the story usually ended with some woman throwing a lamp at George and driving him out of the house. Everybody used to laugh at George and no one believed him[.][2]

These stories continued in the twentieth century, though Moore had abandoned the *Confessions* persona in favour of that of a worldly avuncular bachelor figure, what Grubgeld calls the role of the 'wise fool', and Adrian Frazier a 'Don Juan of the mind'.[3]

In his autobiographical trilogy *Hail and Farewell* (1911–14), he writes: 'I am penetrated through and through by an intelligent, passionate, dreamy interest in sex, going much deeper than the mere rutting instinct'.[4] And yet at the end of this same work Moore announced his intention to embrace his increasing sexual impotence – to hasten the onset of involuntary debility with voluntary celibacy. Richard Cave has read this episode as an introduction of comedy into the otherwise touchingly serious episode of his leaving a partner, a kindly way of directing satire towards himself rather than the abandoned woman.⁵ But Moore also represents his newly continent state as having two purposes. The first is the preservation of health: 'I must cease to be your lover unless my life is to be sacrificed', he claims (vol. 3, 277). And secondly, his altered sexuality leads into the revelation of his supposed destiny: to write his great book, *Hail and Farewell*. Having moved to Ireland ten years before to join the Irish Literary Revival, he claimed that continence would allow him to write 'a work of liberation [...] liberation from ritual and priests, a book of precept and example' that would be 'a turning-point in Ireland's destiny' (361).

Impotence (whether involuntary or affected) was a position of mysterious power and authority for Moore: 'Chastity is the prerogative of the prophet', he declares, 'why no man can tell' (289). The tone is tongue-in-cheek, but Moore had a habit of taking his jokes seriously: if I seem to deal with Moore's delicate, complex tones with a too-heavy hand, it is only to accentuate the hitherto unrecognized seriousness in this jest. When he returned to England in 1911 – to escape scandal resulting from unflattering portraits of Irish literary figures in *Hail and Farewell* – sexual debility became a keynote of his public persona. In 1913 Carl Von Vechten remembers Moore having, at a dinner party, 'referred to his impotency in the most careless manner possible', and Yeats reported Moore's saying to a lady, 'how I regret, for your sake, that I'm impotent'.⁶

What did Moore hope to gain from public avowal of sexual dysfunction? Could he have been sincere in his claim that lack of sexual activity would improve both his physical and mental wellbeing and creative functioning, that it was essential to his literary career? Alongside their sexually daring content, Moore's novels also explored his career-long preoccupation with continence, from the celibate Cecilia in *A Drama in Muslin* (1886) (said to be based on Vernon Lee, whom he met at the house of Mary Robinson and described as speaking 'with extraordinary eloquence' about Pater's *Marius*)⁷ to the thrice-rewritten short story collection first entitled *Celibates* (1895), then *In Single Strictness* (1922), and finally *Celibate Lives* (1927). He was fascinated also by religious celibacy, despite (or perhaps because of) his supposed hatred of Roman Catholicism, and made it the subject of several works of fiction: the two-novel series *Evelyn Innes* (1898) and *Sister Teresa* (1901), *The Lake* (1905), and *The Brook Kerith* (1916). But these fictional examinations of celibacy are mostly negative, portraying continence as evidence of a widespread failure in life. Is it possible to reconcile this scorn for the continence of others with his portrayal of his own impotence as necessary to health, creativity, and wellbeing?

Unlike Pater, Johnson, and Lee, whose explorations of sex are relatively consistent, Moore is often openly opportunistic in his employment of sexual discourses. Like much Victorian writing about sexual health, he switched between different models of bodily function as it suited his purposes. Nevertheless, his turn from sexual promiscuity to continence can be understood as a plausible development of a lifelong pattern of thinking about art's relation to sex. An important, and hitherto unrecognized, part of Moore's thinking on this subject is his engagement with the tradition of sexually continent Decadence explored by this book. This chapter argues that this discourse – in which the artist is imagined as happy, healthy, and social – acted for Moore as a compromise between two artistic discourses that he found equally persuasive: that art was essentially and necessarily sexual, and that the artist was inevitably isolated from mankind by the principle of 'art for art's sake'.

This engagement differs interestingly from that outlined in previous chapters. Moore's pro-sexual attitude means that he is comfortable with the perception of a relationship between aesthetic and sexual experience, and so has no need to justify aesthetic pleasure by separating sensuousness from sensuality. His continence, as we will see, is closer to the Decadent sublimation described by Ellis Hanson as 'a spiritualization and an intensification of desire'.[8] He also differs in his explicit employment of a related but significantly more misogynistic, anti-domestic discourse, what Herbert Sussman calls an 'apprehension about bourgeois marriage sapping male energy and domesticity vitiating male creative potency'.[9] In the French Decadent writing that Moore spent his youth reading, there was a tradition of embracing sexual impotence as 'yet another means to prove one was not bourgeois'.[10]

But Moore's writing can also (like that of Pater, Johnson, and Lee) be read as an effort to synthesize various late nineteenth-century social, aesthetic, and sexual ideas into an ethic, a theory of living that allowed both individual self-cultivation and an ideal of communality. And although he often reaches different solutions to those explored in previous chapters, he also employs a similar discourse of productive sexual continence – in which continence is connected to personal health, sociability, and the evils of modernity (for Moore a tone of anti-individualist convention in late nineteenth-century English and Irish society) – when describing the sexuality, not of all artists necessarily but certainly of what he calls the 'great artist'. It has frequently been said that Moore cannot be read as a philosopher, and as far as systematic philosophy is concerned this is true.[11] Yet ethics are an essential part of both his writing and his strategy of self-cultivation, and while the systems he evolves are often broken, incomplete, and contradictory, it is nevertheless possible to deduce a group of consistently privileged ideas. Among these is an ideal of productive sexual continence for the great artist.

Moore is a transitional figure in the history of sexuality, blending an older discourse of productive continence with the permissiveness which, though comparatively rare in the nineteenth century, would come in the twentieth to dominate popular thinking. To untangle these discourses, I begin by examining some of the idiosyncratic connections that Moore habitually drew between sex, art, and the network of values contributory to what he calls 'humanity', essential for understanding the significance he attributes to sex in general. I then look at the points at which contradictory models of sex and the body cause Moore's theories to fracture. These tensions occur most frequently in representations of the artist's sexuality, and lead Moore to evolve an ideal of continent artistry – defined by the inward cultivation of desire through sexual reminiscence – related to, yet very different from, that of Pater, Johnson, and Lee.

Sex, Art, and Humanity

Moore had a long career in which he moved through many stylistic phases. He has been accused of lacking coherence, of exhibiting a bewildering conglomeration of styles, the majority of which can be traced to one or another of his artistic influences: his early Decadence to Baudelaire and Gautier; the Naturalism that superseded it to Zola; and the later writing composed according to his principle of the 'melodic line' to Pater and Turgenev. This 'unabashed eclecticism' has recently been reappraised as constituting Moore's importance rather than his derivativeness, and Moore himself refashioned as 'the precursor rather than the disciple', influencing writers such as James Joyce and D. H. Lawrence.[12] Grubgeld has written of the ambivalence cultivated by Moore, particularly in his autobiographical prose, as 'a self-reflective mode of narrative, one that typically queries its own explanations, thereby giving voice to both perspectives and settling upon neither'.[13] Moore evolved what many would have identified as a Paterian relationship to truth as constant flux, strengthened and modified by a Schopenhauerian vision of life as eternal struggle between competing claims. His was, as Frazier says, an art that 'cared for truth, while never believing that it can be finally found'.[14] Moore acted and wrote as if the world consisted of competing and contradictory, yet equally valid, truths.

There is a great deal yet to be said about the development of this world view and its impact upon his shifting artistic style.

But although Moore was fundamentally experimental both in style and content, his work nevertheless follows a clear trajectory. Raffaella Maiguashca Uslenghi has argued for an underlying 'unity' in Moore's artistic principles, with freedom of artistic expression, formal perfection, and a commitment to artistic integrity constituting a constant artistic ideal towards which he strove.[15] The same can be said of Moore's ethics. From the late 1880s onwards Moore, like Lee and many of their contemporaries, used the word 'life' to express the epitome of all that he valued: in his case, as in Lee's, a sense of interconnectedness between all things.[16] For Moore, 'life' by no means implied the comprehensive philosophical system that we see in the work of many others at the *fin de siècle*; the 'life force' of Shaw, the *élan vital* of Bergson, the 'life' of Nietzsche, or the Schopenhauerian 'Will' that influenced them all. Moore regularly refers to a universal energy, force, Will or rhythm, but his indiscriminate use of these terms suggests that it is the principle of *connection* between things, the fact of relationship, that Moore is primarily concerned with rather than the agent of such connection.[17]

The interconnectedness of things is, in Moore's work, most intensely figured through three concepts: art, sex, and 'humanity'. These concepts are sometimes described as if they were kinds of experience, through which an individual might access the universal 'life'. Occasionally, however, they are treated as if they were diffuse elements existing in the world, much in the same way that we saw Lee use the term 'love'. All three are essential to Moore's ideal mode of life, and are themselves intimately interconnected, so that failure in one is frequently presented as entailing failure in the others. It was primarily through these categories and the relationship between them that Moore attempted to reconcile individual liberty of experience and self-cultivation with a need to connect to a wider human community. It is also through these categories that Moore can be seen to face his biggest intellectual challenge: how to develop a model of artistic integrity and isolation that also satisfies the claims of sex and humanity.

Moore's use of the word 'sex' is both more frequent than and different from that of Pater, Johnson, and Lee. In the 1880s and 1890s, the decades in which Moore began to publish prose, the word itself was undergoing semantic change. It had previously referred to the gender of a particular person (i.e. his or her sex) or the grouping together of people with similar gender qualities (the female or male sex). Pater, Johnson, and Lee primarily use it in this manner, preferring words such as 'passion', 'sensuality', or 'love' to refer to much that we now recognize as 'sex'. But 'sex' was also increasingly used at this time to refer to any behaviour that was coloured by the fact of another person's genital organization, from copulation to a woman's pleasure in being taken in to dinner by a man, or a man's pleasure in being read to by a woman. For example, an 1895 article entitled 'Sex in Fiction' uses 'sex' to mean broadly 'the relations of the sexes'. Though this relation includes something that constitutes, in the writer's words, 'moral ravages', it must also mean more than that if, as he claims, it makes up 'a good half of human experience'.[18] From the late 1880s, Moore increasingly used the word 'sex' in this expanded, as well as in the narrower, sense. The early 1880s novels use the word primarily in reference to gender, almost always in women: 'the triumphs of her sex',[19] 'the intimate fibres of her sex',[20] 'all the characteristics of her sex'.[21] But in 1888 he uses it differently. In describing the presence of women in a Paris studio, the narrator of *Confessions* approves of 'that sense of sex which is so subtle a mental pleasure, and which is, in its outward aspect, so interesting to the eye – the gowns, the hair lifted, showing the neck; the earrings, the sleeves open at the elbow'.[22] 'Sex' has become something created and experienced between people, more specifically between a man and a woman, though both parties need not be aware. This widened 'sex' is still highly gendered. Though not unaware of sensual feelings between members of the same gender, and indeed writing about it explicitly in the story 'Hugh Monfert' (1922), Moore relates his idealized, widened 'sex' to heterosexual experience only. As we will see later in this chapter, Moore treats homosexuality as entirely outside of his privileged ideological nexus, as much alienated from 'life' as the experience of those who have never known sensual feeling.

The 1894 novel *Esther Waters*, with which Moore finally achieved popular success, avoids the word 'sex' entirely. But his next effort, the novel pair *Evelyn Innes* and *Sister Teresa*, brought a veritable orgy. From then on, and in much of his autobiographical work, 'sex' often referred to a radically expanded category of experience that, while including copulative acts, also epitomized, and sometimes offered access to, all experience that Moore believed to be worthwhile. See, for example, a passage first published in 1890, which describes a young couple dancing:

> There is no denying it, that in these moments of sex one does feel more conscious than at any other time of rhythm, and, after all, rhythm is joy. It is rhythm that makes music, that makes poetry, that makes pictures; what we are after all is rhythm, and the whole of the young man's life is going to a tune as he walks home, to the same tune as the stars are going over his head.[23]

Sex in this passage has become an example of a universal experience, as well as a way of accessing this universality.

'Humanity' is another concept that Moore never explicitly theorized, and yet burdened with meaning. Whereas Pater and Johnson had used the words 'human', 'humanities', and 'humane' to indicate a continuity with a cultural humanism to which sexual continence, at least for the few, was integral, Moore uses it to bring together apparently contradictory ideas which, though less scholarly, are not entirely alien to Pater and Johnson's visions. The first is a commitment to individualism, a creed that privileged self-cultivation over social development. For Moore, as for many of his contemporaries, the liberty to cultivate 'self' was 'humane'; he never, however, politicized this desire for liberty into what we would now call a 'human right' as many socialist individualists such as Shaw did.

Moore also, however, uses 'humanity' to indicate a universal human nature. Grubgeld has identified the competing claims of individualism and community as an animating concern in Moore's autobiographies, as he struggles to assert individual experience in the face of a late Victorian British and Irish society perceived to be constructed on collectivist lines, and in the face of his own recognition of the force of environment in shaping character: 'His wish to fully author himself is offset by a profound historical consciousness that cannot ignore the nagging probability of determinate forces outside the self.'[24] While generally agreeing with this account, I would add that in Moore's later work at least, this struggle for individual expression and cultivation in an oppressive society often gave way to an insistence upon the importance of what was common to all people in all periods. As he proclaimed faith in 'life' in post-1890s work, he more frequently gestured towards a common humanity underpinning individualism that could enable communication between very different individuals. For example, in *Memoirs of My Dead Life* (1906), he writes that 'Every character creates its own stories; we are like spools, and each spool fills itself up with a different-coloured thread' (121). But by *Avowals* (1919) the focus had shifted from the individual spool to the common thread: 'human nature does not change in essentials' and 'We are ourselves only in the pattern we weave'.[25] Individualism is still important – indeed, the impulse to individuation is itself part of common humanity – but only so far as universal humanity is acknowledged.

This vision of 'life' as interconnection is represented most clearly when Moore highlights the relations between sex and humanity. It is overtly explored in Moore's autobiographies, where it is brought into relation with another of Moore's highly valued categories: art. In *Confessions*, Moore had not yet explicitly articulated this idea of universal interconnectedness: the word 'life' is used frequently in *Confessions*, but it does not carry the metaphysical weight that it does in later work. But *Confessions* – a tribute to what Grubgeld calls the 'autogenous self', self-creation, or self-realization – already connects art, sex, and humanity. This individualism is furthered by what Moore calls 'instinct', an irrational will present from birth that guides one through life (guiding, however, along principles that are very different from Lee's 'instinct'). 'Intricate, indeed', the narrator says, 'was the labyrinth of my desires; all lights were followed with the same ardour, all cries were eagerly responded to'. Yet 'one cry was more persistent, and as the years passed I learned to follow it with increasing vigour' (2). This persistent cry is said to be art, and for this narrator, instinct and art become one impulse.

It is in *Confessions* that sex, art, and humanity first come together as mutually sustaining values. The narrator claims: 'I am a sensualist in literature. I may see perfectly well that this or that book is a work of genius, but if it doesn't "fetch me," it doesn't concern me, and I forget its very existence' (139). He goes on to equate this irrational, 'sensual' pleasure with the pleasures of sex: 'there are affinities in literature corresponding to, and very analogous to, sexual affinities' (140). Other attempts to connect art and sex reference the humanity of both. After being forced to leave Paris the narrator returns to London, where he indulges in angry musings on the neglect of art by English society. A persistent theme is the fall of 'the Tavern' and the rise of 'the Club': 'Some seventy years ago the Club superseded the Tavern, and since then all literary intercourse has ceased in London' (233). Such 'literary intercourse' is, he believes, essential to artistic culture; art cannot develop on its own but is dependent on humanity, on free communion with other artists as in the cafés of Paris. What the café and the Tavern have in common is what he calls 'Bohemianism' (287), productive of 'audacity of thought and expression' (240). Sexual liberty is implicit in this ideal, as well as anti-domesticity. He regrets that 'you can't bring a lady to a club, and you have to get into a corner to talk about them' (234), while more explicitly asking, 'If lovers were not necessary for the development of poet, novelist, and actress, why have they always had lovers?' (235–6). Comradeship and communication are needed for art to flourish, and sex is an essential part of this licence.

Against 'bohemianism' he sets 'respectability', 'the hearth', and 'the villa'. Convention in England is hostile to free human intercourse, and therefore strangles art: 'everyone can go to the tavern, and no place in England where everyone can go is considered respectable' (234). It is also hostile to sex: 'the villa made known its want', the 'certainty that nothing would come into the hands of dear Kate and Mary and Maggie that they might not read', in response to which demand 'English fiction became pure' (249). This change, he claims, was affected by circulating libraries, which in suppressing sex in literature had also suppressed humanity. Like Lee, but with very different intentions, he claims that 'Human nature has from the earliest time shown a liking for dirty stories; dirty stories have formed a substantial part of every literature' (250). In 1885 Moore expressed similar sentiments in a pamphlet entitled *Literature at Nurse; or, Circulating Morals*, a tract which, along with his pioneering of the six-shilling one-volume novel, helped to break the monopoly that circulating libraries such as Mudie's and Smith's held on English literature.[26] This criticism was undoubtedly opportunistic; both Mudie's and Smith's had banned several of Moore's novels. Yet Moore's reuse of these sentiments in *Avowals* (1919); in an article of the same year entitled 'Literature and Morals'; and finally in *A Communication to My Friends* (1933) suggests an enduring commitment well after circulating libraries had lost their hold.[27]

This free sexual and artistic intercourse is summed up in the 1916 edition of *Confessions* in the phrase 'blithe humanities',[28] suggesting that there is something essentially humane in personal artistic-sexual expression and development, in the 'self-realisation' of the artistic individual. In modern England, he claims, this atmosphere of 'communal enjoyment' and 'spontaneity' can only be found in the music hall, and it is thus there that he finds most promise for art: 'it is irritating, it is magnetic, it is symbolic, it is art. Not art, but a sign, a presentiment of art' (256). This springing up of art out of an intercourse that is represented as the expression of human nature was a note sounded repeatedly in Moore's later work: for example, his valuation in *Hail and Farewell* of the 'boon companion' (vol. 1, 57), and his adoption in *Avowals* of the dialogue form, an illustration of art as a dialectic between two artistically inclined friends.

The affinities between art, sex, and humanity are elaborated upon in *Memoirs of My Dead Life* (1906), a collection of partly new, partly revised essays which, like *Confessions*, hover between autobiography and fiction. By this time Moore's persona was decidedly less Decadent but certainly still sexually risqué. Again he explicitly connects art with sex: 'what would art be', he imagines his admired Verlaine asking, 'without life, without love?' (83). 'Life' in *Memoirs* more often has the metaphysical meaning that he tended to give it later, as can be seen in the chapter 'In the Luxemburg Gardens'. A girl, Mildred, seems to have no interests beyond men, about whom she chatters unceasingly. But the narrator cannot quite believe it: 'the thought rose up in my mind that one so interested in sex as Mildred was could not be without interest in art' (239–40). He is vindicated when Mildred unexpectedly

produces a violin and plays a stirring melody, of which he says, 'she was playing out of the great silence that is in every soul' (252). As someone with artistic talent and predilection for sexual flirtation, Mildred is not only possessed
of an essential humanity, but is also able to communicate that humanity to
others, and this regardless of the apparent triteness of her personality. Moore
finishes the chapter by claiming, 'I have written this account of [Mildred]
because it seems to me to throw a gleam into the mystery of life, without,
however, doing anything to destroy the mystery' (255).

The identification of this art-sex-humanity nexus as a 'mystery' suggests that Moore was becoming aware of the rational deficiency of his
'life', though not that he recognized this as an argument against such a
world view. He continued to use words like 'energy' and 'will' to express
a sense of interconnectedness, and to use both art and sex, especially in
conjunction, to exemplify his point. An instance of this manoeuvre can be
found in his preface for the 1907 American edition of *Memoirs*. This edition suppressed the most sexually explicit passages, to which Moore finally
agreed on the condition that he would include a preface.[29] The result was
the coyly entitled 'Apologia Pro Scriptis Meis', perhaps the most explicit
expression of his belief in the affinity between art and sex, from which the
value of humanity was never long absent.

The preface begins with a possibly fictional letter from a reader of
Memoirs (presumably English), who objects that 'Your outlook on life is
so different from mine that I can hardly imagine you being built of the
same stuff as myself', to which Moore replies: 'Let me assure you that we
are "built of the same stuff." Were it not so you would have put my book
aside.'[30] Common humanity is again revealed through art. This universal
human nature is then elaborated as a common individualism, as he regrets
'the fallacy, which till now [the correspondent] has accepted as a truth, that
there is one immutable standard of conduct for all men and all women'
(1907; xi). Instead of a common standard, Moore imagines a world in
which each individual lives to their own inevitably different moral standards. But as usual he vacillates between individualism and universality,
suggesting of the letter-writer that 'if there be no moral standard he will
nevertheless find a moral idea if he looks for it in Nature', even if 'the idea
changes and adapts itself to circumstance, and sometimes leaves us for long
intervals' (1907; xiii). Moore struggles here to accommodate both a need
for individual freedom for oneself and a need for protection from the freedom of others, and reaches for the latter in the form of an unquestionable
base standard of behaviour. Like so many other turn-of-the-century 'life'
theories, Moore's suggests not only a cosmology but also an ethic.

The word 'Nature' here is as vague as, if not more so than, the word 'life'. These fuzzy terms are often used by Moore, as by many in this period, to gesture emotively towards a revolutionary extreme without committing; that is, to suggest extremes without ruling out more moderate positions to which one could retreat if needed. Moore allows readers to decide whether by 'Nature' he means to idealize the domination of the weak by the strong that many in the period saw as a Darwinist view of Nature as competition, or whether he is indicating a more communal, mutual dependency of the kind that Darwin came to in his later work. It is a word which, conveniently for Moore, stretches to extremes of both individualism and community, and holds them in uneasy combination. In *Confessions*, a view of the world as competition temporarily won out, expressed as 'the antique world, the bare, barbarous soul of beauty and of might' (206). This idealization of the ancient world, borrowed primarily from Gautier, constituted a great part of Moore's very early artistic persona, especially when he wrote *Pagan Poems* (1881). But interconnectedness comes to the forefront in the 'Apologia'. The sexual-moral objections of his correspondent allow Moore to use sex as an example of false moral standards, with *Esther Waters* and prostitution as examples of how the world is degraded by the rejection of sex. 'We have come to speak of it as part of our lower nature', he regrets, 'permissible, it is true, if certain conditions are complied with, but always looked upon askance' (1907; xix). With sleight of hand, he then equates sexual desire with the desire for beauty, considering his correspondent as 'one incapable of the effort necessary to understand me if I were to tell him, for instance, that the desire of beauty is in itself a morality'. This he reinforces with all the weight of antiquity: 'It was, perhaps, the only morality the Greeks knew, and upon the memory of Greece we have been living ever since.' However, Greece here does not, as it did in *Confessions*, imply an ethic of competition, but rather the universal 'desire for beauty' that connects sex with art. His examples of Greek 'distributors' of this desire are Aspasia, Lais, Phryne, and Sappho, and the inclusion of a poet in this list of courtesans leads into his praise, next, of Gautier's *Mademoiselle de Maupin* as a book in which 'art and sex are not estranged' (1907; xx–xxi). Finally, describing this ideal relationship, he returns to the vocabulary of 'life':

> There is but one energy, and the vital fluid, whether expended in love or in a poem, is the same. The poet and the lover are creators, they participate and carry on the great work begun billions of years ago when the great Breath breathing out of chaos summoned the stars into being (1907; xxi).

Again, many questions are left unanswered. In what way is energy a vital fluid? Is this a common force, or a material substance? Or is it, rather, a spirituality, and the 'great Breath' a supernatural being? Otherwise, is 'great Breath' a metaphor that makes it seem more spiritual than is literally intended? Moore appears committed to keeping these questions unanswered, stressing the connection rather than defining the connecting substance. In a manner that we will see more later, his outline of art's relation to sex resembles Victorian sexual health discourses that gestured towards a vital substance lost during sex, while refraining from insisting that this substance was literally semen.

After the turn of the century, when Moore moved to Ireland and interested himself in the Irish literary scene, his ethical theories underwent minor but significant changes. Increasingly it was mystery itself, rather than an energy, fluid, or rhythm, which he figured as connecting all things. In *Avowals*, the keynotes are 'mystery' and 'the eternal', and the ultimate mystery of everything is cited as the most persuasive proof of eternality. But again, this unchanging eternality is most intensely seen in sex, art, and humanity. 'The Anglo-Saxon race cannot understand', he complains, 'that man's sexual conduct has not varied during the centuries, and cannot vary' (107). This is because 'some things are for all time and never lose their significance, being part and parcel of humanity' (108). Art, too, or at least good art, is unchanging: 'progress in aesthetics is impossible' (288). Consequently he prizes 'that sense of the eternal which gives mystery and awe to a work of art' (81). It is by this standard that he judges all artists in *Avowals*; Turgenev has it because he realizes that 'below the surface, in our instincts there is a calm immortality' (132), and Pater has it because 'in writing about Marius' he writes 'about mankind rather than about the mere individual' (193). Tolstoy, however, does not have it, and in denying the eternal becomes 'lord over what is actual and passing' (147): an inferior lordship, Moore would have us believe, to that of Turgenev and Pater. Moore was evidently attending to Pater's emphasis on the eternal over the fleeting in *Marius* and elsewhere in a way similar to that outlined in Chapter 2. Further, Tolstoy is too concerned with didactic morality for Moore: 'moral ideas are always changing, and what is wrong in one age is right in another, whereas beauty may be said to be eternal' (162). As in the 'Apologia', moral relativity is attended by the establishment of relativity itself as an eternal law of 'Nature'.

His descriptions of eternity in *Avowals*, however, lead either to contradiction or to a declaration of inexpressibility. In attempting to outline Pater's personality he concludes that he will always be 'a mystery' (210).

In later chapters he appeals to the superiority of irrational over rational truth; on Kipling he says that 'He writes with the eye that appreciates all that the eye can see, but of the heart he knows nothing, for the heart cannot be observed', and he 'has seen much more than he has felt, and we prefer feeling to seeing' (167, 170). In a fictional dialogue with American playwright John Balderston, he denies that art can be described in a logical manner. Yet 'A thing does not cease to exist because it cannot be defined'. He continues, 'Let us talk about art, and in the course of conversation you will gather my reasons' (289). The truth can only be approached through accumulation of example, of anecdote, through which the sympathetic listener will trace common feeling. This concept of truth throws much light upon Moore's use of autobiography and dialogue.

Moore, then, repeatedly suggested that sex, art, and humanity could be traced to one impulse. After about 1890 he associated this impulse with a larger conception of 'life', in which everything was similarly connected by a mysterious something, though he was reluctant to investigate the exact nature of this something, preferring more as time went on to maintain its 'mystery'. This idea of universal interconnectedness also often implied an ethic, in which Moore valued experience that promised connection, whether to other people or to the natural world. In a world where sex (in the expanded sense) was experienced as, essentially, a kind of communion, a mysterious connection regarded as one intense example of the connections between all things, an individual's alienation from it suggested a deficiency also in potential for all other forms of connection, and thus all experience of 'life'.

Moore's stories about 'celibates' – people who, for one reason or another, refrain from sexual relationships – constitute a negative expression of his understanding of sex as a universal and universalizing experience, since physical continence is shown to preclude all intimate knowledge of others, of the world, and even of oneself. Mark Llewellyn describes how, for Moore, celibacy was not simply a sexual state, but 'the ultimate form of otherness or difference which the individual consciousness feels about itself when it encounters the world around it'.[31] And each story contains a failure to either produce or appreciate art. The foundering of Mildred Lawson's painting career in Paris is unsurprising given her belief that 'in the studio a woman puts off her sex. There's no sex in art'; John Norton reflects on a woman for whom he is trying to whip up a passion that 'he hardly perceived any sex in her; she was sexless as a work of art'; and Wilfred Holmes' inability to form meaningful relationships, either with family and friends or in business, is synecdochally represented in his flute-playing, which fails because, although he can compose a melody or topline, he has no ear for harmony.[32]

Moore was evidently fascinated by celibacy's ability to confound his privileged nexus of art, sex, and humanity. When he re-wrote and added to his collection as *In Single Strictness* (1922), these personalities increasingly began to seem not quite an absolute failure, but rather a position of privileged access to the 'mystery' that he was starting to see at the heart of all 'life'. Instead of exceptions that proved the rule, his characters acted as symbols for a mysterious principle of non-communication or disruption in Moore's eternal, universal humanity. In 'Henrietta Marr', a rewriting of 'Mildred Lawson', Etta's would-be lover Morton says over her deathbed: 'and what can we know of her motives? hardly anything … very little about our own'.[33] Moore stated in the 'Advertisement' to *In Single Strictness* that these 'temperaments' (vii) are mysteriously predisposed towards continence, a condition that environment may have accentuated, but has not caused. Temperamental continence, for Moore, not only symbolizes an essential mystery in humanity, but also stands as evidence of an original, rather than acquired, absence of those qualities that he considered to be the most intense expression of 'life'.

There was another character, other than the temperamental celibate but overlapping to a certain degree with that type, who seemed to Moore to resist his required valuation of art, sex, and humanity. The good or great artist was also for Moore characterized by self-containment or self-sufficiency that was the ethical equivalent of 'art for art's sake'. As Uslenghi has shown, Moore often claimed that he 'aimed at an art free from any extraneous element and having the creation of beauty as its unique goal'.[34] This narrative, counter to Moore's valuation of art elsewhere as an example of universal impulse towards connection, combined with an alternative conception of sex and the body to produce deep tensions in Moore's thinking about the artist's sexuality. It is these tensions – between art as necessarily sexual and art as necessarily contained and separate – that led Moore to utilize a Decadent discourse of productive continence, as a form of (in his conception) non-genital sexuality that can combine artistic prowess, personal health, social influence, and an embodiment of the eternal element in humanity.

The Artist

Moore's work strained to assimilate ideals of the artist's sexuality that directly conflicted with his privileged nexus of art, sex, and humanity. While he found it easy enough to theorize the connection of art as an abstract concept to sex and humanity, his commitment to an ideal of self-contained, self-justifying art – 'art for art's sake' – was forever confounding Moore's conception of an interconnected world. This was particularly true in his considerations of the life of the artist in the world.

Moore frequently observed the tendency for the artist – particularly the great artist – to become socially and sexually isolated, and for the practical and material processes of making art to interrupt both the artist's sexuality and humanity. The artist constantly frustrated Moore's ideals of communality, in which art relies on and, he implies, expresses sex and sociality. In *Confessions* he writes: 'in me the impulse is so original to frequent the haunts of men that it is irresistible [...]. Contact with the world is in me the generating force; without this what invention I have is thin and sterile' (144–5). Yet earlier in the book he had presented a different view:

> Like the midges that fret the surface of a shadowy stream, these men and women seemed to me; and though I laughed, danced, and made merry with them, I was not of them. [...] my friend became to me a study, a subject for dissection. [...] I used him without shame, without stint. I used him as I have used all those with whom I have been brought into close contact (40, 42).

Artistic observation interrupts social interaction, which thus becomes coldly scientific, a 'dissection'. This word was often used to disparage Naturalism as a mode of naïve literary realism, and may have been meant disparagingly here. Anxiety about the detached artist was never far from Moore's work, though it is expressed in different ways. In *Memoirs* he notes that 'On account of his genius Verlaine was a little slow to see things outside of himself – all that was within him was clear, all without him obscure' (81). It is the isolation of the artist that provides much of the tension, particularly in *Confessions*, between individualism and community.

Moore frequently represented this separation as sexual as well as social. Like many others he used the words 'sterile' and 'lifeless' to describe bad art. In *Confessions* he describes Balzac and Shakespeare's styles as 'deeply impregnated with the savour of life', while George Meredith created 'sterile nuts' (271). Though ostensibly metaphorical, these pronouncements do imply a defective relationship between the bad artist and 'life' which became increasingly literal. To Moore art was clearly akin to sex, yet the artist, like the temperamental celibate, was constantly and mysteriously refusing this connection. In *Confessions* he worries over an obscure but admired musician: 'a blameless life is yours, no base thought has ever entered there, not even a woman's love; art and friends, that is all' (162).

The young Moore idealizes the musician as a prophet of artistic comrade-ship, but the equation of 'a woman's love' with 'base thought' does not chime with Moore's other writing about sex.

The potential reading of 'not even a woman's love' here as indicating homosexuality rather than continence would make little difference within Moore's sexual schema. Moore consistently associated homosexuality with temperamental celibacy. He depicted a series of male homosexual char-acters, the first of which – John Norton in *A Mere Accident* (1887) – was rewritten as 'John Norton' in *Celibates* (1895) and 'Hugh Monfert' in *In Single Strictness*. Moore claimed that these characters were based on his cousin Edward Martyn, who also featured in *Hail and Farewell*. Moore believed Martyn to be homosexual in inclination though celibate in prac-tice, and in *Hail and Farewell* Moore, in the words of Frazier, 'danced around [this], planting his brightly beribboned darts like a mincing ban-derillero around a stumbling bull'.[35] However, homosexuality was not the *kind* of sex that Moore saw as involving 'life', and so not the kind that held a kinship to art. Frazier has described Moore himself as 'a homosexual man who loved to make love to women', but his rationale is Moore's attrac-tion to non-reproductive forms of sexuality and to Paterian Aestheticism.[36] Throughout his writings Moore associates his expanded sense of sex as a universalizing experience, especially when connected to art, exclusively with women. In *Hail and Farewell* he objects to Martyn's misogyny in terms only semi-ironic: 'Without women we should be all reasonable, Edward; there would be no instinct, and a reasonable world – what would it be like? A garden without flowers, music without melody' (vol. 1, 189). Martyn's rejection of women is expressed as a rejection of all real sensuality.

The disruption that the artist caused to Moore's ethical system is evi-dent in his depiction of his relationship with Pater in *Avowals* and the 1916 preface to *Confessions*.[37] He begins in *Avowals* by praising *Marius* as an essentially 'human' book, exploring the universality of human nature rather than its individual manifestation. Yet on meeting its author, he is surprised to find that he is without Moore's highly valued 'blithe humani-ties'. Pater's manner is a 'parade of courtesy and politeness', a 'quiet, old-maidish way' that the narrator feels sure conceals a 'real self' (189–90). He describes Pater as one 'who wished above all things to preserve his real self for himself and to present to the world, even to his friends, a carefully prepared aspect – a mask' (188). By 1919 the 'mask' had become a recog-nized way of referring to Pater's personality, as James famously called him the 'mask without the face' and Gosse referred to Pater's 'courteous and gentle mask'.[38] It is now common to read the 'mask' as coded reference to

Pater's homosexuality, but Moore's emphasis is firmly upon detachment rather than its possible cause. He sets himself to overcome this withdrawal, declaring that 'to attach Pater to other human beings, to rescue him from isolation, shall be my task' (202).

In this narrative he represents himself as failing in his task. He eventually begins to 'weary of Pater – of his shyness' (209). Yet by transposing Pater's story into art, he claims that he has, in a sense, understood him, and in transmitting this understanding to others has indeed connected Pater to other people. Though in life Pater was 'a mystery to us all' (210), through imaginative sympathy, the humanity of art, he can reveal the man behind the mask. Observations of the personality of another from the outside are not, he claims, any less valid for being imaginative, as they chime with his experience of the universal humanity: 'how human', he says of Pater's *Renaissance*; 'so human that it must have been as I dreamt it' (202). And the same seems to go for Pater's inner life. Pater was 'a man who perhaps sought to open his heart to others, who wished to take the world into his confidence perhaps, but who, if he did, found himself unable even for a single unaffected friendship' (210). 'Behind the mask', Moore continues, 'that he did not lift, that he could not lift was a shy, sentimental man'. Somehow, Pater's detachment from 'life' is allowed to be consistent with artistic prowess. He was 'all powerful in written word, impotent in life' (212).

This reconciliation, however, of the socially and emotionally continent man with the 'humane' artist is not so successful as the narrator would have us believe. It chafes against all that Moore has elsewhere written about the similarities between art, sex, and humanity. In order that we may not forget that the continent artist is generally a failure, Moore intersperses his portrait of Pater in later editions of *Avowals* with comments on what he sees as the failure of James' writing due to sexual coldness. In the 1924 version Moore describes James, with reference to Matthew 19:12, as a 'eunuch' who 'made himself a eunuch in the belief that to put manhood off would give him the power to observe mankind without guile'; but 'the kingdom of heaven is not for the mutilated'.[39] Moore never directly addresses Pater's sexual orientation, though it is gestured towards, as he describes Pater at dinner struggling to entertain 'two ladies whose bosoms overflowed their bodies, large full-blown roses' (209). As with Martyn, it is the lack of interest in women and, it is implied in the flower imagery, in sensuality in general that is emphasized, rather than a potential interest in men; but it is likely that Moore was aware of the rumours concerning Pater's homosexual inclination, especially after his death.[40] Pater's writing is, after all, used as an indicator of homosexuality, though continent homosexuality, in *A Mere Accident* and 'Hugh Monfert'. Again, homosexuality does not constitute the 'sex' that Moore values, and is therefore treated as effectively equal to sexual continence in its relation to 'life'. But if James' continence makes him a bad artist, why, we may ask, does not Pater's?

The idea of Pater as a man trapped inside his own continence is undermined in Moore's narrative by the suggestion that Pater's withdrawal had been deliberate, something that he 'wished above all things'. This conscious withdrawal is explicitly addressed in the 1916 preface to *Confessions*:

> Pater always held the end in view; and his rule of life never to separate himself wholly from his art came out of an instinct; his art was to him what the nest is to the sitting bird; were he to remain away for long, he might find the nest disarrayed or himself might be changed.[41]

Though the rationale here is unclear – Moore is attempting to describe a delicate sense of artistic integrity – what is clear is that Pater has reserved himself from humanity and sex, and that this reserve is crucial to his art. The word 'instinct', so often coupled by Moore with sensuality and women, is especially important here. This theory of artistic production is not as alien to Moore as his louder statements on the importance of sex to art may suggest. In the 1907 'Apologia', alongside his declarations that 'there is but one energy, and the vital fluid, whether expended in love or in a poem, is the same', he also reports that Balzac had refrained from sex to accentuate his artistic ability, 'maintaining that great spiritual elation could be gained by restraint' (1907, xxii). Such restraint, Moore claims, need not be applied to everyone as a moral standard; we do not find Balzac 'praising chastity as a virtue, but extolling the results that may be gotten from chastity as a Yogi might' (1907, xxiii).

In the 'Apologia' he does not ask whether Balzac is right in his supposition that restraint in sex can heighten artistic ability. Elsewhere, however, Moore explicitly claims exactly that. In an 1892 article 'Sex in Art', collected in the volume *Modern Painting* (1893), Moore discusses the place that sex must take in the life of the artist. 'Sex', he writes, 'is as important an element in a work of art as it is in life; all art that lives is full of sex'.[42] So far this is consistent with the 'one energy' of the 'Apologia': but he continues, 'I do not mean that the artist must have led a profligate life; I mean, indeed, the very opposite'. He offers in explanation a radical reimagining of 'sex' that conflates it with 'life', but in a particularly materialistic form. 'I mean by sex', he says, 'that concentrated essence of life which the great artist jealously reserves for his art, and through which it pulsates'. As usual when Moore invokes 'life', and as when Lee did the same, we are left with an abundance of unanswered questions. The connection between sex and life, and their importance to art, seems tautologically clear: 'art that lives' is 'full of sex' because sex is a vital force, an intense form of 'life' (whatever that is). What is not so clear is what life or sex actually are; whether, for example, 'sex' in this sense includes intercourse, and how it is transferred into art or elsewhere. This confusion increases as Moore continues with a concession: 'Profligate, I am afraid, history proves the artist sometime to have been', and 'his profligacy is only ephemeral and circumstantial; what is abiding in him is chastity of mind, though not always of body' (222). In typical Moore fashion, what had sounded very material, even literally seminal – the phrase 'concentrated essence of life' could have been taken from a quack medical pamphlet – within a few sentences becomes much more elusive, an emotional rather than physical state, 'chastity of mind, though not always of body', reminiscent instead of Frederick Faber's anxiety over whether there may not be a '*moral* continence' as well as a physical one. In 'Sex in Art', this expansion of continence to include the mental as well as the physical aspects of sexual experience leads Moore to connect a misogynistic, anti-domestic, anti-bourgeois discourse with that of Decadent continence (to a degree foreign to Pater, Johnson, and Lee). 'It is certain', he goes on, 'that woman occupies but a small part in the life of an artist. She is never more than a charm, a relaxation, in his life; and even when he strains her to his bosom, oceans are between them' (222).[43]

Moore expands upon this theory in *Hail and Farewell*. In the first volume he admires the writer John Eglinton for his bachelor life. Though, he says, 'we are all inclined to think that man is never so much man as when he is in pursuit of the female [...] Perhaps he is never less man than at that moment' (vol. 1, 163). He continues:

> The man of whom I am dreaming, shy, unobtrusive and lonely, whose interests are literary, and whose life is not troubled by women, feels intensely and hoards in his heart secret enthusiasms and sentiments which in other men flow in solution here and there down any feminine gutter (vol. 1, 164).

Moore's attitude towards women has recently been reassessed as 'progressive', or even 'feminist'.[44] But sometimes we see his association of women with sensuality shading into misogyny. The 'feminine gutter' is evidently not a worthy receptacle for those 'secret enthusiasms and sentiments'. We see here an opposite rhetorical movement from that in 'Sex in Art'; instead of a seemingly physical continence becoming emotional, the emotional continence of a man who 'hoards in his heart' becomes material, with the seminal image of 'flow in solution'. Again we see a return of Victorian medical discourse in describing the sexuality of the artist, as relationships with women threaten a loss of something that would otherwise mature into an intense, personal, artistic experience. 'Sex in Art' claims that 'The great artist and Don Juan are irreparably antagonistic; one cannot contain the other' (222), a statement which suggests that some limitation of physical sexuality is certainly desirable in the artist. This sits uneasily with the notion that the 'chastity' required is purely an emotional erotic continence, and that an artist need merely refrain from emotional attachment to retain 'sex' for his art. It is difficult to escape the conclusion that, in Moore's representation, the good artist's life will not include much sexual activity and that his rationale for this includes, even if it is not limited to, the idea that abstinence from sexual acts has positive benefits for the artist.

Moore, however, is less anxious than Pater, Johnson, and Lee that his continence be understood as *not* sexual or sensual. While it is possible to read the continence elaborated by the other three as distinguishing between sensuous and sensual experience, no such reading of Moore's work is possible. For him, that which is contained, whether a material substance or an emotional quality, remains sexual. It is, in fact, precisely because this mysterious substance or force is imagined as part of 'sex' (in the widened sense in which he uses the term) that continence can be used to reconcile artistic withdrawal with Moore's high valuation of sex, and Moore is able to sustain his idea of sex and art as categories intimately related and enabling access to universal 'life'. In imagining continence as an intensification and redirection of sex rather than its effective bypass or transformation, Moore partakes in a shift in sexual discourse. 'Sex' was increasingly imagined as an all-encompassing quantity, moving towards what Arnold I. Davidson calls psychiatric 'sexuality' as opposed to anatomical 'sex', and its potential transformation into something else, or even total eradication, was greeted with increasing scepticism, a shift of which Freud's theory of 'sublimation' would become the most enduring product. Moore's engagement with the discourse of Decadent productive sexual continence, however, suggests a continued attraction to that discourse despite frequent repetition of seemingly contrary ideas.

This manner of conceiving of the successful artist as one who abstains from sexual acts, but in doing so retains and even intensifies something also called 'sex' which contributes towards his art, explains Moore's otherwise strange announcement of his own impotence in *Hail and Farewell*. Again Moore offers a range of contradictory explanations for his sexual debility. One was the excessive amorousness of his current lover: it 'would have been the same earlier in my life as it was now' (vol. 3, 275). Another is that he has reached a time of life when attempts at sexual activity swiftly and directly damage his health. He tells of a final attempt: 'the encounter of our lips sent the blood rushing to my head, and so violently that for ten minutes I lay where I had fallen on the sofa, holding my splitting temples. "My time for love encounters is over," I said, reaching out my hand to her sadly' (vol. 3, 287–8). The association of sexual excess with both blood and the head is particularly reminiscent of Victorian medical discourse, with its echoes of old theories concerning the relationship of semen with blood and the brain. He then represents himself as deliberately renouncing an activity that is undignified for older men. 'Love', he writes, 'is for the young and for the middle-aged, and I was growing old, the love of the senses was burning out, and it would be better to quench it by a sudden resolve than to keep blowing upon the ashes, undignified and unhealthy, the folly of fools' (vol. 3, 284). This element of choice gives the impression that Moore's impotence is, like that of Pater ('impotent in life'), at least partly elective, and so qualifies as sexual continence. William Acton had offered similar advice to the aging man: 'The ordinary rule seems to be that sexual power is not retained by the male to any considerable amount after the age of sixty or sixty-five.' Those desiring to extend sexual activity beyond this age should be warned of the threat both to their health and to that of their partners and are told that though 'no immediate mischief has yet occurred', nevertheless 'Libertinage is [...] bad enough at any age; in an elderly man it is a crime, and one that I will not lend myself to abet'.[45]

Finally, Moore considers, as if none of the previous conclusions had occurred, whether to take a wife to keep him company in old age, to have a child whom he could educate to become a great musician, and in this way to leave a legacy behind him. This fantasy quickly becomes a symbolic decision between a life of sex and sensuality, associated as usual with 'blithe humanities', and one of withdrawn and continent art. He imagines looking around a French villa (Grubgeld has indicated that often for Moore 'French is used as a secret sexual code'), the garden suggestively full of flowering but currently fruitless pomegranate trees ('*grenadier*' (vol. 3, 359)) and looking out over a town that the owner tells him is the birthplace of the infamously bawdy Rabelais.[46] He considers buying it as a home for himself and his imaginary wife and child. 'Why not?' he asks himself; but an inner voice returns the answer: 'Because *Hail and Farewell* must be written' (vol. 3, 360). He then represents himself as nobly giving up his potential family, his friends, his native country to write a book that will ironically connect him to people, particularly the people of Ireland, in a way that would be impossible without such sacrifice. *Hail and Farewell* will (he claims) 'be the turning-point in

Ireland's destiny' (vol. 3, 361), a new 'sacred book' (vol. 3, 291). This matches his earlier assertions that his new impotence, whether imposed by nature or freely chosen, will give him a new kind of influence, especially with the Irish, as 'celibacy is set above all the other virtues in Ireland'. 'Nature is not a humorist', he continues; 'She intends to redeem Ireland from Catholicism and has chosen me as her instrument, and has cast chastity upon me so that I may be able to do her work'. He draws on the common association of Decadent productive continence with the idea of 'the few and the many' to suggest that the artist's continence is necessary to the liberated sexuality of the Irish people. 'I have come', he imagines himself declaring, 'to the most impersonal country in the world to preach personality – personal love and personal religion'; but he can preach individualism in this manner only if he is himself detached, impersonal (vol. 3, 290). His melting together of different rationalizations forces his readers' attention all the more clearly towards the essential, continuous elements: that he is renouncing sex, along with some personal humanity, and expects to gain some sort of prophetical authority, a mysterious access to universal humanity which will enable him to write his masterpiece. There is clearly an element of comedy here, but with Moore it is difficult to judge where self-parody ends, if it ever ends, and seriousness begins. One may remember that Pater, Johnson, and Lee all associate continence with the universal, the general, in a way that gives one a special position and authority to speak: of Johnson's imagining himself as a continent priest guiding all humanity, and Lee's representations of continence as a way of accessing the 'general life'. One may also remember Moore's description of Pater as 'all powerful in written word, impotent in life': but what there registered as both admiration and frustration is here deliberately cultivated.

But is Moore really renouncing sex entirely, as he understands it, or just physical sexual activity? Even if 'between fifty and sixty we discover that our love-life is over and done', still, he continues, 'Our interest in sex [...] remains the same, but it is an intellectual interest, changed, transformed, lifted out of the flesh'. For Moore this interest, however 'intellectual' and 'transformed', is still 'sex' because it is directed towards women: 'Our eyes follow the movement of the body under the silken gown, a well-turned neck and shapely bosom please us, and we like to look into feminine eyes and read the feminine soul' (vol. 3, 288). As in 'Sex in Art', we see 'sex' divided into two possible manifestations: the one uncongenial towards art, but the other artistically beneficial because it is physically restrained. Throughout his work, it is possible to read Moore as playing with the idea of an artistically productive continent sexuality, particularly through his use of aesthetic reminiscence in the autobiographical form.

Memory

In 1916 Max Beerbohm caricatured Moore standing next to a tombstone, dressed in mourning clothes, with the legend:

> Elegy on <u>Any</u> Lady, by G. M.
> That she adored me as the most
> Adorable of males
> I think I may securely boast.
> Dead women tell no tales.[47]

The implication – that Moore's tales of amorous adventures were not only conveniently not provably false, but also impossible to prove as true – shows just how deeply Moore's literary and public persona had become associated with a particular type of sexual reverie, 'rooted', in Frazier's words, 'in actual relationship, but elaborated apart and away from basic family-founding acts of procreation'.[48] Moore's most sustained effort to reconcile the continent artist with the ideal of an interconnected world is identifiable in his use of this kind of sexual reminiscence. Moore was in his thirties when he wrote his first autobiography, *Confessions*. By 1905, according to Frazier, he recognized that his strength lay in this genre, though 'he never got over wanting to be a great novelist and a great playwright'.[49] As we have seen, each of his autobiographical works used the events and people of his life to weave a self-consciously artistic work, at the centre of which was his own changing persona. A core component of this persona was sexual reminiscence, regardless of whether the memories were of actual or fictional experiences. As Frazier puts it, 'The sexual impulse to rarify and prolong and decorate a desire was interwoven with the literary impulse itself', and 'in his case, art is the protraction into the future of a past desire, or into the present of a future possible desire, so that its beauty might be endlessly re-examined'.[50] Katherine Snyder has examined the bachelor attitude of sexual nostalgia or reverie as a late nineteenth-century literary motif or technique, related to a particular mode of masculinity that preserves its ambivalent relationship with both sexual transgression and normativity: 'The bachelor in his reveries is defined by the intensity of his inner life, inner life which imaginatively crosses the divides between fantasy and reality, and between self and other.'[51] Moore both takes on and parodies this role through a sexual continence that he portrays alternately as self-imposed and involuntary.

Memory was essential to Moore's conception of artistic practice. This becomes particularly explicit during his time in Ireland, when he was heavily influenced by Irish friends such as Yeats and AE (George Russell), and their emphasis on the relationship between literary narrative and oral story-telling.

But Moore's attraction to memory had long been evident. Llewellyn looks at Moore's privileging of remembered rather than immediate experience in his early poetry, while Uslenghi has shown the centrality of memory to Moore's post-1890s artistic style, an argument which Grubgeld has elaborated upon.[52] Memory, Uslenghi claims, not only allowed Moore to detach his art from all extraneous connections, but also acted as a filtering tool, allowing the artist, when representing a past event artistically, to perceive the formally necessary elements of a narrative and thus create a streamlined simplicity.[53] This relationship between the methods of art and of memory also occasionally allowed him to pass off the necessary labour of selection and reworking of art as the more involuntary filtering of memory, as seen in the preface to the 1925 edition of *Hail and Farewell*, 'Art without the Artist', in which Moore claims that the book was simply a transcription from 'Nature': 'for years I believed myself to be the author of *Hail and Farewell*, whereas I was nothing more than the secretary'.[54] Cave questions this representation of the artistic process, saying of the three-volume work that 'a studied artistry guides the seemingly artless fluctuations of the narrative'.[55]

Sexual reminiscence in Moore's work is often found alongside depreciation of marriage and reproduction, as he developed an ideal of diffuse, self-justifying sexual pleasure which, though it relied on the idea of initial experience (whether actual or fictional), was made more intense not through repeated experience, but through autoerotic acts of memory. Frazier writes that:

> Love for Moore only becomes an art when it ceases to be reproductive. He is happiest when sex is polymorphous: that is, when it is transferred from genital intercourse to touch and talk, to sight and speculation, where it can be indefinitely prolonged through thought.[56]

These comments were made in relation to Moore's personal sex life; but it is also enlightening when applied to his writing, and the indefinite prolongation of sex that he cultivated through rumination. In *Confessions*, for example, a non-reproductive ideal is defined through a Decadent antipathy to domesticity and marriage:

> Marriage – what an abomination! Love – yes, but not marriage. Love cannot exist in marriage, because love is an ideal; that is to say, something not quite understood – transparencies, colour, light, a sense of the unreal. But a wife – you know all about her – who her father was, who her mother was, what she thinks of you and her opinion of the neighbours across the way. Where, then, is the dream, the *au delà*? [...] The unknown, the unreal ... Thus love is possible. There is a delusion, an *au delà* (168, 169).

In the 1889 version here quoted, the difference between love and marriage is one of domestic familiarity and disillusion, the strangling of the imaginative ideal by everyday experience. In the 1904 edition, however, this difference is explicitly related to reproduction: 'Marriage means a four-post bed and papa and mama'. Marriage is scorned for its boring, reproductive sexuality, while the ideal relationship seems even further from consummation: 'But the woman one has never seen before', he cries, 'that one will never see again!'[57] 'Love' for the narrator of the *Confessions* is almost entirely an autoerotic experience, barely relying on another person at all, an act of imagination more than relation.

This model of non-reproductive, imaginative sexuality is returned to and expanded on in *Memoirs*. 'We humans are more complicated than animals', he writes, 'and we love through the imagination'. This time imagination is represented as contributing to an original experience, rather than constituting the whole of it: 'at least', he continues, 'the imagination stimulates the senses, acting as a sort of adjuvant' (59–60). The memoir, in this understanding of 'love', is an imaginative elaboration upon something already, in the moment of experience, heavily augmented by imagination. The long chapter entitled 'The Lovers of Orelay', in which the memory of a probably real encounter (with Maud Cunard in Aix-le-Bains, 1894) is liberally embroidered upon, is almost entirely constituted of sexual delay and temporary impotence.[58] And as accident upon accident further obstructs the movement of the couple towards consummation, a gap opens between narrator and protagonist despite the two nominally being identical, as the protagonist's frustration seems at odds with the narrator's lingering over the details of postponement. Though sexual intercourse is eventually achieved, it is constantly suggested by the narrator that the protagonist's focus on this end is degrading. As he becomes increasingly focused upon consummation, we see also his appreciation of both humanity and art degenerating. 'Wherever human beings collect', he says, 'there is always to be found somebody of interest, but when one's interest is centred in a lady everyone else becomes an enemy' (173). His interest in aesthetics and landscape suffers, as he moans 'I am in no mood to describe the Leonardo-like mountains enframing the azure bay' (174). As sex is limited to intercourse it ceases to be a communicative power, an epitome of 'life'. In another chapter, the narrator remembers visiting a lover who has grown old. He soon determines to visit her no more, to cease mitigating his memory with fresh experience. 'In order to possess her', he realizes, 'I must never see her again' (72).

Models of minimal interaction and subsequent autoeroticism through reverie are found throughout Moore's autobiographical work, though not in his fiction. This discrepancy is partly due to the autobiographical form, in which all sexual encounters are necessarily remembered ones. But it also suggests that this is an ideal not for humanity in general, for the very various people represented in his novels, but specifically for the artist. Moore is of course aware that a non-reproductive ideal cannot be carried out by a large number of people if a nation's population is to be maintained. The narrator of *Confessions* says to himself:

> But it is you who are monstrous, you who expect to fashion the whole world in conformity with your aestheticisms … a vain dream, and if realised it would result in an impossible world. A wife and children are the basis of existence (167).

Only an aesthetic elite, he suggests, can or even should realize an ideal of a detached, intellectual, or imaginative sexuality, indulged through memory more than experience.

Moore's declaration of sexual impotence in *Hail and Farewell* can be read as an attempt to reconcile sex and art by enforcing the cultivation of non-reproductive, imaginative, 'intellectual' sexuality. Reading in this way makes it possible to understand the connection he makes between his sexual continence and individualism (his preaching of 'personality – personal love, personal religion') as well as his imagining of himself as introducing contraception to Ireland, since impotence is represented as the ultimate non-reproductive sexual state. Such a reading also makes sense of his repeated assertion that continence is less aesthetically offensive than actual sexual activity, especially for an ugly man such as himself (as he claims), and after the age of fifty. Reimagining again the 'Lovers of Orelay' episode (and emphasizing especially his initial inability to consummate the relationship), he writes: 'this love-story was no frolic of nymph and satyr, but a disgraceful exhibition of Beauty and the Beast' (vol. 3, 287). Aesthetic beauty is connected not to lack of sexuality, but to a sexuality intensified and prolonged through restraint. The connection between art and sex is represented as being essentially limited to the realm of imagination, with the real experience being marred by the world's refusal to be always beautiful.

It is appropriate, therefore, that Moore follows his meditation on the advantages of continence with an explicit account of the process of writing; we are encouraged to view the narrator as one who, sexually and otherwise, reflects and represents rather than experiences. He portrays the three volumes of *Hail and Farewell* as a delicately planned artistic structure, and himself more as one who crafts this structure than as the inventor of the content: 'Any straying', he says, 'would have been fatal, so intricate are the windings of the story I had been chosen to tell' (vol. 3, 292). Between the lines of Moore's grandiose claims to have been nominated by the Gods as Ireland's saviour, we see him gradually shaping himself as a credible artist whose book, if not perhaps the 'sacred book' that he claims it to be, will plausibly be good. This episode signals the final development of Moore's persona, adopted after the publication of *Hail and Farewell*, in which the worldly uncle became a combination of the Grand Old Man of Letters and an impersonal prophet, a medium for what is universal or eternal in the world. Sexual continence was crucial to this persona.

This last evolution in Moore's character included a renewed attention to religious celibacy. Throughout his career Moore had made frequent statements against the Catholic Church to which his family belonged, including a public declaration of his apostasy in a letter to the *Irish Times* in 1903.[59] Criticism of the enforced celibacy of the priesthood and religious houses made up a large part of his vitriol. *The Lake* (1905, rewritten 1921) revolves around an Irish priest's simultaneous discovery of sex and 'life', while *Evelyn Innes* (1898, rewritten 1908) and its sequel *Sister Teresa* (1901, rewritten 1909) portray an opposite movement, with Evelyn's attraction to the convent presented as the result of her fear of both sex and 'life'. The ending to *Hail and Farewell* is also anti-Catholic in tone: 'the Irish people will listen to my exhortations now that I have become the equal of the priest, the nun, and the ox' (vol. 3, 289). But Moore's public embracing of impotence, and comparison of this state to that of religious celibacy, was more than mere mockery of Catholicism. In 1914 he travelled to the Holy Land as research for a book on the subject, and in 1916 published *The Brook Kerith*, a revision of the life of Jesus in which he does not die on the cross but is rescued and goes on to live as a shepherd in a celibate community. Moore's treatment of this community, the Essenes, is far more ambivalent than his treatment of similar subjects in earlier works. Like his later 'celibate' stories, this novel connects celibacy rather than sex with the mystery and unity at the heart of everything; the brook itself, next to which the community is established, seeming 'to rise out of the very centre of the earth'.[60] And although Jesus finally realizes that God 'put into the heart of man love of woman, and into the heart of woman love of man' because 'he wishes both to enjoy that love', this newfound tolerance does not extend to himself. Jesus remains, like Moore at the end of *Hail and Farewell*, the celibate prophet preaching the wisdom that his separation from mankind has allowed him to discover.[61]

Moore may, however, have misjudged the ability of the next generation to read his self-proclaimed impotence through this nineteenth-century discourse of productive sexual continence. He was not ignored by the younger literary elite: Virginia Woolf, reviewing a new edition of *Esther Waters,* wrote that 'Mr. Moore is a born writer; and, though great novelists are rare, of how many people in a generation can one say truthfully that?'[62] Yet those who paid court at Ebury Street in London often characterized Moore as cold and inhumane. Ford Madox Ford, for example, wrote that Moore 'seemed as aloof as if he had been a denizen of another world where there was neither sun nor wind. The impression was so strong that I was relieved that he did not remove his hand from the door knob and offer it to me'. His writings, Ford continues, offer the same impression. While admitting that they are excellently written, he complains 'you felt even mentally distressed at merely remembering the writings of George Moore – as if you were making acquaintance of what goes on in the mind behind the glacial gaze of the serpent that is the Enemy of Man'.[63] Charles Morgan (playwright and Moore's appointed biographer, though a full-length biography was never written) in his 1935 *Epitaph for George Moore* wrote of the 'physical repulsion' that some felt on visiting Moore. Morgan claims that Moore had, in the effort to squash his irresponsible former self and become instead a Great Artist, somehow sacrificed his humanity to art. 'Self-creation was the end', he says, 'self-discipline the means, and the penalty he had to pay for this everlasting labour of the spirit, compelling the man he had been to bring forth the man he would become, was an exhaustion of the vital energy given by others to the joy, the ease, the warmth, the natural humanity of living'.[64]

Osbert Burdett, in a 1915 poem called 'The Choice', attributed this inhumanity directly to Moore's sexual lack. The choice in question is between the lifestyle of George Borrow and that of George Moore. The first offers 'green lanes or corn-fields,/The steaming, hot sex of the earth'; the latter 'The life in the Temple, the lonely/The bookish, the bachelor hours'.[65] For the literary generation coming of age after the death of Victoria, sexual continence no longer so readily signalled discipline and production. They did not, it seems, generally read Moore's insistence on his impotence as evidence that he was a great artist, for whom sex had come to mean 'that concentrated essence of life' which he 'jealously reserves for his art, and through which it pulsates'. Instead, they read him as one of his own celibates, failing in humanity and art as he failed in sex, and so ultimately failing too in 'life'.

Conclusion

'Pater *won't* vote, and objects to being counted as a vote against.'[1]

Benjamin Kahan, in his study of twentieth-century celibacy, writes that 'there is a slipperiness about celibacy that we can't wrap our minds around. We always take it for a phantom or imagine it as something else'. Although the object of this book differs from Kahan's, the challenge of slipperiness remains for any discourse of sexual restraint. Kahan refers to celibacy's 'definitional instability' – 'its meanings are as variable and myriad as those of sex' – and this inherent wobbliness has its inevitable linguistic equivalent: there is no word that can unproblematically embrace all forms of sexual refusal (itself an uncomfortably negative phrase).[2] The available terms of description – restraint, celibacy, virginity, abstinence, continence, asexuality – are so racy with moral and physiological implications that their use involves an imposition of meaning upon forms of experience that frequently have surprising physiological underpinnings and unpredictable ethical associations. And then there is the difficulty of describing something so often defined by absence and silence; that can be cruelly enforced or express agency; that can serve progressive or reactionary purposes; and the very existence of which can always be doubted.

This book has sought to mitigate (temporarily, hypothetically, pragmatically) slipperiness by focusing on a relatively stable discourse, and by attempting to identify its boundaries within a literary movement. It has attempted to circumvent some of the trickier problems of object isolation (who is to say when/where/how sexual continence was practiced?) by focusing on how sex and its absence were represented and written about rather than acted upon. The result has been a novel perspective on Decadent sexuality that traces previously unexplored connections both within Decadent literature itself and with non-literary nineteenth-century writing about sexual health. Pursuing the significance given to productive sexual continence within this literature has led to authors, texts, and sometimes even paragraphs within texts that are rarely addressed in critical work on Decadent sexuality: not because they have previously been unfairly ignored or side-lined, but because the discourses explored by that work do not find their most typical expression there as does that of productive continence. The recent focus on radical queer Decadence has developed a new canon, the core texts of which are Walter Pater's earlier essays, Vernon Lee's supernatural fiction, and of course the works of Oscar Wilde. This rediscovery of a canon defined by a marginalized sexual identity serves a clear political function that it is not the business of this book to undermine. In describing a different, co-existent canon of productive continence it adds a further complexity to narratives of Decadent sexuality, including queer Decadence.

'Sex and its effects are perhaps not so easily deciphered.'[3] Foucault's warning to proponents of the repressive hypothesis should serve as a salutary motto to every study of historical sexuality. There will undoubtedly be those who are dissatisfied with the prioritizing of structuralist over deconstructive reading methods in this book, the way it focuses on delineating a discourse rather than lingering over the raggedness of its edges. The boundaries of productive continence were not by any means hard borders; just as the line separating sex from its absence is at once the strongest and weakest of lines, at almost every point this discourse bleeds into myriad other sexual discourses, some familiar to us, some very unfamiliar. It is also perhaps precisely the 'slipperiness' of continence that has made it so often attractive in the face of what to most people must seem like the more obvious discursive pleasures of sex. Chapter 1 touched on the opportunities that changing conceptions of sexuality, and the instability that this introduced within the language of continence, provided for late nineteenth-century apologists of same-sex desire to voice an identity based on socially proscribed forms of eroticism. There is ample scope for further readings that emphasize the full political potential of a discourse that could harbour such contradictory, even opposite, meanings; the way in which it allowed a writer to consciously play not only with ambiguity, but also with simultaneous inhabitancy of multiple or mutually exclusive positions.

A broader approach can be especially enlightening when exploring the work of late nineteenth- and early twentieth-century writers whose relationship to both continence and to what they so often saw as Paterian Decadence (of both the sensual and sensuous kinds) was more equivocal than that of the writers addressed here. What would a reading informed by Decadent productive continence make of the frequently puzzling sexual statements of George Bernard Shaw, Coventry Patmore, W. B. Yeats,

Frank Harris, and perhaps – above all – Henry James? Wendy Graham, rather than interpret James' life as either entirely celibate or consciously homosexual, has described him as 'one who practised sexual abstinence both to forestall nervous collapse and to conserve energy for work', suggesting a sexual practice related to the Decadent discourse of productive continence.[4] Like Moore and others – Bridges, Symonds, Yeats, and Shaw, to name a few – James can be read as continuing to assimilate various sexual models as he aged into the twentieth century, and as reconciling those with elements of nineteenth-century productive sexual continence that remained attractive even where their physiological implications were doubted. Reading his work – especially novels that consider artistic ethics such as *Roderick Hudson* (1875) and *The Tragic Muse* (1890) – as an engagement with a tradition of productive sexual continence within late nineteenth-century Decadence would bring a fresh perspective to the relationship between James' vacillating response to sexuality and his attempts to form an ethics of artistry outside of Paterian Decadence.

A similar approach can also supplement our understanding of the diffidence with which Modernist writers responded to, assimilated, and adapted Victorian models of artistry and sexuality. In 1921 Ezra Pound was, according to a biographer, 'speculating about a possible proof from natural science for his conviction that the mind was energized by the power of sex'.[5] Fascinated throughout his career with the possibility of a physical basis of artistic genius, Pound oscillated between sexual theories as the mood took him. Occasionally he references the nineteenth-century discourse of sexual continence as artistically productive, but this context has not been fully recognized by biographers, who have often read his insistence on the importance of sex to art as validating the artist's promiscuity. That another approach is possible can be seen from Pound's 1922 postscript to his translation of Remy de Gourmont's *The Natural Philosophy of Love*, in which he produced a text that reads almost as a parody of Gourmont's system-making, and at the same time as a compilation of similar attempts, from Victorian medical texts to twentieth-century anthropology and psychology. Despite a lifestyle that was far from continent, Pound nevertheless reminds us that 'man has for centuries nibbled at this idea of connection, intimate connection between his sperm and his cerebration', and offers as a contribution to the ongoing debate surrounding this idea the theory that the brain is itself made of coagulated sperm, 'a sort of great clot of genital fluid held in suspense or reserve'. This absurdly (and surely intentionally so) imitates the folk belief derided by William Acton that loss of sperm could in extreme cases entail loss of actual brain matter, and Pound acknowledges this medical heritage, writing that he is proposing only 'an idea which really surprises no one, but seems as if it might have been lying on the study table of any physician or philosopher'. From this he derives a blurred and occasionally self-contradictory theory of continence as a means to intensify energy, figuring the 'genius, the "strong-minded"' as 'discharging apparently only a surplus at high pressure' of the 'fluid' that lies in the brain.[6] He creates, by means of a fantasy physiology, a sexual theory similar to that of George Moore, in which retention and rechannelling of semen is appropriate for the male artist because it strengthens the mind, and especially the impulses in the mind that lead to the creation of art. Sexual continence results in the 'bathing of the cerebral tissues in the residuum, in *la mousse* of the life sap', and this bathing, roughly, creates the energy necessary for creation, whether sexual or artistic.

It is unclear how serious Pound was being in this postscript. By March 1922, he was apparently 'happy to dismiss most of the scientific or pseudo-scientific postulates of his "Postscript" as "various statements now anti-quated" and "speculations neither supported nor disproved"'.[7] And yet, according to one biographer, Pound's American publisher James Laughlin remembered him expounding similar theories in the 1930s, and speculated that this was why Pound always sat with his head as far back as possible: '"Fluids don't run uphill," observes Laughlin. "The poet reclined as much as possible to facilitate and increase the flow of spermatozoa from his balls to his bean"'. Whatever one's opinion on this point, it seems unlikely that the postscript could have been written without an awareness of both the nineteenth-century discourse of productive sexual continence – at least the part thereof which associated continence with artistic and intellectual gain – and its rewriting into the Freudian theory of sublimation. (This despite Pound's supposed labelling of Freud's writing as 'unmitigated shit [...] laid out in most elegant arabesques'.[8]) Attentiveness to this context can enhance readings of Pound's thinking about sexuality and art, especially when combined, for example, with his admiration for the work of Lionel Johnson, whose poems he edited and used as an example of the value of 'hardness' in poetry.[9] Can Pound's continued interest in an out-dated medical theory tell us anything about his complex relationship with the literature of the previous generation?

The 'slipperiness' of continence is, ultimately, the slipperiness of other people: their tendency to do one thing and say another; to make con-tradictory statements; to make of the discourses available to them some-thing entirely unexpected; and to vote all ways or not at all. This book has attempted to find a new coherence in the tangle of discourse that makes up Victorian writing about sexuality, and to match that to a coherence that can be found in late nineteenth-century Decadent literature. As a contribution to the already vibrant fields of the History of Sexuality and Decadent Studies, this tracing of discursive coherence should not be read as an indefensible claim to universal truth, but rather as an argument for complexity, and for the necessity of the constant writing of alternative narratives. In the words of Foucault:

> To reveal in all its purity the space in which discursive events are deployed is not to undertake to re-establish it in an isolation that nothing could overcome; it is not to close it upon itself; it is to leave oneself free to describe the interplay of relations within it and outside it.[10]

Like productive continence itself this book has (like most scholarship) played at closing in, in order to ultimately facilitate an increased freedom (or 'sense of freedom') and breadth.[11] In the spirit of Paterian 'kindly love' it hopes to give rise to an enriched understanding of Decadence, of late nineteenth-century culture, and of sexuality itself.

Notes

Introduction

1 Walter Pater, 'Hippolytus Veiled: A Study from Euripides', *Macmillan's Magazine*, 60:358 (August 1889), 294–306; 304, 301, 304, 302. Later published in *Greek Studies: A Series of Essays*, ed. Charles L. Shadwell (London: Macmillan, 1910; first published 1895), 152–86.

2 Eve Kosofsky Sedgwick, *Epistemology of the Closet* (Hemel Hempstead: Harvester Wheatsheaf, 1991), 188.

3 Yopie Prins, '"Lady's Greek" (with the Accents): A Metrical Translation of Euripides by A. Mary F. Robinson', *Victorian Literature and Culture*, 34:2 (2006), 591–618; 601.

4 See, for instance, Linda Dowling, *Hellenism and Homosexuality in Victorian Oxford* (Ithaca: Cornell University Press, 1994) and Timothy D'Arch Smith, *Love in Earnest: Some Notes on the Lives and Writings of English 'Uranian' Poets from 1889 to 1930* (London: Routledge & Kegan Paul, 1970).

5 Prins, '"Lady's Greek"', 599.

6 Lene Østermark-Johansen, 'Pater's "Hippolytus Veiled": A Study from Euripides?' in Charles Martindale *et al.*, eds., *Pater the Classicist: Classical Scholarship, Reception, and Aestheticism* (Oxford: Oxford University Press, 2017), 183–99; 189.

7 Pater, 'Hippolytus Veiled', 304. See D. G. Paz, *Popular Anti-Catholicism in Mid-Victorian England* (Stanford: Stanford University Press, 1992), 275.

8 Pater, 'Hippolytus Veiled', 304–5.

9 Heather Love, 'Exemplary Ambivalence', *Pater Newsletter: A Queer Theory Roundtable*, 52 (Spring 2007), 25–30; 26. In referring to Pater's 'circumspection and displacement', Love is quoting James Eli Adams, 'An Introduction' in Laurel Brake *et al.*, eds., *Walter Pater: Transparencies of Desire* (Greensbro: ELT Press, 2002), 1–11; 3. For more about this recent trend in Paterian Studies, see Chapter 2.

10 Benjamin Morgan, *The Outward Mind: Materialist Aesthetics in Victorian Science and Literature* (Chicago: University of Chicago Press, 2017), 134.

11 Bruce Haley, *The Healthy Body and Victorian Culture* (Cambridge, MA: Harvard University Press, 1978), 4.

12 For the history of virginity, see Anke Bernau, *Virgins: A Cultural History* (London: Granta Books, 2007) and Judith Fletcher and Bonnie MacLachlen, eds., *Virginity Revisited: Configurations of the Unpossessed Body* (Toronto: University of Toronto Press, 2007); for a more popular history of celibacy, see Elizabeth Abbott, *A History of Celibacy* (Cambridge: De Capo, 2001; first published 1999).

13 The phrase 'sexual continence' is common from the 1880s onwards. Before this, the word 'continence' was most often used alone to refer to abstinence from sexual activity. I prioritize the latter phrase partly because it is in keeping with my focus on the latter part of the century, and partly to distinguish it from the more urinary associations with 'continence' in today's usage.

14 I use the term 'non-sexual' rather than 'asexual' in order to describe the deliberate control of existing sexual feelings, rather than their absence. For an introduction to asexuality in literature and as a theoretical approach, see Karli June Cerankowski and Megan Milks, eds., *Asexualities: Feminist and Queer Perspectives* (New York: Routledge, 2014).

15 Sigmund Freud, 'Leonardo Da Vinci and a Memory of His Childhood' (originally published in German as 'Eine Kindheitserinnerung des Leonardo da Vinci', 1910), in James Strachey *et al.* ed. and trans., *The Standard Edition of the Complete Psychological Works of Sigmund Freud*, 24 vols. (London: The Hogarth Press, 1953–74), vol. 11: *Five Lectures on Psycho-Analysis; Leonardo Da Vinci; and Other Works* (1957), 63–137; 77–8, 136.

16 Freud, *ibid.*, vol. 21, *Civilization and Its Discontents* (1961, originally published in German as 'Das Unbehagen in der Kultur', 1930), 64–145.

17 Freud, 'Leonardo', 132.

18 Kate Hext, *Walter Pater: Individualism and Aesthetic Philosophy* (Edinburgh: Edinburgh University Press, 2014), 117.

19 Ellis Hanson, *Decadence and Catholicism* (Cambridge, MA: Harvard University Press, 1997), 23.

20 Jeff Nunokawa, *Tame Passions of Wilde: The Styles of Manageable Desire* (Princeton: Princeton University Press, 2003), 3, 5.

21 Pater, 'Hippolytus', 302, 301.

22 Walter Pater, *The Collected Works of Walter Pater*, 10 vols., general eds. Lesley Higgins and David Latham (Oxford: Oxford University Press, 2019–), vol. 4: *Gaston De Latour*, ed. Gerald Monsman (2019), 114.

23 Dennis Denisoff, 'Decadence and Aestheticism', in Gail Marshall, ed., *The Cambridge Companion to the Fin de Siècle* (Cambridge: Cambridge University Press, 2007), 31–52; 32, 31.

24 Richard Dellamora, 'Productive Decadence: "The Queer Comradeship of Outlawed Thought": Vernon Lee, Max Nordau, and Oscar Wilde', *New Literary History*, 35:4 (Autumn, 2004), 529–46; 529; Richard Dellamora, ed., *Victorian Sexual Dissidence* (Chicago: University of Chicago Press, 1999).

25 Stefano Evangelista, 'Vernon Lee and the Gender of Aestheticism', in Catherine Maxwell and Patricia Pulham, eds., *Vernon Lee: Decadence, Ethics, Aesthetics* (Basingstoke: Palgrave Macmillan, 2006), 91–111; 91.

26 Sara Lyons, *Algernon Swinburne and Walter Pater: Victorian Aestheticism, Doubt, and Secularisation* (London: Legenda, 2015), 9.

27 Michel Foucault, *History of Sexuality*, vol. 2: *The Use of Pleasure*, trans. Robert Hurley (London: Penguin, 1992; this translation first published 1985; originally published in French as *L'Usage des plaisirs*, 1984), 10–11.

28 Ruth Livesey, *Socialism, Sex, and the Culture of Aestheticism in Britain, 1880–1914* (Oxford: Oxford University Press, 2007), 4; Matthew Potolsky, *Decadent Republic of Letters: Taste, Politics, and Cosmopolitan Community from Baudelaire to Beardsley* (Philadelphia: University of Philadelphia Press, 2012), 10.

29 Regenia Gagnier, *Individualism, Decadence and Globalization: On the Relationship of the Part to the Whole, 1859–1920* (Basingstoke: Palgrave Macmillan, 2010), 3.

30 Harry Quilter, 'The New Renaissance; or the Gospel of Intensity', *Macmillan's Magazine*, 42:251 (September 1880), 391–400; 392.

31 For 'civic' and 'civil humanism' as moral codes, see J. G. A. Pocock, *Virtue, Commerce, and History: Essays on Political Thought and History, Chiefly in the Eighteenth Century* (Cambridge: Cambridge University Press, 1985). For the application of these codes to gender and sexuality, see Andrew Elfenbein, *Romantic Genius: The Prehistory of a Homosexual Role* (New York: Columbia University Press, 1999), 20–27. For its residual influence upon nineteenth-century sexual discourse, see Dowling, *Hellenism and Homosexuality*, 1–31.

32 Robert Buchanan, *The Fleshly School of Poetry: And Other Phenomena of the Day* (London: Strahan, 1872), 70, 19, ix, 90, 33.

33 [W. H. Mallock], *The New Republic: Or, Culture, Faith, and Philosophy in an English Country House*, 2 vols. (London: Chatto and Windus, 1877), vol. 1, 24.

34 *Ibid.*, vol. 2, 101, 178; vol. 1, 78.

35 [Robert Hichens], *The Green Carnation* (London: Heinemann, 1894), 5, 3.

36 John Addington Symonds, *The Memoirs*, ed. Phyllis Grosskurth (London: Hutchinson, 1984), 96.

37 Paz, *Popular Anti-Catholicism*, 275.

38 Katherine V. Snyder, *Bachelors, Manhood and the Novel, 1850–1925* (Cambridge: Cambridge University Press, 1999), 3.

39 Lee Edelman, *No Future: Queer Theory and the Death Drive* (Durham and London: Duke University Press, 2004), 4.

40 Sheila Jeffreys, *The Spinster and Her Enemies: Feminism and Sexuality, 1880–1930* (London: Pandora Press, 1985), 27.

41 Lesley A. Hall, 'Sexual Cultures in Britain: Some Persisting Themes', in Franz X. Eder *et al.*, eds., *Sexual Cultures in Europe: National Histories* (Manchester: Manchester University Press, 1999), 29–52; 29.

42 Pamela K. Gilbert, 'The Other "Other Victorians": Normative Sexualities in Victorian Literature', in Clark Lawlor and Andrew Mangham, eds., *Literature and Medicine: The Nineteenth Century* (Cambridge: Cambridge University Press, 2021), 211–29; 211.

43 Walter Pater, *The Renaissance: Studies in Art and Poetry: The 1893 Text*, ed. Donald Hill (Berkeley: University of California Press, 1980; first published 1873), xix–xx.

44 W. S. Lilly, 'The New Gospel', *Time*, 1 (May 1879), 169–75; 175.

45 Frank Harris, 'Walter Pater', in *Contemporary Portraits: Second Series* (New York: Frank Harris, 1919), 203–26; 203.

46 Frank Harris, *My Life and Loves*, 5 vols. (London: W. H. Allen, 1964).

47 Edgar Jepson, *Memories of a Victorian* (London: Victor Gollancz, 1933), 102. The phrase 'monochronos hedonist' or 'hedonism' was in common use in Victorian classical scholarship to describe the Cyrenaic privileging of momentary and bodily pleasure over the intellectual pleasure of Plato. Pater uses a version of it in the 'New Cyrenaicism' chapter of *Marius the Epicurean*: 'one who had taken for his philosophic ideal the μονόχρονος ἡδονή of Aristippus – the pleasure of the ideal present, of the mystic *now*' (Walter Pater, *Marius the Epicurean: His Sensations and Ideas*, 2 vols. (London: Macmillan, 1910; first published 1885), vol. 1, 154). Oscar Wilde also uses the phrase to refer to 'the divine μονόχρονος ἡδονή of another cigarette' (Oscar Wilde, 'The Critic as Artist', in *The Complete Works of Oscar Wilde*, general eds. Ian Small and Russell Jackson, 7 vols. (Oxford: Oxford University Press, 2000–13) vol. 4: *Intentions*, ed. Josephine M. Guy (2006; first published 1891), 123–206; 142. Jepson's use seems closer to that of Wilde than that of Pater.

48 Edmund Gosse, 'Walter Pater', in *Critical Kit-Kats* (London: William Heinemann, 1896), 239–72; 258.

49 [Mallock], *The New Republic*, vol. 2, 139.

50 Richard Le Gallienne, *Young Lives* (London: The Bodley Head, 1899), 155–60.

51 *Ibid.*, 160. See Pater, *Marius the Epicurean*, vol. 1, 187.

52 T. S. Eliot, 'Arnold and Pater' in *Selected Essays* (London: Faber & Faber, 1999; essay first published 1932), 431–43; 431.

53 W. B. Yeats, *The Collected Works of W. B. Yeats*, 14 vols., general eds. Richard J. Finneran and George Mills Harper (New York: Scribner, 1984–), vol. 3: *Autobiographies*, eds. William H. O'Donnell and Douglas N. Archibald (1999; this section first published 1922), 335.

54 *Ibid.*, 235; W. B. Yeats, *Memoirs*, ed. Denis Donoghue (London: Macmillan, 1972), 97.

55 Yeats, *Autobiographies*, 235.

56 Lionel Johnson, 'Mr. Pater's Humour', in Thomas Whittemore, ed., *Post Liminium: Essays and Critical Papers* (London: Elkin Mathews, 1912), 11–14; 11.

57 Richard Le Gallienne, *The Romantic '90s* (New York: Doubleday, Page & Co: 1925), 98.

58 Catherine Maxwell, *Second Sight: The Visionary Imagination in Late Victorian Literature* (Manchester: Manchester University Press, 2008), 73.

59 Arthur Galton, 'Walter Pater', in *Acer In Hostem* (Windermere: A. W. Johnson & Sons, 1913), 37–43; 37.

60 Johnson, 'The Work of Mr. Pater', in *Post Liminium*, 19–41; 29, 30.

61 A. C. Benson, *Walter Pater* (London: Macmillan, 1906), 27, 204, 86.

62　For Benson's own sexuality and his private comments on that of Pater, see Laurel Brake, 'Judas and the Widow: Thomas Wright and A. C. Benson as Biographers of Walter Pater: The Widow', *Prose Studies: History, Theory, Criticism*, 4:1 (1981), 39–54.

63　Benson, *Walter Pater*, 203; Harris, 'Walter Pater', 222; Gosse, 'Walter Pater', 266.

64　Gosse, 'Walter Pater', 267; Le Gallienne, *The Romantic '90s*, 101.

65　Oliver S. Buckton, *Secret Selves: Confession and Same-Sex Desire in Victorian Autobiography* (Chapel Hill: University of North Carolina Press, 1998), 39.

66　Frederick Roden, *Same-Sex Desire in Victorian Religious Culture* (Basingstoke: Palgrave Macmillan, 2002), 11–34.

67　Benjamin Kahan, *Celibacies: American Modernism and Sexual Life* (Durham: Duke University Press, 2013), 33.

68　Nunokawa, *Tame Passions*, 14, 12. Alternative readings can be found in Dustin Friedman, *Before Queer Theory: Victorian Aestheticism and the Self* (Baltimore: John Hopkins University Press, 2019) and Michael R. Doylen, *Homosexual Askesis: Representations of Self-Fashioning in the Writings of Walter Pater, Oscar Wilde, and John Addington Symonds*, unpublished doctoral dissertation (Berkeley: University of California, 1998).

69　Billie Andrew Inman, 'Estrangement and Connection: Walter Pater, Benjamin Jowett, and William M. Hardinge', in Laurel Brake and Ian Small, eds., *Pater in the 1990s* (Greensboro: ELT Press, 1991), 1–20.

70　More information about the range of sexualities attributed to these writers by critics and biographers can be found in the respective chapters of this book.

71　Adrian Frazier, *George Moore, 1852–1933* (New Haven: Yale University Press, 2000), 347.

72　For political radicalism and aesthetic sexuality, see Livesey, *Socialism, Sex, and the Culture of Aestheticism*. For the dominant role of this identification of sexual license with liberation in post-twentieth-century Western culture, see Michel Foucault, 'We "Other" Victorians' in *History of Sexuality*, vol. 1, *The Will to Knowledge*, trans. Robert Hurley (London: Penguin, 1998; first published as *La volanté de savoir*, 1976), 1–13.

73　Grant Allen, 'The New Hedonism', *Fortnightly Review*, 55:327 (March 1894), 376–92; 391, 384.

74　Elfenbein, *Romantic Genius*, 34.

75　*Ibid.*, 30, 18.

76　*Ibid.*, 34.

77　George Bernard Shaw, *Love among the Artists* (London: John Murray, 2012; first published 1900; written c. 1880), 159–60.

78　Francis Galton, *Hereditary Genius: An Inquiry into Its Laws and Consequences* (London: Macmillan, 1869), 225, 227.

79　Elfenbein, *Romantic Genius*, 32.

80　Galton, *Hereditary Genius*, 227.

81　Frank Kermode, *The Romantic Image* (Routledge, 2001; first published 1957), 4.

82 Robert Bridges, *The Testament of Beauty* (Oxford: Clarendon Press, 1929), 76 (book 3, lines 329–30, 332–34). The author's eccentric system of orthography is preserved.

83 Henry David Thoreau, *Walden*, ed. J. Lyndon Shanley (Princeton: Princeton University Press, 1971; first published 1854), 219–20.

84 *Ibid.*, 220.

85 Leo Tolstoy, 'The Kreutzer Sonata', in *Tolstoy Centenary Edition*, general eds. Aylmer Maude *et al.*, 21 vols. (Oxford: Oxford University Press, 1929–37), vol. 16: *The Devil and Cognate Tales*, ed. and trans. Aylmer Maude (1934; originally published in Russian as *Kreitzerova Sonata*, 1889), 109–231; 133.

86 Leo Tolstoy, 'Marriage, Morality, and Christianity: A Reply to Critics of "The Kreutzer Sonata"', trans. E. J. Dillon, *The Universal Review*, 7:26 (June 1890), 154–62; 154, 157, 155. An exploration of similar sexual discourses in Russian literary culture can be found in Jenifer Presto, *Beyond the Flesh: Alexander Blok, Zinaida Grippius, and the Symbolist Sublimation of Sex* (Madison: University of Wisconsin Press, 2008).

87 Tolstoy, 'Kreutzer Sonata', 132.

88 Bridges, *The Testament of Beauty*, 76 (book 3, lines 325–27, 331–32).

89 See Catherine Edwards, *The Politics of Immorality in Ancient Rome* (Cambridge: Cambridge University Press, 1993), 63–97.

90 James Eli Adams, *Dandies and Desert Saints: Styles of Victorian Masculinity* (Ithaca: Cornell University Press, 1995), 2; Herbert Sussman, *Victorian Masculinities: Manhood and Masculine Poetics in Early Victorian Literature and Art* (Cambridge: Cambridge University Press, 1995), 2.

91 See Kristina Gupta, 'Compulsory Sexuality: Evaluating an Emerging Concept', *Signs*, 41:1 (Autumn 2015), 131–54. The term has become common in studies of asexuality and beyond.

92 Cerankowski and Milks, 'Why Asexuality? Why now?' in *Asexualities*, 1–14; 13.

93 Donald E. Hall *et al.*, 'Introduction' in Hall *et al.*, eds., *The Routledge Queer Studies Reader* (London: Routledge, 2013), xiv–xx; xvi.

94 Cerankowski and Milks, 'Why Asexuality? Why now?', 3.

95 Kahan, *Celibacies*, 4, 3.

96 Cerankowski and Milks, 'Why Asexuality? Why now?', 13, 2, 3.

97 Kahan, *Celibacies*, 68, 1, 143.

98 *Ibid.*, 1, 2, 145, 153.

99 *Ibid.*, 8.

100 Annamarie Jagose, 'The Trouble with Antinormativity', *Differences*, 26:1 (May 2015), 26–47; 26, 43, 40. For further discussion of normativity in recent theoretical writing, see Peter Cryle and Elizabeth Stephens, *Normality: A Critical Genealogy* (Chicago: University of Chicago Press, 2017), 1–15.

101 Foucault, 'We "Other" Victorians', 7.

102 Kahan, *Celibacies*, 9, 53.

103 Peter Cryle and Alison Moore, *Frigidity: An Intellectual History* (Basingstoke: Palgrave Macmillan, 2011), 2, 10, 3, 4.

104 Sharon Marcus, *Between Women: Friendship, Desire, and Marriage in Victorian England* (Princeton: Princeton University Press, 2007).

105 Carolyn Oulton, *Romantic Friendship in Victorian Literature* (Aldershot: Ashgate, 2007), 154.

106 *Ibid.*, 155, 153.

107 Arnold I. Davidson, *The Emergence of Sexuality: Historical Epistemology and the Formation of Concepts* (Cambridge, MA: Harvard University Press, 2001), xii. Davidson adapts the phrase 'styles of reasoning' from the work of Ian Hacking.

108 See Davidson, 'Closing Up the Corpses' in *The Emergence of Sexuality*, 1–29.

109 Davidson, 'Sex and the Emergence of Sexuality' in *The Emergence of Sexuality*, 30–65; 32.

1 Loss and Gain: The Victorian Sexual Body

1 Lesley A. Hall, *Sex, Gender and Social Change in Britain since 1880*, 2nd ed. (Basingstoke: Palgrave Macmillan, 2012; first ed. 2000), 1.

2 Simon Szreter, *Fertility, Class, and Gender in Britain, 1860–1940* (Cambridge: Cambridge University Press, 1996).

3 For changing categorizations of venereal diseases and the uneven distribution of that knowledge, see Anne R. Hanley, *Medicine, Knowledge and Venereal Diseases in England, 1886–1916* (Basingstoke: Palgrave Macmillan, 2017).

4 Michel Foucault, *History of Sexuality*, vol. 1: *The Will to Knowledge*, trans. Robert Hurley (London: Penguin, 1998; first published as *La volanté de savoir*, 1976), 17, 43.

5 Arnold I. Davidson, *The Emergence of Sexuality: Historical Epistemology and the Formation of Concepts* (Cambridge, MA: Harvard University Press, 2001), 13, 21, 32.

6 Hall, *Sex, Gender, and Social Change*, 3, 7.

7 Lesley A. Hall and Roy Porter, *The Facts of Life: The Creation of Sexual Knowledge in Britain, 1650–1950* (New Haven: Yale University Press, 1995), 132.

8 Michael Mason, *The Making of Victorian Sexual Attitudes* (Oxford: Oxford University Press, 1994), 3.

9 Herbert Sussman, *Victorian Masculinities: Manhood and Masculine Poetics in Early Victorian Literature and Art* (Cambridge: Cambridge University Press, 1995), 3, 4.

10 Sussman, *Victorian Masculinities*; James Eli Adams, *Dandies and Desert Saints: Styles of Victorian Masculinity* (Ithaca: Cornell University Press, 1995); Trev Broughton, *Men of Letters, Writing Lives: Masculinity and Literary Auto/Biography in the Late-Victorian Period* (London: Routledge, 1999).

11 Pamela K. Gilbert, *The Citizen's Body: Desire, Health, and the Social in Victorian England* (Columbus: The Ohio State University Press, 2007).

12 Hall, *Sex, Gender, and Social Change*, 30.

13 James Richard Smyth, 'Miscellaneous Contributions to Pathology and Therapeutics: Impotence and Sterility', *The Lancet*, 36:939 (1841), 779–85; 784.

14 'Medical Graduations in Edinburgh', in *The Edinburgh Medical and Surgical Journal*, 40 (Edinburgh: Adam and Charles Black, 1833), 491.

15 'Smyth, James Richard', in *The London Medical Directory* (London: C. Mitchell, 1845), 149.

16 James Richard Smyth, *Miscellaneous Contributions to Pathology and Therapeutics* (London: Simpkin, Marshall, & Co., 1844); [unsigned], 'Review: Miscellaneous Contributions to Pathology and Therapeutics, by James Richard Smyth, M.D.', *The Medico-Chirurgical Review*, 41:82 (1 October 1844), 349–55; 349.

17 Michael Mason, *The Making of Victorian Sexuality* (Oxford: Oxford University Press, 1994). For more on the Victorian medical fringe, see Sylvia Pamboukian, *Doctoring the Novel: Medicine and Quackery from Shelley to Doyle* (Athens: Ohio University Press, 2012) and Roy Porter, *Quacks: Fakers and Charlatans in English Medicine* (Stroud: Tempus, 2000), 200–6.

18 Although I refer here to masturbation only as a form of sexual excess, it is evident that the Victorian fear of the practice goes far beyond this explanation. See Diane Mason, *The Secret Vice: Masturbation in Victorian Fiction and Medical Culture* (Manchester: Manchester University Press, 2009); Thomas Laqueur, *Solitary Sex: A Cultural History of Masturbation* (New York: Zone Books, 2003); Paula Bennet and Vernon A. Rosario, eds., *Solitary Pleasures: The Historical, Literary and Artistic Discourses of Autoeroticism* (London: Routledge, 1995); Lesley A. Hall, 'Forbidden by God, Despised by Men: Masturbation, Medical Warnings, Moral Panic, and Manhood in Great Britain, 1850–1950', *Journal of the History of Sexuality*, 2:3 (January 1992), 365–87.

19 Smyth, 'Impotence and Sterility' (1841), 779, 780, 784.

20 For more about the history of impotence, see Angus McLaren, *Impotence: A Cultural History* (Chicago: University of Chicago Press, 2007).

21 Mason, *Victorian Sexuality*, 222, 227.

22 John Addington Symonds, *The Memoirs*, ed. Phyllis Grosskurth (London: Hutchinson, 1984), 152. Although Symonds later diagnosed himself at this period as suffering from 'unhealthily repressed' homosexual desires (128), it is not clear whether he thought of his illness in this way at the time or represented it as such to Spencer Wells.

23 James Paget, 'Sexual Hypochondriasis', in *Clinical Lectures and Essays*, ed. Howard Marsh (London: Longmans, Green & Co., 1875), 268–92; 286.

24 See Mason, *Victorian Sexuality*, 217.

25 [Unsigned], 'Review: Miscellaneous Contributions to Pathology and Therapeutics', 353–4, 355.

26 Mason, *Victorian Sexuality*, 208.

27 See Aline Rouselle, *Porneia: On Desire and the Body in Antiquity*, trans. Felicia Pheasant (Oxford: Basil Blackwell, 1988; originally published in French as *Porneia*, 1983), 13.

28 James Richard Smyth, 'Miscellaneous Contributions to Pathology and Therapeutics: Impotence and Sterility', *The Lancet*, 39:1010 (1843), 531–6; 535.

29 See, for instance, Thomas Laqueur's broad overview in *Solitary Sex*, 185–246.

30 Ben Barker-Benfield, 'The Spermatic Economy: A Nineteenth Century View of Sexuality', *Feminist Studies*, 1:1 (Summer 1972), 45–74. Although Barker-Benfield coins the phrase 'spermatic economy', a similar thesis concerning semen and Victorian economics had been forwarded by Peter Cominos: 'Late Victorian Sexual Respectability and the Social System', *International Review of Social History*, 8:1 (1963), 18–48.

31 Sussman, *Victorian Masculinities*; Broughton, *Men of Letters, Writing Lives*, 136–65; Elizabeth Stephens, 'Coining Spermatorrhoea: Medicine and Male Body Fluids, 1836–1866', *Sexualities*, 12:4 (2009), 467–85; 474. For more on spermatorrhoea, see Mason, 'Appendix III: The Medical Standing of "Spermatorrhoea"', in *Victorian Sexuality*, 295–8 and Ellen Bayuk Rosenman, 'Body Doubles: The Spermatorrhea Panic', *Journal of the History of Sexuality* 12:3 (2003), 365–99.

32 Rouselle, *Porneia*, 14, 13.

33 Laqueur, *Solitary Sex*, 462 (n. 18). See also 38.

34 Smyth, 'Impotence and Sterility' (1841), 784.

35 See Vern Bullough, *Science in the Bedroom: A History of Sex Research* (New York: Basic Books, 1994), 19–21.

36 For more about semen in eighteenth-century medical writing, see Laqueur, *Solitary Sex*, 190–200. For the discourse of 'energy' in the nineteenth century, see Anson Rabinbach, *The Human Motor: Energy, Fatigue, and the Origins of Modernity* (New York: Basic Books, 1990).

37 Lesley A. Hall, *Hidden Anxieties: Male Sexuality, 1900–1950* (Cambridge: Polity Press, 1991), 54–62.

38 Henry Smith, *The Warning Voice: Or, Private Medical Friend*, 63rd ed. (London: self-published: 1860), 15. Italics in the original.

39 F. B. Courtenay, *Revelations of Quacks and Quackery: A Series of Letters by 'Detector' Reprinted from 'The Medical Circular'*, 10th ed. (London: Bailliere, Tindall & Cox, 1885; first published 1865), 18. Italics in the original.

40 Harvey & Co., *Short Account of Sir Astley Cooper's Vital Restorative* (London: Harvey & Co., 1863), 10, 15.

41 Paget, 'Sexual Hypochondriasis'; 286–7, 284–5.

42 Havelock Ellis, *Studies in the Psychology of Sex*, vol. 6, *Sex in Relation to Society*, 2nd ed. revised (Philadelphia: F. A. Davis, 1921; first published 1910), 191; Robert Darby, 'William Acton's Antipodean Disciples: A Colonial Perspectives on His Theories of Male Sexual (Dys)function', *Journal of the History of Sexuality*, 13:2 (April 2004), 157–82.

43 Ivan Crozier, 'William Acton and the History of Sexuality: The Medical and Professional Context', *Journal of Victorian Culture*, 5:1 (2000), 1–27; Hall, *Hidden Anxieties*, 15–17.

44 Symonds, *The Memoirs*, 151.

45 William Acton, *The Functions and Disorders of the Reproductive Organs in Youth, in Adult Age, and in Advanced Life: Considered in their Physiological, Social, and Psychological Relations*, 2nd ed. revised (London: John Churchill, 1858; first published 1857), 23, 42–3.

46 For spermatorrhoea and Acton's career, see Crozier, 'William Acton and the History of Sexuality', 9–10.

47 In his account of secretion in sexual function Acton follows William Carpenter's *The Principles of Human Physiology*, 5th ed. (London: John Churchill, 1855 edition; first published 1842), 779–80. Carpenter originally stressed the healthfulness of moderate sexual intercourse within marriage but toned this down in subsequent editions.

48 Acton, *Functions and Disorders*, 15, 19, 20, 44, 8. For more on the history of masturbation as a dangerous activity, see Laqueur, *Solitary Sex*.

49 See Rabinbach, *The Human Motor*, 64–8.

50 Acton, *Functions and Disorders*, 39.

51 Davidson, 'Closing up the Corpses', 3–10.

52 Acton, *Functions and Disorders*, 35.

53 *Ibid.*, 14.

54 For the early awareness of continental sexology among British psychologists, see Ivan Crozier, 'Nineteenth-Century British Psychiatric Writing about Homosexuality before Havelock Ellis: The Missing Story', *Journal of the History of Medicine and Allied Sciences*, 68:1 (January 2008), 65–102.

55 Henry Maudsley, *The Physiology of Mind* (London: Macmillan & Co., 1876), 355, 398, 372.

56 Henry Maudsley, *The Pathology of Mind* (London: Macmillan & Co., 1879), 46.

57 *Ibid.*, 225, 46. Arthur N. Gilbert has written persuasively of the ideological values behind Maudsley's fear of masturbation: 'Masturbation and Insanity: Henry Maudsley and the Ideology of Sexual Repression', *Albion*, 12:3 (Autumn 1980), 268–83. While Maudsley's anti-masturbation stance is overtly based in its solitary nature, his concern about excessive sexual intercourse for men especially is more complex.

58 Maudsley, *The Pathology of the Mind*, 335, 226, 370.

59 Davidson, *The Emergence of Sexuality*, 35.

60 *Ibid.*, 3.

61 Lesley A. Hall, 'Sexual Cultures in Britain: Some Persisting Themes', in Franz X. Eder, *et al.*, eds., *Sexual Cultures in Europe: National Histories* (Manchester: Manchester University Press, 1999), 29–52; 41.

62 Phyllis Grosskurth, *Havelock Ellis: A Biography* (London: Allen Lane, 1980), 220.

63 Ellis, *Sex in Relation to Society*, 144.

64 *Ibid.*, 169.

65 *Ibid.*, 197.

66 *Ibid.*, 170, 155, 172.

67 Edward Carpenter, *Love's Coming of Age* (Manchester: Labour Press, 1896), 11.

68 A body of work exists on homosexuality in early sexology. The most relevant to my current argument are Benjamin Kahan, *The Book of Minor Perverts: Sexology, Etiology, and the Emergences of Sexuality* (Chicago: University of Chicago Press, 2019), Heike Bauer, *English Literary Sexology* (Basingstoke: Palgrave Macmillan, 2009), and Lucy Bland and Laura Doan, eds., *Sexology in Culture: Labelling Bodies and Desires* (Cambridge: Polity, 1998).

69 Homosexual chastity can also be found, though with Catholic justification, in Marc-André Raffalovich, *Uranisme et unisexualité: étude sur différentes manifestations de l'instinct sexuel* (Paris: Masson, 1896). Like Ellis and Symonds, Raffalovich had close relationships with many British Decadent writers and published Decadent poetry in English.

70 John Addington Symonds, *A Problem in Modern Ethics* (London: Privately Printed, 1896; first printed 1891), 13.

71 Carolyn Oulton, *Romantic Friendship in Victorian Literature* (Aldershot: Ashgate, 2007), 129–52. Although mid-Victorian sexual discourse made it easier to draw boundaries between the sexual and non-sexual, I do not deny that earlier romantic friendships were often consciously or unconsciously sexual in nature.

72 The porous boundaries of sexuality and friendship in relation to ideal models of citizenship at stake here are explored at length by Richard Dellamora, *Friendship's Bonds: Democracy and the Novel in Victorian England* (Philadelphia: University of Pennsylvania Press, 2004).

73 Symonds, *A Problem in Modern Ethics*, 116–21.

74 Havelock Ellis, *Studies in the Psychology of Sex*, 2nd ed. revised (Philadelphia: F. A. Davis, 1908), vol. 2: *Sexual Inversion* (first published 1897), 216, 202–3.

75 *Ibid.*, 168, 179.

76 Benjamin Kahan, *Celibacies: American Modernism and Sexual Life* (Durham: Duke University Press, 2013), 27.

77 Ellis, *Sex in Relation to Society*, 172–6.

78 Havelock Ellis, *Studies in the Psychology of Sex*, 2nd ed. revised (Philadelphia: F. A. Davis, 1913) vol. 3: *Analysis of the Sexual Impulse, Love and Pain, The Sexual Impulse in Women* (first published 1903), 18.

79 Ellis, *Sexual Inversion*, 18.

80 Rabinbach, *The Human Motor*, 9.

81 Freud, *Civilization and Its Discontents*, 103, 78.

82 Freud, 'Leonardo Da Vinci', 75.

83 Freud, *Civilization and Its Discontents*, 104.

84 *Ibid.*, 103.

85 Norman Vance, *The Sinews of the Spirit: The Ideal of Christian Manliness in Victorian Literature and Religious Thought* (Cambridge: Cambridge University Press, 1985), 169.

86 Frederick Atkins, *Moral Muscle and How to Use it: A Brotherly Chat with Young Men* (London: James Nisbet & Co., 1890), v.

87 Charles Sayle, 'Diary 1864–96', Cambridge University Library, *Charles Edward Sayle: Diaries and Letters*, GBR/0012/MS Add. 8501, 264.

88 John Stuart Blackie, *On Self-Culture*, 3rd ed. (Edinburgh: Edmonston and Douglas, 1874), 74.

89 John Thain Davidson, *Talks with Young Men* (London: Hodder & Stoughton, 1884), 78.

90 H. Sinclair Paterson, *Life, Function, Health: Studies for Young Men* (London: Hodder & Stoughton, 1885), 34, 134–35, 136, 127, 136.

91 According to an unsigned review in the *Spectator* (29 January 1881), 26.

92 [Unsigned], 'Direct Teaching to Men Upon Personal Purity', *The Sentinel*, 50 (June 1883), 206.

93 Quoted by Edward J. Bristow in *Vice and Vigilance: Purity Movements in Britain Since 1700* (Dublin: Gill & Macmillan, 1977), 132.

94 This figure taken from Ed Cohen, *Talk on the Wilde Side: Towards a Genealogy of a Discourse on Male Sexualities* (New York: Routledge, 1993), 88.

95 Lord (Robert) Baden-Powell, *Rovering to Success: A Book of Life-Sport for Young Men*, 2nd ed. revised (London: Herbert Jenkins, 1930; first published 1922), 104.

96 Bristow, *Vice and Vigilance*, 140.

97 *Ibid.*, 127.

98 See Joseph Bristow, *Empire Boys: Adventures in a Man's World* (London: Harper Collins Academic, 1991); Philip Holden and Richard Ruppel, eds., *Imperial Desire: Dissident Sexualities and Colonial Literature* (Minneapolis: University of Minnesota Press, 2003); John Kucich, *Imperial Masochism: British Fiction, Fantasy, and Social Class* (Princeton: Princeton University Press, 2007).

99 Mason, *Victorian Sexuality*, 178–9.

100 Sally Ledger, *The New Woman: Fiction and Feminism at the Fin de Siècle* (Manchester: Manchester University Press, 1997), 94–121; Talia Schaffer, *The Forgotten Female Aesthetes: Literary Culture in Late-Victorian England* (Charlottesville: University Press of Virginia, 2000), 15–25; Ana Parejo Vadillo, *Women Poets and Urban Aestheticism: Passengers of Modernity* (Basingstoke: Palgrave Macmillan, 2005); Ruth Livesey, *Socialism, Sex, and the Culture of Aestheticism in Britain, 1880–1914* (Oxford: Oxford University Press, 2007), 73–101, 132–60.

101 See Lucy Bland, *Banishing the Beast: English Feminism & Sexual Morality, 1885–1914* (Harmondsworth: Penguin, 1995), xiii.

102 *Ibid.*, 16, 172.

103 *Ibid.*, 15–17.

104 *Ibid.*, 68.

105 Sheila Jeffreys, *The Spinster and Her Enemies: Feminism and Sexuality, 1880–1930* (London: Pandora Press, 1985), 27–53.

106 Sarah Grand, *The Heavenly Twins* (London: William Heinemann, 1894), 350.

107 [Henrietta Müller], 'The Future of Single Women', *Westminster Review*, 121:241 (January 1884), 151–62; 162, 158.

108 *Ibid.*, 159.

109 See, for example, Gideon Nisbet, *Greek Epigram in Reception: J. A. Symonds, Oscar Wilde, and the Invention of Desire, 1805–1929* (Oxford: Oxford University Press, 2014); Whitney Davis, *Queer Beauty: Sexuality and Aesthetics from Winckelmann to Freud and Beyond* (New York: Columbia University Press, 2010); Stefano Evangelista, *British Aestheticism and Ancient Greece: Hellenism, Reception, Gods in Exile* (Basingstoke: Palgrave Macmillan, 2009).

110 For the influence of ancient philosophy upon Christian sexual continence in particular, see Peter Brown, *The Body and Society: Men, Women, and Sexual Renunciation in Early Christianity*, 2nd ed. revised (New York: University of Columbia Press, 2008; first published 1988).

111 Michel Foucault, *History of Sexuality*, vol. 2: *The Use of Pleasure*, trans. Robert Hurley (London: Penguin, 1992; this translation first published 1985; originally published in French as *L'Usage des plaisirs*, 1984), 10; and vol. 3: *The Care of the Self*, trans. Robert Hurley (London: Penguin, 1990; first published 1986; originally published as *Le Souci de soi*, 1984).

112 See Martha C. Nussbaum, *The Therapy of Desire: Theory and Practice in Hellenistic Ethics* (Princeton: Princeton University Press, 1994) and Rouselle, *Porneia*, 3.

113 See, for instance, Evangelista, *British Aestheticism and Ancient Greece*.

114 See Kyriakos Demetriou, *Studies on the Reception of Plato and Greek Political Thought in Victorian Britain* (Farnham: Ashgate, 2011) and Anna P. Baldwin and Sarah Hutton, eds., *Platonism and the English Imagination* (Cambridge: Cambridge University Press, 1994).

115 John M. Dillon, 'Rejecting the Body, Refining the Body: Some Remarks on the Development of Platonist Asceticism', in Valantasis and Wimbush, eds., *Asceticism* (Oxford: Oxford University Press, 2002), 80–7; 80.

116 Plato, *Phaedo* (67A), quoted in Dillon, 'Rejecting the Body, Refining the Body', 2002, 81.

117 *Ibid.*, 82.

118 Carolyn Oulton, *Romantic Friendship in Victorian Literature* (Aldershot: Ashgate, 2007), 155.

119 Plato, 'Phaedrus', in *Euthyphro, Apology, Crito, Phaedo, Phaedrus*, trans. Harold North Fowler (Cambridge, MA: Harvard University Press, 1995; this translation first published 1914), 193–404; 475 (247B).

120 Plato, 'Symposium', in *Lysis, Symposium, Gorgias,* trans. W. R. M. Lamb (Cambridge, MA: Harvard University Press, 1991; this translation first published 1925), 73–246; 55 (211C).

121 Symonds, *The Memoirs*, 99, 101; A. C. Benson, diary for 1913, quoted in Vance, *The Sinews of the Spirit*, 188.

122 Stefano Evangelista, '"Lovers and Philosophers at Once": Aesthetic Platonism in the Victorian *Fin de Siècle*', *The Yearbook of English Studies*, 36:2 (2006), 230–44; 231.

123 *Ibid.*, 234.

124 John Addington Symonds, *A Problem in Greek Ethics* (London: Privately Printed, 1901; first published 1883, written 1873), 52.

125 H. Montgomery Hyde, ed., *The Trials of Oscar Wilde* (London: William Hodge and Co., 1949), 236.

126 Symonds, *A Problem in Greek Ethics*, 52, 54.

127 George Ridding, *Purity* (Derby: Bemrose & Sons, 1883), 6.

128 Linda Dowling, *Hellenism and Homosexuality in Victorian Oxford* (Ithaca: Cornell University Press, 1994), 68–9.

129 Lesley Higgins, 'Jowett and Pater: Trafficking in Platonic Wares', *Victorian Studies*, 37:1 (Autumn 1993), 43–72; 48.

130 Dowling, *Hellenism and Homosexuality*, 73, 71.

131 See Higgins, 'Jowett and Pater'.

132 See Evangelista, '"Lovers and Philosophers at Once"', 231–35.

133 Higgins, 'Jowett and Pater', 45; Stefano Evangelista, 'Against Misinterpretation: Benjamin Jowett's Translations of Plato and the Ethics of Modern Homosexuality', *Recherches anglaises et nord-américaines*, 36:3 (2003), 13–25. For the details of Pater's involvement with Balliol undergraduate William Money Hardinge, and Jowett's intervention, see Billie Andrew Inman, 'Estrangement and Connection: Walter Pater, Benjamin Jowett and William M. Hardinge', in Laurel Brake and Ian Small, eds., *Pater in the 1990s* (Greensboro: ELT Press, 1991), 1–20.

134 Higgins, 'Jowett and Pater', 53.

135 Walter Pater, *Plato and Platonism: A Series of Lectures* (London: Macmillan, 1910; first published 1893), 143.

136 Benjamin Jowett, 'Symposium: Introduction' in *The Dialogues of Plato: Translated into English with Analyses and Introductions*, 3rd ed. revised, 5 vols. (Oxford: Clarendon Press, 1892; first published 1871) vol. 1, 515–40; 537.

137 Benjamin Jowett, 'Phaedrus: Introduction' in *The Dialogues of Plato*, 393–423; 412.

138 *Ibid.*, 411, 415.

139 *Ibid.*, 411.

140 *Ibid.*, 408.

141 Jowett, 'Symposium: Introduction', 525.

142 M. L. Holbrook, *Chastity: Its Physical, Moral, and Intellectual Advantages* (London: L. N. Fowler & Co., 1894), 55.

143 Symonds, *A Problem in Greek Ethics*, 50.

144 Jowett, 'Symposium: Introduction', 533.

145 David J. DeLaura, *Hebrew and Hellene in Victorian England: Newman, Arnold, and Pater* (Austin: University of Texas Press, 1969), xi; see also Hilary Fraser, *Beauty and Belief: Aesthetics and Religion in Victorian Literature* (Cambridge: Cambridge University Press, 1986).

146 See Martin Lockerd, *Decadent Catholicism and the Making of Modernism* (London: Bloomsbury Academic, 2020); Alex Murray, 'Recusant Poetics: Rereading Catholicism at the Fin de Siècle', *English Literature in Transition, 1880–1920*, 56:3 (2013), 355–73; Ellis Hanson, *Decadence and Catholicism* (Cambridge, MA: Harvard University Press, 1998).

147 Owen Chadwick, ed., *The Mind of the Oxford Movement* (London: Adam Charles Black, 1960), 11.

148 Fraser, *Beauty and Belief*, 11. See also Stephen Prickett, *Romanticism and Religion: The Tradition of Coleridge and Wordsworth in the Victorian Church* (Cambridge: Cambridge University Press, 1976), and David Goslee, *Romanticism and the Anglican Newman* (Athens: Ohio University Press, 1996).

149 Chadwick, *The Mind of the Oxford Movement*, 27; Stephen Prickett, 'Tractarian Poetry', in Richard Cronin *et al.*, eds., *A Companion to Victorian Poetry* (Malden: Blackwell, 2002), 279–90; 279.

150 Fraser, *Beauty and Belief*, 2.

151 Vance, *The Sinews of the Spirit*, 39; D. G. Paz, *Popular Anti-Catholicism in Mid-Victorian England* (Stanford: Stanford University Press, 1992), 2.

152 See David Hilliard, 'Unenglish and Unmanly: Anglo-Catholicism and Homosexuality', *Victorian Studies*, 25:2 (Winter 1982), 181–210.

153 Dominic Janes, 'When "Perverts" Were Religious: The Protestant Sexualization of Asceticism in Nineteenth-Century Britain, India and Ireland', *Cultural and Social History*, 11:3 (2014), 425–39; 426.

154 DeLaura, *Hebrew and Hellene*, 303–46.

155 R. W. Church, *The Oxford Movement: Twelve Years, 1833–1845* (London: Macmillan, 1891), 321.

156 Geoffrey Faber, *Oxford Apostles: A Character Study of the Oxford Movement* (London: Faber & Faber, 1954; first published 1933), 213.

157 See, for example, Frederick Roden, *Same-Sex Desire in Victorian Religious Culture* (Basingstoke: Palgrave Macmillan, 2002).

158 James Eli Adams has discussed the importance of the doctrine of reserve to Newman's ethical thinking, but does not connect this with celibacy specifically. See *Dandies and Desert Saints*, 83–106.

159 Duc Dau, 'Perfect Chastity: Celibacy and Virgin Marriage in Tractarian Poetry', *Victorian Poetry*, 44:1 (2006), 77–92; 78; Kirstie Blair, 'Breaking Loose: Frederick Faber and the Failure of Reserve', *Victorian Poetry*, 44:1 (Spring 2006), 25–41. For more about the importance of reserve to Newman specifically, see Robin C. Selby, *The Principle of Reserve in the Writings of John Henry Newman* (Oxford: Oxford University Press, 1975).

160 For the extent to which Newman's celibacy made sense in an Anglican as well as a later Catholic context, see B. W. Young, 'The Anglican Origins of Newman's Celibacy', *Church History*, 65 (1996), 15–27.

161 John Henry Newman, *Apologia Pro Vita Sua,* ed. Ian Ker (London: Penguin, 1994; first published 1864), 28. For the gendered and sexual controversy surrounding this work, see Oliver S. Buckton, '"An Unnatural State": Gender, "Perversion", and Newman's "Apologia Pro Vita Sua"', *Victorian Studies*, 35:4 (Summer 1992), 359–83.

162 Letter to F. W. Faber, 27 October 1840, in Ian Ker *et al.*, eds., *The Letters and Diaries of John Henry Newman*, 32 vols. (1995), vol. 7: Gerard Tracey, ed., 421–22, 422; letter to Simon Lloyd Pope, 9 April 1832, in *ibid.*, vol. 3: eds. Ian Ker and Thomas Gornall, S. J. (1979), 42–43, 43. Italics in the original.

163 Letter from Newman to George Ryder, 22–23 July 1832, in *ibid.*, 70.
164 Letter from Faber to J. B. Morris, 21 October 1840, in John Edward Bowden, ed., *The Life and Letters of Frederick William Faber D. D.* (London: Thomas Richardson & Son, 1869), 79–80, 79; letter from Faber to Newman, 24 October 1840, in *The Letters and Diaries of John Henry Newman*, vol. 7, 419–20; 419. Italics in the original.
165 Letter from Newman to Henry Wilberforce, 26 February 1832, *ibid.*, vol. 3, 22–24; 23.
166 DeLaura, *Hebrew and Hellene*, 311, x. For more on the notion of an intellectual 'clerisy' in early and mid-Victorian prose writing, see Ben Knights, *The Idea of the Clerisy in the Nineteenth Century* (Cambridge: Cambridge University Press, 1978).
167 DeLaura, *Hebrew and Hellene*, 307, 339–44; John Henry Newman, 'Many Called, Few Chosen', in *Parochial and Plain Sermons*, 8 vols. (London: Longmans, Green, & Co, 1907; first published 1868), vol. 5, 254–68; 268.
168 Frank Turner, *John Henry Newman: The Challenge to Evangelical Religion* (New Haven: Yale University Press, 2002), 426.
169 Letter from Newman to Simon Lloyd Pope, 9 April 1832, 43.

2 'A Passionate Coldness': Walter Pater

1 See, for example, Richard Dellamora, *Masculine Desire: The Sexual Politics of Victorian Aestheticism* (Chapel Hill: University of North Carolina Press, 1990); Dennis Denisoff, *Aestheticism and Sexual Parody, 1840–1940* (Cambridge: Cambridge University Press, 2001); Laurel Brake, 'Print and Gender: The Publishing Career of Walter Pater, 1866–95', in *Print in Transition, 1850–1910: Studies in Media and Book History* (Basingstoke: Palgrave Macmillan, 2001), 183–282; Stefano Evangelista, *British Aestheticism and Ancient Greece: Hellenism, Reception, Gods in Exile* (Basingstoke: Palgrave Macmillan, 2009).
2 Linda Dowling, 'Ruskin's Pied Beauty and the Constitution of a "Homosexual Code"', *The Victorian Newsletter*, 75 (Spring 1989), 1–8; 4; Linda Dowling, *Hellenism and Homosexuality in Victorian Oxford* (Ithaca: Cornell University Press, 1994), 115.
3 Gerald Monsman, 'The Platonic Eros of Walter Pater and Oscar Wilde: "Love's Reflected Image" in the 1890s', *English Literature in Transition, 1880–1920*, 45:1 (2002), 26–45; Adam Lee, 'Platonic Communion in Pater's "Unfinished Romance"', *The Pater Newsletter*, 63 (Fall 2012), 25–44.
4 William F. Shuter, 'The "Outing" of Walter Pater', *Nineteenth-Century Literature*, 48:4 (March 1994), 480–506; 502.
5 Kate Hext, *Walter Pater: Individualism and Aesthetic Philosophy* (Edinburgh: Edinburgh University Press, 2013), 117.
6 Herbert Sussman, *Victorian Masculinities: Manhood and Masculine Poetics in Early Victorian Literature and Art* (Cambridge: Cambridge University Press, 1995), 174.
7 Hext, *Walter Pater*, 85.

8 Walter Pater, 'Conclusion' in Donald Hill, ed., *The Renaissance: Studies in Art and Poetry: The 1893 Text* (Berkeley: University of California Press, 1980), 186–90; 186. This edition of the 1893 text is the preferred critical edition; all references will be to this edition unless otherwise stated and will be given in the text. I will note where variants between editions are of significance to my argument.

9 Hext, *Walter Pater*, 5; Whitney Davis, 'Eternal Moment: Pater on the Temporality of the Classical Ideal in Art', in Charles Martindale *et al.*, eds., *Pater the Classicist: Classical Scholarship, Reception, and Aestheticism* (Oxford: Oxford University Press, 2017), 81–98; 83.

10 Hext, *Walter Pater*, 7.

11 Walter Pater, *Marius the Epicurean: His Sensations and Ideas*, 2 vols. (London: Macmillan, 1910; first published 1885), vol. 2, 70. All references will be to this edition unless otherwise stated and will be given in the text.

12 Walter Pater, 'Hippolytus Veiled: A Study from Euripides', *Macmillan's Magazine*, 60:358 (August 1889), 304.

13 Frank Harris, 'Walter Pater' in *Contemporary Portraits: Second Series* (New York: Frank Harris, 1919), 203–26; 203.

14 Richard Le Gallienne, *Young Lives* (London: The Bodley Head, 1899), 156.

15 Carolyn Williams, *Transfigured World: Walter Pater's Aesthetic Historicism* (Ithaca: Cornell University Press, 1987), 12, 26.

16 Hext, *Walter Pater*, 15.

17 The protagonist of *Gaston de Latour* does marry and conceive a child, but under rites of a religion not his own. Pater insists that the relationship does not seem a genuine marriage to Gaston.

18 For more on the place of modern scientific thought in Pater's writing, see Benjamin Morgan, *The Outward Mind: Materialist Aesthetics in Victorian Science and Literature* (Chicago: University of Chicago Press, 2017) and Gowan Dawson, 'Walter Pater's *Marius the Epicurean* and the Discourse of Science in *Macmillan's Magazine*: "A Creature of the Nineteenth Century"', *English Literature in Transition, 1880–1920*, 48:1 (2005), 38–54.

19 Sara Lyons, *Algernon Swinburne and Walter Pater: Victorian Aestheticism, Doubt and Secularisation* (Leeds: Legenda, 2015), 7. See Williams, *Transfigured World*, 11–77, for a more epistemologically focused reading of the 'Conclusion'.

20 The phrase 'we are all under a sentence of death but with a sort of indefinite reprieve' is added in the 1888 edition, in rough translation of the French of Victor Hugo given from the first: '*les hommes sont tous condamnés a morte avec des sursis indéfinis*'. Walter Pater, *The Renaissance: Studies in Art and Poetry*, 3rd ed. revised (London: Macmillan, 1888), 251.

21 Lyons, *Algernon Swinburne and Walter Pater*, 6, 30.

22 John Morley, 'Mr Pater's Essays' (April 1873), in R. M. Seiler, ed., *Walter Pater: The Critical Heritage* (London: Routledge & Kegan Paul, 1980), 63–73; 68, 63.

23 The change between the first and third editions from 'high' to 'great' passions is presumably due to the repeated use of the phrase 'high passions' across two sentences. Both words suggest an element of ennoblement that would be absent from, for instance, the word 'heightened'. See Pater, *The Renaissance* (1888), 252.

24 [Sidney Colvin], review, *Pall Mall Gazette* (1 March 1873), in Seiler, ed., *Walter Pater: The Critical Heritage*, 47–54; 54.

25 The reference is to Luke 16:8, 'for the children of this world are in their generation wiser than the children of light'. It is added in the third (1888) edition and introduces, in true Paterian equivocal manner, the potential for religious experience to be considered either wiser or less wise than embodied artistic experience, depending on how ironic one feels Pater is being.

26 The first (1873) edition reads 'art for art's sake'.

27 John Addington Symonds, review, *Academy* (15 March 1873), in Seiler, ed., *Walter Pater: The Critical Heritage*, 57–61; 57; letter to Mary Robinson, 30 March 1885, *ibid.*, 124.

28 There is disagreement among Pater scholars as to whether this footnote represented a genuine sense of having been misunderstood, a change of heart inspired by responses to the first edition, or a cover that allowed for the republication of an essentially radical text. Pater's actual motivations matter less here than the form of the semi-retraction.

29 The change from 'fervid' to 'fervent' from the second (1877) edition onwards more firmly links Winckelmann's friendships to his relationship with sculpture: 'Suddenly he is in contact with that life, still fervent in the relics of plastic art' (146).

30 Stefano Evangelista and Katherine Harloe, 'Pater's "Winckelmann": Aesthetic Criticism and Classical Reception', in Martindale *et al.*, eds., *Pater the Classicist*, 63–80; 76.

31 Richard Dellamora, 'The Androgynous Body in Pater's "Winckelmann"', *Browning Institute Studies*, 11 (1983), 51–68, 65; Evangelista, *British Aestheticism and Ancient Greece*, 35, 34.

32 Dustin Friedman, *Before Queer Theory: Victorian Aestheticism and the Self* (Baltimore: John Hopkins University Press, 2019), 35, 50.

33 Walter Pater, 'Winckelmann', *Westminster Review*, 31:1 (January 1867), 80–110; 88.

34 Friedman, *Before Queer Theory*, 46.

35 A. C. Benson, *Walter Pater* (London: Macmillan, 1906), 14.

36 Harris, 'Walter Pater', 203, 226.

37 Stefano Evangelista, '"Lovers and Philosophers at Once": Aesthetic Platonism in the Victorian *Fin de Siècle*', *The Yearbook of English Studies*, 36:2 (2006), 230–44; 238.

38 Walter Pater, *Plato and Platonism: A Series of Lectures* (London: Macmillan, 1910; first published 1893), 136, 143.

39 Lee, 'Platonic Communion', 38.

40 Pater, *Plato and Platonism*, 134, 137, 140, 136.

41 For more on Pater's 'Winckelmann' as a direct response to Arnold (1869), see David DeLaura, *Hebrew and Hellene in Victorian England: Newman, Arnold, and Pater* (Austin: University of Texas Press, 1969), 206.

42 See F. C. McGrath, *The Sensible Spirit: Walter Pater and the Modernist Paradigm* (Tampa: University of South Florida Press, 1986), 215–30 and James Eli Adams, *Dandies and Desert Saints: Styles of Victorian Masculinity* (Ithaca: Cornell University Press, 1995), 176–7.

43 Lionel Johnson, 'Mr. Pater and His Public' (first published 1900), in Thomas Whittemore, ed., *Post Liminium: Essays and Critical Papers* (London: Elkin Mathews, 1912), 14–19; 15.

44 Walter Pater, 'Style' in *Appreciations: With an Essay on Style* (London: Macmillan, 1910; first published 1889), 5–38; 12.

45 Megan Becker-Lackrone, 'Same-Sex and the Second Sex in "Style"', *The Pater Newsletter*, 52 (Spring 2007), 37–44. See also James Eli Adams, 'Pater's Muscular Aestheticism', in Donald Hall, ed., *Muscular Christianity: Embodying the Victorian Age* (Cambridge: Cambridge University Press, 1994), 215–38.

46 Both of these sentences were altered for the 1888 edition: 'proper' had formerly been 'pure', and 'restraint' was 'limitation'. The latter change would certainly have increased the association of 'passion' with sexuality and its control with continence for late nineteenth-century readers.

47 For divergent readings see Lee, 'Platonic Communion', 38 and Stefano Evangelista, '"Lovers and Philosophers at Once"', 230–44. The phrase is translated from the Greek only in the third edition.

48 Arthur Symons, 'Introduction', in Arthur Symons, ed., *Walter Pater, The Renaissance* (New York: The Modern Library, 1919), xi–xiv; xiii.

49 Pater, 'Diaphaneitè', read at Oxford in 1864, first published in Charles L. Shadwell, ed., *Miscellaneous Studies: A Series of Essays* (London: Macmillan, 1910; first published 1895), 247–54; 253. Benson, *Walter Pater*, 10.

50 See Dellamora, 'The Androgynous Body', 51–68.

51 [Walter Pater], 'Poems by William Morris', *Westminster Review*, 34:2 (October 1868), 300–12; 303, 302.

52 The first edition reads not 'practical or intellectual', but 'religious, moral, political', a change that reflects a softening of the secular context. Pater, *The Renaissance* (1873), 155.

53 For an alternative reading of Pater's engagement with Goethe with regard to sexuality, see Stefano Evangelista, '"Life in the Whole": Goethe and English Aestheticism', *Publications of the English Goethe Society*, 82:3 (1 October 2013), 180–92.

54 Benjamin Morgan, 'Aesthetic Freedom: Walter Pater and the Politics of Autonomy', *ELH*, 77:3 (Fall 2010), 731–56; 747, 749.

55 Benson, *Walter Pater*, 18.

56 *Ibid.*, 47.

57 Walter Pater, 'The Aesthetic Life', Cambridge, Harvard University, Houghton Library, *The Pater Manuscripts*, bMS.Eng1150(7), 1. All references will be given in the text. I have preserved Pater's punctuation, or lack of such, in this manuscript, though it evidently does not always represent a final decision.

58 Gowan Dawson has pointed out Pater's engagement with the principle of energy conservation in nineteenth-century physics, but not in relation to sexuality. See Dawson, '"A Creature of the Nineteenth Century"', 44.

59 Arthur Symons, 'Walter Pater' in *Figures of Several Centuries* (London: Constable & Company, 1916), 316–35; 324.

60 Friedman, *Before Queer Theory*, 44.

61 *Ibid.*, 50.
62 Evangelista, *British Aestheticism and Ancient Greece*, 48.
63 Hext, *Walter Pater*, 104.
64 Walter Pater, 'Diaphaneitè', 247, 251.
65 *Ibid.*, 248, 251.
66 *Ibid.*, 248–9, 254.
67 Williams, *Transfigured World*, 185.
68 DeLaura, *Hebrew and Hellene*, xvii.
69 For instance, Monsman, 'The Platonic Eros', 35.
70 *Ibid.*, 32.
71 Matthew Potolsky, 'Fear of Falling: Walter Pater's "Marius the Epicurean" as a Dangerous Influence', *ELH*, 65:3 (Fall 1998), 701–29; 714, 717.
72 Friedman, *Before Queer Theory*, 79.
73 Potolsky, 'Fear of Falling', 715.
74 See William F. Shuter, *Rereading Walter Pater* (Cambridge: Cambridge University Press, 1997), 92–108, and Lee Behlman, 'Burning, Burial, and the Critique of Stoicism in Walter Pater's *Marius the Epicurean*', *Nineteenth-Century Prose*, 31:1 (Spring 2004), 133–56.
75 Friedman, *Before Queer Theory*, 80, 79.
76 John Henry Newman, *An Essay in Aid of a Grammar of Assent* (London: Burns, Oates & Co., 1870).
77 Walter Pater, *Marius the Epicurean: His Sensations and Ideas*, ed. Gerald Monsman (Kansas City: Valancourt Books, 2008), 230; Ernest Renan, *Histoire des origines du Christianisme*, 8 vols. (Paris: Calmann Lévy, 1863–83), vol. 7: *Marc-Aurèle et la fin du monde antique* (1882), 91.
78 Sussman, *Victorian Masculinities*, 16–72.
79 Richard Dellamora, *Masculine Desire: The Sexual Politics of Victorian Aestheticism* (Chapel Hill: University of North Carolina Press), 165, 168.
80 Heather Love, *Feeling Backward: Loss and the Politics of Queer History* (Cambridge, MA: Harvard University Press, 2007), 67.
81 *Ibid.*, 64.
82 Potolsky, 'Fear of Falling', 718.
83 The extant material has been edited by Gerald Monsman: *The Collected Works of Walter Pater*, 10 vols., general eds. Lesley Higgins and David Latham (Oxford: Oxford University Press, 2019–), vol. 4: *Gaston de Latour*, ed. Gerald Monsman (2019). All references will be to this edition and will be given in the text.
84 Letter from Lionel Johnson to Campbell Dodgson, 26 September 1888, in *Some Letters of Lionel Johnson*, ed. Raymond Roseliep, unpublished doctoral dissertation (South Bend, IN: University of Notre Dame, 1955), 65.
85 Monsman, 'The Platonic Eros', 41.
86 Lee, 'Platonic Communion', 26–31.
87 *Ibid.*, 32.
88 *Ibid.*, 34.
89 For the Platonic implications of this term see Monsman, 'The Platonic Eros', 34–41.

90 See Gerald Monsman, 'Introduction', in Gerald Monsman, ed., *Gaston de Latour: The Revised Text* (Greensboro: ELT Press, 1995), xvii–xlvi, xvii.

91 More about Pater's use of this idea from Plato's *Phaedrus* in *Gaston de Latour* can be found in Lee, 'Platonic Communion', and Monsman, 'The Platonic Eros'.

92 Lee, 'Platonic Communion', 35.

3 'A Holy Indifference and Tolerant Favour': Lionel Johnson

1 Ezra Pound, 'Preface' in *Poetical Works of Lionel Johnson* (London: Elkin Mathews, 1915), v–xix; v.

2 Richard Whittington-Egan, *Lionel Johnson: Victorian Dark Angel* (Great Malvern: Capella Archive, 2012), 285.

3 George Santayana, *Persons and Places: The Autobiography in One Volume,* ed. Daniel Cory (New York: Scribner, 1963; first published 1944–53), 57–62; Ernest Rhys, *Everyman Remembers* (London: J. M. Dent, 1931), 227; Edgar Jepson, *Memories of a Victorian* (London: Victor Gollancz, 1933), 213; Cornelius Weygandt, *Tuesdays at Ten* (Philadelphia: University of Philadelphia Press, 1928), 72.

4 W. B. Yeats, *Collected Works,* general eds. Richard J. Finneran and George Mills Harper, 14 vols. (New York: Scribner, 1984–), vol. 3: *Autobiographies,* eds. William H. O'Donnell and Douglas N. Archibald (1999; this section first published 1922), 185, 241.

5 W. B. Yeats, *Memoirs,* ed. Denis Donoghue (London: Macmillan, 1972), 97.

6 Sarah Green, 'The Undeveloped Body of Lionel Johnson', *Notes and Queries,* 63:2 (June 2016), 281–3.

7 Ezra Pound, '"Siena Mi Fe": Disfecemia Maremma' (from the sequence 'Hugh Selwyn Moberly'), in *Collected Shorter Poems* (London: Faber, 1952), 210, lines 7–12.

8 Barbara Charlesworth *Dark Passages: The Decadent Consciousness in Victorian Literature* (Madison: University of Wisconsin Press, 1965), 122, 95.

9 Ian Fletcher, 'Lionel Johnson and "The Dark Angel"' in *W. B. Yeats and His Contemporaries,* ed. Ian Fletcher (Brighton: The Harvester Press, 1987), 303.

10 R. K. R. Thornton, *The Decadent Dilemma* (London: Edward Arnold, 1983), 111; Murray Pittock, 'The Poetry of Lionel Johnson', *Victorian Poetry,* 28:3/4 (Autumn/Winter 1990), 43–60, 44.

11 Alex Murray, 'Recusant Poetics: Rereading Catholicism at the Fin de Siècle', *English Literature in Transition, 1880–1920,* 56:3 (2013), 355–73; 367.

12 Lionel Johnson, 'An Old Debate', *The Anti-Jacobin,* 25 (8 July 1891), 589–90; 589, 590.

13 Lionel Johnson, *The Art of Thomas Hardy* (London: Elkin Mathews & John Lane, 1894), 225. All references will be given in the text.

14 [Frank Russell], ed., *Some Winchester Letters of Lionel Johnson* (London: George Allen & Unwin, 1919), 190. All references are given in the text.

15 After Johnson's death, his friend Arthur Galton collected his papers with view to a biography. On Galton's death in 1921, and the death of his own literary executor Frederic Manning in 1933, these were sent to Johnson's sister Isabella, biography unwritten. Isabella loaned these papers, in 1943, to an interested scholar, Adrian Earle, who also planned a biography. Not only were they never returned, but Earle seems to have spent the next ten years visiting prominent 1890s archives and relieving them of Johnson-related material, including the John Gray archive held by the Dominican Library at Edinburgh and the Selwyn Image papers held by Image's widow. Ian Fletcher had access to these papers at some point between his two editions of Johnson's poems, and references some of them in his revised introduction, though claiming that he no longer knew their whereabouts. Earle was found deceased in a hotel in Madrid on Christmas Day 1977, and the Johnson papers have not been seen since. Though seemingly sincere in his interest in Johnson, Earle effectively wiped his presence from the archive. More information on Earle's interest in Johnson can be found in Whittington-Egan, *Victorian Dark Angel*, 303–4.

16 For more on Johnson's relationship with his correspondents, especially Frank Russell, see Ruth Derham, *Bertrand's Brother: The Marriages, Morals and Misdemeanours of Frank, 2nd Earl Russell* (Stroud: Amberly Publishing, 2021), 48–73.

17 Murray Pittock, 'Introduction', in Lionel Johnson, *Selected Letters* (Edinburgh: Tragona Press, 1988), 5–7; 6.

18 The originals can be found in Dubuque, IA, Loras College Library, *Roseliep Personal Papers*, Cabinet A, Drawer 1, Folders 3–7; and in Cambridge University Library, *Charles Edward Sayle: Diaries and Papers*, GBR/0012/MS Add. 8548. See Derham, *Bertrand's Brother*, 65–73.

19 Letter to Oswald Carnagey Johnson (undated, but evidently March 1889), *Roseliep Personal Papers*, Cabinet A, Drawer 1, Folders 1–2, letter 14.

20 Murray, 'Recusant Poetics', 370.

21 Pittock, 'The Poetry of Lionel Johnson', 43, 47.

22 Mark Knight and Emma Mason, *Nineteenth-Century Religion and Literature: An Introduction* (Oxford: Oxford University Press, 2006), 9.

23 *Ibid.*, 89.

24 Letter to Campbell Dodgson, December 1891, in *Some Letters of Lionel Johnson*, ed. Raymond Roseliep, unpublished doctoral dissertation (South Bend, IN: University of Notre Dame, 1953), 117.

25 George Ridding, *Purity* (Derby: Bemrose & Sons, 1883), 4, 8.

26 I am joined in this interpretation by Ruth Derham; see *Bertrand's Brother*, 62–3.

27 Letters to Oswald Carnagey Johnson (undated, early summer 1888; undated, March 1889), in *Roseliep Personal Papers*, letters 12 and 14, respectively.

28 *Ibid.*, letters 14 and 15.

29 Thomas à Kempis, *The Imitation of Christ*, trans. William Atkynson (books 1–3) and Princess Margaret, Countess of Richmond (book 4) (London: Dent, 1910, reprinted 1937; this translation first published by Wynkyn de Worde, 1504; first Latin printing 1471), book 1, Chapter 16, 27–8; 27.

30 Lionel Johnson, *A Letter to Edgar Jepson*, ed. Ian Fletcher (Norfolk: Daedalus Press, 1979), 7.

31 *Ibid.*, 8.

32 Walter Pater, *Marius the Epicurean: His Sensations and Ideas*, 2 vols. (London: Macmillan, 1910; first published 1885), vol. 2, 17.

33 Letter to Campbell Dodgson, 15 April 1889, in *Some Letters*, 80.

34 Letter to Campbell Dodgson, 5 February 1891, *ibid.*, 109.

35 Letter to W. B Yeats, 23 October 1894, *ibid.*, 154. Brackets indicate illegibility.

36 Lionel Johnson, 'The Work of Mr. Pater' (first published 1894), in *Post Liminium: Essays and Critical Papers*, ed. Thomas Whittemore (London: Elkin Mathews, 1912), 19–42; 34.

37 Johnson, 'Mr Pater's Humour' (first published 1897), in *Post Liminium*, 11–9; 11.

38 Johnson, 'The Work of Mr. Pater', 28–9.

39 Letter to Campbell Dodgson, 12 September 1894, in *Some Letters*, 150.

40 'Lionel Johnson, *The Collected Poems of Lionel Johnson*, ed. Ian Fletcher, 2nd ed. (London: Garland, 1982), 246–54.

41 Gary H. Paterson makes a similar point in *At the Heart of the 1890s: Essays on Lionel Johnson* (New York: AMS Press, 2008), 34.

42 David DeLaura, *Hebrew and Hellene in Victorian England: Newman, Arnold, and Pater* (Austin: University of Texas Press, 1969), 338.

43 Johnson, 'Mr. Pater Upon Plato' (amalgamation of two review essays, both first published 1893), in *Post Liminium*, 1–10; 3.

44 *Ibid.*, 5–6.

45 Christopher R. Wilson and Michela Calore, *Music in Shakespeare: A Dictionary* (London: Thoemmes Continuum, 2005), 111.

46 Johnson, 'Mr. Pater Upon Plato', 6.

47 Fletcher, *Collected Poems*, 225–6; 226 (line 23).

48 Johnson, 'The Work of Mr. Pater', 25.

49 *Ibid.*, 26, 25.

50 *Ibid.*, 25.

51 *Collected Poems*, ed. Fletcher, 225 (lines 1–6).

52 [Lionel Johnson], 'The Way of Writing', *The Anti-Jacobin*, 15 (9 May 1891), 347–8; 347.

53 Stephen Cheeke, *Transfiguration: The Religion of Art in Nineteenth-Century Literature Before Aestheticism* (Oxford: Oxford University Press, 2016), 191.

54 *Collected Poems*, ed. Fletcher, 52–3; 53 (lines 41–4).

55 Kempis, *The Imitation of Christ*, book 1, Chapter 13, 20–2; 20.

56 *Collected Poems*, ed. Fletcher, 53–4; 54 (lines 9–12).

57 Ian Fletcher, 'Lionel Johnson and "The Dark Angel"', 311.

58 See Arthur W. Patrick, *Lionel Johnson (1867–1902): Poète et Critique*, unpublished doctoral dissertation (Paris: L. Rodstein, 1939), 67; Yeats, *Autobiographies*, 243; Raymond Roseliep, 'Introduction', in *Some Letters*, 1–9c; 9b.

59 Brian Reade, *Sexual Heretics: Male Homosexuality in English Literature from 1850 to 1900* (London: Routledge & Kegan Paul, 1970), 39; Ellis Hanson, *Decadence and Catholicism* (Cambridge, MA: Harvard University Press, 1997), 88.

60 Thornton, *The Decadent Dilemma*, 125; Ronald Schuchard, *Eliot's Dark Angel: Intersections of Life and Art* (Oxford: Oxford University Press, 1999), 5.

61 Pittock, 'The Poetry of Lionel Johnson', 45.

62 *Collected Poems*, ed. Fletcher, 52 (lines 21–4).

63 *Ibid.*, (lines 5–6, 15–6).

64 Knight and Mason, *Nineteenth-Century Religion and Literature*, 102.

65 *Collected Poems*, ed. Fletcher, 137–8; 138 (lines 17, 21–4).

66 *Ibid.*, 53 (line 38).

67 *Ibid.*, 53 (lines 3–4).

68 *Ibid.*, 152–3; 152 (lines 5–6, 9, 11–2), 153 (lines 17–20).

69 *Ibid.*, 53 (lines 55–6).

70 *Ibid.*, 132–4; 132 (lines 1–2), 133 (lines 26–7, 46, 47, 32–3).

71 R. L. Stevenson, 'Our Lady of the Snows', in *Collected Poems*, ed. Roger C. Lewis (Edinburgh: Edinburgh University Press, 2003; poem first published 1887), 89–90; 89 (lines 12, 9).

72 *Collected Poems*, ed. Fletcher, 75–6; 75 (lines 25–6), 76 (lines 68, 69–70).

73 *Ibid.*, 216–7; 217 (lines 5, 6–7, 9).

74 R. K. R. Thornton, 'Johnson, Lionel Pigot (1867–1902)', *Oxford Dictionary of National Biography* (Oxford: Oxford University Press, 2004); online edition, May 2007, www.oxforddnb.com/view/article/34204 (accessed 2 May 2016); *Collected Poems*, ed. Fletcher, 24–5; 24 (line 1).

75 Knight and Mason, *Nineteenth-Century Religion and Literature*, 206–12.

76 [Walter Pater], 'Poems by William Morris', *Westminster Review*, 34:2 (October 1868), 300–12; 303.

77 *Collected Poems*, ed. Fletcher, 25 (lines 19–20).

78 *Ibid.*, 160–1; 161 (lines 5–6), 160 (line 4).

79 See, for instance, letter to Katharine Tynan, 8 October 1901, Manchester, John Rylands Library, *The Tynan/Hinkson Collection*, KTG 1/463/1b.

80 John S. North, ed., *Waterloo Directory of English Newspapers and Periodicals: 1800–1900*, 3rd series (Waterloo: Waterloo Academic Press 1976–). Accessed online at victorianperiodicals.com (4 March 2019).

81 DeLaura, *Hebrew and Hellene.*

82 For Newman's thinking about the relationship between art and religion, see Hilary Fraser, *Beauty and Belief: Aesthetics and Religion in Victorian Literature* (Cambridge: Cambridge University Press, 1986), 26–8.

83 Paterson, *At the Heart of the 1890s*, 141.

84 See Owen Chadwick, ed., *The Mind of the Oxford Movement* (London: Adam Charles Black, 1960), 38–41.

85 Richard Le Gallienne, *Retrospective Reviews: A Literary Log*, 2 vols. (London: John Lane, 1896), vol. 2, 234.

86 [Lionel Johnson], 'Inspirers and Teachers', *The Anti-Jacobin*, 26 (25 July 1891), 611.

87 John Henry Newman, 'The Tamworth Reading Room', in *Discussions and Arguments on Various Subjects* (London: Pickering, 1872), 254–305, 294; first published in *The Times* (5 and 27 February 1841).

88 Johnson, 'Inspirers and Teachers', 611.
89 Johnson, 'The Way of Writing', 347–8; 347.
90 *Ibid.*, 348.
91 *Ibid.*, 347.
92 [Lionel Johnson], 'Of the Spirit of Books', *The Anti-Jacobin*, 13 (25 April 1891), 299–300; 299.
93 *Ibid.*, 300.
94 Walter Pater, 'Style', in *Appreciations: With an Essay on Style* (London: Macmillan, 1910; first published 1889), 5–38.
95 [Lionel Johnson], 'Criticism in Corruption', *The Anti-Jacobin*, 6 (7 March 1891), 131–2; 132.
96 [Lionel Johnson], 'The Cultured Faun', *The Anti-Jacobin*, 7 (14 March 1891), 156–7; 156.
97 *Ibid.*, 157.
98 Hanson, *Decadence and Catholicism*.
99 'The Cultured Faun', 157.
100 *Ibid.*, 156.
101 Lionel Johnson, 'A Note upon the Practice and Theory of Verse at the Present Time Obtaining in France', *Century Guild Hobby Horse*, 5:22 (April 1891), 61–6; 61, 64, 65, 61.
102 *Ibid.*, 64.
103 Johnson, 'The Inimitable Lucian' (first published 1900), in *Post Liminium*, 188–93, 193, 188–9; 'Thoughts on Bacon' (first published 1900), in *ibid.*, 131–6, 132.
104 Johnson, 'Marie Bashkirtseff' (first published 1891), in *Post Liminium*, 245–50; 245, 248–9.
105 Johnson, 'Saint Francis' (amalgamation of two articles, first published 1899 and 1901), in *Post Liminium*, 90–7; 91, 96.
106 Johnson, 'Thomas à Kempis' (amalgamation of two articles, first published 1891 and 1901), in *Post Liminium*, 276–83; 279, 280, 282.
107 Johnson, 'Charlotte Brontë and Her Champion' (amalgamation of two articles, both first published 1900), in *Post Liminium*, 42–50; 44, 44–5, 46.
108 Johnson, 'Santo Virgilio' (first published 1900), in *Post Liminium*, 223–9; 228.
109 Lionel Johnson, 'Erasmus, My Darling' (first published 1902), in *Post Liminium*, 161–5; 163.

4 'An Ascetic Epicureanism': Vernon Lee

1 Vernon Lee, 'A Dialogue on Poetic Morality', in *Belcaro: Being Essays on Sundry Aesthetical Questions* (London: W. Satchell & Co, 1881), 229–74; 274. All references will be to this edition and given in the text.
2 Mary Robinson published at this time under the name A. Mary F. Robinson, and later as Madame Darmesteter, and Madame Duclaux. Similar opinions were voiced by Lee in two letters to Robinson, dated 19 and 20 November 1880. In *Selected Letters of Vernon Lee, 1856–1935*, vol. 1, eds. Amanda Gagel *et al.* (London: Routledge, 2017), 267–75.

3 Though 'Vernon Lee' was the pseudonym of Violet Paget, she was often known by the assumed name both in public and private. I use 'Vernon Lee' throughout this chapter in accordance with my focus on her public utterances rather than psychology.

4 Vernon Lee, *Baldwin: Being Dialogues on Views and Aspirations* (London: T. Fisher Unwin, 1886), 13–4. All references will be to this edition and given in the text.

5 Letter from Lee to Frances Power Cobbe, 26 April 1885, in *Selected Letters of Vernon Lee (1856–1935)*, ed. Mandy Gagel, unpublished doctoral dissertation (Boston: Boston University, 2008), 363–4.

6 Burdett Gardner, *The Lesbian Imagination (Victorian Style): A Psychological and Critical Study of 'Vernon Lee'* (New York: Garland, 1987; written 1954).

7 Jo Briggs, 'Plural Anomalies: Gender and Sexuality in Bio-Critical Readings of Vernon Lee', in Catherine Maxwell and Patricia Pulham, eds., *Vernon Lee: Decadence, Ethics, Aesthetics* (Basingstoke: Palgrave Macmillan, 2006), 160–73; 161.

8 Sally Newman, 'The Archival Traces of Desire: Vernon Lee's Failed Sexuality and the Interpretation of Letters in Lesbian History', *Journal of the History of Sexuality*, 14:1/2 (January–April 2005), 51–75; 55.

9 For example, Sophie Geoffroy, ed., *Women and Political Theory: Vernon Lee and Radical Circles* (Paris: Michel Houdiard Editeur, 2017); Benjamin Morgan, *The Outward Mind: Materialist Aesthetics in Victorian Science and Literature* (Oxford: Oxford University Press, 2017); Kirsty Martin, *Modernism and the Rhythms of Sympathy: Vernon Lee, Virginia Woolf, D.H. Lawrence* (Oxford: Oxford University, 2013); Kristen Mahoney, 'Vernon Lee at the Margins of the Twentieth Century: World War 1, Pacifism, and Post-Victorian Aestheticism', *English Literature in Transition, 1880–1920*, 56:3 (2013), 313–42.

10 Martha Vicinus, for example, has represented Lee's relationships as consciously sexual, whether or not genital-based sex acts took place: *Intimate Friends: Women Who Loved Women, 1778–1928* (Chicago: University of Chicago Press, 2004), 143–70.

11 Kathy Alexis Psomiades, '"Still Burning from This Strangling Embrace": Vernon Lee on Desire and Aesthetics', in Richard Dellamora, ed., *Victorian Sexual Dissidence* (Chicago: University of Chicago Press, 1999), 21–42, 37; Stefano Evangelista, 'Vernon Lee and the Gender of Aestheticism', in Maxwell and Pulham, eds., *Vernon Lee*, 91–111, 92.

12 See Ardel Haefele-Thomas, *Queer Others in Victorian Gothic: Transgressing Monstrosity* (Cardiff: University of Wales Press, 2012), 120–48; Margaret Stetz, 'The Snake Lady and the Bruised Bodley Head: Vernon Lee and Oscar Wilde in the Yellow Book', in Maxwell and Pulham, eds., *Vernon Lee*, 112–22; Catherine Anne Wiley, '"Warming Me Like a Cordial": The Ethos of the Body in Vernon Lee's Aesthetics', in *ibid.*, 58–74; Christa Zorn, *Vernon Lee: Aesthetics, History, & the Victorian Female Intellectual* (Athens: Ohio University Press, 2003), 78; Patricia Pulham, 'The Castrato and the Cry in Vernon Lee's Wicked Voices', *Victorian Literature and Culture*, 30:2 (January 2002), 421–37; 'Duality and Desire in *Louis Norbert*', in Maxwell and Pulham, eds., *Vernon Lee*, 123–42; Psomiades, 'Vernon Lee on Desire and Aesthetics'.

13 Vineta Colby, *Vernon Lee: A Literary Biography* (Charlottesville: University of Virginia Press, 2003), 209.

14 *Ibid.*, 280, 4.

15 Darmesteter's exact condition is unknown. Colby mentions stunted growth from 'childhood spinal disease' (Colby, *Vernon Lee*, 121). Robinson herself, in her entry for her husband in the *Jewish Encyclopedia*, claims that this lack of growth was due to the family's poverty during his formative years (Mary Robinson Duclaux, 'James Darmesteter', in Isidore Singer *et al.*, eds., *The Jewish Encyclopedia*, 12 vols. (1901–1906), vol. 4, 444–7; 444). Lee's family letters assume the problem to be acquired rather than congenital, suggesting Lamarckian rather than Darwinian evolution, in which acquired characteristics are passed to offspring. See Colby, *Vernon Lee*, 121–9, and Shaftquat Towheed, 'Creative Evolution of Scientific Paradigms: Vernon Lee and the Debate over the Hereditary Transmission of Acquired Characters', *Victorian Studies*, 49:1 (Autumn 2006), 33–61. See also Lee's objection on the same grounds when her brother, having spent a considerable number of years paralyzed from the waist down, recovered after their mother's death, married, and had a child (Colby, 148).

16 Letter from Lee to Matilda Paget, 27 September 1887, *Vernon Lee: Letters Home*, 333, https//digitalcommons.colby.edu/letters_home/333 (consulted 23 June 2022). In transcribing this letter I agree with Gardner (*The Lesbian Imagination*, 190–1) in reading 'common instinct', against Amanda Gagel's more recent 'error on instinct' (*Selected Letters*, ed. Gagel (dissertation), 449).

17 Lee's phrasing does not necessarily exclude masturbation, but it seems unlikely that she would not have considered masturbation to be a means of 'indulging passion'.

18 Vernon Lee, 'Two Books on Social Evolution', *The Academy*, 732 (15 May 1886), 340–1; 340.

19 Letter from Lee to Karl Pearson, 13 March 1886, in *Selected Letters*, ed. Gagel (dissertation), 395–400; 398–9. This is the only letter from Lee to Pearson known to survive, and Gagel thinks it likely to have been the only one written, 49.

20 Colby, *Vernon Lee*, 125.

21 Letter from Lee to Pearson, 13 March 1886, 398. For Lee's visit to Clapperton, see the letter from Vernon Lee to Matilda Paget, 17 July 1887, *Vernon Lee: Letters Home*, 305, https//digitalcommons.colby.edu/letters_home/305 (accessed 9 March 2019).

22 Letter from Lee to Cobbe, 26 April 1885, *Selected Letters*, ed. Gagel (dissertation), 363–5; 364.

23 Letter from Lee to Pearson, 13 March 1886, 397.

24 Lucy Bland, *Banishing the Beast: English Feminism & Sexual Morality, 1885–1914* (Harmondsworth: Penguin, 1995), 197; see also 189, 196. Hera Cook has argued that this anti-contraception bias among feminist writers was the result of a common movement towards preferred sexual abstinence among women of all classes in the late nineteenth century. See Hera Cook, *The Long Sexual Revolution: English Women, Sex, and Contraception, 1800–1975* (Oxford: Oxford University Press, 2005), 115.

25 An example can be found in the work of George Moore; see Chapter 5.

26 Vineta Colby, *The Singular Anomaly: Women Novelists of the Nineteenth Century* (New York: University of New York Press, 1970), 294.

27 Bland, *Banishing the Beast*, 81–91; Sheila Jeffreys, *The Spinster and Her Enemies: Feminism and Sexuality, 1880–1930* (London: Pandora Press, 1985), 27–53.

28 Jane Hume Clapperton, *Scientific Meliorism and the Evolution of Happiness* (London: Kegan Paul & Trench, 1885), ix.

29 Havelock Ellis, *Studies in the Psychology of Sex*, 6 vols., 2nd ed. revised (Philadelphia: F. A Davis, 1921; first published 1910), vol. 6: *Sex in Relation to Society* (1910), 145.

30 Richard von Krafft-Ebing, *Psychopathia Sexualis*, trans. F. J. Rebman, 10th ed. (Chicago: Keener, 1901; originally published in German, 1886), 3, 2.

31 See Regenia Gagnier, *Individualism, Decadence and Globalization: On the Relationship of the Part to the Whole, 1859–1920* (Basingstoke: Palgrave Macmillan, 2010), 15; Rob Boddice, *The Science of Sympathy: Morality, Evolution, and Victorian Civilization* (Chicago: University of Illinois Press, 2016); Bland, *Banishing the Beast*, 86–91.

32 Vernon Lee, 'The Use of the Soul', in *Althea: Dialogues on Aspirations and Duties* (London: Osgood, McIlvaine & Co, 1894), 267–304; 302, 287. All references will be to this edition and will be given in the text.

33 Vernon Lee, 'The Spiritual Life', in *Althea* (first published in 1892), 223–66.

34 Vernon Lee, 'Introduction: Juvenilia', in *Juvenilia: Being a Second Series of Essays on Sundry Aesthetical Questions*, 2 vols. (London: T. Fisher Unwin, 1887), vol 1., 1–22; 18. All references will be to this edition and will be given in the text.

35 George Eliot, *Middlemarch: A Study of Provincial Life*, 4 vols. (Edinburgh: William Blackwood, 1871), vol. 2, 308.

36 Lee, 'Ruskinism', in *Belcaro*, 197–229.

37 Letter from Lee to Robinson, 7 November 1880, in *Selected Letters*, ed. Gagel et al., 262–5; 263.

38 Vernon Lee, 'Medieval Love', in *Euphorion: Being Studies of the Antique and the Medieval in the Renaissance*, 2nd ed. revised (London: T. Fisher Unwin, 1885; first published 1884), 337–431; 353. All references will be to this edition and will be given in the text.

39 See Christa Zorn for a reading of Lee's dialogues as a rejection of Platonic homoeroticism. Zorn interprets this as a rewriting of the genre in lesbian terms. Zorn, *Vernon Lee*, 96–110.

40 Vernon Lee, 'Love of the Saints', in *Renaissance Fancies and Studies: Being a Sequel to Euphorion* (London: Smith, Elder & Co., 1895), 1–64; 15–16. All references will be to this edition and will be given in the text.

41 Evangelista, 'Vernon Lee and the Gender of Aestheticism', 93.

42 Vernon Lee, 'Chapelmaster Kreisler: A Study of Musical Romanticists', in *Belcaro* (first published 1878), 106–28.

43 [Walter Pater], 'Poems by William Morris', *Westminster Review*, 34:2 (October 1868), 300–12; 303.

44 *Ibid.*

45 Vernon Lee, 'Valedictory', *Renaissance Fancies and Studies*, 233–60.
46 See *Vernon Lee Collection*, The British Institute of Florence, VL 143 BEN, VL 143 BER, VL 170 BER, VL 113 BER, and VL 128.2 BER.
47 Anne Fernihough, *Freewomen and Supermen: Edwardian Radicals and Literary Modernism* (Oxford: Oxford University Press, 2013), 25.
48 Vernon Lee, 'The Use of Beauty', in *Laurus Nobilis: Chapters on Art and Life* (London: John Lane, 1909), 1–40; 11–2, 22, 33–4.
49 Vernon Lee, 'Epilogue', *Euphorion*, 435–48.
50 Vernon Lee, 'In Umbria: A Study in Artistic Personality', in *Belcaro* (first published 1881), 156–96.
51 Walter Pater, *Marius the Epicurean: His Sensations and Ideas*, 2 vols. (London: Macmillan, 1910; first published 1885), vol. 1, 22.
52 Vernon Lee, 'Of Novels', in *Baldwin* (first published 1885), 185–246.
53 Laurel Brake, 'Vernon Lee and the Pater Circle', in Maxwell and Pulham, eds., *Vernon Lee*, 40–57, 41; Evangelista, 'Vernon Lee and the Gender of Aestheticism', 104.
54 See especially Vernon Lee, 'The Aesthetics of the Novel', in *The Handling of Words and Other Studies in Literary Psychology* (London: John Lane, 1923), 66–72.
55 William F. Shuter, *Rereading Walter Pater* (Cambridge: Cambridge University Press, 1997).
56 Vernon Lee, *Miss Brown: A Novel* (London: Blackwood, 1884).
57 Letter from Henry James to Vernon Lee, 10 May 1884, quoted in Peter Gunn, *Vernon Lee: Violet Paget, 1856–1935* (London: Oxford University Press, 1964), 104; [unsigned review], *Spectator*, 13 December 1884, quoted in Colby, *Vernon Lee*, 109.
58 Letter from Henry James to Vernon Lee, 10 May 1884, quoted in Gunn, *Vernon Lee*, 104–5.
59 *Ibid.*, 105, 106.
60 Psomiades, 'Vernon Lee on Desire and Aesthetics', 27, 29, 27, 25.

5 'Men Have Died of Love': George Moore

1 Elizabeth Grubgeld, *George Moore and the Autogenous Self: The Autobiography and Fiction* (Syracuse: Syracuse University Press, 1994), 16.
2 Quoted in Charles Morgan, *Epitaph on George Moore* (London: Macmillan, 1935), 15.
3 Grubgeld, *The Autogenous Self*, ix; Adrian Frazier, *George Moore, 1852–1933* (New Haven: Yale University Press, 2000), 161. For the bachelor uncle as a stock figure in nineteenth-century literature, see Katherine V. Snyder, *Bachelors, Manhood and the Novel, 1850–1925* (Cambridge: Cambridge University Press, 1999), 182.
4 George Moore, *Hail and Farewell*, 3 vols. (London: Heinemann, 1911–14), vol. 1, 232. All references will be to this edition unless otherwise stated and will be given in the text.

5 Richard Cave, 'George Moore's "Stella"', *Review of English Studies*, 28:110 (May 1977) 181–8; 184.

6 Frazier, *George Moore*, 387, 563 (n. 68).

7 George Moore, *Avowals* (London: privately printed, 1919), 181. All references will be to this edition, unless otherwise specified, and given in the text. For Lee as inspiration for Cecilia, see Frazier, *George Moore*, 107.

8 Ellis Hanson, *Decadence and Catholicism* (Cambridge, MA: Harvard University Press, 1997), 23.

9 Herbert Sussman, *Victorian Masculinities: Manhood and Masculine Poetics in Early Victorian Literature and Art* (Cambridge: Cambridge University Press, 1995), 5. For more on the gendered implications of Moore's impotence, see Sarah Green, 'Impotence and the Male Artist: The Case of George Moore', *Journal of Victorian Culture*, 24:2 (April 2019), 179–92.

10 Angus McLaren, *Impotence: A Cultural History* (Chicago: University of Chicago Press, 2007), 118.

11 For example, Patrick Bridgwater, *George Moore and German Pessimism* (Durham: University of Durham, 1988), 40; Helmut Gerber, ed., *George Moore in Transition: Letters to T. Fisher Unwin and Lena Milman, 1894–1910* (Detroit: Wayne State University Press, 1968), 101.

12 Fabienne Dabrigeon-Garcier and Christine Huguet, 'Introduction', in Fabienne Dabrigeon-Garcier and Christine Huguet, eds., *George Moore: Across Borders* (Amsterdam: Rodopi, 2013), 1–12; 2, 3.

13 Grubgeld, *The Autogenous Self*, x.

14 Frazier, *George Moore*, 163. For Moore's relationship to and influence from Pater, see Robert Porter Sechler, *George Moore: A Disciple of Walter Pater*, unpublished doctoral dissertation (Oxford: University of Oxford, 1931); for his reading of Schopenhauer, see Bridgwater, *George Moore and German Pessimism*, 11–56.

15 Raffaella Maiguashca Uslenghi, 'A Perspective of Unity in George Moore's Writings', *English Literature in Transition, 1880–1920*, trans. Jack W. Weaver, 27:3 (1984), 201–24; 214.

16 For discourses of 'life' and vitalism in the late nineteenth and early twentieth centuries, see Jonathan Rose, *The Edwardian Temperament, 1895–1919* (Athens: Ohio University Press, 1986), 74–116.

17 For further discussion of Moore's use of the word 'life', see Grubgeld, *The Autogenous Self*, 200–31.

18 D. F. Hannigan, 'Sex in Fiction', *Westminster Review*, 143 (January 1895), 616–25; 618, 616, 618.

19 George Moore, *A Modern Lover*, 2nd ed. (London: Vizetelly, 1885; first published 1883), 178.

20 George Moore, *A Mummer's Wife* (London: Vizetelly, 1885), 320.

21 George Moore, *A Drama in Muslin* (London: Vizetelly, 1886), 3.

22 George Moore, *Confessions of a Young Man*, 2nd ed. (London: Swan Sonnenschein, 1889), 31. *Confessions* was first published in 1888. It was,

however, almost immediately heavily revised. All references, unless otherwise specified, will be to the 1889 version and will be given in the text.

23 George Moore, 'Bring in the Lamp', in *Memoirs of My Dead Life* (London: Heinemann, 1906), 269–85; 274. All references, unless otherwise specified, will be to this edition and given in the text.

24 Grubgeld, *The Autogenous Self*, 2.

25 Moore, *Avowals*, 178, 204.

26 George Moore, *Literature at Nurse: Or, Circulating Morals* (London: Vizetelly, 1885). For more on Moore and censorship, see Jane Jordan, '"Literature at Nurse": George Moore, Ouida, and *Fin-de-Siècle Literary Censorship*', in *George Moore: Influence and Collaboration*, eds. Ann Heilmann and Mark Llewellyn (Newark: University of Delaware Press, 2014), 69–82. For the effect of the circulating libraries on the English literary market, see Guinevere L. Griest, *Mudie's Circulating Library and the Victorian Novel* (Bloomington: Indiana University Press, 1970).

27 See Edwin Gilcher, *A Bibliography of George Moore* (Dekalb: Northern Illinois University Press, 1970), 16, 103, 212.

28 George Moore, *Confessions of a Young Man*, 4th ed. (London: Heinemann, 1916), 151.

29 Gilcher, *A Bibliography of George Moore*, 73.

30 George Moore, 'Apologia Pro Scriptis Meis', in *Memoirs of My Dead Life* (New York: D. Appleton & Co., 1907), viii, x.

31 Mark Llewellyn, 'Introduction', in Mark Llewellyn and Ann Heilmann, eds., *The Collected Short Stories of George Moore: Gender and Genre*, 5 vols., eds. (London: Pickering & Chatto, 2007), vol. 5: *In Single Strictness (1922)*, ed. Mark Llewellyn, vii–xlii; ix.

32 George Moore, *Celibates* (London: Walter Scott, 1895), 168, 396; George Moore, *In Single Strictness* (New York: Boni and Liveright, 1922), 5.

33 Moore, *In Single Strictness*, 286.

34 Uslenghi, 'A Perspective of Unity', 208.

35 Frazier, *George Moore*, 368.

36 *Ibid.*, 347.

37 George Moore, 'Preface', in *Confessions* (1916), vii–xiii.

38 Letter from Henry James to Edmund Gosse, 13 December 1894, in *The Letters of Henry James*, ed. Percy Lubbock, 2 vols. (London: Macmillan, 1920), vol. 1, 228; Edmund Gosse, 'Walter Pater', in *Critical Kit-Kats* (London: Heinemann, 1896), 239–72; 26.

39 George Moore, *Avowals*, 2nd ed. (London: Heinemann, 1924), 198.

40 For the circulation of these rumours, see Denis Donoghue, *Walter Pater: Lover of Strange Souls* (New York: Knopf, 1995), 58–61.

41 Moore, 'Preface,' in *Confessions of a Young Man* (1916), vii–xiii; ix.

42 George Moore, 'Sex in Art', in *Modern Painting* (London: Walter Scott, 1893), 220–31; 221. All references will be to this edition and given in the text. First published as 'Sex in Art: I', *The Speaker*, 5 (18 June 1892), 737–8 and 'Sex in Art: II', 5 (25 June, 1892), 766–78.

43 For further discussion of gender in 'Sex in Art', see Green, 'Impotence and the Male Artist'.

44 See, for example, Ann Heilmann and María Elena Jaime de Pablos, 'Alice Barton: A Portrait of the Artist as a Young (New) Woman?' in Heilmann and Llewellyn, eds., *George Moore: Influence and Collaboration*, 99–121; Mary Pierse, 'No More Than a Sketch', in Dabringeon-Garcier and Huguet, eds., *George Moore: Across Borders*, 161–76; 167.

45 William Acton, *The Functions and Disorders of the Reproductive Organs*, 2nd ed. (London: John Churchill, 1858; first published 1857), 99, 98.

46 Grubgeld, *The Autogenous Self*, 13.

47 N. John Hall, ed., *Max Beerbohm Caricatures* (New Haven: Yale University Press, 1997), 46. For discussion of this caricature and more on Moore's relationship with Beerbohm, see Marie-Claire Honard, 'Max the Caricature and Moore: Crossing the Boundaries of Friendship', in Dabringeon-Garcier and Huguet, eds., *George Moore: Across Borders*, 161–76.

48 Frazier, *George Moore*, 183.

49 *Ibid.*, xv, 206–7.

50 *Ibid.*, 183.

51 Snyder, *Bachelors, Manhood and the Novel*, 62.

52 Mark Llewellyn, '"Pagan Moore": Poetry, Painting, and Passive Masculinity in George Moore's *Flowers of Passion* (1877) and *Pagan Poems* (1881)', *Victorian Poetry*, 45:1 (Spring 2007), 77–92.

53 Uslenghi, 'A Perspective of Unity', 213–21; see also Grubgeld, *The Autogenous Self*, 232–50.

54 George Moore, 'Art without the Artist', in Richard Cave, ed., *Hail and Farewell* (Gerrards Cross: Colin Smyth, 1976; first published 1925), 47–53; 51.

55 Cave, 'Introduction', *ibid.*, 11–44; 23.

56 Frazier, *George Moore*, 356.

57 George Moore, *Confessions of a Young Man*, 3rd ed. (London: T. Werner Laurie, 1904), 130.

58 For Moore's affair with Maud Cunard in Aix-le-Bains, see Frazier, *George Moore*, 245–48.

59 George Moore, 'Mr. George Moore and the Roman Church', *Irish Times* (24 September 1903), 5. For more on this incident, see Frazier, *George Moore*, 332–3.

60 George Moore, *The Brook Kerith: A Syrian Story* (London: T. Werner Laurie, 1916), 293.

61 *Ibid.*, 434.

62 Virginia Woolf, 'A Born Writer', *Times Literary Supplement*, 967 (29 July 1920), 485.

63 Quoted in Morgan, *Epitaph*, 17, 18.

64 *Ibid.*, 14.

65 Osbert Burdett, 'The Choice', in *Songs of Exuberance, Together with The Trenches* (London: A. C. Fifield, 1915), 137–8; 137 (lines 9–10, 5–6).

Conclusion

1 Falconer Madan, 'Private Account of College Matters, esp. College Meetings, MS [57–61]', in R. M. Seiler, ed., *Walter Pater: A Life Remembered* (Calgary: University of Calgary Press, 1987), 59.

2 Benjamin Kahan, *Celibacies: American Modernism and Sexual Life* (Durham: Duke University Press, 2013), 1, 2.

3 Michel Foucault, *History of Sexuality*, vol. 1, *The Will to Knowledge*, trans. Robert Hurley (London: Penguin, 1998; first published as *La volanté de savoir*, 1976), 6.

4 Wendy Graham, *Henry James's Thwarted Love* (Stanford: Stanford University Press, 1999), 1.

5 A. David Moody, *Ezra Pound: Poet*, 3 vols. (Oxford: Oxford University Press, 2014), vol. 2: *The Epic Years*, 9.

6 Ezra Pound, 'Translator's Postscript', in Remy de Gourmont, ed. and Ezra Pound, trans., *The Natural Philosophy of Love* (New York: Boni and Liveright, 1922; originally published in French as *Physique de l'Amour: Essai sur l'Instinct Sexuel*, 1903), 206–19; 218, 206, 207, 206.

7 Moody, *Ezra Pound*, vol. 2, 10.

8 Humphrey Carpenter, *A Serious Character: The Life of Ezra Pound* (London: Faber & Faber, 1988), 394, 395.

9 Lionel Johnson, *Poetical Works*, ed. Ezra Pound (London: Elkin Mathews, 1915); Ezra Pound, 'The Hard and the Soft in French Poetry', *Poetry*, 11:5 (February 1918), 264–71; 267.

10 Michel Foucault, *The Archaeology of Knowledge*, trans. A. M. Sheridan Smith (London: Routledge, 2002; this trans. first pub. 1972; originally pub. as *L'Archéologie du savoir*, 1969), 32.

11 Walter Pater, 'Winckelmann' in Donald Hill, ed., *The Renaissance: Studies in Art and Poetry: the 1893 Text* (Berkeley: University of California Press, 1980), 141–85; 184.

Bibliography

Manuscripts

Johnson, Lionel, letters to Charles Sayle, Cambridge, University Library, *Charles Edward Sayle: Diaries and Papers*, GBR/0012/MS Add. 8548.

Johnson, Lionel, letters to Frank Russell, Dubuque IA, Loras College Library, *Roseliep Personal Papers*, Filing Cabinet A, Drawer 1, Folders 3–7.

Johnson, Lionel, letter to Katharine Tynan, 8 October 1901, Manchester, John Rylands Library, *The Tynan/Hinkson Collection*, KTG 1/463/1b.

Johnson, Lionel, letters to Oswald Carnagey Johnson, Dubuque IA, Loras College Library, *Roseliep Personal Papers*, Filing Cabinet A, Drawer 1, Folder 2.

Lee, Vernon, Letter to Matilda Paget, 17 July 1887, *Vernon Lee: Letters Home*, 305, https//digitalcommons.colby.edu/letters_home/305 (accessed 9 March 2019).

Lee, Vernon, Letter to Matilda Paget, 27 September 1887, *Vernon Lee: Letters Home*, 333, https//digitalcommons.colby.edu/letters_home/333 (accessed 18 February 2018).

Pater, Walter, '*The Aesthetic Life*', undated, probably 1890s, Cambridge MA, Harvard University, Houghton Library, *The Pater Manuscripts*, bMS. Eng1150(7).

Sayle, Charles, '*Diary 1864–96*', Cambridge, University Library, *Charles Edward Sayle: Diaries and Letters*, GBR/0012/MS Add. 8501, 264.

Primary

[Unsigned], 'Direct Teaching to Men Upon Personal Purity', *The Sentinel*, 50 (June 1883), 206.

[Unsigned], 'Medical Graduations in Edinburgh', in *The Edinburgh Medical and Surgical Journal*, 40 (Edinburgh: Adam and Charles Black, 1833), 491.

[Unsigned], 'Review: Miscellaneous Contributions to Pathology and Therapeutics, by James Richard Smyth, M.D.', *The Medico-Chirurgical Review*, 41:82 (1 October 1844), 349–55.

[Unsigned], 'Review [of Hugh Sinclair Paterson's *Life, Function, Health: Studies for Young Men*]', *Spectator* (29 January 1881), 26.

[Unsigned], 'Smyth, James Richard', in *The London Medical Directory* (London: C. Mitchell, 1845), 149.

Acton, William, *The Functions and Disorders of the Reproductive Organs in Youth, in Adult Age, and in Advanced Life: Considered in Their Physiological, Social, and Psychological Relations*, 2nd ed. revised (London: John Churchill, 1858; first published 1857).

Allen, Grant, 'The New Hedonism', *Fortnightly Review*, 55:327 (March 1894), 376–92.

Atkins, Frederick, *Moral Muscle and How to Use It: A Brotherly Chat with Young Men* (London: James Nisbet & Co., 1890).

Baden-Powell, Lord (Robert), *Rovering to Success: A Book of Life-Sport for Young Men*, 2nd ed. revised (London: Herbert Jenkins, 1930; first published 1922).

Beerbohm, Max, *Max Beerbohm Caricatures*, ed. N. John Hall (New Haven: Yale University Press, 1997).

Benson, A. C., *Walter Pater* (London: Macmillan, 1906).

Blackie, John Stuart, *On Self-Culture: Intellectual, Physical, and Moral: A Vade Mecum for Young Men and Students*, 3rd ed. (Edinburgh: Edmonston and Douglas, 1874).

Bridges, Robert, *The Testament of Beauty* (Oxford: Clarendon Press, 1929).

Buchanan, Robert, *The Fleshly School of Poetry: And Other Phenomena of the Day* (London: Strahan & Co., 1872).

Burdett, Osbert, *Songs of Exuberance, Together with The Trenches* (London: A. C. Fifield, 1915).

Carpenter, Edward, *Love's Coming of Age* (Manchester: Labour Press, 1896).

Carpenter, William, *The Principles of Human Physiology*, 5th ed. (London: John Churchill, 1855 ed.; first published 1842).

Church, R. W., *The Oxford Movement: Twelve Years, 1833–1845* (London: Macmillan, 1891).

Clapperton, Jane Hume, *Scientific Meliorism and the Evolution of Happiness* (London: Kegan Paul & Trench, 1885).

Courtenay, F. B., *Revelations of Quacks and Quackery: A Series of Letters by 'Detector' Reprinted from 'The Medical Circular'*, 10th ed. (London: Bailliere, Tindall & Cox, 1885; first published 1865).

Davidson, John Thain, *Talks with Young Men* (London: Hodder & Stoughton, 1884).

Eliot, George, *Middlemarch: A Study of Provincial Life*, 4 vols. (Edinburgh: William Blackwood, 1871).

Eliot, T. S., *Selected Essays* (London: Faber & Faber, 1999).

Ellis, Havelock, *Studies in the Psychology of Sex*, 2nd ed. revised, 6 vols. (Philadelphia: F. A Davis, 1921; first published 1897–1910).

Faber, Frederick, *The Life and Letters of Frederick William Faber, D.D.*, ed. John Edward Bowden (London: Thomas Richardson & Son, 1869).

Freud, Sigmund, *The Standard Edition of the Complete Psychological Works of Sigmund Freud*, 24 vols., ed. and trans. James Strachey (London: The Hogarth Press, 1953–1974).

Galton, Arthur, *Acer In Hostem* (Windermere: A. W. Johnson & Sons, 1913).

Galton, Francis, *Hereditary Genius: An Inquiry into Its Laws and Consequences* (London: Macmillan, 1869).

Gosse, Edmund, 'Walter Pater', *Critical Kit-Kats* (London: William Heinemann, 1896), 239–72.

Gourmont, Remy de, *The Natural Philosophy of Love,* trans. Ezra Pound (New York: Boni and Liveright, 1922; originally published in French as *Physique de l'Amour: Essai sur l'Instinct Sexuel,* 1903).

Grand, Sarah, *The Heavenly Twins* (London: William Heinemann, 1894).

Greenslet, Ferris, *Walter Pater* (New York: McClure, Phillips & Co., 1903).

Hannigan, D. F., 'Sex in Fiction', *Westminster Review,* 143 (January 1895), 616–25.

Harris, Frank, *Contemporary Portraits: Second Series* (New York: Frank Harris, 1919).

Harris, Frank, *My Life and Loves,* 5 vols. (London: W. H. Allen, 1964).

Harvey & Co., *Short Account of Sir Astley Cooper's Vital Restorative* (London: Harvey & Co., 1863).

[Hitchens, Robert], *The Green Carnation* (London: Heinemann, 1894).

Holbrook, M. L., *Chastity: Its Physical, Moral, and Intellectual Advantages* (London: L. N. Fowler & Co., 1894).

James, Henry, *The Letters of Henry James,* ed. Percy Lubbock, 2 vols. (London: Macmillan, 1920).

Jepson, Edgar, *Memories of a Victorian* (London: Victor Gollancz, 1933).

Johnson, Lionel, *A Letter to Edgar Jepson,* ed. Ian Fletcher (Norfolk: Daedalus Press, 1979).

[Johnson, Lionel], 'An Old Debate', *The Anti-Jacobin,* 25 (8 July 1891), 589–90.

Johnson, Lionel, 'A Note upon the Practice and Theory of Verse at the Present Time Obtaining in France', *Century Guild Hobby Horse,* 5:22 (April 1891), 61–6.

[Johnson, Lionel], 'Criticism in Corruption', *The Anti-Jacobin,* 6 (7 March 1891), 131–2.

[Johnson, Lionel], 'Inspirers and Teachers', *The Anti-Jacobin,* 26 (25 July 1891), 611.

Johnson, Lionel, *Ireland: With Other Poems* (London: Elkin Mathews, 1897).

[Johnson, Lionel], 'Of the Spirit of Books', *The Anti-Jacobin,* 13 (25 April 1891), 299–300.

Johnson, Lionel, *Poems* (London: Elkin Mathews, 1895).

Johnson, Lionel, *Poetical Works,* ed. Ezra Pound (London: Elkin Mathews, 1915).

Johnson, Lionel, *Post Liminium: Essays and Critical Papers by Lionel Johnson,* ed. Thomas Whittemore (London: Elkin Mathews, 1912).

Johnson, Lionel, *Selected Letters,* ed. Murray Pittock (Edinburgh: Tragara Press, 1988).

Johnson, Lionel, *Some Letters of Lionel Johnson,* ed. Raymond Roseliep, unpublished doctoral dissertation (South Bend, IN: University of Notre Dame, 1953).

Johnson, Lionel, *Some Winchester Letters of Lionel Johnson,* ed. [Frank Russell] (London: George Allen & Unwin, 1919).

Johnson, Lionel, *The Art of Thomas Hardy* (London: Elkin Mathews & John Lane, 1894).

Johnson, Lionel, *The Collected Poems of Lionel Johnson*, ed. Ian Fletcher, 2nd ed. (London: Garland, 1982).

[Johnson, Lionel], 'The Cultured Faun', *The Anti-Jacobin*, 7 (14 March 1891), 156–7.

[Johnson, Lionel], 'The Way of Writing', *The Anti-Jacobin*, 15 (9 May 1891), 347–8.

Jowett, Benjamin, *The Dialogues of Plato: Translated into English with Analyses and Introductions*, 3rd ed. revised, 5 vols. (Oxford: Clarendon Press, 1892; first published 1871).

Kempis, Thomas à, *The Imitation of Christ*, trans. William Atkynson (books 1–3) and Princess Margaret, Countess of Richmond (book 4) (London: Dent, 1910, reprinted 1937; this translation first published by Wynkyn de Worde, 1504; first Latin printing 1471).

Krafft-Ebing, Richard von, *Psychopathia Sexualis, with Especial Reference to Antipathic Sexual Instinct: A Medico-Forensic Study*, trans. F. J. Rebman, 10th ed. (Chicago: Keener, 1901; originally published in German, 1886).

Lee, Vernon, *Althea: Dialogues on Aspirations and Duties* (London: Osgood, McIlvaine & Co, 1894).

Lee, Vernon, *Baldwin: Being Dialogues on Views and Aspirations* (London: T. Fisher Unwin, 1886).

Lee, Vernon, *Belcaro: Being Essays on Sundry Aesthetical Questions* (London: W. Satchell & Co, 1881).

Lee, Vernon, *Euphorion: Being Studies of the Antique and the Medieval in the Renaissance*, 2nd ed. revised (London: T. Fisher Unwin, 1885; first published 1884).

Lee, Vernon, *Hortus Vitae: Essays on the Gardening of Life* (London: John Lane, 1903).

Lee, Vernon, *Juvenilia: Being a Second Series of Essays on Sundry Aesthetical Questions*, 2 vols. (London: T. Fisher Unwin, 1887).

Lee, Vernon, *Laurus Nobilis: Chapters on Art and Life* (London: John Lane, 1909).

Lee, Vernon, *Limbo and Other Essays* (London: Grant Richards, 1897).

Lee, Vernon, *Miss Brown: A Novel* (London: Blackwood, 1884).

Lee, Vernon, *Renaissance Fancies and Studies: Being a Sequel to Euphorion* (London: Smith, Elder & Co., 1895).

Lee, Vernon, *Selected Letters of Vernon Lee (1856–1935)*, ed. Mandy Gagel, unpublished doctoral dissertation (Boston: Boston University, 2008).

Lee, Vernon, *Selected Letters of Vernon Lee, 1856–1935*, vol. 1, eds. Amanda Gagel *et al.* (London: Routledge, 2017).

Lee, Vernon, *The Handling of Words and Other Studies in Literary Psychology* (London: John Lane, 1923).

Lee, Vernon, 'Two Books on Social Evolution', *The Academy*, 732 (15 May 1886), 340–1; 340.

Le Gallienne, Richard, *Retrospective Reviews: A Literary Log*, 2 vols. (London: John Lane, 1896).

Le Gallienne, Richard, *The Romantic '90s* (New York: Doubleday, Page & Company, 1925).

Le Gallienne, Richard, *Young Lives* (London: John Lane: The Bodley Head, 1899).

Lilly, W. S., 'The New Gospel', *Time*, 1 (May 1879), 169–75.

[Mallock, W. H.], *The New Republic: Or, Culture, Faith, and Philosophy in an English Country House*, 2 vols. (London: Chatto & Windus, 1877).

Maudsley, Henry, *The Pathology of Mind* (London: Macmillan & Co., 1879).

Maudsley, Henry, *The Physiology of Mind* (London: Macmillan & Co., 1876).

Moore, George, *A Communication to My Friends* (London: Nonesuch Press, 1933).

Moore, George, *A Drama in Muslin* (London: Vizetelly, 1886).

Moore, George, *A Modern Lover*, 2nd ed. (London: Vizetelly, 1885; first published 1883).

Moore, George, *A Mummer's Wife* (London: Vizetelly, 1885).

Moore, George, *Avowals* (London: privately published, 1919).

Moore, George, *Avowals*, 2nd ed. (London: Heinemann, 1924).

Moore, George, *Celibate Lives*, 2nd ed. (London: Heinemann, 1937; first published 1927).

Moore, George, *Celibates* (London: Walter Scott, 1895).

Moore, George, *Confessions of a Young Man*, 2nd ed. (London: Swan Sonnenschein, 1889).

Moore, George, *Confessions of a Young Man*, 3rd ed. (London: T. Werner Laurie, 1904).

Moore, George, *Confessions of a Young Man*, 4th ed. (London: Heinemann, 1916).

Moore, George, *Evelyn Innes* (London: T. Fisher Unwin, 1898).

Moore, George, *George Moore in Transition: Letters to T. Fisher Unwin and Lena Milman, 1894–1910*, ed. Helmut Gerber (Detroit: Wayne State University Press, 1968).

Moore, George, *Hail and Farewell*, 3 vols. (London: Heinemann, 1911–14).

Moore, George, *Hail and Farewell*, ed. Richard Cave (Gerrards Cross: Colin Smyth, 1976).

Moore, George, *In Single Strictness* (New York: Boni and Liveright, 1922).

Moore, George, *Literature at Nurse: Or, Circulating Morals* (London: Vizetelly, 1885).

Moore, George, *Memoirs of My Dead Life* (London: Heinemann, 1906).

Moore, George, *Memoirs of My Dead Life* (New York: D. Appleton & Co., 1907).

Moore, George, *Modern Painting* (London: Walter Scott, 1893).

Moore, George, 'Mr. George Moore and the Roman Church', *Irish Times* (24 September 1903), 5.

Moore, George, 'Sex in Art, I', *The Speaker*, 5 (18 June 1892), 737–8.

Moore, George, 'Sex in Art, II', *The Speaker*, 5 (25 June 1892), 766–78.

Moore, George, *Sister Teresa* (London: T. Fisher Unwin, 1901).

Moore, George, *The Brook Kerith: A Syrian Story* (London: T. Werner Laurie, 1916).

Moore, George, *The Lake*, ed. Richard Cave (Gerards Cross: Colin Smyth, 1980; this ed. first published 1921; originally published 1905).

Morgan, Charles, *Epitaph on George Moore* (London: Macmillan, 1935).

[Müller, Henrietta], 'The Future of Single Women', *Westminster Review*, 121:241 (January 1884), 151–62.

Newman, John Henry, *An Essay in Aid of a Grammar of Assent* (London: Burns, Oates & Co., 1870).

Newman, John Henry, *Apologia Pro Vita Sua*, ed. Ian Ker (London: Penguin, 1994; first published 1864).

Newman, John Henry, *Discussions and Arguments on Various Subjects* (London: Pickering, 1872).

Newman, John Henry, *Parochial and Plain Sermons*, 8 vols. (London: Longmans, Green, & Co., 1907; first published 1868).

Newman, John Henry, *The Letters and Diaries of John Henry Newman*, eds. Ian Ker *et al.*, 32 vols. (Oxford: Clarendon Press, 1963–2008).

Paget, James, *Clinical Lectures and Essays*, ed. Howard Marsh (London: Longmans, Green & Co., 1875), 268–29.

Pankurst, Christabel, *The Great Scourge and How to End It* (London: E. Pankhurst, 1913).

Paterson, H. Sinclair, *Life, Function, Health: Studies for Young Men* (London: Hodder & Stoughton, 1885).

Pater, Walter, *Appreciations: With an Essay on Style* (London: Macmillan, 1910; first published 1889).

Pater, Walter, *Gaston de Latour: The Revised Text*, ed. Gerald Monsman (Greensboro: ELT Press, 1995).

Pater, Walter, *Greek Studies: A Series of Essays*, ed. Charles L. Shadwell (London: Macmillan, 1910; first published 1895).

Pater, Walter, 'Hippolytus Veiled: A Study from Euripides', *Macmillan's Magazine*, 60:358 (August 1889), 294–306.

Pater, Walter, *Imaginary Portraits* (London: Macmillan, 1887).

Pater, Walter, *Marius the Epicurean: His Sensations and Ideas*, 2 vols. (London: Macmillan, 1910; first published 1885).

Pater, Walter, *Marius the Epicurean: His Sensations and Ideas*, ed. Gerald Monsman (Kansas City: Valancourt Books, 2008).

Pater, Walter, *Miscellaneous Studies: A Series of Essays*, ed. Charles L. Shadwell (London: Macmillan, 1910; first published 1895).

Pater, Walter, *Plato and Platonism: A Series of Lectures* (London: Macmillan, 1910; first published 1893).

[Pater, Walter], 'Poems by William Morris', *Westminster Review*, 34:2 (October 1868), 300–12.

Pater, Walter, *Studies in the History of the Renaissance* (London: Macmillan, 1873).

Pater, Walter, *The Renaissance*, ed. Arthur Symons (New York: The Modern Library, 1919).

Pater, Walter, *The Renaissance: Studies in Art and Poetry*, 2nd ed. revised (London: Macmillan, 1877).

Pater, Walter, *The Renaissance: Studies in Art and Poetry*, 3rd ed. revised (London: Macmillan, 1888).

Pater, Walter, *The Renaissance: Studies in Art and Poetry: The 1893 Text*, ed. Donald Hill (Berkeley: University of California Press, 1980).

Pater, Walter, *The Collected Works of Walter Pater*, 10 vols., general eds. Lesley Higgins and David Latham (Oxford: Oxford University Press, 2019–).

Pater, Walter, 'Winckelmann', *Westminster Review* 31:1 (January 1867), 80–110.

Plato, *Euthyphro, Apology, Crito, Phaedo, Phaedrus*, trans. Harold North Fowler (Cambridge, MA: Harvard University Press, 1995; this translation first published 1914).

Plato, *Lysis, Symposium, Gorgias*, trans. W. R. M. Lamb (Cambridge, MA: Harvard University Press, 1991; this translation first published 1925).

Pound, Ezra, *Collected Shorter Poems* (London: Faber, 1952).

Pound, Ezra, 'The Hard and the Soft in French Poetry', *Poetry*, 11:5 (February 1918), 264–71.

Quilter, Harry, 'The New Renaissance; or the Gospel of Intensity', *Macmillan's Magazine*, 42:251 (September 1880), 391–400.

Raffalovich, Marc-André, *Uranisme et Unisexualité: Etude sur différentes manifestations de l'instinct sexuel* (Paris: Masson, 1896).

Renan, Ernest, *Histoire des origines du Christianisme*, 8 vols. (Paris: Calmann Lévy, 1863–1883).

Rhys, Ernest, *Everyman Remembers* (London: J. M. Dent, 1931).

Ridding, George, *Purity* (Derby: Bemrose & Sons, 1883).

Robinson Duclaux, Mary, 'James Darmesteter', in Isidore Singer *et al.* eds., *The Jewish Encyclopedia*, 12 vols. (London and New York: Funk & Wagnalls Co., 1901–1906), vol. 4, 444–7.

Santayana, George, *Persons and Places: The Autobiography in One Volume*, ed. Daniel Cory (New York: Scribner, 1963; first published 1944–53).

Seiler, R. M. ed., *Walter Pater: The Critical Heritage* (London: Routledge & Kegan Paul, 1980).

Shaw, George Bernard, *Love among the Artists* (London: John Murray, 2012; first published 1900; written c. 1880).

Smith, Henry, *The Warning Voice: Or, Private Medical Friend*, 63rd ed. (London: self-published, 1860).

Smyth, James Richard, *Miscellaneous Contributions to Pathology and Therapeutics* (London: Simpkin, Marshall, & Co., 1844).

Smyth, James Richard, 'Miscellaneous Contributions to Pathology and Therapeutics: Impotence and Sterility', *The Lancet*, 36:939 (1841), 779–85.

Smyth, James Richard, 'Miscellaneous Contributions to Pathology and Therapeutics: Impotence and Sterility', *The Lancet*, 39:1010 (1843), 531–6.

Stevenson, R. L., *Collected Poems*, ed. Roger C. Lewis (Edinburgh: Edinburgh University Press, 2003).

Symonds, John Addington, *A Problem in Greek Ethics* (London: privately printed, 1883).

Symonds, John Addington, *A Problem in Modern Ethics* (London: privately printed, 1896; first printed 1891).

Symonds, John Addington, *The Memoirs of John Addington Symonds*, ed. Phyllis Grosskurth (London: Hutchinson, 1984).

Symons, Arthur, *Figures of Several Centuries* (London: Constable & Company, 1916), 316–35.

Thoreau, Henry David, *Walden*, ed. J. Lyndon Shanley (Princeton: Princeton University Press, 1971; first published 1854).

Tolstoy, Leo, 'Marriage, Morality, and Christianity: A Reply to Critics of "The Kreutzer Sonata"', trans. E. J. Dillon, *The Universal Review*, 7:26 (June 1890), 154–62.

Tolstoy, Leo, 'The Kreutzer Sonata', in *Tolstoy Centenary Edition*, general eds. Aylmer Maude *et al.*, 21 vols. (Oxford: Oxford University Press, 1929–37), vol. 16: *The Devil and Cognate Tales,* ed. and trans. Aylmer Maude (1934; originally published in Russian as *Kreitzerova Sonata*, 1889), 109–231.

Weygandt, Cornelius, *Tuesdays at Ten: A Garnering from the Talks of Thirty Years on Poets, Dramatists, and Essayists* (Philadelphia: University of Pennsylvania Press, 1928).

Wilde, Oscar, *Complete Works of Oscar Wilde*, general eds. Ian Small and Russell Jackson, 7 vols. (Oxford: Oxford University Press, 2000–13).

Woolf, Virginia, 'A Born Writer', *Times Literary Supplement*, 967 (29 July 1920), 485.

Yeats, W. B., *Memoirs*, ed. Denis Donoghue (London: Macmillan, 1972).

Yeats, W. B., *The Collected Works of W. B. Yeats*, general eds. Richard J. Finneran and George Mills Harper, 14 vols. (New York: Scribner, 1984–).

Secondary

Abbott, Elizabeth, *A History of Celibacy* (Cambridge: De Capo, 2001; first published 1999).

Adams, James Eli, *Dandies and Desert Saints: Styles of Victorian Manhood* (Ithaca: Cornell University Press, 1995).

Baldwin, Anna P. and Sarah Hutton eds., *Platonism and the English Imagination* (Cambridge: Cambridge University Press, 1994).

Barker-Benfield, Ben, 'The Spermatic Economy: A Nineteenth Century View of Sexuality', *Feminist Studies*, 1:1 (Summer 1972), 45–74.

Bauer, Heike, *English Literary Sexology* (Basingstoke: Palgrave Macmillan, 2009).

Becker-Lackrone, Megan, 'Same-Sex and the Second Sex in "Style"', *The Pater Newsletter*, 52 (Spring 2007), 37–44.

Behlman, Lee, 'Burning, Burial, and the Critique of Stoicism in Walter Pater's *Marius the Epicurean*', *Nineteenth-Century Prose*, 31:1 (Spring 2004), 133–56.

Bennet, Paula and Vernon A. Rosario eds., *Solitary Pleasures: The Historical, Literary and Artistic Discourses of Autoeroticism* (London: Routledge, 1995).

Bernau, Anke, *Virgins: A Cultural History* (London: Granta Books, 2007).

Blair, Kirstie, 'Breaking Loose: Frederick Faber and the Failure of Reserve', *Victorian Poetry*, 44:1 (Spring 2006), 25–41.

Bland, Lucy, *Banishing the Beast: Sexuality and the Early Feminists* (Harmondsworth: Penguin, 1995).

Bland, Lucy and Laura Doan eds., *Sexology in Culture: Labelling Bodies and Desires* (Cambridge: Polity, 1998).

Boddice, Rob, *The Science of Sympathy: Morality, Evolution, and Victorian Civilization* (Chicago: University of Illinois Press, 2016).

Brake, Laurel, 'Judas and the Widow: Thomas Wright and A. C. Benson as Biographers of Walter Pater: The Widow', *Prose Studies: History, Theory, Criticism*, 4:1 (1981), 39–54.

Brake, Laurel, *Print in Transition, 1850–1910: Studies in Media and Book History* (Basingstoke: Palgrave Macmillan, 2001).

Brake, Laurel and Ian Small eds., *Pater in the 1990s* (Greensboro: ELT Press, 1991).

Brake, Laurel, *et al.* eds., *Walter Pater: Transparencies of Desire* (Greensboro: ELT Press, 2002).

Bridgwater, Patrick, *George Moore and German Pessimism* (Durham: University of Durham, 1988).

Bristow, Edward J., *Vice and Vigilance: Purity Movements in Britain since 1700* (Dublin: Gill & Macmillan, 1977).

Bristow, Joseph, *Empire Boys: Adventures in a Man's World* (London: Harper Collins Academic, 1991).

Broughton, Trev, *Men of Letters, Writing Lives: Masculinity and Literary Auto/Biography in the Late-Victorian Period* (London: Routledge, 1999).

Brown, Peter, *The Body and Society: Men, Women, and Sexual Renunciation in Early Christianity*, 2nd ed. revised (New York: University of Columbia Press, 2008; first published 1988).

Buckton, Oliver S., '"An Unnatural State": Gender, "Perversion", and Newman's "Apologia Pro Vita Sua"', *Victorian Studies*, 35:4 (Summer 1992), 359–83.

Buckton, Oliver S., *Secret Selves: Confession and Same-Sex Desire in Victorian Autobiography* (Chapel Hill: University of North Carolina Press, 1998).

Bullough, Vern, *Science in the Bedroom: A History of Sex Research* (New York: Basic Books, 1994).

Carpenter, Humphrey, *A Serious Character: The Life of Ezra Pound* (London: Faber & Faber, 1988).

Cave, Richard, 'George Moore's "Stella"', *The Review of English Studies*, 28:110 (May 1977), 181–8.

Cerankowski, Karli June and Megan Milks eds., *Asexualities: Feminist and Queer Perspectives* (New York: Routledge, 2014).

Chadwick, Owen ed., *The Mind of the Oxford Movement* (London: Adam Charles Black, 1960).

Charlesworth, Barbara, *Dark Passages: The Decadent Consciousness in Victorian Literature* (Madison: University of Wisconsin Press, 1965).

Cheeke, Stephen, *Transfiguration: The Religion of Art in Nineteenth-Century Literature Before Aestheticism* (Oxford: Oxford University Press, 2016).

Cohen, Ed, *Talk on the Wilde Side: Towards a Genealogy of a Discourse on Male Sexualities* (New York: Routledge, 1993).

Colby, Vineta, *The Singular Anomaly: Women Novelists of the Nineteenth Century* (New York: University of New York Press, 1970).

Colby, Vineta, *Vernon Lee: A Literary Biography* (Charlottesville: University of Virginia Press, 2003).

Cominos, Peter, 'Late Victorian Sexual Respectability and the Social System', *International Review of Social History*, 8:1 (1963), 18–48.

Cook, Hera, *The Long Sexual Revolution: English Women, Sex, and Contraception 1800–1975* (Oxford: Oxford University Press, 2005).

Crozier, Ivan, 'Nineteenth-Century British Psychiatric Writing about Homosexuality before Havelock Ellis: The Missing Story', *Journal of the History of Medicine and Allied Sciences*, 68:1 (January 2008), 65–102.

Crozier, Ivan, 'William Acton and the History of Sexuality: The Medical and Professional Context', *Journal of Victorian Culture*, 5:1 (2000), 1–27.

Cryle, Peter and Elizabeth Stephens, *Normality: A Critical Genealogy* (Chicago: University of Chicago Press, 2017).

Cryle, Peter and Alison Moore, *Frigidity: An Intellectual History* (Basingstoke: Palgrave Macmillan, 2011).

Dabrigeon-Garcier, Fabienne and Christine Huguet eds., *George Moore: Across Borders* (Amsterdam: Rodopi, 2013).

Darby, Robert, 'William Acton's Antipodean Disciples: A Colonial Perspectives on His Theories of Male Sexual (Dys)function', *Journal of the History of Sexuality*, 13:2 (April 2004), 157–82.

D'Arch Smith, Timothy, *Love in Earnest: Some Notes on the Lives and Writings of English 'Uranian' Poets from 1889 to 1930* (London: Routledge & Kegan Paul, 1970).

Dau, Duc, 'Perfect Chastity: Celibacy and Virgin Marriage in Tractarian Poetry', *Victorian Poetry*, 44:1 (Spring 2006), 77–92.

Davidson, Arnold I., *The Emergence of Sexuality: Historical Epistemology and the Formation of Concepts* (Cambridge, MA: Harvard University Press, 2001).

Davis, Whitney, *Queer Beauty: Sexuality and Aesthetics from Winckelmann to Freud and Beyond* (New York: Columbia University Press, 2010).

Dawson, Gowan, 'Walter Pater's Marius the Epicurean and the Discourse of Science in Macmillan's Magazine: "A Creature of the Nineteenth Century"', *English Literature in Transition, 1880–1920*, 48:1 (2005), 38–54.

DeLaura, David, *Hebrew and Hellene in Victorian England: Newman, Arnold, and Pater* (Austin: University of Texas Press, 1969).

Dellamora, Richard, *Friendship's Bonds: Democracy and the Novel in Victorian England* (Philadelphia: University of Pennsylvania Press, 2004).

Dellamora, Richard, *Masculine Desire: The Sexual Politics of Victorian Aestheticism* (Chapel Hill: University of Carolina Press, 1990).

Dellamora, Richard, 'Productive Decadence: "The Queer Comradeship of Outlawed Thought": Vernon Lee, Max Nordau, and Oscar Wilde', *New Literary History*, 35:4 (Autumn 2004), 529–46.

Dellamora, Richard, 'The Androgynous Body in Pater's "Winckelmann"', *Browning Institute Studies*, 11 (1983), 51–68.

Dellamora, Richard ed., *Victorian Sexual Dissidence* (Chicago: University of Chicago Press, 1999).

Demetriou, Kyriakos, *Studies on the Reception of Plato and Greek Political Thought in Victorian Britain* (Farnham: Ashgate, 2011).

Denisoff, Dennis, *Aestheticism and Sexual Parody, 1840–1940* (Cambridge: Cambridge University Press, 2001).

Denisoff, Dennis, 'Decadence and Aestheticism', in Gail Marshall ed., *Cambridge Companion to the Fin de Siècle* (Cambridge: Cambridge University Press, 2007), 31–52.

Derham, Ruth, *Bertrand's Brother: The Marriages, Morals and Misdemeanours of Frank, 2nd Earl Russell* (Stroud: Amberly Publishing, 2021).

Donoghue, Denis, *Walter Pater: Lover of Strange Souls* (New York: Knopf, 1995).

Dowling, Linda, *Hellenism and Homosexuality in Victorian Oxford* (Ithaca: Cornell University Press, 1994).

Dowling, Linda, 'Ruskin's Pied Beauty and the Constitution of a "Homosexual Code"', *The Victorian Newsletter*, 75 (Spring 1989), 1–9.

Doylen, Michael R., *Homosexual Askesis: Representations of Self-Fashioning in the Writings of Walter Pater, Oscar Wilde, and John Addington Symonds*, unpublished doctoral dissertation (Berkeley: University of California, 1998).

Edelman, Lee, *No Future: Queer Theory and the Death Drive* (Durham and London: Duke University Press, 2004).

Eder, Franz X. *et al.* eds., *Sexual Cultures in Europe: National Histories* (Manchester: Manchester University Press, 1999).

Edwards, Catherine, *The Politics of Immorality in Ancient Rome* (Cambridge: Cambridge University Press, 1993).

Elfenbein, Andrew, *Romantic Genius: The Prehistory of a Homosexual Role* (New York: Columbia University Press, 1999).

Evangelista, Stefano, 'Against Misinterpretation: Benjamin Jowett's Translations of Plato and the Ethics of Modern Homosexuality', *Recherches anglaises et nord-américaines*, 36:3 (2003), 13–25.

Evangelista, Stefano, *British Aestheticism and Ancient Greece: Hellenism, Reception, Gods in Exile* (Basingstoke: Palgrave Macmillan, 2009).

Evangelista, Stefano, '"Life in the Whole": Goethe and English Aestheticism', *Publications of the English Goethe Society*, 82:3 (1 October 2013), 180–92.

Evangelista, Stefano, '"Lovers and Philosophers at Once": Aesthetic Platonism in the Victorian "Fin de Siècle"', *The Yearbook of English Studies*, 36:2 (2006), 230–44.

Faber, Geoffrey, *Oxford Apostles: A Character Study of the Oxford Movement* (London: Faber & Faber, 1954; first published 1933).

Fernihough, Anne, *Freewomen and Supermen: Edwardian Radicals and Literary Modernism* (Oxford: Oxford University Press, 2013).

Fletcher, Ian ed., *W. B. Yeats and his Contemporaries* (Brighton: Harvester Press, 1987).

Fletcher, Judith and Bonnie MacLachlen eds., *Virginity Revisited: Configurations of the Unpossessed Body* (Toronto: University of Toronto Press, 2007).

Foucault, Michel, *The Archaeology of Knowledge*, trans. A. M. Sheridan Smith (London: Routledge, 2002; this translation first published 1972; originally published as *L'Archéologie du savoir*, 1969).

Foucault, Michel, *History of Sexuality*, vol. 1, *The Will to Knowledge*, trans. Robert Hurley (London: Penguin, 1998; first published as *La volanté de savoir*, 1976).

Foucault, Michel, *History of Sexuality*, vol. 2: *The Use of Pleasure*, trans. Robert Hurley (London: Penguin, 1992; this trans. first published 1985; originally published in French as *L'Usage des plaisirs*, 1984).

Foucault, Michel, *History of Sexuality*, vol. 3: *The Care of the Self*, trans. Robert Hurley (London: Penguin, 1990; this translation first published 1986; originally published in French as *Le Souci de soi*, 1984).

Fraser, Hilary, *Beauty and Belief: Aesthetics and Religion in Victorian Literature* (Cambridge: Cambridge University Press, 1986).

Frazier, Adrian, *George Moore: 1852–1933* (New Haven: Yale University Press, 2000).

Friedman, Dustin, *Before Queer Theory: Victorian Aestheticism and the Self* (Baltimore: John Hopkins University Press, 2019).

Gagnier, Regenia, *Individualism, Decadence and Globalization: On the Relationship of the Part to the Whole, 1859–1920* (Basingstoke: Palgrave Macmillan, 2010).

Gardner, Burdett, *The Lesbian Imagination (Victorian Style): A Psychological and Critical Study of 'Vernon Lee'* (New York: Garland, 1987; written 1954).

Geoffroy, Sophie ed., *Women and Political Theory: Vernon Lee and Radical Circles* (Paris: Michel Houdiard Editeur, 2017).

Gijswijt-Hofstra, Marijke and Roy Porter eds., *Cultures of Neurasthenia from Beard to the First World War* (Amsterdam: Rodopi, 2001).

Gilbert, Arthur N., 'Masturbation and Insanity: Henry Maudsley and the Ideology of Sexual Repression', *Albion*, 12:3 (Autumn 1980), 268–83.

Gilbert, Pamela K., *The Citizen's Body: Desire, Health, and the Social in Victorian England* (Columbus: The Ohio State University Press, 2007).

Gilbert, Pamela K., 'The Other "Other Victorians": Normative Sexualities in Victorian Literature', in Clark Lawlor and Andrew Mangham eds., *Literature and Medicine: The Nineteenth Century* (Cambridge: Cambridge University Press, 2021), 211–29.

Gilcher, Edwin, *A Bibliography of George Moore* (Illinois: Northern Illinois University Press, 1970).

Goslee, David, *Romanticism and the Anglican Newman* (Athens: Ohio University Press, 1996).

Graham, Wendy, *Henry James's Thwarted Love* (Stanford: Stanford University Press, 1999).

Green, Sarah, 'Impotence and the Male Artist: The Case of George Moore', *Journal of Victorian Culture*, 24:2 (April 2019), 179–92.

Green, Sarah, 'The Undeveloped Body of Lionel Johnson', *Notes and Queries*, 63:2 (June 2016), 281–3.

Griest, Guinevere L., *Mudie's Circulating Library and the Victorian Novel* (Bloomington: Indiana University Press, 1970).

Grosskurth, Phyllis, *Havelock Ellis: A Biography* (London: Allen Lane, 1980).

Grubgeld, Elizabeth, *George Moore and the Autogenous Self: The Autobiography and Fiction* (Syracuse: Syracuse University Press, 1994).

Gunn, Peter, *Vernon Lee: Violet Paget, 1856–1935* (London: Oxford University Press, 1964).

Gupta, Kristina, 'Compulsory Sexuality: Evaluating an Emerging Concept', *Signs*, 41:1 (Autumn 2015), 131–54.

Haefele-Thomas, Ardel, *Queer Others in Victorian Gothic: Transgressing Monstrosity* (Cardiff: University of Wales Press, 2012).

Haley, Bruce, *The Healthy Body and Victorian Culture* (Cambridge, MA: Harvard University Press, 1978).

Hall, Donald E. ed., *Muscular Christianity: Embodying the Victorian Age* (Cambridge: Cambridge University Press, 1994).

Hall, Donald E. *et al.* eds., *The Routledge Queer Studies Reader* (London: Routledge, 2013).

Hall, Lesley A., 'Forbidden by God, Despised by Men: Masturbation, Medical Warnings, Moral Panic, and Manhood in Great Britain, 1850–1950', *Journal of the History of Sexuality*, 2:3 (January 1992), 365–87.

Hall, Lesley A., *Hidden Anxieties: Male Sexuality, 1900–1950* (Cambridge: Polity Press, 1991).

Hall, Lesley A., *Sex, Gender and Social Change in Britain since 1880*, 2nd ed. (Basingstoke: Palgrave Macmillan, 2012; first ed. 2000).

Hall, Lesley A., 'Sexual Cultures in Britain: Some Persisting Themes', in Franz X. Eder *et al.* eds., *Sexual Cultures in Europe: National Histories* (Manchester: Manchester University Press, 1999), 29–52.

Hall, Lesley A. and Roy Porter, *The Facts of Life: The Creation of Sexual Knowledge in Britain, 1650–1950* (New Haven: Yale University Press, 1995).

Hanley, Anne R., *Medicine, Knowledge and Venereal Diseases in England, 1886–1916* (Basingstoke: Palgrave Macmillan, 2017).

Hanson, Ellis, *Decadence and Catholicism* (Cambridge, MA: Harvard University Press, 1997).

Heilmann, Ann and Mark Llewellyn eds., *George Moore: Influence and Collaboration* (Newark: University of Delaware Press, 2014).

Hext, Kate, *Walter Pater: Individualism and Aesthetic Philosophy* (Edinburgh: Edinburgh University Press, 2013).

Higgins, Lesley, 'Jowett and Pater: Trafficking in Platonic Wares', *Victorian Studies*, 37:1 (Autumn 1993), 43–72.

Hilliard, David, 'Unenglish and Unmanly: Anglo-Catholicism and Homosexuality', *Victorian Studies*, 25:2 (Winter 1982), 181–210.

Holden, Philip and Richard Ruppel eds., *Imperial Desire: Dissident Sexualities and Colonial Literature* (Minneapolis: University of Minnesota Press, 2003).

Hyde, H. Montgomery ed., *The Trials of Oscar Wilde* (London: William Hodge and Co., 1949).

Jagose, Annamarie, 'The Trouble with Antinormativity', *Differences*, 26:1 (May 2015), 26–47.

Janes, Dominic, 'When "Perverts" Were Religious: The Protestant Sexualization of Asceticism in Nineteenth-Century Britain, India and Ireland', *Cultural and Social History*, 11:3 (2014), 425–39.

Jeffreys, Sheila, *The Spinster and Her Enemies: Feminism and Sexuality 1880–1930* (London: Pandora Press, 1985).

Kahan, Benjamin, *Celibacies: American Modernism and Sexual Life* (Durham: Duke University Press, 2013).

Kahan, Benjamin, *The Book of Minor Perverts: Sexology, Etiology, and the Emergences of Sexuality* (Chicago: University of Chicago Press, 2019).

Kermode, Frank, *The Romantic Image* (Routledge, 2001; first published 1957).

Knight, Mark and Emma Mason, *Nineteenth-Century Religion and Literature: An Introduction* (Oxford: Oxford University Press, 2006).

Knights, Ben, *The Idea of the Clerisy in the Nineteenth Century* (Cambridge: Cambridge University Press, 1978).

Kucich, John, *Imperial Masochism: British Fiction, Fantasy, and Social Class* (Princeton: Princeton University Press, 2007).

Laqueur, Thomas, *Solitary Sex: A Cultural History of Masturbation* (New York: Zone Books, 2003).

Ledger, Sally, *The New Woman: Fiction and Feminism at the Fin de Siècle* (Manchester: Manchester University Press, 1997).

Lee, Adam, 'Platonic Communion in Pater's "Unfinished Romance"', *The Pater Newsletter*, 63 (Fall 2012), 25–44.

Llewellyn, Mark, 'Introduction', in *The Collected Short Stories of George Moore: Gender and Genre*, 5 vols., eds. Mark Llewellyn and Ann Heilmann (London: Pickering & Chatto, 2007), vol. 5: *In Single Strictness (1922)*, ed. Mark Llewellyn, vii-xlii.

Llewellyn, Mark, '"Pagan Moore": Poetry, Painting, and Passive Masculinity in George Moore's *Flowers of Passion* (1877) and *Pagan Poems* (1881)', *Victorian Poetry*, 45:1 (Spring 2007), 77–92.

Livesey, Ruth, *Socialism, Sex, and the Culture of Aestheticism in Britain, 1880–1914* (Oxford: Oxford University Press, 2007).

Lockerd, Martin, *Decadent Catholicism and the Making of Modernism* (London: Bloomsbury Academic, 2020).

Love, Heather, *Feeling Backward: Loss and the Politics of Queer History* (Cambridge, MA: Harvard University Press, 2007).

Love, Heather, 'Exemplary Ambivalence', *Pater Newsletter: A Queer Theory Roundtable*, 52 (Spring 2007), 25–30.

Lyons, Sara, *Algernon Swinburne and Walter Pater: Victorian Aestheticism, Doubt, and Secularisation* (London: Legenda, 2015).

McGrath, F. C., *The Sensible Spirit: Walter Pater and the Modernist Paradigm* (Tampa: University of South Florida Press, 1986).

McLaren, Angus, *Impotence: A Cultural History* (Chicago: University of Chicago Press, 2007).

Mahoney, Kristen, 'Vernon Lee at the Margins of the Twentieth Century: World War I, Pacifism, and Post-Victorian Aestheticism', *English Literature in Transition, 1880–1920*, 56:3 (2013), 313–42.

Marcus, Sharon, *Between Women: Friendship, Desire, and Marriage in Victorian England* (Princeton: Princeton University Press, 2007).

Martindale, Charles *et al.* eds., *Pater the Classicist: Classical Scholarship, Reception, and Aestheticism* (Oxford: Oxford University Press, 2017).

Martin, Kirsty, *Modernism and the Rhythms of Sympathy: Vernon Lee, Virginia Woolf, D.H. Lawrence* (Oxford: Oxford University, 2013).

Mason, Diane, *The Secret Vice: Masturbation in Victorian Fiction and Medical Culture* (Manchester: Manchester University Press, 2009).

Mason, Michael, *The Making of Victorian Sexual Attitudes* (Oxford: Oxford University Press, 1994).

Mason, Michael, *The Making of Victorian Sexuality* (Oxford: Oxford University Press, 1994).

Maxwell, Catherine and Patricia Pulham eds., *Vernon Lee: Decadence, Ethics, Aesthetics* (Basingstoke: Palgrave Macmillan, 2006).

Maxwell, Catherine, *Second Sight: The Visionary Imagination in Late Victorian Literature* (Manchester: Manchester University Press, 2008).

Monsman, Gerald, 'The Platonic Eros of Walter Pater and Oscar Wilde: "Love's Reflected Image" in the 1890s', *English Literature in Transition, 1880–1920*, 45:1 (2002), 26–45.

Moody, A. David, *Ezra Pound: Poet*, 3 vols. (Oxford: Oxford University Press, 2014).

Morgan, Benjamin, 'Aesthetic Freedom: Walter Pater and the Politics of Autonomy', *ELH*, 77:3 (Fall 2010), 731–56.

Morgan, Benjamin, *The Outward Mind: Materialist Aesthetics in Victorian Science and Literature* (Chicago: University of Chicago Press, 2017).

Murray, Alex, 'Recusant Poetics: Rereading Catholicism at the Fin de Siècle', *English Literature in Transition, 1880–1920*, 56:3 (2013), 355–73.

Newman, Sally, 'The Archival Traces of Desire: Vernon Lee's Failed Sexuality and the Interpretation of Letters in Lesbian History', *Journal of the History of Sexuality*, 14:1/2 (January–April 2005), 51–75.

Nisbet, Gideon, *Greek Epigram in Reception: J. A. Symonds, Oscar Wilde, and the Invention of Desire, 1805–1929* (Oxford: Oxford University Press, 2014).

North, John S. ed., *Waterloo Directory of English Newspapers and Periodicals: 1800–1900*, 3rd series (Waterloo: Waterloo Academic Press 1976–). (accessed online at victorianperiodicals.com, 4 March 2019).

Nunokawa, Jeff, *Tame Passions of Wilde: The Styles of Manageable Desire* (Princeton: Princeton University Press, 2003).

Nussbaum, Martha C., *The Therapy of Desire: Theory and Practice in Hellenistic Ethics* (Princeton: Princeton University Press, 1994).

Oulton, Carolyn, *Romantic Friendship in Victorian Literature* (Aldershot: Ashgate, 2007).

Pamboukian, Sylvia, *Doctoring the Novel: Medicine and Quackery from Shelley to Doyle* (Athens: Ohio University Press, 2012).

Paterson, Gary H., *At the Heart of the 1890s: Essays on Lionel Johnson* (New York: AMS Press, 2008).

Patrick, Arthur W., *Lionel Johnson (1867–1902): Poète et Critique*, unpublished doctoral dissertation (Paris: L. Rodstein, 1939).

Paz, D. G., *Popular Anti-Catholicism in Mid-Victorian England* (Stanford: Stanford University Press, 1992).

Pittock, Murray G. H., 'The Poetry of Lionel Johnson', *Victorian Poetry*, 28:3/4 (Autumn/Winter 1990), 43–60.

Pocock, J. G. A., *Virtue, Commerce, and History: Essays on Political Thought and History, Chiefly in the Eighteenth Century* (Cambridge: Cambridge University Press, 1985).

Porter, Roy, *Quacks: Fakers and Charlatans in English Medicine* (Stroud: Tempus, 2000).

Potolsky, Matthew, *Decadent Republic of Letters: Taste, Politics, and Cosmopolitan Community from Baudelaire to Beardsley* (Philadelphia: University of Philadelphia Press, 2012).

Potolsky, Matthew, 'Fear of Falling: Walter Pater's "Marius the Epicurean" as a Dangerous Influence', *ELH*, 65:3 (Fall 1998), 701–29.

Presto, Jenifer, *Beyond the Flesh: Alexander Blok, Zinaida Grippius, and the Symbolist Sublimation of Sex* (Madison: University of Wisconsin Press, 2008).

Prickett, Stephen, *Romanticism and Religion: The Tradition of Coleridge and Wordsworth in the Victorian Church* (Cambridge: Cambridge University Press, 1976).

Prickett, Stephen, 'Tractarian Poetry', in Richard Cronin *et al.* eds., *A Companion to Victorian Poetry* (Malden: Blackwell, 2002), 279–90.

Prins, Yopie, '"Lady's Greek" (with the Accents): A Metrical Translation of Euripides by A. Mary F. Robinson', *Victorian Literature and Culture*, 34:2 (2006), 591–618.

Psomiades, Kathy Alexis, *Beauty's Body: Femininity and Representation in British Aestheticism* (Stanford: University of Stanford Press, 1997).

Pulham, Patricia, 'The Castrato and the Cry in Vernon Lee's Wicked Voices', *Victorian Literature and Culture*, 30:2 (January 2002), 421–37.

Rabinbach, Anson, *The Human Motor: Energy, Fatigue, and the Origins of Modernity* (New York: Basic Books, 1990).

Reade, Brian, *Sexual Heretics: Male Homosexuality in English Literature from 1850 to 1900* (London: Routledge & Kegan Paul, 1970).

Roden, Frederick, *Same-Sex Desire in Victorian Religious Culture* (Basingstoke: Palgrave Macmillan, 2002).

Rose, Jonathan, *The Edwardian Temperament: 1895–1919* (Athens: Ohio University Press, 1986).

Rosenman, Ellen Bayuk, 'Body Doubles: The Spermatorrhea Panic', *Journal of the History of Sexuality* 12:3 (2003), 365–99.

Rouselle, Aline, *Porneia: On Desire and the Body in Antiquity*, trans. Felicia Pheasant (Oxford: Blackwell, 1988; originally published in French as *Porneia*, 1983).

Schaffer, Talia, *The Forgotten Female Aesthetes: Literary Culture in Late-Victorian England* (Charlottesville: University of Virginia Press, 2000).

Schuchard, Ronald, *Eliot's Dark Angel: Intersections of Life and Art* (Oxford: Oxford University Press, 1999).

Sechler, Robert Porter, *George Moore: A Disciple of Walter Pater*, unpublished doctoral dissertation (Oxford: University of Oxford, 1931).

Sedgwick, Eve Kosofsky, *Epistemology of the Closet* (Hemel Hempstead: Harvester Wheatsheaf, 1991), 188.

Selby, Robin C., *The Principle of Reserve in the Writings of John Henry Newman* (Oxford: Oxford University Press, 1975).

Showalter, Elaine, *Sexual Anarchy: Gender and Culture at the Fin de Siècle* (New York: Viking, 1990).

Shuter, William F., *Rereading Walter Pater* (Cambridge: Cambridge University Press, 1997).

Shuter, William F., 'The "Outing" of Walter Pater', *Nineteenth-Century Literature*, 48:4 (March 1994), 480–506.

Snyder, Katherine V., *Bachelors, Manhood and the Novel, 1850–1925* (Cambridge: Cambridge University Press, 1999).

Stephens, Elizabeth, 'Coining Spermatorrhoea: Medicine and Male Body Fluids, 1836–1866', *Sexualities*, 12:4 (2009), 467–85.

Sussman, Herbert, *Victorian Masculinities: Manhood and Masculine Poetics in Early Victorian Literature and Art* (Cambridge: Cambridge University Press, 1995).

Szreter, Simon, *Fertility, Class, and Gender in Britain, 1860–1940* (Cambridge: Cambridge University Press, 1996).

Thornton, R. K. R., 'Johnson, Lionel Pigot (1867–1902)', *Oxford Dictionary of National Biography* (Oxford: Oxford University Press, 2004); online edition, May 2007, www.oxforddnb.com/view/article/34204 (accessed 2 May 2016).

Thornton, R. K. R., *The Decadent Dilemma* (London: Edward Arnold, 1983).

Towheed, Shaftquat, 'Creative Evolution of Scientific Paradigms: Vernon Lee and the Debate over the Hereditary Transmission of Acquired Characters', *Victorian Studies*, 49:1 (Autumn 2006), 33–61.

Turner, Frank, *John Henry Newman: The Challenge to Evangelical Religion* (New Haven: Yale University Press, 2002).

Uslenghi, Raffaella Maiguashea, 'A Perspective of Unity in George Moore's Writings', trans. Jack W. Weaver, *English Literature in Transition, 1880–1920*, 27:3 (1984), 201–24.

Vadillo, Ana Parejo, *Women Poets and Urban Aestheticism: Passengers of Modernity* (Basingstoke: Palgrave Macmillan, 2005).

Valantasis Richard and Vincent L. Wimbush eds., *Asceticism* (Oxford: Oxford University Press, 1998).

Vance, Norman, *The Sinews of the Spirit: The Ideal of Christian Manliness in Victorian Literature and Religious Thought* (Cambridge: Cambridge University Press, 1985).

Vicinus, Martha, *Intimate Friends: Women Who Loved Women, 1778–1928* (Chicago: University of Chicago Press, 2004).

Whittington-Egan, Richard, *Lionel Johnson: Victorian Dark Angel* (Great Malvern: Cappella Archive, 2012).

Williams, Carolyn, *Transfigured World: Walter Pater's Aesthetic Historicism* (Ithaca: Cornell University Press, 1987).

Wilson, Christopher R. and Michela Calore, *Music in Shakespeare: A Dictionary* (London: Thoemmes Continuum, 2005).

Young, B. W., 'The Anglican Origins of Newman's Celibacy', *Church History*, 65:1 (1996), 15–27.

Zorn, Christa, *Vernon Lee: Aesthetics, History, & the Victorian Female Intellectual* (Athens: Ohio University Press, 2003).

Index

CAMBRIDGE STUDIES IN NINETEENTH-CENTURY LITERATURE AND CULTURE

GENERAL EDITORS:
Kate Flint, *University of Southern California*
Clare Pettitt, *King's College London*

Titles published